# EMPOWERING BHARAT

## Urban Co-operative Banks (UCBs) as Engines of Inclusive Growth & Technology Triggers a Banking Revolution A Case Study

*Dr. Mahendra P. Kalyankar*
*M.Sc., DBM, LLB., Ph.D*

HIMALAYA PUBLISHING HOUSE PVT. LTD.

**Author:**
*Dr. Mahendra P. Kalyankar*



**ISBN No.: 978-93-5051-777-2**

**First Edition : Oct. 2011**

**Price : ₹ 495/-**

**Published by:**
HIMALAYA PUBLISHING HOUSE PVT. LTD.
"Ramdoot", Dr. Bhalerao Marg, Girgaon, Mumbai - 400 004.
Phones: 2386 0170 / 2386 3863, Fax: 022-2387 7178
Email: **himpub@vsnl.com** Website: **www.himpub.com**

**Designed & Printed by :**
Jayant Printery, Mumbai

*To*

*Kala, Kaustubh & Saanvi*

*I do not believe in the doctrine of the greatest good of the greatest number. The only real, dignified, human doctrine is the greatest good of all.*

***- Mahatma Gandhi***

*If you go out into the real world, you cannot miss seeing that the poor are poor not because they are untrained or illiterate but because they cannot retain the returns of their labor. They have no control over capital, and it is the ability to control capital that gives people the power to rise out of poverty."*

***- Nobel Laureate Muhammad Yunus***

# Contents

# *Preface*

I would like to trace the origins of this book to a doctoral thesis I had written a few years ago. The thrust of that study was on the far-reaching impact of Information Technology (IT) on banking practices among Urban Co-operative Banks (UCBs). As a sample, I chose two UCBs - Thane Janata Sahakari Bank Ltd., Mumbai and Apna Sahakari Bank Ltd, Mumbai – to prove how IT and IT-related software packages transformed their working, making them competitive, efficient and transparent. In that exhaustive thesis, done under the able guidance of Dr. P.B. Ashturkar of K.R.M. Mahila Mahavidyalaya, Nanded, I had emphasized the need for every UCB to prepare a vision document and action plan on Information Technology for its adoption and implementation.

My stint with the Maharashtra Government has broadened my vision of what UCBs as a whole can accomplish. I have come to the conclusion that these banks, especially in Maharashtra, have a great potential to reach out to the poor, the underprivileged and the unbanked population. That brings me to the most important banking topic of our times - inclusive finance and inclusive growth. I sincerely believe, that UCBs, by virtue of their being associated with the less privileged, compared with the commercial banks, can emerge as instruments of inclusive finance and inclusive growth.

The crux of my thesis as mentioned earlier was on the impact of Information Technology on banking operations. Over the years, my belief in technology has further deepened as it can help banks deliver their products more efficiently to a vast number of people. The combination of the two issues most critical to banking operations - Inclusive Finance and Technology - have formed the basis of this book, supported by my earlier thesis, which has turned out to be a very valuable case study. Precisely from this point of view, I have added a prologue on inclusive finance and micro-finance and a chapter on technology at the beginning and an Epilogue at the end on what UCBs could do in promoting both the concepts and their implementation. In this context, I have strived to present material covering the global as well as national policies.

A word about the title - **Empowering Bharat.** Mahatma Gandhi once said that India lived in her villages. The connotation, with its undercurrent of age-old tradition, sounds appropriate for a study encompassing co-operative movement and co-operative banks in a country, which was and is, and shall always remain **Bharat.**

I trust the book will be of use for the bankers, especially those in the co-operative banking sector, the general readers, scholars studying the co-operative movement and the functioning of Urban Co-operative Banks in the country and the policy makers ushering in inclusive development.

Many people have helped me in turning this venture, a blurred vision in the beginning, into a concrete reality. I wish to place an record my deep sense of gratitude to Dr. Ashturkar, Dr. K. Ramesha of National Institute of Banking Management, Pune, Dr. R.M. Tungare, Director, MILS, Mumbai and Dr. Kadukar, Lecturer MILS, Mumbai, who have rendered me all the co-operation required. Special thanks to Prof. Viral V. Acharya, C. V. Starr Professor of Economics, New York University Stern School of Business for his appreciation of the book.

I must place on record my deep appreciation of the outstanding support extended by Himalaya Publishing House Pvt. Ltd. I also wish to thank designed & printed Shashank Shah for making this venture a reality. I thank my friends Arvind Shah for his support in many ways, Himanshu Acharya for his good advice and Deva for his valuable comments and editorial input.

I also acknowledge various UN and other agencies dealing with microfinance as important sources of information for the book. The online www.microfinancefocus.com has been of great help in citing the latest developments concerning microfinance.

Overall, the book - Empowering Bharat - has been a collective effort.

Finally, I must mention with deep affection the names of my Aai and Baba - Sou. Jijabai P. Kalyankar & Dr. Punjarao G. Kalyankar who have forever encouraged and motivated me in my quest for achiving higher goals in life.

Date : 24 October, 2011

Mumbai

**Dr. Mahendra P. Kalyankar**

**RATNAKAR GAIKWAD**
*Chief Secretary*

Chief Secretary's Office
Mantralaya, Mumbai-400 032

Date. 16/09/2011

# Foreword

Today, India is an acknowledged economic power house. The country's overall economic progress and its annual GDP growth rate of more than 8.0% is applauded the world over. But the question that policy makers administrators and economic analysts face is whether or not the benefits of India's stupendous economic achievement have reached the poorest of poor across the country. The reality is that governments, both the Central and state, are seized of the matter and they have introduced various schemes to bring into the fold of economic growth the weaker and marginal sections of the society, hitherto neglected by the organized banking sector. Thus the issue of inclusive finance is born out of the concerns for equitable growth and the development has become imperative to the country's economic policies. No wonder in the last few years, the concepts of microfinance and micro credit have taken deep roots in the economic system and become a reality in terms of their implementation and spread at the grassroots' level in rural and semi-urban areas.

In this context, Dr. Mahendra Kalyankar's book **Empowering Bharat** - is very timely. Interestingly, Dr. Kalyankar has chosen as the focus for the book, his doctoral thesis on the role of Information Technology and how it has helped urban co-operative banks (UCBs) in vastly changing for the better their functioning and overall performance with the help of a case study he expanded on this theme arguing forcefully how these banks can and should reach out the poorest of poor and help them. This argument holds good for the entire banking sector as a whole operating in the rural and semi urban areas across the country, that is BHARAT. That makes the title of the book very thoughtful.

Also right at the outset the book stresses on the role of Information Technology and Financial inclusion in India. This makes Dr. Kalyankar's book further relevant at a time when Bharat is vying with India for equal share in economic growth, banking on the strength of Information Technology, the very sector which has put India on a global map as a technology powerhouse. Also, the book throws light on the very aspect of Information Technology, which when used in Urban Co-operative Banks, it is of immense help for them as well as the public at large. The Reserve Bank of India, has also published high-level committee report - Information Technology Vision Document ( 2011-2017) - recently, which shows that this subject carries lot of importance in the banking arena.

I congratulate Dr. Mahendra Kalyankar, an officer in the Maharashtra Government, for his initiative in writing this book, espousing boldly the course of both inclusive finance and Information Technology in it, thus making Empowering Bharat, truly a significant work of our times.

I wish Dr. Kalyankar success and recommend **Empowering Bharat** as a must-read for policy-makers and administrators concerned with inclusive growth.

**Ratnakar Gaikwad**
I.A.S.
Chief Secretary,
Government of Maharashtra

**U. C. Sarangi**
*Additional Chief Secretary*

# Introduction

Here is a comprehensive book that attempts to bring into focus the working of Urban Co-operative Banks and their critical role as instruments of inclusive finance and engines of economic growth.

The book, **Empowering Bharat**, straight away raises two most important issues that will provoke policy-makers and bankers into thinking of promoting inclusive finance and incredibly helpful technology that makes it smooth and possible.

The book traces the history of banking, co-operative movement and co-operative banking. It lays special emphasis on the working of Urban Co-operative Banks and what they could do promote inclusive finance.

This is a burning topic which is very relevant to policies of governments both at the state and Central level. The Union Budgets presented in the last two years testify the Government's determination to promote inclusive growth through various initiatives to alleviate poverty and foster economic growth.

More importantly, the book deals with the most crucial subject of technology. In a well-researched case study, the book highlights how Information Technology (IT) has transformed two Urban Co-operative Banks - Thane Janata Sahakari Bank Ltd., Mumbai and Apna Sahakari

Bank Ltd., Mumbai - into efficient, profitable and customer-friendly institutions. This case study approach has amply aided the author to investigate and assess the impact of Information Technology on business growth, profitability, productivity, deposit mobilization and customer satisfaction.

The thrust of the book is on the IT and various related banking products and how these have opened up opportunities for UCBs to meet the rising expectations of customers. It is true that IT has bestowed on Urban Co-operative Banks, a host of benefits; IT has helped them to reduce costs, improve productivity and profitability and expand their operations, making them more economical. The book argues that UCBs as a whole can be instruments of inclusive growth.

The book points out that by installing e-governance structures, Urban Co-operative Banks can effectively and efficiently handle operations of functional areas of management, MIS and IT. The Urban Co-operative Banks can also provide on-line services because of a dynamic revolution in IT and communication systems which has made everything possible in today's e-banking world, the book adds.

Overall, the book is a scholarly and well-researched effort that will be very useful to bankers and research scholars. I wish Dr. Mahendra Kalyankar all the best.

**(Umeshchandra Sarangi)**
**Additional Chief Secretary (Home)**
**Government of Maharashtra**
**(Ex- Chairman, NABARD)**

# Prologue

## An Overview & The Importance of Inclusive Finance

India is truely an emerging economic powerhouse, as Shri Ratnakar Gaikwad, Chief Secretary, Government of Maharashtra, has pointed out at the start of his foreword to this book. When most countries of the world have barely shown signs of recovery from the recent economic meltdown, India has not only braved the crisis but maintained the pace of its GDP growth at an impressive 8.6 percent in 2010-11, up from 8.0 percent from the previous year. While the growth rate had been steep in agriculture at 5.4 percent in 2010-11 against a low of 0.4 percent in 2009-10, it was more or less steady in industry and services sectors at 8.0 percent and 9.6 percent respectively, according to the Central Statistics Office (CSO).

Quoting the World Investment Report (WIR) 2010 of the United Nations Conference on Trade and Development (UNCTAD), the Union Finance Ministry's Economic Survey for 2011-12, says, 'India is today rated as one of the most attractive investment destinations across the globe.' In its analysis of the global trends and sustained growth of Foreign Direct Investment (FDI) inflows, WIR rated India to be the second most attractive location for FDI for 2010-2012.

India's share of world FDI inflows shot up from 0.78 percent in 2005 to 3.11 percent in 2009. Moreover, India attracted FDI equity inflows of US$ 1,042 million in January 2011. The cumulative amount of FDI equity inflows from April 2000 to January 2011 stood at US$ 189.8 billion, according to the data released by the Department of Industrial Policy and Promotion (DIPP).

The humungous increase in investment mirrors the foreign investors' faith in the Indian markets, says the Economic Survey, tabled in Indian Parliament on 25 February 2011 by the Union Finance Minister, Mr Pranab Mukherjee.

### Banking Sector

Indian banking too has withstood the global financial turmoil of recent years with little disruption and continued to grow at a healthy pace. According to the Economic Survey, one aspect that stood out in glittering perspective was a rise of 59 percent in Net Bank Credit in 2010-11 over the previous year. This reflects the fact that the Indian banking sector has not only been an integral part of the country's overall economic growth story but actively supported the development of all other segments of the economy, such as agriculture, industry and services.

Most importantly, the policy regulatory thrust of both the Union Government and the Reserve Bank of India (RBI) has been to promote financial inclusion to widen the reach of the banking sector.

The Indian Government has identified financial inclusion as one of its top economic priorities, in order to promote inclusive growth. Financial exclusion remains an area of concern for the Government, given the low levels of financial penetration and deepening in India compared with other countries across the globe.

Recent data from the World Bank suggest that India ranks low when compared with developed countries with regard to financial penetration. When compared with select Asian peer group countries, the difference in financial access is much less striking as far as access to bank branches is concerned but it is prominent with regard to access to ATMs. Further, the size and depth of the banking sector when measured taking private credit to GDP ratio also works out to be much lower for India than many of its Asian peer group countries. These trends underline the need for strengthening the financial inclusion process in India in the years to come.

In tune with the Government's policy direction, the Reserve Bank of India (RBI) has put financial inclusion process into a mission mode, given that it can effectively help in addressing the concern of inclusive growth.

Financial inclusion in banking terms simply means taking banking services to the common man, part of the hitherto unbanked population. An inclusive financial system is one that services all clients - not just the relatively well-off. This means reaching out to poor and low-income clients and providing them with affordable financial services tailored to their needs. An inclusive financial sector will support the full participation of lower income households in the financial system. In many poor and developing countries including India, poor and low-income people do not have access even to basic savings accounts, let alone more advanced financial services. So, an inclusive financial system is one that recognizes both the market potential and the development opportunities of learning to bank the poor.

Financial inclusion in the Indian context has been defined as the provision of affordable financial services, viz., access to payments and remittance facilities, savings, loans and insurance services by the formal financial system to those who tend to be excluded. The Indian policy approach towards financial inclusion since early 2000s has been focused on ensuring inclusion at the individual and household level.

Accordingly, the scheme of no-frills accounts (no pre-condition, low minimum balance maintenance) was initiated by the Reserve Bank in 2005 to provide an easy financial savings facility to the population at large, which can act as a means of their entry into the formal banking system. At end-March 2010, 50.6 million no-frills accounts were opened by the banking system. While no-frills accounts have grown phenomenally, an important challenge before the banking system is to keep these accounts operational, as many such accounts are found to be dormant since the poor often find it difficult to save and deposit money into these accounts. In order to keep these accounts operational, banks have been advised to provide small overdrafts in such accounts; up to March 2010, Rs. 27.54 crore were provided as overdrafts by banks in such accounts.

**RBI Guidelines**

The Reserve Bank has taken several initiatives in recent years for promoting financial inclusion. A significant step in this direction was the issue of RBI guidelines in January 2006 for engagement of Business Correspondents (BCs) by banks for providing banking and financial services in addition to the traditional 'brick and mortar' model. Under this BC Model, banks have been permitted to use the services of various entities like Non-Governmental Organizations/Self Help Groups (NGOs/SHGs), Micro Finance Institutions (MFIs) and other Civil Society Organizations (CSOs), companies registered under Section 25 of the Companies Act, 1956, retired Government/bank employees and ex-servicemen to act as BCs.

Based on the recommendations of the Working Group constituted to examine the experience of the BC Model and suggest measures to enlarge the category of persons that can act as BCs. Keeping in view the regulatory and supervisory framework and consumer protection issues, the banks were allowed to appoint as BCs: individual owners of kirana/medical/Fair Price shops/individual PCO operators, agents of small savings schemes of the Government of India, Insurance companies, individuals who own petrol pumps, retired teachers, authorized functionaries of well run self help groups which are linked to banks and any other individuals including those operating common service centre as BCs.

A committee set up by RBI to look into issues relating to the Indian micro finance sector had already submitted its report. The Government is considering putting in place an appropriate framework to protect the interests of small borrowers.

**Union Budget 2011**

In the Union Budget for 2011-12 presented to Parliament on 28 February 2011, the Finance Minister, Mr. Pranab Mukherjee made significant statements relating to Financial Inclusion and Microfinance. He said that Micro Finance Institutions (MFIs) had emerged as an important means to financial inclusion, adding, that the creation of a dedicated fund for providing equity to smaller MFIs would help them maintain growth and achieve scale and efficiency in operations.

Called the 'India Microfinance Equity Fund', it is expected to be created in 2011-12. The Rs 100-crore Fund will be operated by the Small Industries Development Bank of India (SIDBI).

The Finance Minister also said that to empower women and promote their Self Help Groups (SHGs), he intended to create a 'Women's SHG Development Fund' with a corpus of Rs 500 crore.

In the last Budget (2010-11) too, the Finance Minister had advised banks to provide banking facilities to habitations with a population of over 2000 by March, 2012. The banks identified about 73,000 such habitations for providing banking facilities using appropriate technologies

A multi-media campaign, "Swabhimaan", had been launched to inform, educate and motivate people to open bank accounts. During 2010-11, banks would cover 20,000 villages and the rest in 2011-12, said the Finance Minister.

**Unorganized Sector**

Mr. Mukherjee had announced a co-contributory pension scheme 'Swavalamban' in the Budget of 2010-11. The scheme had been welcomed by the workers in unorganized sector. Over 400,000 applications had already been received and on the basis of the feedback received, he relaxed the exit norms whereby a subscriber under Swavalamban would be allowed exit at the age of 50 years instead of 60 years, or a minimum tenure of 20 years, whichever was later. He also made a proposal to extend the benefit of Government contribution from three to five years for all subscribers of Swavalamban who enroll during 2010-11 and 2011-12. An estimated 20 lakh beneficiaries will join the scheme by March 2012 said the Finance Minister.

**Financial Sector Legislative Initiatives**

Mr. Mukherjee said that in his last Budget speech, he had announced that Reserve Bank of India would consider giving some additional banking licenses to private sector players. Accordingly, RBI had issued a discussion paper in August, 2010, inviting feedback from the public. RBI proposed some amendments in the Banking Regulation Act. He intended to bring suitable legislative amendments in this regard in the session. RBI was planning to issue the guidelines for banking licenses before the close of the financial year of 2011.

**MSMEs & NABARD**

Micro and small enterprises play a crucial role in furthering the objective of equitable and inclusive growth said the Finance Minister. He explained that last year, Rs 4,000 crore was provided to SIDBI for refinancing incremental lending by banks to these enterprises and for 2011-12, he proposed to provide Rs 5,000 crore to SIDBI for the same purpose out of the shortfall of banks on priority sector lending targets.

Mr. Mukherjee said that handloom weavers had been facing economic stress and consequently, many of them had not been able to repay debts to handloom weaver co-operative societies, which in turn, had become financially unviable. He intended to make a provision of Rs 3,000 crore to NABARD, in phases for the co-operative societies. The initiative would benefit 15,000 co-operative societies and about 300,000 handloom weavers. The details of the scheme would be worked out by the Ministry of Textiles in consultation with Planning Commission, the Finance Minister said.

### Housing Sector Finance

Speaking about housing and finance sector, the Finance Minister said that provision of housing finance to targeted groups in rural areas at competitive rates and enhancing the provision under Rural Housing Fund to Rs 3,000 crore from the existing Rs 2,000 crore was required.

Mr. Mukherji said that credit enablement of Economically Weaker Sections (EWS) and low income group (LIG) households was a serious challenge. To address this issue, he made a proposal to create a Mortgage Risk Guarantee Fund under Rajiv Awas Yojana. The scheme would guarantee housing loans taken by EWS and LIG households and enhance their credit worthiness.

### Agriculture Credit

The Finance Minister argued that to get the best returns from their land, farmers needed access to affordable credit. Banks had been consistently meeting the targets set for agriculture credit flow in the past few years. For 2011-12, he set a higher target of credit flow to the farmers at Rs 4,75,000 crore, against Rs 3,75,000 crore in 2010-11. Banks had been asked to step up direct lending for agriculture and credit to small and marginal farmers, he said.

In view of the enhanced target for flow of agriculture credit, the Finance Minister proposed to strengthen NABARD's capital base by infusing Rs 3,000 crore, in a phased manner, as Government equity. This would raise its paid-up capital to Rs 5,000 crore. To enable NABARD refinance the short-term crop loans of the co-operative credit institutions and RRBs at concessional rates, he intended contribution of Rs 10,000 crore to NABARD's Short-term Rural Credit Fund for 2011-12 from the shortfall in priority sector lending by Scheduled Commercial Banks.

### Can UCBs be Instruments of Inclusive Finance?

Yes. With a large network in urban and semi-urban areas, UCBs can be very effective tools of promoting inclusive finance and development. The urban co-operative banking sector comprises a number of institutions which vary in terms of their size, nature of business and geographic spread while concentrating on credit delivery in urban areas. As an outcome of the on-going consolidation of the sector, there was a decline in the number of UCBs at end-March 2010 to 1,674 from 1,721 in the previous year, but the sector has emerged stronger.

The latest RBI report on the Trends and Progress of Banking in India (2010), says that in response to measures undertaken in the UCB sector, their financial performance witnessed considerable improvement over the last one decade. The scheduled UCB sector started reporting overall net profits since 2003-04 as compared with net losses prior to it, keeping in tune with the overall trends in the banking industry.

The Indian banking industry as a whole has made tremendous strides in terms of volume and spread in the last few decades. In spite of making significant improvement in all the areas relating to financial viability, profitability and competitiveness, the banking industry has not reached out to vast segments of the population, especially the poor and underprivileged sections of the society.

The issue inclusive finance is global concern. Hectic efforts are being made worldwide to ensure financial inclusion of the poor and disadvantaged in the banking and financial systems of nations. The reasons may vary from country to country and hence the strategy could also vary but all out efforts are being made as financial inclusion can truly lift the financial condition and standards of life of the poor and the disadvantaged.

Financial inclusion can be achieved through state-driven intervention by way of statutory enactments and also through voluntary effort by the banking industry itself by drawing up various strategies to bring large sections of society into its fold. The Indian Government and the Reserve Bank of India have placing a lot of emphasis on financial inclusion to ensure that the banking industry extends the desired attention to the neglected sections of society.

In India the focus of the financial inclusion at present is confined to ensuring a bare minimum access to a savings bank account without frills.

The concept of financial inclusion has taken deep roots in the financial systems of countries since the launch of International Year of Microcredit, which was 2005.

Ever since, Microcredit has been changing people's lives and revitalizing communities. Currently micro-entrepreneurs use loans as small as $100 (Rs 4,500) to grow thriving business and, in turn, provide their families, leading to strong and flourishing local economies. The year of Microcredit 2005 called for building inclusive financial sectors and strengthening the powerful, but often untapped, entrepreneurial spirit existing in communities across the world.

Going by various global studies, there is enough evidence that access to financial services is a critical tool for both economic growth and human development. Global experience also shown that the poor can be reliable clients and institutions that service them right do good business, as the experience of Grameen Bank in Bangladesh and scores of microfinance institutions (MFIs) in India have proved in recent years.

**Inclusive Finance - A Global Perspective**

**Vision & Mission**

The United Nations Capital Development Fund (UNCDF) has defined its vision of inclusive finance as large-scale access to a variety of financial services for poor and low-income people and micro and small enterprises.

Inclusive financial sectors are defined by a continuum of financial institutions that together offer appropriate financial products and services to all segments of the population. To operate effectively, inclusive financial sectors need to be supported by sound policy, legal and regulatory frameworks. Overall they are characterized by:

a. Access at a reasonable cost of all households and enterprises to a broad range of financial services including savings, short and long-term credit, leasing and factoring, mortgages, insurance, pensions, payments, local money transfers and international remittances;

b. Sound institutions guided by appropriate internal management systems, industry performance standards, performance monitoring, institutional transparency, accountability and sound prudential regulation;

c. Financial and institutional sustainability as a means of providing access to financial services over time; and

d. Multiple providers of financial services, wherever feasible, so as to bring cost-effective and a wide variety of alternatives to customers.

Financial services for poor and low-income people and micro and small enterprises should be seen as an important and integral component of the financial sector. This sector should also include a variety of financial institutions, each with its own comparative advantages and business models. The provision of financial services is primarily a private sector activity, with the role of government focused on creating an enabling environment.

**Strategy & Approach**

The strategy of the United Nations Capital Development Fund (UNCDF) to implement the above stated vision is to promote a sector-based approach to financial inclusion, as well as a number of thematic initiatives that support and strengthen the impact of this sector-based approach.

UNCDF's sector-based approach to financial inclusion:

UNCDF's Inclusive Finance (IF) practice area made a strategic shift in 2002 to a sector development approach to building inclusive financial sectors. This sector-based approach is aligned with the Paris Declaration on Aid Effectiveness and its call for greater national ownership, donor alignment with national strategies, harmonization of donor support and management for results and mutual accountability.

The sector development approach to building inclusive financial sectors is a flexible tool that can be tailored to the gaps, opportunities and constraints in each country. It follows these key steps: (i) a sector review focused on analyzing the key opportunities and constraints for access to financial services for the poor and low-income people, from the macro- (policy), meso- (financial infrastructure) and micro- (retailer) perspectives; (ii) an assessment of on-going initiatives by key stakeholders (including donors) and of the gaps that need to be filled at those three levels of intervention; and (iii) the development of a programming framework (in the form of a National Microfinance Strategy, Action Plan or other), that stems from the above analysis to build an inclusive financial sector in that country.

Financial sector development programmes are designed to create enabling environments for a variety of retail Financial Service Providers (FSPs). FSPs include commercial banks, non-banking financial institutions (NBFIs), microfinance institutions (MFIs), credit unions, co-operatives, insurance providers, money transfer companies, mobile network operators (MNOs) and other institutions providing financial services. This approach also seeks to address gaps in the supportive infrastructure (meso: audit, ratings, networks) and the policy, legal, and regulatory constraints that prevent a financial sector from being inclusive. This results in a dynamic process, tailored to the realities of each country.

Building inclusive financial sectors is a complex task that requires a range of specialized expertise that goes beyond UNCDF's internal capacities and calls for technical partnerships. For sector approaches to work, a range of actors must all contribute based on their comparative advantage. *UNCDF's role in the promotion of a sector-based approach is both of a facilitator and an investor*.

UNCDF's role as a facilitator stems from being accepted by a range of actors as a neutral broker. Through its strong field presence of technical staff at the national and regional levels, UNCDF is positioned to *facilitate the consultative process that underpins the development of frameworks for a range of actors to coordinate their support*, while encouraging key actors to lead in their respective areas of comparative advantage. This includes UNCDF forming strategic partnerships with key actors who are not based at country level, such as the Alliance for Financial Inclusion (AFI) or CGAP's cadre of policy experts for work in the area of financial regulations.

**An Indian Perspective**

A vast majority of Indian population is very poor and live on an estimated daily income of Rs 20. This segment of population, spread across the country, does not have any access to formal financial institutions such as banks.

As much as 65 percent of the population in the country does not get benefit from the formal financial services offered by the government due to its inability to provide the required collaterals or finding a guarantor standing surety for them against their borrowings.

In this context, the Reserve Bank of India Governor, Dr D. Subbarao urged bankers to meet the four formidable challenges before them: deepening financial inclusion, financing infrastructure, strengthening risk management and improving efficiency.

"Commercial banking in India has not penetrated sufficiently to serve the large mass of rural, illiterate and poor people in any meaningful way," the RBI Governor noted. The intermediation cost in India is still high, largely due to high operating costs, said Dr. Subbarao. The challenge for the Indian banks is to reduce the costs and pass on the benefits to both depositors and lenders.

Thus the big challenge India is facing now is the financial inclusion of a large segment of the population. And this challenge could only be met through the proper application of microfinance.

In the Budget 2010 the Indian Government has set a deadline - March 2012 - to carry out the financial inclusion drive that has the target to cover 60,000 habitations through the Lead Bank Scheme to reach the unbanked people. The scheme is to provide appropriate banking facilities to habitations with more than 2,000 people.

Now the average population coverage by a commercial bank branch in urban areas is 9,400 and in rural and semi urban areas it is 15,900 as on June 30, 2010.

Even by the spread of the commercial banks the financial problem of the masses could not be solved as the commercial banks are based on the minimization of risks and maximization of profits and unfortunately cannot reach the vast majority of the poor.

### *Microfinance*

The Microfinance Movement in India can be traced back to 1992 when National Bank for Agriculture and Rural Development (NABARD) linked SHGs with banks. The working definition of micro-finance is given by NABARD in 1998 which states: "Provision of thrift (saving), credit, and other financial services and products of very small amount to the poor in rural, semi-urban and urban areas for enabling them to raise their income levels and improve living standards." It is a paradigm shift from class banking to mass banking growing at the rate of 60 percent and covers the population earning more than ₹90 a day. Out of 9 crore clients or customers of MFIs in India, 80 percent are women and 90 percent have SC/ST and minority background.

The main point of departure of microfinance from mainstream finance is its alternative approach to collateral and thus becomes the powerful tool to achieve 100 percent financial inclusion. Micro-finance provides financial services to poor and low income people whose low income standing excludes them from formal banking systems. Now-a-days financial credit is treated as a human right. They need financial services to meet their life-cycle events such as birth, marriage, old age and in emergencies.

The Union Finance Minister, Mr. Pranab Mukherjee has said that our economic policies need to be designed in such a manner that the redistributing process does not feed off the public finances and the growth process itself is not hampered.

To achieve this objective, inclusive development needs to be combined with consolidation of public finances, financial stability, employment generation and economic growth, he said, while delivering the inaugural address at a two-day International Conference on 'Economic Policies for Inclusive Development," on 30 November 2010 in New Delhi. The Finance Minister said that some of the aforesaid competing concerns could be addressed through an optimal policy mix which should also be one of the discussion priorities of this international conference.

Nobel laureate, Professor Michal spank, Shri Rangarajan, Chairman Economic Advisory Council to the Prime Minister, Shri Ashok Chawla, Finance Secretary, Dr. Kaushik Basu, Chief Economic Advisor and Shri Govindrao Director of National Institute of Public Finance and Policy were also present on the occasion.

This was the first such International Conference being organized by Department of Economic Affairs, Ministry of Finance in collaboration with National Institute of Public Finance and Policy. The objective of this International Conference was to suggest out of box ideas for financial inclusion and achieving higher GDP growth rate besides containing inflation.

The Finance Minister observed that India had experienced a fairly long period of rapid economic growth and since 2003-04, there had been a further step up in India's GDP growth rate with the economy moving to a high trajectory growth rate of 8.5 percent to 9.0 percent per annum. He said that India's economy has become remarkably resilient to both external and domestic shocks. He said that it has not only recovered rapidly from the global economic downturn but also took the monsoon failure last year in its stride and is now showing robust growth.

### The 11th Five-Year Plan & Inclusive Growth

Mr. Mukherji said that 11th Five Year Plan endorsed a need for inclusive growth to ensure equality of opportunity for all. He said that a multi-pronged strategy was adopted that included rapid growth for reducing poverty and creating employment opportunities, improving access to essential services in health and education especially for the poor, empowerment through education and skill development and creating employment opportunities supplemented by the Mahatma Gandhi National Rural Employment Guarantee Scheme.

The Finance Minister said that in the last few years, "we have created entitlements backed by legal guarantees for an individual's Right to Information and his/her Right to Work. This has been followed-up with the enactment of the Right to Education in 2009-10. As the next step, we are working on the National Food Security Bill which is presently under examination by an Expert Committee set-up by the Prime Minister under the chairmanship of Dr. C. Rangarajan, the Minister said. He further said that to fulfil these commitments the spending on social sector has been rapidly increased. With growth and the opportunities that it generates, we hope to further strengthen the process of inclusive development, the Minister added.

Mr. Mukherjee stated; "Financial inclusion is a key determinant of sustainable and inclusive growth. We have accorded high importance to financial inclusion to cover the entire gamut of financial services pertaining to savings, credit, insurance and transfers. We are conscious that if our efforts have to bear fruit we have to tackle issues of governance and service delivery. We have taken up an ambitious programme of providing unique identities to the people through the Unique Identification Authority of India. Provisión of identity will enhance the access of poor and marginalized to public services and enable efficient delivery of benefits.

Needless to say, much still remains to be done. This is a challenging task in terms of resources, analytical issues, policy design as well as practical aspects of public service delivery. While I am aware that a fair amount of research work has focused on these issues, it is now imperative that their results are projected onto the policy matrix.

We need to design policies in a manner that the redistributive process does not feed off the public finances and the growth process itself is not hampered. To this end, inclusive development needs to be combined with consolidation of public finances, financial stability, employment generation and economic growth. How some of these competing concerns could be addressed through an optimal policy mix should be one of the discussion priorities of this conference."

India's 11$^{th}$ Five-Year Plan endorsed a need for inclusive growth to ensure equality of opportunity for all. A multi-pronged strategy was adopted that included rapid growth for reducing poverty and creating employment opportunities, improving access to essential services in health and education especially for the poor, empowerment through education and skill development and creating employment opportunities supplemented by the Mahatma Gandhi National Rural Employment Guarantee Scheme. The scheme provides for legal guarantee of 100 days of wage employment in a financial year to every rural household whose adult member volunteers to do unskilled manual work at minimum wage rate for agricultural labour. It is estimated that during the current financial year, around 37 million households have been provided employment under this scheme. In all 1.25 billion person-days have been created under the scheme. There has been a substantial attempt to broad base the programme and target weaker sections including Schedule Castes and Schedule Tribes population, with women accounting for nearly 52 per cent of person-days created under this scheme.

The Rashtriya Swasthya Beema Yojana, a scheme for providing health insurance coverage for below poverty line families has been launched. The Rashtriya Krishi Vikas Yojana has been initiated with a view to improve agriculture productivity and ensure food security. We are implementing a four-pronged strategy covering (a) improvement in agricultural production by extending the green revolution to the Eastern part of India while preserving gains in other areas (b) reduction in wastage of produce, (c) credit support to farmers, and (d) a thrust to the food processing sector. There is also a renewed focus on the development of physical infrastructure.

Micro-finance, another important component of the financial inclusion process in India, is defined as provision of thrift, credit and financial services and products of very small amount to the poor in rural, semi-urban and urban areas for enabling them to raise their income levels and improving living standards. The Self-Help Group-Bank Linkage Programme (SBLP), which started as a pilot programme in 1992 has developed with rapid strides over the years. In 2009-10, 1.59 million new SHGs were credit-linked with banks, and bank loan of Rs.14,453 crore was disbursed to these SHGs.

Further, at end-March 2010, around 6.95 million SHGs maintained savings accounts with banks. On an average, the amount of savings per SHG was Rs.‘8,915 as compared to the amount of credit outstanding of Rs‘57,795 in 2009-10. While there was a continued increase in the amount of credit outstanding per SHG, there was a fluctuating trend in the amount of saving per SHG in the recent years.

Alongside SBLP, Micro-finance Institutions (MFIs), such as Non-Governmental Organisations (NGOs), NBFCs, among others, have emerged as important sources of micro-finance delivery in India. In 2009-10, 691 MFIs were provided loans by banks to the tune of Rs ‘8,063 crore. The growth under the MFI-linkage programme in terms of both number of credit-linked institutions and amount of loans was much higher than the corresponding growth under the SHG-Bank Linkage Programme in 2009-10.

**Microfinance: A Review & Outlook**

The Indian Microfinance Sector is heading for revolutionary changes. The Reserve Bank of India will soon be regulating the Indian microfinance sector to enable its orderly growth and development. The ultimate objective of this far-reaching policy measure is to help the microfinance sector to meet the growing banking needs of the poor and underprivileged across the country.

The Bill aims at providing access to financial services for the rural and urban poor and certain disadvantaged sections of the society by promoting the growth and development of micro finance institutions as extended arms of the banks and financial institutions and for the regulation of micro finance institutions.

A draft Microfinance Bill, which has recently been placed prepared by the Ministry of Finance, represents a major step forward in the Government's engagement with the microfinance sector. The draft Bill has since been placed on the Ministry's website for eliciting opinions and suggestions from the concerned agencies and the public.

## Micro Finance Development Council

The Bill provides for setting up of a Micro Finance Development Council to advise the Indian Government on formulation of policies, schemes and other measures required for of the sector's organized growth.

According to the draft Bill, the Union Government may seek to establish State Advisory Councils for Micro Finance at the State level. Under the new Bill, microfinance institutions, including Non-Banking Finance Companies (NBFCs) are required to register themselves with RBI to get involved in microfinance operations. The Bill requires microfinance institutions to create a Reserve Fund and transfer a percentage, of its net profit or surplus realized by providing microfinance services every year as disclosed in the profit and loss account or income and expenditure account before any dividend is declared or surplus is utilized for any other purpose.

## Microfinance Reserve Fund

RBI will also have the power to intervene in matters related to income recognition, accounting standards, provisions for bad and doubtful debts, capital adequacy based on risk weights for assets and credit conversion factors for off-balance-sheet items and deployment of funds by micro finance institutions.

The Central Bank will constitute a fund to be called the Micro Finance Development Fund for issuing grants and making equity investments in microfinance institutions.

The Bill also proposes appointing a Microfinance Ombudsmen for the purpose of looking into grievances of the clients against microfinance institutions.

Response from concerned agencies to the draft Bill has been encouraging. Sa-Dhan, the Association of Community Development Finance Institutions has welcomed the Government's proposal. "It's an important step in defining the framework for microfinance services," said Mathew Titus, Sa-Dhan's Executive Director. "It provides helpful measures for client protection and a direction to the microfinance industry to perform its roles with efficiency and effectiveness," he said.

Sa-Dhan also welcomes inclusion of all legal forms under the proposed Bill, provisions for composite financial services including thrift, RBI as the sole regulator for the sector, developmental and advisory role of the Councils and the ombudsman scheme for client protection and grievance redressal, along with provision for recognition to the self regulatory organizations in promotion and compliance of code of conduct by member-microfinance Institutions.

Sa-Dhan has been a part of the drafting committee in developing the framework of the Bill. Since the Bill is in public domain, the Association has been holding consultations with its members comprising NBFCs, Section-25 Companies, Cooperatives, Societies, Trusts, etc to develop a consolidated response to the proposed regulatory framework. Subsequently, Sa-

Dhan will engage with its membership in developing rules, regulations and compliance to the regulatory guidelines.

Sa-Dhan is the Association of Community Development Finance Institutions with 251 members across region. It has a total client outreach of over 26 million and a portfolio of Rs 22,000 crore.

Women's World Banking (WWB) President and CEO, Mary Ellen Iskenderian believes regulations will help microfinance institutions. In an interview with Microfinance Focus Online, Ms. Iskenderian said: "Becoming a regulated financial institution can have a tremendous positive impact for both the institution and its clients, if done properly. In most countries, by becoming regulated, an MFI can tap additional external capital sources and begin to mobilize savings deposits, allowing it to reach more people. The additional regulatory oversight also tends to make for more transparent financial reporting and interaction with clients, resulting in better governance and more effective and accountable boards of directors for MFIs."

However, Ms. Iskenderian cautions: "Institutions must be extremely careful about their choice of partners. MFIs should seek like-minded investors that are committed to helping them achieve their mission and vision in addition to growth and sustainability. For example, investors may need to commit to forgoing short term growth for longer-term gains that help clients grow, such as business development services, committing to maintaining loans small enough to be available to women. The manner in which investors conduct due diligence, construct loan covenants and reporting requirements and maintain the post-investment relationship with an MFI can shape the MFI's direction, particularly with regard to maintaining its mission focus. Institutions that choose investors who are passionate about preserving the mission, while earning a reasonable economic return in the process, can help ensure mission-focus."

**Growing Activity**

In 2011, there has been a lot of activity on the microfinance front. Larger and profitable microfinance institutions have been successful in raising funds. Notable among these are NBFC-MFI Janalakhmi which received an equity investment worth Rs 65 crores from Citi Venture Capital International. Kolkata- based microfinance institution Bandhan has announced a $35 million funding commitment from World Bank's financial arm IFC (International Finance Corporation).

Some other major players have taken the securitization route to ease their liquidity crunch. Recently, Avendus Capital made a debt investment worth Rs. 108 million (USD 2.4 million) by buying out 11, 304 microloans of Tamil Nadu-based Grama Vidiyal Micro Finance. Bangalore based NBFC-MFI, Ujjivan Financial Services has also raised Rs 173 million through a securitisation transaction in May, 2011.

India's largest and the only listed microfinance institution, SKS securitized a loan worth Rs 50 crores with YES Bank. BlueOrchard Private Equity Fund, through its subsidiary in

Mauritius, invested Rs 4.5 crores in the second round of equity funding of Svasti Microfinance Private Limited, Mumbai-based NBFC.

Also, in July 2011, lending banks recently approved restructuring of loans worth Rs 5240 crores of five microfinance institutions including Spandana, Share Microfinance, Asmitha, Trident and Future Financial.

While profitable MFIs with diversified portfolios are showing signs of recovery, funding picture for smaller, concentrated microfinance institutions continues to remain bleak.

Microfinance has played an important role in providing sustainable finance and supporting the poor and underprivileged in India. There have been reports in the media about some microfinance institutions harassing their clients.

**Profit Motives**

In recent years, microfinance has received a lot of investor support, because MFIs have been openly offering them high returns. Criticism of such blatant profiteering by MFIs has raised issues of their social responsibility and commitment to help the poor. It has also brought into focus the role of venture capitalists about funding such MFIs.

Talking about such criticism, the head of Vienna based Dual Return Fund - Vision Microfinance, Dr. Varadanyan has in an interview with Microfinance Focus Online, says: "We have quite a rigorous selection procedure for MFIs. They go through complete due diligence and credit risk assessment by our investment advisors Symbiotics and Bank in the diocese of Essen, Germany. We make sure that all MFIs that we are investing in have clear social mission and objectives. We use Symbiotics investment assessment methodology and Symbiotics social responsibility ratings or tools to make sure that we invest in socially responsible institutions. This includes both examinations of policy statement and internal process and procedures and social performance. We also visit MFI branches and meet micro-entrepreneurs to check implementations of client protection principles.

For various commissions and omissions, MFIs have under attack from media in both India and Bangladesh. Responding to this charge against the MF industry, Dr. Vardanyan says: "There has been a lot of bad press and negative coverage about microfinance in India and Bangladesh. Of course there were problems with some of the MFIs in some of the regions and nobody can justify the irresponsible behaviour of some of the institutions towards their clients. But instead of generalizing the idea we need to try and find the root cause of the problem." He said it was not correct to blame the entire microfinance industry because some MFIs had made immense contribution to the cause of helping the poorest of the poor in the Indian sub-continent.

Arnaud Ventura, Vice President of PlaNet Finance & Founder & CEO of MicroCred Group, says: "I am very worried by the situation in India. This situation is in large part due to the market structure and the fact that policy makers have put pressure to decrease microfinance interest rates driving MFIs to accelerate growth. This accelerated growth has led to a major risk of over-indebting clients, loan officers not being able to market aggressively as well as to monitor adequately their existing loans. I am very concerned that this type of situation could happen again in India and/ or elsewhere."

WWB President and CEO Iskenderian says: "The commercialization of microfinance institutions has been concurrent with the trend of a decline in the percent of borrowers who are women. WWB's research shows that one reason is the increased focus among microfinance providers on profitability, a consequent shift up-market by offering larger loans. This has meant that growth in the sector has not been shared equally among men and women, a contrast to the first 30 years of microfinance, which prioritized women. Meanwhile, a significantly more challenging problem persists. Even when women have access to services, they often do not have control over their loans or savings, inhibiting their full economic participation and empowerment."

She further adds: "Much criticism has been lobbed at the sector for being too supply driven, with rigid lending methodologies that allow for massive scale but limited tailoring of the product to individual customer needs. MFIs who have broken this mold and have built strong marketing departments have become market leaders. While there remains an underinvestment in marketing as a capability in the sector, we believe there is an increased recognition of its importance. Marketing is essential for innovation in financial services and is essential to delivering on reaching and impacting women. As much as anything, the crisis in Andhra Pradesh is the result of a gradual drift away from that deeply customer-focused finance. If MFIs are to enjoy future success, it won't be because they are well regulated by a protective government. It will come down to good customer information, transparency of governance, and a commitment to knowing and serving clients well.

On the criticism for growing commercialization in the microfinance sector, Ms Iskenderian says, "It is our belief that there will never be enough donor capital to bring microfinance to the scale it must reach if we are to address the needs of the billions of people who remain unbanked worldwide. Yet as critical as commercial capital is to reach scale, we are acutely conscious of the impact commercial capital can have on the choices MFIs make on who to serve, and how they are served.

**SHGs : A Case Study**

**Multi-Dimensional Support for SC Members**

Members of the scheduled castes are among the poorest of the poor in India. Sampark is a microfinance organization that has been working with 230 self-help groups (SHGs) and 3,300 women in Koppal district of India's southern State of Karnataka.

In a paper written on the basis of Sampark's experience of working with these people, researchers Smita Premchander and V. Prameela have said that while the SC and minorities constitute just about 3.0 percent of the population in this area, Sampark's focus on reaching out to the poorest has resulted in 20 percent of the SHG members being SCs.

The SCs are among the poorest and most neglected, lack physical, financial and human capital, and are caught up in a vicious cycle of poverty. Their SHGs and federations tend to take much longer to become creditworthy, viable financial forums. Working with these groups requires the programme strategies to be flexible and multi-dimensional. Above all, it needs long term and consistent support.

These results are validated in Orissa, Bihar, tribal belts of Andhra Pradesh and Nepal, where Sampark has done research and evaluation assignments with projects covering over 200,000 households. Income poverty is highly linked with caste, and minority and low income status combines to result in a cycle of poverty which is difficult to break, requiring significant and consistent external support.

**Following are the findings of the study:**

**Vicious Cycle of Poverty -** Scheduled caste people struggle in the vicious cycle of poverty. Due to low literacy, low income levels, and lack of time, they are not even able to participate in SHGs. Nor are they able to take other opportunities offered by NGOs such as vocational training. They do not have the time or resources to be able to give up their wages and augment their own skills, even for a day, leave alone for several months as needed in skill training. So they are not able to build their capacities. As they lack risk bearing capacity, they are not able to take large loans for business and earn more money so they remain poor.

**Lack of Assets -** Those who belong to Scheduled castes are typically landless or marginal farmers, depend fully or partly on casual farm labour, migrate frequently for short or long periods, and have few assets other than human labour to earn from.

Typically, SCs are less educated and have fewer skills than those belonging to other castes. The cycle begins in childhood. When children are unable to cope with studies, they lose interest, absenteeism increases; teachers lose patience, eventually the children drop out of school. They also drop out because household chores need to be done, siblings need to be cared for, goats or cows need to be grazed, or the child has to go for farm labour to earn for the daily food requirements of the family.

Due to many handicaps, organization building is much more difficult when working with SCs. SHGs of SCs take longer to stabilize, and federations of SC groups are slower to form and stabilize too, compared to those where the general castes predominate.

**MFIs : Funding from Global Agencies**

In spite of the problems that some MFIs have been facing, the microfinance industry has been receiving the much-needed assistance from international funding institutions. In May 2011, media reported that the International Finance Corporation (IFC) was planning to invest $45 million to an Indian NBFC (Non-Banking Financial Company) to provide increased access to micro, small and medium entrepreneurs in the rural and semi-urban areas across the country. With this investment, IFC intends to help the NBFC in setting up and expanding its low income housing finance business through a subsidiary in India. It is also expected assist the company in executing its plan to enter select countries in South Asia and Africa.

A Bangalore-based NBFC-owned MFI, Janalakshmi Financial Services, has also announced an equity hike of Rs 65 crore. Citi Venture Capital International (CVCI), a global investment firm has taken a majority stake in the company as part of this round; other participants are existing investors in the company.

Janalakshmi Financial Services Private Limited is among the MFIs that focus on the urban microfinance space in India. It is an Indian MFI that has a structure of a Social Business, with the entire promoter stake being held in a Not-For-Profit Section 25 Company, Janalakshmi Social Services.

CVCI, a part of Citi Capital Advisors, is involved in the business of private equity investing. It currently manages over $7 billion in equity investments and committed capital. CVCI has presence in Singapore, Mumbai, New Delhi, Hong Kong, London, New York and Santiago.

**Women in the Forefront of Microfinance Revolution - WWB's Role**

Serving over 24 million clients, WWB is a microfinance network of 39 financial organizations from across the globe. Focused on developing a broader array of financial products and services, including savings and insurance, WWB conducts market researches and share best practices with its member organizations.

Along with designing financial products and services, WWB offers its network members advisory and technical assistance. The Technical Assistance and Programs division of WWB offers research, development and roll out of microfinance products including placing individual lending into group lenders; housing finance; rural finance; savings and Microinsurance. The division also supports microfinance institutions in defining and refining their strategic positioning and transforming into regulated financial institutions.

WWB's Centre for Microfinance Leadership formed in partnership with The Wharton School of the University of Pennsylvania and Creative Metier Limited offers executive education programs and coaching for senior managers and executive directors of microfinance institutions.

Women are more reliable borrowers because they often follow a more conservative investment strategy, which in turn results in lower default rates for MFIs. We see an opportunity to develop new ways to better serve women.

**Grameen Bank, Bangladesh & Prof Muhammad Yunus**

Grameen Bank (GB) has reversed conventional banking practice by removing the need for collateral and created a banking system based on mutual trust, accountability, participation and creativity. GB provides credit to the poorest of the poor in rural Bangladesh, without any collateral. At GB, credit is a cost effective weapon to fight poverty and it serves as a catalyst in the over all development of socio-economic conditions of the poor who have been kept outside the banking orbit on the ground that they are poor and hence not bankable. Professor Muhammad Yunus, the founder of "Grameen Bank" and its Managing Director, reasoned that if financial resources can be made available to the poor people on terms and conditions that are appropriate and reasonable, "these millions of small people with their millions of small pursuits can add up to create the biggest development wonder."

As of July, 2011, it has 8.37 million borrowers, 97 percent of whom are women. With 2,565 branches, GB provides services in 81,379 villages, covering more than 97 percent of the total villages in Bangladesh.

Grameen Bank's positive impact on its poor and formerly poor borrowers has been documented in many independent studies carried out by external agencies including the World Bank, the International Food Research Policy Institute (IFPRI) and the Bangladesh Institute of Development Studies (BIDS).

The origin of Grameen Bank can be traced back to 1976 when Professor Yunus, Head of the Rural Economics Program at the University of Chittagong, launched an action research project to examine the possibility of designing a credit delivery system to provide banking services targeted at the rural poor, mainly women.

The Grameen Bank Project (Grameen means "rural" or "village" in Bangla language) came into operation with the objectives of:

- Extending banking facilities to poor men and women;
- Eliminating the exploitation of the poor by money lenders;
- Creating opportunities for self-employment for the vast multitude of unemployed people in rural Bangladesh;
- Bringing the disadvantaged, mostly the women from the poorest households, within the fold of an organizational format which they can understand and manage by themselves; and
- Reversing the age-old vicious circle of "low income, low saving & low investment", into virtuous circle of "low income, injection of credit, investment, more income, more savings, more investment, more income".

The work done in Bangladesh on the microcredit front received global recognition. Together, Prof. Yunus and the Grameen Bank made history, when they were jointly awarded the Nobel Peace Prize for 2006.

## Global Scenario

Paris-based Investment Company MicroCred was formed by PlaNet Finance in 2005 with an aim of creating a group of microfinance institutions which can offer financial services to the under-banked across the world. In a span of five years, MicroCred created six subsidiaries in Madagascar, Senegal, Nigeria, Côte d'Ivoire, Nanchong and Sichuan.

In 2010, MicroCred reported a 73 percent increase of the outstanding portfolio to EUR 43.3 million. The group's savings deposits increased 451 percent with an outstanding savings portfolio of EUR 12.7 million and almost 87,000 savers.

DWM, AXA Belgium, the European Investment Bank (EIB), the French Development Agency (Agence Française de Développement, AFD), the International Finance Corporation (IFC) and PlaNet Finance are among the shareholders of MicroCred S.A.

Talking to Microfinance Focus, Arnaud Ventura, Vice President of PlaNet Finance & Founder & CEO of MicroCred Group explains his organization's mission. "MicroCred's mission is to provide financial services to micro entrepreneurs excluded from the traditional financial sector by building a group of leading microfinance banks and finance companies. MicroCred is a group of responsible finance institutions, created in 2005 by the group PlaNet Finance. MicroCred specializes in the creation of bank of microfinance in emerging countries. Concentrating especially on Africa and China, MicroCred manages six institutions, nearly 900 collaborators, offers today, to more than 65,000 clients, financial products. The Group focus exclusively on China and Africa, because these markets had clearly emerged as the pillars of future development.

**European Scenario**

Given that in the European Union 99 percent of start-ups are micro or small enterprises and that one-third of those were launched by unemployed individuals, effective support for the European micro-finance sector is an important instrument in developing this young market segment.

Established in March 2010, The European Progress Microfinance Facility (EPMF) is a microfinance initiative with EUR 200 million of funding from the European Commission and the European Investment Bank. Targeting all EU-27 Member States, EPMF aims to increase access to finance for individuals who have lost or are at risk of losing their job or have difficulties entering or re-entering the labour market.

Along with targeting disadvantaged individuals, including people at risk of social exclusion. Progress Microfinance supports micro-enterprises, including those in the social economy providing jobs for the unemployed or the disadvantaged.

Experts believe that microfinance in Europe will have a considerable impact on job creation and entrepreneurship, particularly in the aftermath of the financial crisis.

Per-Erik Eriksson, Head of Microfinance Investments, European Investment Fund, is quoted on Microfinance Focus, online as saying that in Europe, microfinance consists mainly of micro-credits, loans below EUR 25,000 tailored towards micro-enterprises and people who want to become self-employed but do not have access to traditional banking services. The market is heterogeneous with a wide range of different providers of micro-credit ranging from small non-bank Microfinance institutions (MFIs), via various forms of banks to regional and national development agencies, he says.

According to Eriksson, the business models supporting the various intermediaries also differ, some applying commercially priced micro-loans seeking to reach sustainability, some applying heavily subsidized loans and relying to a large extent on grant funding to cover its operating costs and the business support services provided.

Talking about his organization - European Investment Fund (EIF), Eriksson says that EIF has developed its know-how in the microfinance sector, managing several joint European Union initiatives (mandates) on behalf of the European Commission and the European Investment Bank (EIB), such as the European Parliament Preparatory Action (EPPA), Risk Capital Mandate (RCM) Micro, Competitiveness and Innovation Framework Programme (CIP), the Joint European Resources for Micro to Medium Enterprises (JEREMIE) and the Joint Action to Support Microfinance Institutions in Europe (JASMINE).

According to him, EIF had in 2010, significantly scaled up its microfinance activity with the launch of the European Progress Microfinance Facility, an initiative established in March 2010 with EUR 200 million of funding from the European Commission and the European Investment Bank which now serves as an "umbrella" initiative to group EIF's microfinance activities. Under Progress Microfinance, EIF manages a wide range of financial instruments aimed at supporting the diverse needs of Europe's microfinance intermediaries, he says.

This facility, which targets the 27-European Union Member-States, has a particular focus on micro-borrowers, micro-entrepreneurs, including the self-employed and other groups with limited access to the conventional banking system (ethnic minorities, young entrepreneurs, female entrepreneurs, etc.).

Additionally, EPMF seeks to have a different angle of impact through its particular focus on boosting employment while promoting social inclusion, especially in light of the adverse effects of the current financial environment.

### Role of Grass-root Cooperatives

It was announced in the RBI's Annual Policy Statement for the year 2010-11 that there was a need for better understanding of the functioning of grass-root level rural co-operatives, which have the potential to play an important role in financial inclusion. Accordingly, it was decided to conduct a study of select 'well functioning' rural co-operatives (around 220) across the country through the Regional offices in association with the Regional offices of NABARD and the concerned State Governments under the overall RBI guidance.

In November 2009, RBI has advised banks to draw up a roadmap to provide banking services through a banking outlet in every village having a population of over 2,000 by March 2011. Such banking services may not necessarily be extended through a brick and mortar branch but can be provided through any of the various forms of ICT-based models including through BCs. The target date for achievement of above has been revised to March 2012 in alignment with the Budget announcements. Banks are further advised that March 2011 may be considered as an intermediate target. As at end June 2010, about 73,000 villages have been allocated to various banks for the provision of banking facilities in villages having population of more than 2000.

With a view to increasing banking penetration and promoting financial inclusion domestic commercial banks, both in the public and private sectors, were advised in January 2010 to draw up specific Board approved Financial Inclusion Plans (FIP) with a view to rolling them out over the next three years. Banks were advised to devise FIPs matching with their business strategy and to make the FIPs an integral part of their corporate plans. RBI has not imposed a uniform model to allow each bank to build its own strategy in line with its business model and comparative advantage.

Given the strategic positioning of RRBs, the RBI directed their sponsor banks to implement Core Banking Solutions (CBS) in all RRBs speedily and fully as well as adhere to the deadline of September 2011. This is expected to give a further fillip to financial inclusion efforts given the penetrative outreach of the RRBs in the rural areas.

**Self-Help Groups (SHGs)**

- During 2001-02 several studies examined cost of promoting SHGs and the emerging SHG federations. Estimates for *cost of SHG promotion* under different promotion regimes in two studies were in the range of Rs. 1,200 to Rs. 20,400 and Rs. 4000 to Rs. 16,000 per SHG.
- Also reported costs in the range of Rs.15,000 to 25,000 per SHG up to the federation stage for the development of structures of SHGs linked to livelihoods; and Rs. 15,000 per SHG for development of the three-tier structure of SHGs, village organizations and the financial intermediary mandal samakhyas under the UNDP-SAPAP – the forerunner of the Velugu/IKP in A.P.

Thereafter no major attempt at estimation of cost of SHG promotion and development of SHG federations has been made but this segment of inclusive finance has played a vital role in improving the economic condition of the poor, especially, women.

**Role of ICT**

Technology, especially Information Technology (IT), has played a key role in the Indian banking sector's growth and reach in recent years. According to RBI figures released in 2010, around 90 percent of the public sector branches have been updated with core banking software, while around 97.8 percent of the public sector banks branches have been fully computerized. The trend of transactions too can be seen to have shifted from paper-based to electronic based. In FY10, the share of electronic transactions to total transactions stood at around 89 percent in value terms and around 40 percent in volume terms.

The banking sector business has grown at a CAGR of around 23 percent between 2005 and 2010. In the current financial year the growth rate is expected to be around 20 percent. With the overall economy expected to grow more than 8.0 percent in 2011, and services and industry expected to grow at an even faster pace of around 10 percent and more than 9.0 percent respectively, bank credit is expected to continue at a healthy rate.

**Mobile Banking**

Bankers say the next leg of growth is expected to be driven by mobile banking technology. This would also be in corroboration with the RBI's thrust on financial inclusion. There were around 525.9 million mobile connections in India as of Nov 10, compared with around 69,160 branches and 60,153 ATMs. Mobile technology is expected to widen the reach of the banking network on one side along with providing for ease of transactions on the other. Corroborated with the business correspondent model and UID, the same is expected to making banking services accessible to very small habitations by utilizing mobile technology where setting up a branch is unfeasible.

In recent decades, technology has revolutionized human lives, their living and working conditions, improving them beyond recognition and imagination. A key sector that affects the people most is banking, which has undergone a massive change, thanks mainly to application of Information (Technology) to its various services.

Till recently, the conventional banking systems adopted IT-enabled services to provide better services and products to their existing clientele. But with the integration of IT and communication technology into ICT, the conventional banking system is now equipped with a wide range of force multipliers. These include mobile banking, conventional cards, smart cards, common service centres, low cost ATMs, hand held devices, etc.

Now, time is ripe for the ICT to play a major and decisive role in reaching out to vast sections of the country's poor into the fold of financial inclusion.'

ICT can affectively help realize the fundamental objectives of Financial Inclusion. It can help the the formal banking system to reach out to the hitherto 'unreached and unbanked' sections of society. In Financial Inclusion ICT can be applied:

- to mop up micro deposits
- to provide affordable credit
- to provide micro insurance covering not only life and death but also crops, assets and accidents.
- to provide safe money transfers
- to provide financial advice and counseling
- to provide add-on services like agriculture-portals, etc.

With the explosion of ICT services, especially in data processing and communication, banking has entered a phase where the above issues could be effectively addressed.

With ICT playing a big role, the stipulated goal of providing access to financial services to 50 percent of the excluded rural cultivator and non-cultivator households across the country different Stales, estimated at 56 million by 2012 and 100 percent by 2017, looks achievable.

The interface between banking and ICT has already resulted in the following:

- Financial service providers have access to technologies which help them to reach new customers, track their operations to increase transparency, thereby improving the efficiency of financial services for the new customers.
- It has ensured the need for a paradigm shift in banking business fundamentals so as to enable them to implement new delivery channels of financial services.
- Due to availability of a variety of technologies, it is easier than before to select the right technology so as to get the most out of the investments made in such technologies.

**Mobile Banking**

With a telecom revolution sweeping India, the mobile phone has reached almost every village across the country. As competition between various mobile phone service providers increases, their services are expected to become cheaper and cheaper. According to an estimate, about 737 million people in India will own cell phones by 2012. A recent announcement of TRAI has said that there is going to be a significant decrease in the messaging prices, which will bring down the cost of transactions on mobile phones drastically.

Implementation of banking services on mobile phones can be done by providing them a user portal through which they can do the balance checks, cash transfers and payments by simple messages. However, there is need for ensuring that the transactions are as safe as internet banking transfers. It also calls for increased mobile literacy and the use of vernacular languages on the mobile phone.

**IIM-UNDP-Nabard Workshops on ICT's Role in Financial Inclusion**

In order to provide a neutral platform for discussions to various stakeholders of Finaincial Inclusion, IIM, Ahmedabad, the National Agricultural Bank for Rural Development (NABARD), United Nations Development Programme (UNDP) have joined hands. Accordingly, IIM, Ahmedabad has planned a series of workshops, funded by UNDP and NABARD.

The first workshop in the series was held on 7 March 2011 at IIM, Ahmedabad to provide a common platform for discussions on the various business and technology issues and challenges in the existing ITC-enabled FI initiatives faced by difference stakeholders.

The findings from the first workshop provided a basis for discussion to carry forward in the second workshop, held on 21 April 2011 in Ahmedabad.

The second Workshop on the Role of ICT in Financial Inclusion was held in Ahmedabad under the auspices of the Indian Institute of Management)

**Underlying Challenges of Technology-Enabled FI Initiatives**

The underlying challenges of this IT enabled Financial Inclusion have been manifold. During an experience sharing initiative of NABARD, following are the challenges and issues that came up from the presentations made by the eleven commercial banks

- *State Bank of India* portrayed a situation where, no. of unbanked villages to be covered : 1 lakh; Customer base to increase by 4 crores; No. of rural branches to go up to 10,000; No. of ATMs in rural areas to go up to 6,000; pointing towards an immediate need for robust technologies and fast scale up.
- *Indian Bank* mentioned few challenges like, Multiple vendors and technologies involved; Changing Technology trends; Vendor selection and valuation of vendor; Standards / Specifications prescribed to be followed by the service providers; Negotiation and Fixation of Commercials; Proper data storage and retrieval framework; Operation through third party switches.
- *Bank of India* gave a picture that, 45.9 million farmer households in the country out of the total of 89.3 million households, do not have access to credit.at all; Cash-less transactions can also be conducted this solution, by using similar Smart devices at the merchant locations; Payment of insurance premiums can be explored with this solution; Other investment products like mutual funds can be rolled out thru this solution; Utility payments can also conducted thru this solution.
- *Punjab National Bank* stated, Extend the Banking to the unbanked villages; Offer the financial products (Deposit, Loan, Remittance )& empower the under privileged; with the technology enabled solution ; Reduce the transaction cost and provide affordable credit; Offer branchless banking; Reach at least seven crore customers; Provide seamless transactions through the delivery channels also; Brick and Mortar model, Financial Inclusion, BC model & Kiosk model, All the Models will be Technology driven; All delivery points will be computerized. Biometric and Rural ATMs shall be deployed; Kiosk will be at Locations without Branch or at a distance more than 15 kms (say 30kms) from the existing PNB branch.
- *Andhra Bank* felt, Enrollment of large numbers; Wide geographic spread; High maintenance costs for accounts; Small ticket size of transaction; Illiteracy and use of vernacular product & service pricing; Trust and acceptance; Lack of electricity; Poor telecommunications are challenges for scaling up of financial inclusion initiatives.

Given that the access to financial services to a rural citizen is broad based than the presence of the formal bank network only, pre-workshop consultation was done comprising of a sample of stakeholders. There was a selection of few stakeholders with whom interviews were conducted. Stakeholders of Public sector bank (SBI), Private sector bank (ICICI and YES bank), Regulatory authorities (NABARD), Credit rating agencies (CIBIL) and microfinance institutions (SKS Microfinance) were included in the interview list.

### Mobile Financial Services (MFS)

The term "Mobile Financial Services" (MFS) encompasses a broad range of financial activities that consumers engage in or access using their mobile phones. MFS can be divided into two distinct categories: mobile banking (m-banking) and mobile payments (m-payments)

(Boyd & Jacob, 2007). Mobile banking is defined as "a channel whereby the customer interacts with a bank via a mobile device, such as a mobile phone or personal digital assistant (PDA)" (Barnes & Corbitt, 2003). Mobile payments on the other hand are defined as the use of a mobile device to conduct a payment transaction in which money or funds are transferred from a payer to a receiver via an intermediary, or directly without an intermediary (Niina Mallat, 2006). Mobile devices can be used in a variety of payment scenarios, such as payment for digital content (e.g., ring tones, logos, news, music, or games), tickets, parking fees and transport fares, or to access electronic payment services to pay bills and invoices. Payments for physical goods are also possible, both at vending and ticketing machines, and at manned point-of-sale (POS) terminals (Dahlberg, Mallat, The terms "mobile banking" and "mobile payments" describe distinct but in some cases overlapping sets of products. Some m-banking platforms provide services, such as money transfers, that are considered forms of mobile payment, while some m-payments products are so closely linked to bank accounts as the source of funds that they assume m-banking functions (Boyd & Jacob, 2007). MFS refer collectively to a set of applications that enable people to use their mobile telephones to manipulate their bank account, store value in an account linked to their handsets, transfer funds, or even access credit or insurance products (Donner & Tellez, 2008).

Penetration of mobile in India is witnessing an impressive growth. The following figure shows the growth of subscriber base and tele-density in Indian market. The growth is impressive which includes both wired and wireless subscribers.

In urban region the teledensity is 119.73 percent where as in rural region, it is 24.29 percent 21. That is why, mobile based technology is also considered to be a viable medium to conduct transaction of money. The MFS initiatives for FI in India are currently at pilot stage. There had been instances where various entities like banks, telecom operators, and other service providers have been conducting MFS pilots from time to time at various locations across India (refer Appendix – I for details on some of the MFS pilots in India). The regulators have put forward various regulatory guidelines for ensuring safe and secured financial transactions through MFS (refer Appendix – II for the regulatory guidelines related to MFS). There are various modes in which mobile financial services are delivered:

**Short Message Service (SMS)**

This is a text message service that enables short messages (140-160 characters) that can be transmitted from a mobile phone. Short messages are stored and forwarded by SMS centers. SMS messages have a channel of access to phone different from the voice channel (Valcourt, Robert and Beaulieu, 2005). SMS can be used to provide information about the status of one's account with the bank (informational) or can be used to transmit payment instructions from the phone (transactional).

# CHAPTER 1

## A Brief History of Banking

There are several views regarding the origin of the word "Bank". The word "Bank in Germany means a joint stock fund. According to some writers, the word "Bank" was derived from 'Banco', 'Bancus', 'Banque' or 'Bane'. All of which mean a bench upon which the early bankers, viz., the medieval European money-lenders and money-changers used to display their coins and transact business across the bench in the market place. In the early days when the cheque system, was not in vogue, the banker's functions was considered to be borrowing and lending it at a profit.

The modern conceptions about the banker are however to be born out of a variety of functions, he performs and the facilities he provides all these functions are taken into consideration to define as "Bank" or "Banker". Hart in his book 'Law of Banking' explained that, "The banker is one who in the ordinary course of his business, receives money, which he repays by honoring the cheque of the persons from whom he received the account of for whose account he receives".[1] As mentioned in English Book Society, "there are three ancestors of the present day banking; the money-lenders, merchants and goldsmiths and the various functions of these three ancestors are performed by the present day banking system. A bank collects savings of persons or a community and gives loans out of saving collected to those persons who require the loans. In other words, a bank borrows and lends money. In this context, Crowther remarks, that "the Institutions, which are themselves are banks, perform no other function than banking"

The Jews, who did not have land, had to keep their assets in a more or less liquid state. They were amoung the first bankers of Europe. European Banking Deposit Banks and Exchange Banks flourished in the continent of Europe. The Baco-di-Fialto was the first public Bank started in the year of 1584, which did the business both in the deposit and exchange branches.[2]

The Bank of Sweden was established in the year of 1556, which was known, as the State bank of Sweden. Exchange Banks were started in Amsterdam in the year 1609 and at Hamburg in 1690. Banking had been very much developed in the Europe and other countries between the years 1700 to 1812.

In India, Bank of Hindustan, set up in 1870, was the earliest Indian Bank. Banking in India on modern lines started with the establishment of three presidency banks under Presidency Banks' Act 1876, namely, Bank of Calcutta, Bank of Bombay and Bank of Madras. In 1921, all presidency banks were amalgamated to form the Imperial Bank of India.

Imperial bank carried out limited central banking functions also prior to establishment of RBI. It engaged in all types of commercial banking business except dealing in foreign exchange.

---

[1] *Ibid*.

[2] Economic Times, 11th June 2002.

The Resrve Bank of India Act was passed in 1934 & Reserve Bank of India (RBI) was constituted as an apex bank without major government ownership. Banking Regulations Act was passed in 1949. This regulation brought Reserve Bank of India under government control. Under the act, RBI got wide ranging powers for supervision & control of banks. The Act also vested licensing powers & the authority to conduct inspections in RBI.

In 1955, the Reserve Bank of India acquired control of the Imperial Bank of India, which was renamed as State Bank of India. In 1959, SBI took over control of eight private banks floated in the erstwhile princely states, making them as its 100 percent subsidiaries. Today the state-owned SBI is the country's largest bank.

The Banking Regulation Act of India, 1949 defines Banking as "accepting, for the purpose of lending or investment of deposits of money from the public, repayable on demand or otherwise and withdrawable by cheques, draft, order or otherwise."

Also, a bank is defined as an institution that carries out the business of banking. Banks perform certain activities which are allied to the business of accepting deposits and lending out of them. Since Banking involves dealing directly with money, governments in most countries regulate this sector and keep it under their control.

Banks provide almost all payment services by conducting checking or current accounts for customers, paying cheques drawn by customers on the bank, and collecting cheques deposited to customers' accounts. Banks also enable customer payments via other payment methods such as telegraphic transfer.

Today, in the age driven by the Information and Communication Technology and the Internet, banks have added new payment channels like Telephone Banking, Internet Banking, Mobile Banking, ATMs etc.

Banking activities can be divided into retail banking, dealing directly with individuals; business banking, providing services to mid-size business; corporate banking dealing with large business entities; private banking, providing wealth management services to High Net Worth Individuals; and investment banking, relates to helping customers raise funds in the Capital Markets and advising on mergers and acquisitions. Today, banks are now moving towards universal banking, which is a combination of commercial banking, investment banking and various other activities including insurance.

Banks are among the main participants of the financial system in India. The commercial banking structure in India consists of: Scheduled Commercial Banks & Unscheduled Banks. The arrival of foreign and private banks with their superior state-of-the-art technology-based services pushed Indian Banks also to follow suit by going in for the latest technologies so as to meet the threat of competition and retain customer base.

The Software Packages for Banking Applications in India had their beginnings in the middle of 80s, when the Banks. spurred on by RBI and the Rangarajan Committee Report, started computerising the branches in a limited manner.

The evolution of IT services outsourcing in the Indian banks has presently moved on to the level of Facilities Management (FM). Banks now looking at business process management (BPM) to increase returns on investment, improve customer relationship management (CRM) and employee productivity. For, these entities sustaining long-term customer relationship management (CRM) has become a challenge with almost everyone in the market with similar products.

**Globalization & Banking**

In the era of globalization, the poor, the vulnerable and the underprivileged will continue to be the responsibility of national governments and hence of concerns to public policy. Sound public policies at the national level in countries like India are very critical in the current context. This challenge is particularly complex in the area of financial services, more so in the case of banks in the larger emerging economies, such as India.

"The financial sector can add competitive strength and growth if reforms in the financial and real sectors keep apace. In other words, flexibility in product and factor markets play a part not only in capturing the gains from financial sector reform but also more generally from globalization," Dr. Reddy added.

**Narasimham Committee on Banking Sector Reforms (1998)**

Soon after initiating economic reforms in 1991, the Government of India set up a banking reforms committee, headed by M. Narasimham, with the task of analyzing India's banking sector and recommending legislation and regulations to make it more effective, competitive and efficient. The committee submitted two reports over the years. Recommendations of the Narasimham Committee-I (1991) report and the Narasimham Committee-II (1998) Report cover the entire issues relating to capital adequacy, bank mergers, the condition of global sized banks, recasting of banks boards etc. some important findings are as follows;

- **Need for Stronger Banking System**: The Narasimham Committee has made out a stronger banking system in country, especially in the context of capital account convertibility (CAC) which would involve large amount of inflow and outflow of capital and consequent complications for exchange rate management and domestic liquidity. To handle this India would need a strong resilient banking and financial system.
- **Experiment with the Concept of Narrow Banking**: The Narasimham Committee is seriously concerned with the rehabilitation of weak public sector banks which have accumulated a high percentage of non-paying assets (NPA), and in some cases, as high as 20 percent of their total assets. They suggested the concept of narrow banking to rehabilitate such weak banks.
- **Small Local Banks**: The Narasimham Committee has argued that "While two or three banks with an international orientation and 8 to 10 of larger banks should take care of their needs of the large and medium corporate sector ad larger of the

small enterprises, there will still be a need for a large number of local banks." The committee has suggested the setting up of small local banks which should be confined to states or clusters of districts in order to serve local trade, small industry etc.

- **Capital Adequacy Ratio**: The Narasimham Committee has also suggested that the government should consider raising the prescribed capital adequacy ratio to improve the inherent strength of banks and to improve their risk taking ability.
- **Public Ownership & Real Autonomy**: The Narasimham Committee has argued that government ownership and management of banks does not enhance autonomy and flexibility in working of public sector banks. Accordingly, the committee has recommended a review of functions of banks boards with a view to make them responsible for enhancing shareholder value through formulation of corporate strategy.
- **Review & Updating Banking Laws**: The Narasimham Committee has suggested the urgent need to review and amended the provisions of RBI Act, Banking Regulation Act, State Bank of act etc so as to bring them on same line of current banking needs.

Recommendations of the two committees not only helped unleash the potential of banking in India, they are also recognized as a factor towards minimizing the impact of global financial crisis starting in 2007. Unlike the socialist-democratic era of the 1960s to 1980s, India is no longer insulated from the global economy and yet its banks survived the 2008 financial crisis relatively unscathed, a feat due in part to the Narasimham Committee.

In 1998, then RBI Governor Bimal Jalan informed the banks that the RBI had a three to four year perspective on the implementation of the Committee's recommendations. Based on the other recommendations of the committee, the concept of a universal bank was discussed by the RBI and finally ICICI bank became the first universal bank of India. The RBI published an "Actions Taken on the Recommendations" report on 31 October 2001 on its own website. Most of the recommendations of the Committee have been acted upon.

## Basel Accords I to III

The Basel Accords refer to the banking supervision Accords containing recommendations on banking laws and regulations. Basel I and Basel II and Basel III were issued by the Basel Committee on Banking Supervision (BCBS). They are called the Basel Accords as the BCBS maintains its secretariat at the Bank for International Settlements in Basel, Switzerland, where the committee normally meets.

Originally, the Basel Committee comprised representatives from central banks and regulatory authorities of the Group of 10 countries plus Luxembourg and Spain. Since 2009, all the other G-20 major economies are represented, as well as some other major banking centres such as Hong Kong and Singapore.

The Basel Committee does not have the authority to enforce recommendations, although most member countries as well as some other countries tend to implement the Committee's policies.

**Key Aspects of India's Financial Sector Reforms**

India initiated important measures for financial sector reforms from the 1990s, and these reforms have major implications for industrial growth in the country. The major aim of the reform process was to improve allocative efficiency in financial markets and, at the same time, ensure macroeconomic stability in the economy. Deregulation of interest rates was considered important for enhancing allocative efficiency in financial markets and for developing interest rate as an instrument for monetary transmission.

The notable aspects of the Indian reforms were the following:

First, they included major steps for liberalization of the country's financial system. The mechanism for interest rate controls in India has been dismantled; the dismantling of administered interest rates occurred in stages. For issuing large loans, banks in India had to obtain prior approval from the RBI; with the reforms, this constraint has been removed. The limits on the levels of Cash Reserve Ratio (CRR) and Statutory Liquidity Ratio (SLR) to be maintained by Indian banks have been relaxed.

Secondly, the reforms have resulted in a considerably reduced role for the state in allocation of credit; the reforms in credit regulation involved a shift in focus from micro-regulation to macro-management of credit (RBI, 2003). In the pre-reform period, targets were assigned to the banking system in India with respect to lending to priority sectors such as agriculture and small-scale industries.

These targets have been relaxed as part of the reform process. On the monetary-fiscal coordination, several reform measures were introduced. In June 1992, an auction system was introduced for the Central Bank's market borrowings, thus ensuring that a larger proportion of fiscal deficit will be financed by borrowings at market-related interest rates. Subsequently, RBI reduced SLR to 25.0 percent by October 1997. In September 1994, the Government and the RBI agreed to eliminate the automatic monetization of the Centre's fiscal deficit; by April 1997, ad hocs would be replaced by a system of ways and means advances to the Central Government at market-related rates.

Thirdly, new measures where introduced that allowed the RBI to contain volatility in the market and facilitate the smooth progression of market borrowings.

Also, important reforms have been initiated with a view to encourage competition and ensure greater transparency in the operations and accounting practices of the financial sector. The private sector including foreign institutional investors (FIIs) have been allowed entry into the Indian financial sector. The Insurance Bill approved by the Indian Parliament in 2000 permitted foreign insurance companies to operate in the Indian market. Investment norms were liberalized in the 1990s following which nationalized banks in India have been offered greater freedom to participate in the financial market, including in the sale of equity to the private sector. Banks were eligible to invest in commercial paper, units of mutual funds and the secondary equity market. By October 1993, they were allowed to invest five percent of their previous year's deposit mobilization in capital markets. The sub-ceiling in regard to corporate equity was withdrawn in May 1994. By May 2001, the limits on bank's exposure to stock markets was set at five per cent of the total advances (including CPs) as on March 31 of the previous year.

Foreign banks have been given permission to access India's domestic market. At the same time, the government specified new norms on capital adequacy and 'bad debts' in the banking sector. The government set up the Securities and Exchange Board of India (SEBI) in 1992 as a regulatory board on stock market transactions in India. However, over the reform years, there has been a progressive relaxation of the regulations set by SEBI. Lastly, the government initiated policies to raise the degree of financial openness in India. The rules for taking money in and out of the country have been relaxed. Non-resident Indians (NRIs) have been offered liberal conditions for making investments in the country. Foreign institutional investors (FIIs) have been allowed to invest in India's stock markets.

# CHAPTER 2

# Computerization in Banks

Banking which forms a core industry of any economy should be growth oriented. Computerization is a positive step to bank growth. With the aid of computers, the bank work can be done faster. Not only the present work load can be reduced to a great extent but also the bank can expand its working area with the same manpower.

Computerization in banking sector/financial sector dates back to 1963 when life insurance corporation introduced computers for maintenance and processing of insurance policies. Later on Reserve Bank of India and State Bank of India installed computer systems for processing reconciliation of inter branch transactions, processing statistical data and for research purposes. The rest of work was left to be handled easily with help of calculators, accounting machines and cash registers.

It was on 1975, when the working group on customer's services headed by T.R. Vardarchay suggested, introduced of modern technology in specific banking area to improve the customer's services. It was a result of changing banking scenario in India that these recommendations were made i.e., with nationalization of 14 major banks in 1969 and subsequent explosion of banks region-wise and service wise the need for varied information system was realized i.e., house keeping and control of macro level information for policy formulation and control by central banking authority. However, despite such a multi dimensional growth, mechanization was still known in the industry in general.

In 1981 Goipara Committee once again echoed the recommendations of working group. However, due to stiff resistance for employee's unions apprehending retrenchment, the recommendations of these two committees could not be implemented. In the same year National Industrial Tribunal presided over be Justice C.T. Dighe, cleared the way for use of computers and other sophisticated machines in Reserve Bank of India. However, Tribunal award also prohibited retrenchment displacement of more than 10 percent of their staff.

In 1966 the first bipartite settlement was signed between Bankers Association and Employees unions on computerization. Chapter (VI) of the agreements permitted use of certain type of machines for banking transactions. Machines like calculators, accounting machines and cash registers were permitted, though they were never put into use intensively by banks. From 1966 to 1983, development in computerization in banks was conspicuous by its absence, despite vibrating banking activities and branch expansion apart from few areas. The various reasons attributes to this were:

- The constraints, obstacles any myths in respect to computerization. It was still help that unemployment would result from computerization.
- Growing pressure of population which was adding to unemployment in the economy. Under such conditions, both government and management could not even dream of computerization:

- Lack of technological advances in computers within India.
- Labour unions were still opposed to computerization because they still believed that, computers would displace humans.

The second bipartite agreement/settlement on computerization and mechanization was signed in 1988. The agreement specified the area of computerization and the number of computers and machines that could be used. It also provided protection of the existing provision relating to computerization which was existing at respective banks. The settlement covered two areas: Computerization and mechanization.

**Mechanization in Banks:**

- Current accounts
- Saving bank accounts
- Cash credit and loan accounts
- Other deposit accounts
- General ledger accounts
- Salary and pay.

The settlement permitted banks to own computer themselves or through consortia. Banks could also hire from other agencies until the main frames or mini computer were installed in the respective banks. For larger computers other than mini computers only one could be installed at one center in each bank and capacity of such should not exceed what was being used in Reserve Bank of India. Banks could use mini computers as warranted by their needs and exigencies. The maximum number of computer a bank could have would be one for each area 1 center and an additional one for every 200 branches / offices or major part, with a minimum of one or 18 computers which is lower. Any individual bank was given liberty to install such a number of computers at various places according to their administrative conveniences. Assurances given be management to the labour union including the following:

(1) No retrenchment of staff as a result of computerization and mechanization. Displacement shall be kept as possible and those affected will be absorbed in the same city or town.

(2) In banks with less than 500 braches, no larger computers shall be installed for a period of 18 months.

(3) Hiring of time in respect to computers will be done only for a period of two years.

(4) If any new categories of employees were appointed due to introduction of computers for performance of higher duties than what was an envisaged in existing settlement, the same was to be settled through mutual discussion.

(5) No accounting machines were allowed to be used in rural branches. Installation of electronic machines with memory was prohibited at semi-urban branches.

(6) Limited purpose of MIS

(7) Specified purpose where clerical strength exceeds 15.

This settlement set the stage ready for commercial banks to extend mechanization and computerization to various operational areas in pursuit of efficiency in operations and customer services.

Another land mark in history of computerization was the setting up of Rangarajan Committee on computerization and mechanization of banking service of 1983. The committee headed by Dr. C. Rangarajan, deputy governor of Reserve Bank of India, was to look onto modalities of drawing a phased plan of mechanization in banks in view of further expansion.

It recommended a tree level mechanization structure-branch, regional and head office level. At branch level, computerization was to improve customer service, house-keeping and generation of data to meet the requirements of control and information system. A target of 30,000 advanced ledger printing machine (ALPM) to be installed in two phases in bank branches was fixed.

At regional level and head quarters, mechanization was to store, analyses and retrieve the data received from the branches so as to generate speedy information for strengthening internal control over branches and policy formulation. A target of 300 micro processors was set for zonal and regional officers. A target of 85 mainframe computers was set at headquarters.

In March 1987 second bipartite agreement and settlement on computerization and mechanization was signed. In this agreement, vide clause 22, it was agreed that further extension of mechanization and computerization in banks will be renewed by the parities after expiry of three years from September 1986 and fresh agreement entered into 6 months. However this agreement was a partial veto on implementation of the 1983 committee. It limited the ALPMs to less than 20 percent i.e., 5700 put to the recommended 30,000. The number of saving accounts to be handled per ALPM was limited to 2200 though its capacity was four or five times more. This agreement however could not make big changes at all levels because its recommendations were inferior to those recommended by the 1983 agreement i.e., by then 18 mini computers had been allowed per bank and installations of one large computer per bank.

Further in 1988, Reserve Bank of India appointed the second Rangarajan Committee to review the progress made in computerization in view of growing volumes of computer technology and problems associated with implementation of recommendations of the first committee. The committee was also interested in the task of drawing a perspective plan of computerization in banks and to suggest modalities for implementation of on line computerization at branch level. The committee submitted its report in 1989 and recommended a thrust of computerization in banks for the next five years by fully computerizing 2000-2500 large branches located at high activities areas and centers. Those branches which were having work load of 750 vouchers per day were computerized in gradual and phased but in an effective way. In the first phase 500 branches with workload of above 1500 vouchers daily were fully computerized. The remaining 1500 to 2000 with work load of 750 to 1500 were computerized in phase two. The committee recommended computerization of regional, zonal and headquarters.

In April, 1989 the third bipartite on mechanization and computerization was signed. The interim agreement on mechanization and computerization was also signed.

In October 1993, settlement on mechanization and computerization was signed between 58banks under IBA and workmen represented by all India Bank Employees Association. According to the agreement banks were free to computerize some, or all operations in branches, administrative offices communication and networking, automated teller machines, notes and cash counting machines, signature verification equipment and pass book printers, demand draft printers and terminals at customer location and equity terminals.

Since then, the process of computerization and mechanization has picked up momentum. By the end of 1996, it was estimated that around 5,000 branches would be computerized. Out of these, 750 will be fully computerized with rest being semi computerized. The implementation of IT Act of computerization further accelerated in banks.

**Computerization in Nationalised Banks:**

The first effort of computerization and mechanization in the banking industry was drawn up in 1983-84. But the process of introducing computerization in the banking industry in India, particularly in public sector banks were very slow. There were so many difficulties inherent in nationalized banks which had hurdles in their endeavor to mechanization/automate their operations.

- Stiff opposition from unions for the introduction of any sort of automation fearing loss of jobs.
- Vast network of branches largely located in rural/semi-urban areas which were set-up post-nationalization to meet the banking needs of a vast rural population. Most of these branches were setup to achieve social objectives without considering their viability.
- The lack of inventive and urge to upgrade skills and the inadequacies in the training system had further compounded the difficulties.
- The large size of banks, in terms of workforce and branches had generally resulted in slow response to the changes in the banking environment.
- The huge branch networks have made it almost impossible to develop centralized software systems simply because of the cost involved. Thus customers denied the facility of anywhere banking which the private sector banks have started making a noise about technology in banking. The following development offer some source of hope:

  RBI is encouraging to nationalized banks regarding computerization.

A number of computerization banks and the SBI have laid put plans to network the computerized branches/ATMs to give customers anytime/anywhere banking services.

Nationalized banks have started looking for software companies to develop integrated solutions to meet the increasing need for technology-oriented services. Despite of all the above developments, nationalized banks have a long way to go to catch up with the new private sector-foreign banks as far as technology is concerned.

## Computerization in New Private Sector/Foreign Banks:

In the early nineties after the liberalization of the Indian economy, a few new private sector banks were set up and this stood to a new chapter in the history of Indian banking. These new entrants had the advantage that they did not inherit any legacy in retail banking and also had a rich understanding of the Indian industry. The main agenda of these banks so as to provide better services to the customer who can afford it. Their approach was termed as cherry picking banking, which aims at the customers. Their perception was also strategically different. They viewed the customers as financial partners rather than custodians of their customers money – a shift from custodianship to companionship. To achieve the goals these banks eliminated the constraints of time and distance by expanding the banking hours from eight to twenty four and reducing the distance from infinity to near zero.

To achieve the above objectives, these banks introduced a high level of automation right from inception. All the branches were computerized from inception to insure efficient on-line transaction processing. Processors were developed to attain the highest level of customer satisfaction.

High speed computer-mediated communication networks were set up to reduce the communication cycle time. Staff was carefully selected to play the role of business of facilitators rather than processing clerks and accountants. Employees attended to the customer proposal and problems, while computer processed all the transaction and displayed the options and assisted the employees by providing customized solutions. The targeted customers were affluent urban dwellers and non-resident Indians (NRIs).

As per the settlement computers, including mini computers were used in banks for following purposes.

- Reconciliation of inter-branch transaction
- Transfer of funds through improved systems
- Foreign exchange transaction
- Management of investment

## Various Committee Reports on Banking Technology

The Liberalization and Globalization of the Indian economy has thrown up new challenges to the banking system in the form of new breed of private sector banks, foreign Banks and other non banking financial institutions, apart from the growing expectation from the customers and the government, and to achieve international standards. The transformation from the totally manual accounting to computerized environment calls for enabling and proactive policy and legal environments. Public policy authorities in the country and international agencies have been alive to this and accordingly the Reserve Bank of India, Government of India and the bank for International Settlements has taken several initiatives in that direction.

The Reserve Bank of India (RBI) has adopted 'development of the banking and financial market' as one of its prime objectives. 'Institutional development' was the hallmark of this approach. In the 1980s, the Reserve Bank focused on 'improvements in the productivity' of the banking sector. Being convinced that technology is the key for improving in productivity, the Reserve Bank took several initiatives to popularize usage of technology by banks in India.

The Reserve Bank's approach in the matter has, as in any other area, been consultative. Periodically, almost once in five years since the early 1980s, the Reserve bank appointed committees and Working Groups to deliberate on and recommend the appropriate use of technology by banks given the circumstances and the need. These Committees were as follows:

- Δ Rangarajan Committee I in early 1980s
- Δ Rangarajan Committee II in late 1980s
- Δ Saraf & Shere Working Groups in early 1990s
- Δ Vasudevan working Group in late 1990s
- Δ Barman Working Group in early 2000s

**Dr. C. Rangarajan Committee Report on Computerization in Banks**

Profile of Indian banking has undergone a metamorphosis in the post-nationalization era. The change is characterised by radical transformation in the role, scope and extent of business operations of banks. The industry has grown dramatically in size as well as complexity of business. Banks have emerged as effective catalytic agents of socio-economic change.

This massive expansion and diversification of the banking system was not without its attended stresses and strains. Housekeeping and control functions got somewhat neglected owing to business pressures. Customer service tended to deteriorate and attracted public attention. Bottlenecks developed in the flow of information compromising control and monitoring on one hand and responsive policy formulation and review on the other. Recovery of advances slipped, thereby sub-optimizing recycling of funds and profitability of banks.

Banks showed exemplary zeal in meeting their social obligations in tune with the national policies. Banks in India have perhaps registered the highest growth in terms of branch network within a span of two decades. The growth in network of branches and volume of business was achieved mostly by enlarging the manpower resources. However, higher and sophisticated technology was not widely used. Banking industry has now entered a phase with accent on consolidation, productivity and qualitative improvement in its operations. Inevitably this has prompted a closer look at the technology in use.

The first blue print for computerization and mechanization in banking industry was drawn up in 1983-84. A Committee was set-up in 1983, under the Chairmanship of Dr. C. Rangarajan, Deputy Governor, Reserve Bank of India to look into the modalities of drawing up a phased plan of mechanization for the banking industry, covering the period 1985-89. The

Committee submitted its report in 1984 and recommended introduction of computerization/ mechanization at Branch, Regional Office/Zonal Office and Head Office levels of banks. The recommendations of the Committee were implemented by banks and progress monitored on a ongoing basis by Reserve Bank of India and the Government.

Against the background of the experience gained in the eighties and the tasks ahead of the banking system, Reserve Bank of India set up in September 1988, another Committee under the chairmanship of Dr. C. Rangarajan, Deputy Governor was to draw a perspective plan of computerization for banking industry for the give year period 1990-94 including introduction on online services, ATMS, EFT, e-mail, training of personnel, etc., and consider other allied issues.

**W.S. Saraf Committee Recommendations on Technological Issues**

The Indian financial sector is now in the fourth year of structural changes and reforms. The process of liberalization of the economy has opened up new opportunities. In response, a number of new financial institutions are coming up and the existing ones are diversifying their functions, the role of the banks is also undergoing major changes. Banks have to face stiff competition from the intermediates. They can no longer afford to neglect the customer service, or technology up-gradation so vital for efficiency, image and growth.

Traditionally, the banking system is the established medium of settlement of economic transactions. In fact, the payment and settlement system holds the key for efficient economic activity. A sluggish payment system act as a limiting factor in an economy, which otherwise has potential for rapid growth. More specifically, it comes in the way of growth of capital market activity, trading and other market operations. It is therefore necessary that in the growing economy, the payment and settlement systems are improved and updated to subserve their role. The nature and type of process, involved in these systems are such that the computer and communication technologies can be adopted with greater advantage in terms of efficiency and speed.

Against this backdrop, the Reserve Bank of India appointed in June 1994 a committee on Technology issues relating to Payment System, cheque clearing and Securities Settlement in the Banking Industry. The committee was required to undertake a critical review of the existing procedure and practices relating to transfer of funds, payments systems and settlement procedures, cheque clearing and the related work flow. The committee was also required to make recommendations containing action-oriented, step-by-step solutions on the different items, keeping in the long-term perspective of widening the use of modern technology in the banking industry.

The committee was headed by Shri W.S. Saraf, Executive Director, Reserve Bank of India, Mumbai and twelve other members from commercial banks and other institutions involved with financial sector.

## Smt. K.S. Shere Committee on Legislative Aspects of Electronic Banking

### Formation of the Committee

Cash and negotiable instruments are treated as the first and second great revolutions respectively, in the history of payments systems; Electronic Payments undoubtedly, has to be recognized as the third.

The advent of electronics in banking, has brought about a sea change in the nature of banker-customer relation and perception of customer service in banking business. The introduction of electronic technology in banking which has resulted in far-reaching changes in the banking systems. Further one of the major recommendation of the Saraf Committee was the introduction of Electronic Fund Transfer in the banking system which prompted the Governor, Reserve Bank of India, to constitute this committee.

The committee formulated was headed by Smt. K.S. Shere, Principal Legal Adviser, Reserve Bank of India, Mumbai, and nine other members to suggest legislative measures needed before introduction of electronic fund transfer and other electronic payments in the banking industry.

## Dr. A. Vasudevan Committee on Technology Upgradation in Banking Sector

### Formation of the Committee

In order to examine the various issues pertaining to technology upgradation in the banking sector and to suggest steps that facilitate implementation of the spirit of the recommendations of the Narasimham Committee II, in this regard in a time-bound manner, the Reserve Bank of India appointed, in September 1998, a 'Committee on Technology Upgradation in the Banking Sector' having representation from the Government, Reserve Bank of India, banks and academic institutions associated with information technology. Dr. A. Vasudevan, (Executive Director), Reserve Bank of India was the Chairman.

The Committee made several recommendations. The Committee's major recommendations were under the following heads:

- INFINET Usage
- Standardization and Security
- Outsourcing Technology and Services
- Computerization of Government Transactions
- Data Warehousing, data Mining and MIS
- Legal framework for electronic banking
- BPR
- HRD

## Recommendations

- The INFINET should be a blend of satellite, microwave and terrestrial links appropriately configured depending upon availability, accessibility and likely volume of message traffic. The use of VSATs will be particularly effective in places, which are inaccessible, and in difficult terrain. The transponder capacity needs to be enhanced to the extent feasible along with the number of outroutes as the demand grows. INFINET may be expanded by using a blend of satellite and land links as media for payment and settlement systems backbone with the growth in network traffic.
- There should be an appropriate institutional arrangement for key management and authentication by way of a certification agency. RBI may consider appointing IDRBT as the certification agency for security management.
- The technology should be allowed to evolve into standard based solutions for multi-vendor heterogeneous environment working co-operatively and collectively for EFTPOS, including the debit, credit and smart cards based operations. Card layout with Europay, Master Card VISA (EMV) specifications appears most suitable.
- The RBI and banks should have a Standing Committee with members having requisite expertise to periodically review standards/security policies/message formats/system software and their implementation.

## Outsourcing of Technology and Services

- Outsourcing software technology would be a better option for banks to resort to in the context of rapid changes taking place in the IT industry.
- Software outsourced could be customized – either in-house or through outside vendors. It is essential that software that has been outsourced is maintained regularly – either by outsourcing maintenance or by in-house maintenance.
- Specific terms and conditions governing the outsourcing activity have to be clearly spelt. Factors such as security, safety for day-to-day operations, integrity of data, liability for third party software, confidentiality obligations, rights of bank personnel to access vendor sites, penalty clauses for delays, etc., should be integral part of agreement with vendors. There is a need for obtaining full sets of documentation – both user and system. The entire source code should be obtained, if need be under an ESCROW arrangement.

## Computerization of Government Transactions

- There is a need to computerize all branches of banks dealing with Government transactions. In the first phase computerization of all focal point branches and State Government Link Cells should be completed by 31st March 2000 to be followed by the second phase of computerization of all branches dealing with Government transaction on an expeditious basis.

- The computerization of Government department should be synchronized with the computerization of bank branches dealing with Government transactions.
- The Public Accounts Departments of the RBI should be connected to Central Accounts Section (CAS), RBI, Nagpur to enable same day reporting and booking of Government transactions. Establishment of connectivity between the CAS, Nagpur and the Reserve Banl's departments (DGBA, IDMC) and the Controller General of Accounts and the Finance departments of State Government is necessary. The RBI should develop the necessary software package for information exchange using the INFINET.
- There is a need to delink the submission of scrolls from the funds settlement by the payee branch. The computerization of Government accounts would require a process re-engineering to upgrade the entire process of Government accounting/funding.

**Data Warehousing, Data Mining and Management Information System**

- A robust MIS founded on data warehousing and data mining, at individual bank level is essential for implementing various regulatory guidelines including the latest one on ALM. The structure, configuration and design of the data warehouse may vary from bank to bank.
- All banks should put in place their data warehouse strategy by 1 January 2001. A Task Force may be set-up by IBA to explore feasible methodology for working out a unique identification system for individual customer data bases at banks.
- The Reserve Bank of India could establish a Data Warehouse on Banking and Finance for the data collected under the regulatory provisions. Data collected by the Department of Banking Supervision, the Department of banking Operations and Development, the Exchange Control Department, the Department of Economic Analysis and Policy and the Department of Statistical Analysis and Computer Services of the RBI can be used for data warehousing and data mining.

**Legal Framework for Electronic Banking**

- The Reserve Bank may promote amendment to the Reserve Bank of India Act, 1934 and assume the regulatory and supervisory powers on payment and settlement systems. Simultaneously, the RBI may promote a new legislation on Electronic Funds Transfer System to facilitate multiple payment systems to be set-up for banks and financial institutions.
- A Standing Committee to examine legal issues on Electronic Banking with members drawn from the Legal Departments of the RBI, IBA and a few banks may be set-up by the Reserve bank.
- Issues on confidentiality of data in the computerized environment and in the context of banker's secrecy obligations require a detailed scrutiny which may be examined by the proposed Standing Committee on legal issues on Electronic Banking.

**Other Related Issues**

- Re-engineering: banks may choose the branches and areas of operations where they have already introduced a certain degree of automation and computerization and review the systems and procedures in these branches/areas to adapt them to the technology that is newly introduced. These banks should now attempt to have a hi-tech bank within the bank, totally distinct and different from the other branches and areas of operation which now perform the routine business without that much of intensity of computerization. The stress should be laid on review of the processes, based on the technology introduced or likely to be introduced in selected areas, dovetailing with the processes at the other branches and, if necessary, there can be a separate manual or work procedure for this purpose, without disturbing the existing situation.
- Human Resource Development: Education of staff on IT should be given due importance. Adequate budgetary allocation for the purpose needs to be given. The training establishments of the banks should be strengthened with adequate personnel and other infrastructure facilities, to impart necessary IT training to all levels of staff. There is a need for an institution specializing in affording training to bank staff exclusively in banking related IT.
- The larger banks should explore the possibilities of giving exposure to their technical staff on the latest developments that are taking place around the world in the area of IT and allied areas by deputing their technical officers to the banks and other specialized institutions abroad and also to the Seminars, Workshops, etc., relating to IT.
- Sharing of Experiences on Technology Implementation: The meetings of Computer Policy and Planning Department (CPPD) Chiefs should be held frequently enough to be effective. The IBA Standing Committee on technology issues may also meet more frequently to ensure the successful implementation of industry level technology projects like ECS, EFT, SPNS and Smart Card. One of the goals should be to make India a good market place for banking software. Such a more would help in driving down the cost of banking technology over a period of time.

**S.R. Mittal Working Group on Internet Banking**

Banks have traditionally been in the forefront of harnessing technology to improve their products, services and efficiency. They have, over a long time, being using electronic and telecommunication networks for delivering a wide range of value added products and services. With the popularity of PCs, easy access to Internet and World Wide Web (WWW), Internet is increasingly used by banks as a channel for receiving instructions and delivering their products and services to their customers. This form of banking is generally referred to as Internet Banking, although the range of products and services offered by different banks vary widely both in their content and sophistication.

## Distinctive Features of I-Banking

1. It removes the traditional geographical barriers as it could reach out to customers of different countries / legal jurisdiction. This has raised the question of jurisdiction of law-supervisory system to which such transactions should be subjected.
2. It has added a new dimension to different kinds of risks traditionally associated with banking, heightening some of them and throwing new risk control challenges.
3. Security of banking transactions, validity of electronic contract, customers' privacy, etc., which have all along been concerns of both bankers and supervisors have assumed different dimensions given that Internet is a public domain, not subject to control by any single authority or group of users.
4. It poses a strategic risk of loss of business to those banks who do not respond in time, to this new technology, being the efficient and cost effective delivery mechanism of banking services.
5. A new form of competition has emerged both from the existing players and new players on the market who are not strictly banks.

Reserve Bank of India constituted a Working Group to examine different issues relating to I-banking and recommend technology, security, legal standards and operational standards keeping in view the international best practices. The Group was headed by S.R. Mittal, the Chief General Manager-in-Charge of the Department of Information Technology and comprised experts from the fields of banking regulation and supervision, commercial banking, law and technology.

The Group made a number of recommendations. A summary of major recommendations is given below:

The Working Group on Internet Banking, appointed by the Reserve bank, in its report had classified the internet products into three types based on the levels of access granted. They are as under:

*(a) Level 1: Information only Systems*: General purpose information like interest rates, branch locations, product features, FAQs, loan and deposit calculators, etc., were provided on the Bank's Website. There was also provision for downloading various types of application forms. The communication is normally done through e-mail. There was no interaction between the Bank's application systems and the customer. No identification or authentication of customers was done.

In this case, the possibility of any hacking or an unauthorized person getting into the production system of the Bank through the internet does not exist.

*(b) Level 2: Electronic Information Transfer System:* These systems provided the customer-specific information in the form of account balances, transaction details, statement of accounts,

etc. The information is still largely 'read only'. Identification and authentication of the customer was through password. The information was fetched from the bank's application systems either in batch mode or off-line.

In this case also, the application systems cannot be directly accessed through the Internet.

*(c) Level 3 : Fully Transactional System*: These system allowed bi-directional transactional capabilities. Transactions could be submitted by the customers for on-line update. These systems required high degree of security and control. Invariably in such environment, web server and the application systems were linked over a secured infrastructure.

The basic requirements in terms of technology covering computerization, networking and security; inter-bank payment gateway and legal infrastructure for introduction of internet banking.

**Dr. R.B. Barman Working Group on Information System Audit & Security**

The application of Information Technology has brought about significant changes in banking and financial sector process and store data. This sector is now poised to countenance various developments such as internet banking, e-money, e-cheque, e-commerce, etc., as the most modern methods of delivery of services to the customers. The telecommunication networks have played a catalytic role in the expansion and integration of the Information System (IS), within and between the institutions, facilitating data accessibility to different users. In view of the critical importance of IS, there is a need to exercise constant vigilance for the safety of the financial systems. Structured, well-defined and documented security policies, standards and guidelines lay the foundation for good IS security and each institution is required to define, document, communicate, implement and audit IS Security to ensure the confidentiality, integrity, authenticity and timely availability of information, which is of paramount importance to business operations.

Reserve Bank of India constituted a 'Working Group for Information Systems Security for the banking and Financial Sector' under the chairmanship of Dr. R.B. Burman, Executive Director, Reserve Bank of India, to discuss and finalize the standards and procedures for IS Audit and IS Security Guidelines for the banking and financial sector. The Working Group had prepared this report on the 'Information Systems Audit Policy' including 'Information Systems Security Guidelines'.

This report discusses various aspects of IS audit such as the objectives, approaches, methodology, charter, planning, standards and guidelines, sampling, evidence and documentation. It discusses the skills, the IS auditors will require to possess as also the way they were required to address the irregularities, observed during auditing. It discussed the issue relating to the corporate governance of Information Systems and Security Controls. It had brought out the primary roles to be performed by the auditor.

Under the 'Information Systems Security Guidelines', the report discusses IS Security Controls relating to computer hardware, software, network, Telecommuting/Tele-Working, Mobile Computing, Computer Media Handling, Voice, Telephone and related equipment, internet and the procedures/methodologies to be adopted to safeguard the information and information systems. It discusses issues such as Change Control Mechanism, Separation of Development and (Production) Operational facilities, Information Handling and Backup, Electronic Mail and Financial Services/Products. It emphasizes the use/implementation of Firewall, Digital Signature, Cryptographic Controls, Business Continuity Planning (BCP) Framework/Disaster Recovery Planning (DRP) including Cryptographic disasters. It also discusses various other issues relating to Certification Authorities (CAs)/Trusted Third parties (TTPs), Compliance with Legal Requirements, Intellectual Property Rights (IPR), Review of IS Security Policy and Human Resources.

**RBI Financial Sector Vision Technology Vision Document 2005**

The Reserve Bank of India published the Financial Sector Technology Vision Document in July 2005. The Vision Document has enumerated the initiatives to be undertaken by the Reserve Bank in the medium-term in order to ensure maintenance of overall systemic efficiency of the financial sector. In a nutshell, the 'Financial Sector Technology Vision' document, elucidates the Technology Vision for the financial sector, under the following four heads:

- IT for regulation and supervision
- IT and IDRBT
- IT for the financial sector
- IT related functions.

The overall vision that the RBI has for the financial sector is captured in its Vision Statement: 'IT for Efficiency and Excellence'. The Corporate Objective ahs been identified to be 'Enabling banks to leverage on It for better customer service, improved housekeeping and overall systemic efficiency'. The Financial Sector Technology Vision document outlines the previews and prospects as envisioned by the Reserve bank for the medium-term period covering the period 2005-08.

**R. Gandhi Working Group on IT Support for UCBs**

The vision document for Urban Co-operative Banks, released in March 2005 proposed signing of Memorandum of Understanding (MOU) between RBI and Central and respective state government for establishing in consultative approach to supervision and regulation of Urban Co-operative Banks. The Reserve Bank has so far signed such MOUs with 16 state governments and the central government.

In terms of the MOUs, the Reserve Bank is committed to facilitate initiatives in Urban Co-operative Banks. In furtherance of the commitment, Governor announced in the mid-term Review of the Annual Policy 2007-08 that 'a working group comprising representatives of the

Reserve Bank, State Governments and the UCB sector, would be constituted to examine the various areas where IT support could be provided by the Reserve Bank.

The Group made number of recommendations summary of these is given below:

(a) In order to implement the minimum level of infrastructure by Urban Co-operative Banks as indicated, core Banking solution would be require to be adopted by the banks. The models for acquiring the IT infrastructure could be one of the following.

(1) Application Service Provider (ASP) model.

In respect of the small banks particularly the unit banks, best method for computerization could be through ASP model as the problems of software development and maintenance, training and retention of IT professionals, installation and maintenance of complex and costly hardware and other logistics like data centers would be addressed by the service provider without need for much initiative or involvement of the UCB.

An agency like IDRB could shortlist/Select one/two few vendors and be the conduit and service quality assuror to the banks.

(2) Outright Purchase Model: If banks seek to go for outright purchase of the core Banking, including data center, the cast would be in the range of 1.5 to 2 crores for 5-10 branches per bank. Further availability and retention of IT savvy professionals are also to be ensured. The banks which are well capitalized and with good track record and which have IT savvy personnel to implement and deal with the vendors. And such banks which have a business of more than 100 crores, CRAR of over 9 percent and have been making profit for last 3 years could be provided support for outright purchase.

(3) Delivery Mechanism: The support will be available for all urban co-op Banks, however it should not be given in the form of a grant, support may be in the form of a loan and not subsidy. Different type of interest free loans, moratorium, less service charge etc. was prescribed by the working group in their report.

**Information Technology Act, 2000**

The Government of India enacted in June 2000. The Information Technology Act, 2000. The Act is as follows:

1. It provides legal recognition for transactions carried out by means of electronic data interchange and other means of electronic communication, commonly referred to as 'electronic commerce',
2. facilities electronic foiling of documents with the Government agencies,
3. suitably amends the Indian penal Code, the Indian Evidence Act, 1872, the Banker's Book Evidence Act, 1891 and the reserve Bank of India Act, 1934 for matters connected therewith or incidental thereto.

The United Nations Commission on International Trade law had recommended to member nations that they adopt the Model Law on Electronic Commerce.

The overall net effect of the It Act, 2000 is that the information, transaction and records in the electronic format have been granted legal validity and sanction, digital signatures have been defined and made legal. It is now possible to retain information in an electronic format. Electronic contract has been recognized to be legal and binding. Some types of cyber crimes have been defined and made punishable offences like hacking, damage to computer source code, publishing of information which is obscene in the electronic form, breach of confidentiality and privacy and publishing digital signature certificate in certain particulars and for fraudulent purpose. The amendments to the Bankers' Books Evidence Act mean that the information, transaction and records kept by banks in the electronic format have been granted legal validity and sanction.

# CHAPTER 3

# Technology: Triggering a Banking Revolution

Today, banking across the world revolves round technology. To say that technology has revolutionized the banking industry is an understatement of the 21st Century. Banking has become increasingly global, with accompanying challenges and opportunities. Among challenges are risks and global consequences. One the opportunities front, the frontier is unlimited; because, technology has enabled banks to redefine their business models, become fiercely competitive, viable, profitable and most important, to serve the customers to their utmost satisfaction.

The world has just witnessed an economic meltdown and some of the biggest names in global investment banking have perished. India and its banking industry has bravely faced the financial crisis and emerged with little bruises and reduced profits. But it has survived the worst-ever crisis. It will need technology more than ever before, to manage its assets and liabilities better, which is the crux of banking business.

This chapter deals with the importance technology, especially Information Technology (IT) and its various products, as said afore, have revolutionized banking operations.

Technology, which offers immense scope for innovation, has formed the backbone of the Indian industry, more so in banking because of its constant interaction with the public, namely its customers.

No wonder then, the banking industry has pioneered the adoption of IT and gained immensely from it. Over the years, banks have been among the first clients to understand how to use technology to simplify procedures and deliver unique services to their customers in the face of intense competition. The role of Information Technology has become so integrated and all encompassing with banking that it is impossible to think of banking processes without an effective IT system in place.

Co-operative banks, including the Urban Co-operative Banks, the focus of this book, are increasingly under pressure to adopt technological solutions in a competitive scenario, both in rural and city environs. As larger commercial banks are setting up branches in the rural areas, the smaller co-operatives are looking at ways to counter this competition and hence, are increasingly opting for better technology solutions. The key area of technology that these banks are looking at is core-banking solutions in order to modernize and provide better customer services. The later chapters of this book deal exclusively with a case study involving two urban co-operative banks to prove how Information Technology has transformed them into efficient and profit-making entities.

### RBI's IT Vision Document (2011-17)

A recent report of the Reserve Bank of India (RBI) acknowledges that Information Technology (IT) has transformed the conduct of businesses in every sector of the economy. Financial sector is one such area where the touch of IT has completely overhauled the nature and accelerated the pace of business. IT has been instrumental in improved communication and connectivity across all segments/players of this sector as well as in enhancing the quality, efficiency and speed of delivery of financial services.

**IT & Inclusiveness of Financial Sector**

RBI, as the Central bank controlling the monetary and banking policies of the country, has played a pivotal role in this process of transformation of the financial sector with the use of IT. It has strived to create a conducive environment for promoting technological adoption encompassing the financial sector. Moreover, being an important institution in the financial sector, RBI too has undergone the process of technological change.

**Most Importantly, RBI has endeavoured to streamline technological change in a manner that would help to enhance the inclusiveness of the financial sector.**

While technology has become an integral part of conducting and managing business in the financial sector, it has constantly remained flexible and fluid. It has evolved over the years and it is important, therefore, that the financial sector too reviews these developments and adapts itself to the same. It is in this context of review and adaptation to technology that the information management requires specific attention.

The Department of Information Technology (DIT) of the Reserve Bank was formed in 1995 to exclusively to look after the Reserve Bank's requirements in the field of computerization and modern communications network and undertake advance planning for technology upgradation in the banking sector. Over a period of 15 years, DIT has satisfactorily fulfilled most of the objectives set to it at the time of formation. It has been instrumental in designing, developing and implementing IT-based systems, which have helped RBI in the discharge of various functions.

During this period, several developments have taken place in the realm of IT and its adoption in the banking sector. The developments largely relate to improvements in back office management in the form of streamlining Management Information System (MIS), strengthening centralised processing and improving communication networks. As these developments have a bearing on the role, functions and organization of the Department, it is necessary to review the objectives of DIT in the light of these developments.

To steer the financial sector to achieve the desired technological goals, RBI has brought out two vision documents encompassing the periods 2005-08 and 2008-10. As the tenure of the previous IT vision document was 2008-10, the department set out to prepare the next version of the vision document for the period 2011-17. Accordingly, RBI set up a high-level committee under the chairmanship of Dr K.C. Chakrabarty, Deputy Governor, RBI, on 16 February 2010 for preparing the Information Technology Vision Document 2011-17. The objective of the Document is to guide RBI for transforming itself into an Information intensive knowledge organization and help the Indian banking sector at large, a step that indicates how serious is RBI in infusing technology into its own working in order to guide the banking sector.

RBI has intensified its focus further. With the increase in transactions in electronic mode, it was also critical to examine the legal implications for banks arising out of cyber laws and steps that were required to be taken to suitably mitigate the legal risks. To consider these issues, the Governor had announced, in the Annual Monetary Policy Statement 2010-11 in April, 2010, the creation of a Working Group on Information Security, Electronic Banking, Technology Risk Management and Tackling Cyber Fraud.

Some of the major recommendations of the group are:

- Banks need to formulate a Board approved IT strategy/plan document. An IT policy needs to be framed for regular management of IT functions and ensure that detailed documentation in terms of procedures and guidelines exists and are implemented. The strategic plan and policy need to be reviewed annually.
- A need was felt to create an exclusive Board level IT Strategy Committee with a minimum of two directors as members, one of whom should be an independent director. All members of the IT Strategy Committee would need to be technically competent while at least one member would need to have substantial expertise in managing/guiding technology initiatives
- IT Steering Committee needs to be created with representations from various IT functions, HR, Legal and business functions as appropriate. The role of the IT Steering Committee would be to assist the Executive Management in the implementation of the IT strategy approved by the Board.
- The IT Steering Committee should assess whether the IT Governance structure fosters accountability, is effective and transparent, has well defined objectives and actions and unambiguous responsibilities for each level in the organization.
- Key focus areas of IT Governance that need to be considered include strategic alignment, value delivery, risk management, resource management and performance management.
- Requirements for trained resources with requisite skill sets for the IT function need to be understood and assessed appropriately. A periodic assessment of the training requirements for human resources should be made to ensure that sufficient, competent and capable human resources are available.
- Banks need to establish and maintain an enterprise information model to enable applications development and decision-supporting activities, consistent with IT strategy. The model should facilitate optimal creation, use and sharing of information by a business, in a way that it maintains integrity, and is flexible, functional, cost-effective, timely, secure and resilient to failure
- There is also a need to maintain an "enterprise data dictionary" that incorporates the organization's data syntax rules. This should enable the sharing of data among applications and systems, promote a common understanding of data among IT and business users and preventing incompatible data elements from being created

- The major role of the Board/ Top Management should involve approving information security policies, establishing necessary organizational processes/ functions for information security and providing necessary resources.
- Each bank needs to create a separate information security function to focus exclusively on information security management. The organization of the information security function should be commensurate with the nature and size of activities of a bank and extent of IT leverage and e-delivery channels. The function should be adequately resourced in terms of the number of staff, their range and level of skills, and tools or techniques.
- Risk assessment is the core competence of information security management for a bank. The risk assessment must, for each asset within its scope, identify the threat/ vulnerability combinations that have a likelihood of impacting the confidentiality, availability or integrity of that asset - from a business, compliance and/or contractual perspective

The Board of Directors and Senior Management should oversee the implementation of a safe and sound IT operations environment. The policies and procedures defined as part of IT operations should support a bank's goals and objectives as well as follow statutory and regulatory requirements.

IT operations include business services which are available to the internal or external customers of the organization using IT as a service delivery component. Instances include Mobile Banking and Internet Banking. IT Operations also include IT components which are used to support IT Operations, which can be service desk application, ticketing tools, event management tools etc. Banks may consider including test environment, quality assurance environment and any other such environment besides production environment within the scope of IT Operations.

The Board of Directors and Senior Management should oversee the implementation of a safe and sound IT operations environment. The policies and procedures defined as part of IT operations should support a bank's goals and objectives as well as follow statutory and regulatory requirements.

IT operations include business services which are available to the internal or external customers of the organization using IT as a service delivery component. Instances include Mobile Banking and Internet Banking. IT Operations also include IT components which are used to support IT Operations, which can be service desk application, ticketing tools, event management tools etc. Banks may consider including test environment, quality assurance environment and any other such environment besides production environment within the scope of IT Operations.

- Over the years, the IT infrastructure in banks has grown and developed, and there may not be a clear picture of all the IT services currently being provided, and the consumers for each service. In order to establish an accurate IT landscape it is recommended that an IT Service Catalogue is defined, produced and maintained. The Service Catalogue can be considered a repository that provides information on all the IT services supported by the IT Operations framework.

- Most retail cyber frauds and electronic banking frauds would be of values less than Rs.1 crore and hence may not attract the necessary attention of the Special Committee of the Board. Since these frauds are large in number and have the potential to reach large proportions, it is recommended that the Special Committee of the Board be briefed separately on this to keep them aware of the proportions of the fraud and the steps taken by the bank to mitigate them. The Special Committee should specifically monitor the progress of the mitigating steps taken by the bank in case of electronic frauds and the efficacy of the same in containing fraud numbers and values.
- Various fraud prevention practices need to be followed by banks. These include fraud vulnerability assessments(for business functions and also delivery channels), review of new products and processes, putting in place fraud loss limits, root cause analysis for actual fraud cases above Rs.10 lakhs, reviewing cases where a unique modus operandi is involved, ensuring adequate data/information security measures, following KYC and Know your employee/vendor procedures, ensuring adequate physical security, sharing of best practices of fraud prevention and creation of fraud awareness among staff and customers.
- The Board of Directors/Senior Management need to be committed to the process of consumer education initiatives by providing adequate resources, evaluating the effectiveness of the process and fine-tuning and improving customer education measures on an ongoing basis.
- To get desired support for the programme, it is important to identify and involve key stakeholders in decision-making, planning, implementation and evaluation. A working group or committee can be created to establish a clear goal for the endpoint in consultation with key stakeholders, clearly define roles, responsibilities and accountabilities, communicate in an open, clear and timely manner, allowing for flexibility in approaches to suit different stakeholder needs, support training and development to ensure a change in behaviour and culture, learn from previous and ongoing experiences and celebrate achievements.
- Banks need to follow a systematic process to develop an awareness programme through the stages of planning and design, execution and management, and evaluation and course correction.
- Since awareness programmes should be customized for the specific audience, it is important to identify and segment the target users for the programmes - like bank customers, employees, law enforcement personnel, fraud risk professionals, media partners, etc.
- Building consensus among decision makers and stakeholders for financial and administrative support is an important step in the programme. In this respect, both fixed and variable costs need to be identified.
- Since the target groups obtain information from a variety of sources, more than one communication channel could be used to engage them successfully.

- A research group should be formed to continually update the communications team with the latest trends and evolving modus operandi. The team would maintain a repository of material such as case studies, sample mails, samples of fraudulent documents, international practice/developments etc.
- Evaluation of the effects of various campaigns for specific target groups can be measured through qualitative (e.g. focus groups, interviews) and/ or quantitative (e.g. questionnaires, omnibus surveys) research. Evaluation against metrics, performance objectives, etc. should also be conducted to check the campaign's effectiveness, and to establish lessons learned to improve future initiatives.
- At the industry level, each bank should have a documented policy, training mechanisms and research units. Material can be pooled from these units to be used on a larger platform towards a common goal

Banking analysts say that today, banks' operations are focused on three areas: meet customers' growing service expectations, cut costs, and manage competition. To meet these challenges, banks are striving to introduce innovative new financial products that would help them bring in more and more customers and business. Any new financial product or service that a bank offers will be intrinsically related to technology, which offers unending scope to innovate.

**SPS Grover**, *Vice President - Technology Sales, Oracle India, in a cyber media interview listed following technology-related trends to prevail in the near future.*

- Growth in **electronic payments** will accelerate. Innovative, multi-channel payments will continue to grow on the retail side.
- Heightened attention to **security and fraud control** - Fraud and security concerns remain top-of-mind for many banks. Several factors are driving banks to invest more heavily in security and identity management and human resources to combat fraud. Such factors include: increasing concern regarding regulatory compliance; vulnerability created by check imaging and the need for new check fraud measures; and continuing attacks against cards at both the POS and ATM.
- **Customer Relationship Management** - CRM has today evolved into a customer-centric philosophy that must permeate an entire organization. In Banking, CRM is about offering a better proposition to the customer after understanding his or her entire portfolio of investments with the bank. Customers nowadays acknowledge CRM as an enterprise wide software solution with back end integration rather than being understood as a stand-alone software module for call center or Sales Force automation or selling on the web.
- **Core banking applications** - Core banking applications helps provide complete front-end and backend automation of banks. Indian Banks are widening their operations increasingly, this means they need to engage in the practice of core banking. Banks are increasingly looking for solutions to manage and operate their core banking functions effectively. Core banking is helping not just the banks to retain customers and lower the

service cost to customers but is also allowing customers to interact with their banks seamlessly.

- **Risk management** is another area where core-banking applications can help. Getting the risk management systems in place and gathering the necessary data for internal ratings-based (IRB) approaches for credit risk and the Advanced Management Approach (AMA) for operational risk are the priority areas for the Indian banking sector. The recent wave of consolidation amongst the smaller banks showcases the importance of compliance to the sector.

Automation is the key thing that banks need to have in place. This industry is very quickly adopting newer technologies to keep pace with growing competition and expanding customer base. It involves a combination of centralized networks, operations, and a core banking application. Automation enables banks to offer round the year service using lesser manpower. But to be really competitive, banks need to think beyond just basic automation.

According to Grover, a prominent issue facing banks is in accurate analysis of financial data to identify business opportunities - whether cross-sell and up-sell opportunities. This is where technologies such as data warehousing or data mining come into play here. These drivers that present a compelling case for banks to consider Business Intelligence (BI) and analytics software tools that can turn data piles into relevant and useful information and enable businesses to take better informed business decisions.

Another key aspect to consider is the need for a centralized database. With multi-branches, the databases should be updated instantaneously, irrespective of the branch.

## IT & Current Scenario

Given the fact that 75 percent of the financial sector assets come from banking services, this industry plays a pivotal role in governing the economy. Indian banking industry, today is in the midst of an IT revolution. A combination of regulatory and competitive reasons have led to increasing importance of total banking, automation in the Indian Banking Industry. Deregulation and the demands of the globalized economy is transforming the Indian banking industry at the speed of thought. In this metamorphosis – technology, customer service, and consolidation have emerged as the key parameters for defining performance. Liberalization in Banking and adoption of technology as one of the means of delivering customers service coincided in the early nineties. Banks in the regulated environments were used to walk-in customers, regulated interest rates on deposits as well as advances, limited involvement in the international banking and moderate scale of operations. Liberalization allowed the entry of Private Banks. These new generation Private Banks were the harbingers of technology adoption from the beginning. Entry of new banks resulted in paradigm shift in the ways of banking in India. The growing competition, and the growing expectations led to increased awareness amongst banks on the role and importance of technology in banking. The arrival of foreign and private banks with their superior state-of-art technology-based services pushed the Indian Banks also to follow suit by going in for the latest technologies so as to meet the threat of competition and retain their customer base. Nationalized banks, co-operative Banks and old generation private banks started adopting the technology thereafter.

**From Branch Automation to Core Banking**

The Software Package for Banking Applications in India had their beginnings in the middle of 80s, when the Banks started computerizing the branches in a limited manner. Branch automation though helped banks in reducing the manual work and balancing the accounts, interest calculations etc., it did not bring transformation in the systems and practices followed by Banks for ages together. Branch automation merely automated the manual processes. Branches continued to be independent islands. Customers had to heavily depend on the Branch functioning for their operations. Collection of outstation cheques, system or carrying cash in excess of requirements and such other inefficiencies continued to be in the system.

The early 90's saw the plummeting hardware prices and advent of cheap and inexpensive but high-powered PCs and servers. The middle of late 90s witnessed the financial reforms, deregulation, globalization etc. It coupled with rapid revolution in communication technologies and evolution of novel concept of 'convergence' of computer and communication technologies, like Internet, mobile / cell phones etc. These changes on the technology front enabled banks to undertake implementation of core banking initiative. Core Banking or any where banking enabled flood gates of opportunities and challenges in the banking industry. The core of the banking at the outset enabled any branch and thereby provided inter-connectivity amongst the branches of banks. Collection of outstation cheques, inter-city or at par cheques became a reality. Customers could get multiple delivery options for availing banking services. ATM not only facilitated withdrawal of cash at any time during the day, but because of connectivity, it became possible to form a consortium of ATM of different banks and facilitate customer to withdraw cash from any ATM set-up in any nook and corner of the globe. Internet Banking facilitated customers to do the banking transactions with a click of mouse on the desktop or laptop from home or office. Customers can not only transfer funds from their account to any other person, but also can take the view of their statement of accounts, log requests for issuance of cheque books, monitor MIS provided by Banks on usage of their limits/balances in the account and instruct bank for such other miscellaneous services as issuance of demand drafts, sending of cheques directly to the vendors etc. Mobile has revolutionized the Banking operations altogether. Customers can get alerts and messages about operations in the account and check their balance in the account using pull message and send requests for issuance of cheque books.

On banks the Bank's front technology had provided many opportunities and benefits to manage operations without increasing staff strength.:

Following liberalization, business volumes of the banks have increased manifold. Regulator too has cast additional obligations on banks such as income recognition norms, capital adequacy norms, risk-based audit and such other prudential norms due to which the complexity in the functioning of the banks has increased. Technology has enabled banks to manage the business volumes as well as the complexities.

Inter-connectivity of branches and centralized database has provided banks with access to Management Information System (MIS) on an on going basis without delay. Banks therefore have been continuously evolving their product to meet their customers changing demands and have also been able to comply with the requirements of regulator for timely submission of returns.

Technology has enabled banks to minimize frauds. ATM transactions have facilitated withdrawal of cash by customers. It is unlikely that customers' PIN would be traced even in cases where card is lost. This is because, after three wrong attempts to key in the PIN, the card is retained in the ATM. Moreover, banks have been sending SMS messages immediately after the cash is withdrawn. On the basis of past history of frauds, Banks have been proactively monitoring the transactions in accounts where the risk is high or medium. Technology has facilitated banks for having built in checks to prevent misuse and committing of frauds by customers and in collusion with the staff members of the Bank.

Technology has poised before banks of many of the challenges as well. Core Banking system has become an in mission critical in nature. The failure of the system will bring to an halt operations of the Banks at all its branches. Apart from pecuniary loss to the bank as well as to its customers, such an event would tarnish the image of the bank. It is therefore essential to have disaster recovery management system in place. Many banks have set up DRS keeping in mind that the data center as well as DRS site do not fall in the same seismic zones. 9-11 event in US showed the ability of many banks to respond to crisis as occurred thereafter.

Internet banking, Mobile Banking and banking through off-site ATMS were fraught with risks. In case of Internet banking, hacking by the intruders would cause substantial damage to the customers and banks own reputation. Banks therefore need to revisit its security measures periodically using ethical hacking, vulnerability testing and such other techniques. In case of ATMs, in addition to physical security, banks are required to equip ATM rooms with hidden cameras to track miscreants.

**Technology at Macro Level**

In India, banks as well as other financial entities entered the world of information technology and with Indian Financial Net (INFINET). INFINET is a wide area satellite based network (WAN) using VSAT (Very Small Aperture Terminals) technology, were jointly set up by the Reserve bank and Institute for Development and research in Banking Technology (IDRBT) in June 1999. The Indian Financial Network (INFINET) which had initially comprised only the public sector banks were opened up for participation by other categories of members. The first set of applications that could benefit greatly from the use of technological advances in the computer and communications area relate to the Payment systems which formed the lifeline of any banking activity. The process of reforms in payment and settlement systems has gained momentum with the implementation of projects such as NDS (Negotiated Dealing System), CFMS (Centralised Funds Management System) for better funds management by banks and SFMS (Structured Financial Messaging Solution) for secure message transfer. This resulted in funds transfers and funds-related message transfer to be routed electronically across banks using the medium of the INFINET. Negotiated dealing system (NDS), which has become operational since February 2002 and RTGS (Real Time Gross Settlement system) in 2003 were other major developments in the area.

The Information Technology Act, 2000 has given legal recognition to creation, transmission and retention of an electronic (or magnetic) data to be treated as valid proof in a the court of law and except in those areas, which continue to be governed by the provisions of the Negotiable Instruments Act, 1881.

**Centralized Funds Management System**

The centralized funds management system (CFMS) provides a centralized viewing of balance positions of the account holders across different accounts maintained at various locations of RBI.

**Certification and Digital Signatures**

The mid-term Review of October 2002 indicated the need for information security on the network and the use of public key infrastructure (PKI) by banks. The Controller of Certifying Authorities, Government of India, have approved the Institute for Development and Research in Banking Technology (IDRBT) as a Certification Authority (CA) for digital signatures. Consequently, the process of setting up of registration authorities (RA) under the CA has commenced at various banks. In addition to the negotiated dealing system (NDS), the electronic clearing services (ECS) and electronic funds transfer (EFT) are also being enhanced in terms of security by means of implementation of PKI and digital signatures using the facilities offered by the CA.

**Multi-application Smart Cards**

Recognizing the need for technology based payment products and the growing importance of smart card based payment flowed, a pilot project for multi-application smart cards in conjunction with a few banks and vendors, under the aegis of the Ministry of Communications and Information Technology, Government of India, has been initiated. The project is aimed at the formulation of standards for multi-application smart cards on the basis of inter-operable systems and technological components of the entire system.

Information Technology has basically been used under two different avenues in Banking. One is the Communication and Connectivity and other is Business Process Reengineering regarding Information technology enables sophisticated product development, better market infrastructure, implementation of reliable techniques for control of risks and helps the financial intermediaries to reach geographically at distant and diversified markets.

Technology has changed the face of banking by bringing a customer-centric approach to the industry. The private sector banks took the initiative in introducing anytime, anywhere banking, to their customers, ATMs, internet banking, and D-MAT, plastic money were the tools that these banks used to woo the customers. The need to use enabling technology is to provide value for money services to the customers and not only helped them reduce operational costs but also helped them in cross selling, which was an imperative need of the hour.

According to projections for 2010 made by IBA, the total deposits of banks in India are expected to increase to Rs. 3,500,000 crore. The implementation of the Basel II accord is expected to strengthen the financial health of banks by adopting globally accepted norms for capital adequacy. Also with the roadmap given to foreign banks and other globally competitive strategies, that will not be a surprise if the Indian banking sector overshoots these projections!

**Cloud Computing – The Next Big Trend in IT- Enabled Services in Banking**

Cloud Computing is the next big trend that will revolutionize information technology enabled services, including banking. As a metaphor for the Internet, "the cloud", when combined with "computing," the meaning gets bigger and fuzzier.

Cloud computing is a way of increasing the capacity of IT services or add capabilities to them without investing in new infrastructure, training new personnel, or licensing new software. Cloud computing encompasses any subscription-based or pay-per-use service that, in real time over the Internet, extends IT's existing capabilities.

Cloud computing is the delivery of computing as a service rather than a product, whereby shared resources, software, and information are provided to computers and other devices as a utility similar to the electricity grid over a network such as the Internet.

Cloud computing provides computation, software, data access, and storage services that do not require end-user knowledge of the physical location and configuration of the system that delivers the services. It is similar to the electricity grid, wherein end-users consume power without needing to understand the devices required to provide the service.

Cloud computing describes a new supplement, consumption, and delivery model for IT services based on Internet protocols, and it typically involves provisioning of dynamically scalable and often virtualized resources. It is a byproduct and consequence of the ease-of-access to remote computing sites provided by the Internet. This may take the form of web-based tools or applications that users can access and use through a web browser as if the programs were installed locally on their own computers.

Cloud computing providers deliver applications via the internet, which are accessed from a web browser, while the business software and data are stored on servers at a remote location. In some cases, legacy applications are delivered via a screen-sharing technology, while the computing resources are consolidated at a remote data center location; in other cases, entire business applications have been coded using web-based technologies such as AJAX.

Most cloud computing infrastructures consist of services delivered through shared data-centers and appearing as a single point of access for consumers' computing needs. Commercial offerings may be required to meet service-level agreements (SLAs), but specific terms are less often negotiated by smaller companies.

**Following are a few examples of Cloud Computing some of which are already in use in the banking sector.**

**SaaS: It is a** type of cloud computing that delivers a single application through the browser to thousands of customers using a multi-tenant architecture. On the customer side, it means no upfront investment in servers or software licensing; on the provider side, with just one app to maintain, costs are low compared to conventional hosting. Salesforce.com is by far the best-known example among enterprise applications, but SaaS is also common for HR apps and has even worked its way up the food chain to ERP, with players such as Workday.

**Utility Computing:** This form of cloud computing is getting new life from Amazon.com, Sun, IBM, and others who now offer storage and virtual servers that IT can access on demand. Liquid Computing's LiquidQ offers similar capabilities, enabling IT to stitch together memory, I/O, storage, and computational capacity as a virtualized resource pool available over the network.

**Web services in the cloud:** Closely related to SaaS, Web service providers offer APIs that enable developers to take advantage of functionality over the Internet, rather than delivering full-blown applications. These could include conventional credit card processing services.

**Platform as a service:** Another SaaS variation, this form of cloud computing delivers development environments as a service. You build your own applications that run on the provider's infrastructure and are delivered to users via the Internet from the provider's servers.

**MSP (Managed Service Providers) :** One of the oldest forms of cloud computing, a managed service is basically an application exposed to IT rather than to end-users, such as a virus scanning service for e-mail or an application monitoring service, which Mercury, among others, provides. Managed security services delivered by SecureWorks, IBM, and Verizon fall into this category, as do such cloud-based anti-spam services as Postini, recently acquired by Google. Other offerings include desktop management services, such as those offered by CenterBeam or Everdream.

**Service commerce platforms:** A mix of SaaS and MSP, this cloud computing service offers a service hub that users interact with. They're most common in trading environments, such as expense management systems that allow users to order travel or secretarial services from a common platform that then coordinates the service delivery and pricing within the specifications set by the user. Examples include Rearden Commerce and Ariba.

**Internet integration :** The integration of cloud-based services is in its early days. OpSource, which mainly concerns itself with serving SaaS providers, recently introduced the OpSource Services Bus, which employs in-the-cloud integration technology from a little startup called Boomi.

Today Cloud Computing can be described as "sky computing," with many isolated clouds of services which IT customers must plug into individually.

# CHAPTER 4

# IT & Urban Co-operative Banks

With the development of information technology, the world has become a global village and it has brought a revolution in the banking industry. The banks appear to be on fast track for IT based products and services. Deregulation and Liberalization in the financial sector which have stimulated financial innovations. Breath taking developments in the technology of telecommunications and electronic data processing have further been accelerated to these changes. Technology has become the fuel for rapid change. IT is no longer considered as mere transaction processing or confined to management information system. In its wider definition, it implies the integration of information system with communication technology and to innovative applications to product manufacturing design and control.

One sector that has undergone fundamental changes as a consequence of the application of IT is banking. The new technology has radically altered the traditional ways of doing banking business. Increasingly, the customers in retail sector are doing business with their banks from the comfortable confines of their homes or offices. Customers can view the accounts and get account statements, transfer funds, purchase drafts by just making a few key punches. Availability of ATMs and plastic cards to a large extent avoid customers going to branch premises. Cards with an embedded micro-processor chip also called smart cards, are adding a new dimension to this scenario. EDI is another development that has made its impact felt in the UCBs. In fact in urban co-op banking, IT is finding its use in five key areas.

- Convenience in product delivery access,
- Managing productivity access,
- Product design,
- Adapting to market and customer needs and
- Access to customer market.

The first serious effort of computerization and mechanization in the urban co-op banking industry was drawn up in 1983-84. But the process of introduction of computerization in the banking industry in India, particularly, in public sector banks, were very slow. As a culmination of the implementation of the recommendations of (Saraf Committee, Share Committee and Vasudevan Committee), today the transactions of all large branches of banks have been fully computerized; banks have moved in the direction of inter-branch and inter-bank connectivity. Electronic Funds transfer and delivery versus payment system have been introduced. Bank customers are becoming very demanding and it is the extensive use of technology that will enable banks to satisfy adequately the requirement of customers. Thus the four major objectives of computerization in the banking are

(a) Improvement in customer service,
(b) Better-house-keeping,
(c) Faster decision making, and
(d) Increase in productivity and profitability.

With the coming into the effort of the IT Act on October 8, 2000, India had reached another significant mile stone on the information super highway. The Act provide legal sanctity. To electronic commerce and lays down penalties for hacking and other crime. India will become the 12th country in the world to have an IT bill in place for recognizing digital signature and facilitating e-commerce.

IT is also helping in cutting costs by providing cheaper ways of delivering products to customers. Banks are moving into the primary services of helping their customers buy things like automobiles, real estates, in all these areas, IT has been an enormous help. The younger age group customers are much more amenable to use electronic delivery channels rather than visiting physical branches. Banks have been cautious in launching new services using IT. The virtual financial services can be largely categorized as follows:

**Automated Teller Machines:**

- ***Cash withdrawals***
- Fast cash
- Details of most recent balance of account
- Mini-statement
- Statement ordering facility
- Deposit facility
- Payments to third parties

**Remote Banking Services:**

- Balance enquiry
- Statement ordering
- Funds transfer (payment to third parties)
- Funds transfer between customers different accounts
- Order traveler's cheques and other financial instruments.

**Services Not Available Through Remote Banking :**

- Cash withdrawal
- Cash /cherub deposit
- Sale of the more complex types of financial services such as life insurance mortgages and pensions.

**Remote Banking Interface:**

- Automated voice-response system
- Interactive television
- Internet terminal

- Screen phone
- Person digital assistant
- Other people provide the information.

**Smart Cards:**

- Stored value cards
- As a replacement for all types of magnetic stripes cards
- ATM cards
- Debit cards
- Charge cards Credit cards
- One smart card to carry out all these functions
- One smart card can contain the functionality of several different types of cards issued by different banks on running of different types of networks.
- Smart card is a truly powerful financial token, giving user access to

Δ ***STM***

Δ Debit facility

Δ Charge facilities

Δ Credit facilities

Δ Electronic purse facilities at national and international level.

**Internet Banking :**

The latest wave in IT is Internet banking. It is becoming more obvious that the Internet has unleashed a revolution that is impacting every sphere of life. Internet is an inter-connection of computer communication networks spanning the entire globe, crossing all geographical boundaries. Touching lifestyles in every sphere the Net has redefined methods of communication, work, study, education inter-action, health, trade and commerce. Net is changing everything. From the way we conduct commerce, to the way we distribute information. Being an interactive two-way medium, the Net, through innumerable websites, enables participation by individual in B2B and B2C commerce, visits to shopping malls, books – stores, entertainment sides and cyberspace.

**Electronic Banking :**

E-banking refers to the use of technology which allows customers to access banking service electronically whether to pay bills, transfer funds, view accounts or to obtain information and advices. It refers to the electronic service that, are made available to the customer through phone, personal computers, television and the Internet. Technology in banking has been used in four major ways:

- To handle a greatly expanded customers ways.
- To reduce substantially to real cost of handling payments.
- To liberate the bank from the traditional constraints on time and place; and
- To introduce new products and services.

The following type of IT is used in the Urban Co-op Banking Industry.

**Electronic Transfer of Funds:**

For years, banks have been effecting inter-city transfer of money for their customers through demand drafts, mail transfer and telegraphic transfers. As each of these mode imposes some limitations, the RBI has devised an EFT system to facilitate speediest transfer to funds electronically.

EFT facilities transfer of funds from the bank accounts of one customer to the bank account of another customer. In this system, the sender and the receiver of funds may be located in different cities and may tie the bank with different banks. Funds transfer within the same city is also permitted. The scheme has been in operation since February 7, 1996.

The account holder having some saving / current / cash credit with the bank can use the EFT facility presently available b/w in Mumbai, Calcutta, New Delhi and Chennai. The upper limit for individual EFT transaction is Rs. 5,00,000 (Rs. Five Lakh only) and for whole Rupee only (paisa not allowed). All the 27 public sector banks are the participating banks under the EFT system.

**Benefits:**

- **Fast:** Funds are transferred within 24 hours. Delays and paper work are avoided.
- **Safe:** Frauds in processing paper instruments is avoided.
- **Secure:** Facilitates funds transfer from account to account with built in security measures. Control practices, Computerization of control records and detailed procedural guidelines make the system absolutely secure.
- **Hassle Free:** Beneficiary needs not to go to the bank. Amount is credited to his bank account directly.

**Electronic Clearing Services (ECS):**

- Electronic Credit Clearing
- Electronic Debit Clearing

**ECS Credit Clearing:**

It is a simple, reliable and cost effective solution for bulk and repetitive payment transaction like salary, pension, interest, commission, divided etc., by public or private companies and Government Departments through banks.

Under the said system Companies who have to make bulk payments to a large number of beneficiaries prepare the credit instructions on the magnetic medic and submit the same to RBI through the bankers. RBI processes the data arrive, at inter-bank settlement and provide bank and branch wise reports containing the details of payments to facilitate fast payment to the beneficiaries. This scheme was introduced in Chennai and Mumbai in April 1995. However, at present ECS (credit clearing) is now available in 46 centers.

**ECS Debit Clearing:**

It was introduced in March 1996 by RBI (Reserve Bank of India) direct debit are

- Telephone and electricity bills.
- Loan installments and insurance premium.
- School, college and club membership fees.
- Credit cards dues.
- Water taxes, property taxes and other regular payments, to your bank account.

**Advantages of ECS to Consumers:**

- Payment on due date.
- No more "loss in transit"
- No fraudulent encashment.
- Effortless receipt.
- No more correspondence with the companies.
- No hassle of standing in long queues for payments.
- No more disconnection of telephone/electricity line.
- Accounts statement/pass book will show the source of credit and debit.

**Advantages of ECS to Corporates:**

- Eliminates of postal loss and delays as well as paper work and lengthy procedures.
- Saves cost on stationary, printing and postage.
- No fraudulent encashment.
- Immediate receipt and payment of dues.
- Automatic reconciliation
- Appreciation from investors/customers.

**Credit Cards/Debit Cards:**

The customer need not carry any cash and is empowered to spend wherever and whenever he wants with his credit card within the fixed limits prescribed by his bank. Debit and unlike credit card which is a post paid is a prepaid card with same stored value. Every time a person uses the card, the merchant who in turn can get the money transferred to this account from the banks of the buyer, debits an exact amount of purchase from the card.

To get a debit card, an individual opens an account with the issuing bank which gives him a debit card along with a personal identification number (PIN). When he makes a purchase, he enters this number on the shop's pin pad. When the card is swiped through the electronic terminal, it dials the acquiring bank system either master card or VISA that validates the PIN and finds out from the issuing bank whether to accept or decline the transaction. The customer can never overspend because the system will reject any transaction that exceeds the balance in his account and the ban will never face a default because the amount spent is debited immediately from the customers account. Debit card limitation is that currently only some 3000-4000 shops country wide accepts it. Also a person can't operate it in case the telephone lines are down. Currently city bank and time bank launched debit cards and may more banks are talking to visa and master card to launch their own cards.

**Smart Cards:**

It is a standard plastic credit card, except that it contains a micro processor and a storage unit. It can hold a lot of information about the card holder, including digital certificates. It can be used in all banking transactions. It can also be used as an Electronic Purse in to which monetary value has been loaded. Bank of America has recently launched a new security and encryption process for corporate clients who use WANDA electronic service to transfer funds, initiate payments and manage global accounts. The smart card given to WANDA user offers encryption and authentication capabilities. Full range of cash management and foreign exchange services are available over the Net to corporate users through the use of smart cards.

**Electronic Cheques:**

It is a mechanism for Internet payments. This facility is Internet vision of FEDI systems which have allowed these functions to be performed over VANs. The electronic cheques provide Internet websites with the ability to perform the following functions

- Present the bill to the payer.
- Allow the payer to initiate payment of the invoice.
- Provide remittance information.
- Allow the payer to initiate automatic payment authorizations for a pre-specified amount or range of amount.
- Interface with financial management software and transactions processing software.
- Allow payments to be made to new businesses with which the payer has never before transacted.

Cyber cash and Edison Electronic Institute (EEI) have also been announced the availability or secure Internet payment services to EEI's electric utility industry member at a discount. This is through pay now secure check service, which enables members to receive payments from consumer over the Internet.

**Banking Technology - Overview**

In the five decades since independence, banking in India has evolved through four distinct phases:

1. Foundation Phase – It can be considered to cover 1950's and 1960's till the nationalization of the banks in 1969. Commercial banking took its first few steps from class banking towards mass banking. The focus, during this stage was to lay the foundation for a sound banking system in the country.
2. Expansion Phase – The banks made a major contribution in both Industrial and Rural development. The fifteen years ..... the bank nationalization in 1969 were dominated by the bank's expansion at a feverish pace, which also saw an upsurge in banking services in rural India.
3. Consolidation Phase – This phase beginning 1985 when a series of policy initiatives were taken by RBI and relaxation of control, over the banks was initiated. During this period, there was marked slowdown in the branch expansion and attention was paid to improving house-keeping, customer service, credit management, staff productivity and profitability of the banks.
4. Reform Phase – Recommendations of the Narsimham Committee (1991) paved the way for this phase in the banking. Introduction of new accounting and prudential norms relating to income recognition, provisioning and capital adequacy, deregulation of Interest rates and easing of norms for the entry in the field of banking.

Entry of new private and foreign banks resulted in a paradigm shift in the ways of banking in India. The growing competition and growing customer expectations led to increased awareness amongst banks on the sole and importance of technology in banking.

In the Indian Banking lot of importance is given to automation, the reasons being combination of regulatory and competitive reasons.

Information Technology has basically been used under two different avenues in Banking.

- one as communication and connectivity and the
- other as Business process re-engineering.

Information technology enables innovative product development, better market infrastructure, implementation of reliable techniques for control of risks and helps financial helps the Financial Intermediaries to reach geographically distant and diversified markets.

Banking Software – the software packages for banking applications in India had their beginnings in the middle of 1980s. When the Banks started computerizing the branches in a limited manner. The early 90 and the plummeting hardware prices and advent of cheap and inexpensive but high powered PCs and servers and banks went in for what was called Total Branch Automation (TBA) packages. The middle and late 90s, deregulation, globalization etc coupled with rapid revolution in communication technologies and evolution of novel concept of 'convergence' of computer and communication technologies, like Internet, mobile, cell phones, etc.

Milestone Changes – In India, banks as well as other financial entities entered the world of Information Technology and with Indian Financial Net (INFINET). INFINET a wide area satellite based network (WAN) using VSAT (very small Aperture Terminals) technology, was jointly set up by Reserve Bank and Institute for Development and Research in Banking Technology (IDRBI) in June 1999.

Internet has significantly influenced delivery channels on the banks. Internet has emerged as an important medium for delivery of banking products and services.

Recognizing the key to quick, safe and efficient funds transfer lies in the use of electronic modes of funds transfers, the Reserve bank has improved the existing facilities under EFT (Electronic Funds Transfer)

The application that could benefit greatly from the use of technological advances in the computer and communications are related to payment systems which forms the lifeline of any banking activity. The process of reforms in payment and settlement systems has gained momentum with the implementation of projects such as NDS (Negotiated Dealing System), CFMs (Centralised Funds Management System) for better funds management by banks and SMFs (Structured Financial Messaging Solution) for secure message transfer. This would result in funds transfer and funds related message transfer to be routed electronically across banks using the medium of INFINET.

**Variance in IT in UCBs**

There is a wide variance among Urban Co-operative Banks with regard to the usage of Information Technology. As on March 31, 2007 – 16 out of 1853 had implemented core banking solution, with some of them even offering to set up share data centers with other UCBs, while over 50 banks did not have even computers. The remaining banks existed somewhere in between.

The Urban Co-op Banking sector is also characterised by heterogeneity in terms of size of the banks, their spread and profitability etc. 77 of 1813 Urban Co-operative Banks for example account for over 50 percent of deposits of the sector while 77 percent of Urban Co-operative Banks i.e., almost 1900 Urban Co-operative Banks accounted for only 19 percent of total deposits. In terms of spread, almost 30 percent of Urban Co-operative Banks are unit banks i.e., having single head office / branch and only 29 banks had 25 branches or more.

Most banks have solutions based on Total Branch Automation. Several banks have implemented locally developed and customized application solutions. While some big Urban Co-operative Banks have in-house IT wings to take care of development and maintenance of systems, most banks have outsourced these services.

Accidental evidences are there about the problems faced by these banks because of their small size, lack of adequate IT knowledge, lack of adequate IT savvy manpower and small time vendors.

**Core Banking**

When core business of the banks i.e., Deposits and lending operations are managed through policies, procedures and technology from a central location of the bank.

Processing of all operations of branches through a centralized system deployed at a data center.

Core Banking Solutions manage Transaction Processing, Accounting and MIS for branch operations for a central location.

In Core Banking Solutions, branches invariably reduce to become another delivery channel and the processes are run from the central host system.

**Benefits of the Core Banking**

Operations Perspective:

- Provide a Single Customer Identity across the bank.
- In CBS, MIS and compliance reports are on-line in head office. RBI Off-Site Surveillance Reports are complex and lengthy, that require a central on-line data source, which core banking can provide
- Controls today are exercised by head Office but implemented by branches.
- In CBS, new schemes, policies and procedures can be implemented on-line across the bank uniformly and without much effort.
- In CBS, new schemes, policies and procedures can be implemented on-line across the bank uniformly and without much effort.
- In Core Banking, there is no need for Technical expertise / System administration in the branches.

**Business Perspective:**

- Most of the banks are already on Core Banking Map thus their competitive advantage is higher.
- Cost of branch network expansion and set up time is much lower in CBS and thus new branches make profit early.
- With processes and compliance left to Central Office, the branches focus on business expansion, customer service and collections.
- Revenue leakages are checked better
- ATM Network, RTGS, Cheque Transaction, Internet Banking, Mobile (SMS) Banking and Wealth Management possible only through core banking solution.

## Emerging Trends

### Tele Banking:

In tele-banking, by using automatic voice recorder for simple queries and transactions and manned phone terminals for complicated queries and transactions, the customer can actually do entire non-cash related banking on telephone. Tele Bank is a free service which makes banking easy from any touch tone telephone 24 hours a day by enabling customers to:

- Obtain checking and savings account balances
- Inquire about a specific check
- Identify the amount and date of the most recent checking and savings account balances.
- Make transfers from checking and savings accounts.
- Obtain the following CD information:
- Current CD balance
- Current maturity date
- Next interest payment date
- Last year's total interest paid
- Obtain the following loan information:
- Posted loan balance
- Next payment amount and due date
- Make loan payments
- Transfer to the Loan Department (during regular business hours)
- Change your security code
    - Δ BALANCE ENQUIRY SERVICE – Balance inquiry on savings or current Account within your ATM card. Balance inquiry is your unit owned.
    - Δ MONEY TRANSFER SERVICE – Money transfer services facilitates fund transfer from and to accounts which are linked by the same ATM card. This can be done since one ATM card can link upto ten accounts under one name, even if the accounts were opened at different branches. Thus, fund transfer can be made from savings to current accounts, or vice versa.
    - Δ CREDIT CARD SERVICE – Inquiries concerning credit card service can be made as follows:

- Available Credit
- Credit Line
- Current Balance
- Due Date, Payment Amount

- Total Current Balance
- Payments can also be made through credit card, if the card can be used as an ATM card.

  Δ ATM and Be1st CARD SERVICE – Bualuang Phone service can be used to

- Cancel ATM and Be 1st Card
- Inquire current purchasing limit per day on your Be 1st card.
- Change current purchasing limit per day on your Be 1st card.
- List Bangkok Bank's ATM location via fax.

  Δ PAYMENT SERVICE – Payments can be made through Phone service, exclusively to the service's business partners.

There are 3 types of payment

- Bill – Payment
- Utility Payment such as Telephone, Electricity
- Credit card Payment

  Δ OPEN END FUND SYSTEM – Bualuang Phone service can be used to make pending orders in BBL Asset Management's Open-end Fund, 24 – hour daily. To obtain this service, simply fill in an application at your Bangkok Bank branch.

FOREIGN EXCHANGE INFORMATION – The exchange rates are available for the following currencies.:

US Dollar

EMU

Pound Sterling

Deutsche Mark

Japanese Yen

Malaysian Dollar

Singapore Dollar

Hong Kong Dollar

Swiss Franc

French Franc

**Asynchronous Transfer mode (ARM):**

Asynchronous transfer mode (ATM) is a high-performance, well oriented switching and multiplexing technology that utilizes fixed – length packets to carry different types of traffic. ATM is a technology that will enable carriers to capitalize on a number of revenue opportunities through multiple ATM classes of services; high-speed local area network (LAN) interconnection; voice, video and future multimedia applications in business markets in the short term; and in community and residential markets in the longer term.

**The benefits of ATM are the following:**

- High performance via hardware switching
- Dynamic bandwidth for bursty traffic
- Class-of-service support for multimedia
- Scalability in speed and network size
- Common LAN/WAN architecture
- Opportunities for simplification via VC architecture
- International standards compliance

**E-Banking :**

Electronic banking has existed for around 20 years, but before the advent of the Internet, was limited to direct-dial services. The rise of the Internet and the increase in e-commerce have speeded up this process in recent years and have made web-based Internet banking available as well as direct-dial. With increasing competition from Internet-only banks and other financial organizations such as insurance companies, building societies and even supermarkets, most high street banks are now offering electronic banking services.

**Types of Electronic Banking :**

(i) Traditional high street bank :

Two different methods of connection to the customer's account are used:

(a) Direct-dial / PC banking : direct – dial works via a dedicated phone number when the customer dials directly into the bank's server. With direct-dial, customers need to use customized software by the bank itself. This allows the customer to download their account details from the bank's network and view them offline.

(b) Web-based Internet banking involves a customer logging onto a bank's online banking via any compatible PC to perform common banking transactions.

(ii) Internet only bank

**Advantages:**

(i) Cost effectiveness

(ii) Cash flow

(iii) Convenience

(iv) Time-saving

**Disadvantages:**

(i) Internet connection speeds

(ii) Extra staff

(iii) Security

**What Kind of Services are on Offer:**

(i) Viewing account balances and recent transactions.

(ii) Paying bills to utilizes companies and suppliers etc. without having to write cheques.

(iii) Scheduling bill payment in advance.

(iv) Transferring money between the business accounts.

(v) Setting up and checking direct debits

(vi) Ordering bank books.

(vii) Setting up and making direct payments to other banks and building societies.

(viii) Viewing the last 40 entries on the bank statement.

(ix) Viewing, activating or canceling standing order details

(x) Sending messages to the bank via e-mail.

Some banks also offer additional services. These may include:

(i) The ability to transfer account information into financial management software packages, e.g., Microsoft Money 2000, Intuit Quicken, Sage Instant Accounting packages and Excel spreadsheets.

(ii) A 'retail park' where the business customer can view and order products such as office furniture and software – making the site a 'one – stop shop' for all the business needs.

(iii) A communication center with free e-mail address available to customers.

**Security:**

(i) Security operates at three different levels.

(ii) Ban's operates at three different levels.

(iii) Access security

(iv) Account holder's vigilance

Security measures to be aware of include:

(i) Not divulging their PIN number of password to any third party.

(ii) Not leaving their PIN number lying around.

(iii) Not leaving their PC while still being logged on the bank website. The customer should not rely on the online bank website to automatically time out.

(iv) Making sure nobody can see their details on screen on ensuring that the equipment will not allow electronic eavesdropping

(v) Not sending e-mails containing their password or membership number.

(vi) Always removing any data that has been exported to a financial management package.

(vii) Taking note when the PC/Internet screen indicates whether the customer is operating in a secure environment.

**Useful Tips:**

(i) Shopping around is a good idea since banks and building societies offer different service and charges. Some of the internet – only bank still offer electronic banking services for personal and not business customers. It is advisable to choose one which fits the business's needs.

(ii) Deciding on either direct – dial or web – based Internet banking depends on the customer's consumers about security and the customer's habitual computer usage. For example, choosing web-based Internet banking may be more suitable if the customer is familiar with using the Internet.

(iii) It is important to remember that electronic banking can benefit the business in terms of time and money. However, electronic banking cannot replace the advice offered by a 'real person.

**Web Banking :**

**Why Bank Online?**

This question is frequently encountered by those who have just ventured into this exciting arena. Hopefully this article will help you make up your mind.

Essentially, your 'brick & mortar' bank offers you three types of services:

*(i)* *Transactional* – Clearing your checks, paying your bills, processing direct payments.

*(ii)* *Credit*- Providing you with credit, either through mortgages, credit cards or basic loans.

*(iii)* *Investments* – Providing you with investment options, including advice. But you would sometimes have to make an appointment, or worse stand in a long queue. No more!

Here's what online banks currently offer:

**(i) Convenience** – Complete your banking at your convenience, in the comfort of your home or at any place you can access the Net.

**(ii) No more Qs** – There are no queues at an online bank.

**(iii) 24/7 service** – Bank online 24 hours a day, 7 day a week and 52 weeks a year.

(i) In addition they also offer:

**(a) Free cheques** – Most online banks now offer you free personalized checks mailed to your home.

**(b) Free stock trading** – Fierce competition among the banks has prompted one major American bank to offer free stock trading. Read all about this unique offer in No. Fee Stock Trading on the Web.

(c) **Free Electronic Fund Transfers** – Most online banks offer you the ability to transfer money between accounts, or sometimes even between banks. Onc bank offers you money to ANYONE, for free! Check out my article – So what does X.com do? Also read my article on Checks, Drafts & P2P.

(d) **Free online bill payment** – Pay your utility, phone, credit card and other bills electronically without standing in a queue. Check out the resources available for this service.

(e) **Export financial data** – Transfer your bank statements electronically to your financial software. For choices in financial software refer to the list of financial software. Electronically balance your checkbook.

(f) **Instant mortgage approvals** – Apply for and obtain your mortgage loan within minutes. Refer to our resources on applying for mortgages online.

(g) **Instant credit card applications** – Apply for credit cards online and get a decision within minutes. Check on these online offers.

(h) **Buy CDs online** – Not the music variety, but the Certificates of Deposit (CD). You can even price the rate of interest if you would prefer on your CD. Try making your own CD.

(i) **Refer to old transactions** – Most online banks will allow you to refer to past transactions, sometimes even up to six months online.

(j) **Free interactive help** – Most online banks provide resources to help you plan a budget, but a new hone and many other financial decisions.

(k) **Your own financial commodity** – One bank even offers its customers likeminded company. Read how Egg.com does banking at A Bank Called Egg.com?

**Internal Control and Housekeeping in Banks:**

(i) Internal Control Systems:

The Bank periodically reviews the steps taken by the public sector banks in the internal control area through analytical reports covering the following areas:

- Reconciliation of inter – branch accounts
- Reconciliation of inter – bank accounts
- Reconciliation of nostro accounts, and
- Status of balancing of books of accounts
- Reconciliation of clearing differences

The banks were given definitive time frame to improve their internal clearing systems and the progress has been closely monitored and followed up by the Department of Banking Supervision.

### (ii) Reconciliation of Inter – Branch Accounts:

The close monitoring and periodical discussions with the chairman of banks by the Deputy Governor had an impact in reduction of old un-reconciled entries in inter-branch accounts of banks, a fraud prone area. The continued pressure on banks has been yielding the desired results in as much as the un-reconciled entries have been substantially reduced over the last three years.

To promote effective concern in reconciliation of debit entries in inter-branch accounts the concept making provision for net debits outstanding for more than three years in inter-branch accounts has been introduced. The cut off period for provisioning has been reduced to more than two years from the period ended March 2001.

Similarly, to have an effective monitoring or remittances transactions, the banks have been advised not to route entries on account of such transactions through normal inter branch account but evolve a separate account for this purpose. The banks have also been asked to ensure that outstanding entries under remittance transactions are reconciled on a weekly basis.

Banks are required to ensure that the practice of forced matching of inter-branch entries should be the subject to appropriate checks and balances. Any forced matching practice adopted by banks for adjustment of old un-reconciled entries in inter-branch accounts should have the approval of their Audit Committee of the Board and the Board of Directors should be apprised of the full details of such practice. The statutory auditors of the bank should also look into the justifiability from the angle of fair accounting practice.

There has been considerable improvement in the reconciliation of inter-branch accounts in public sector banks and the position of un-reconciled entries pending for more than two years. Total number of un-reconciled entries over two years, which stood at 22.58 lakh entries (Rs. 50706 crore) as on March 31, 1996, had declined to 14.74 lakh entries (Rs. 3824 crore) as on March 31, 2000.

### (iii) Balancing of Books:

A related concern that required a close monitoring was the progress in reducing the arrears in balancing of books at branches of banks. A reporting system for banks was introduced in July 1995 for monitoring progress in respect of banks having more than 5 percent of branches having arrears in balancing of books. A detailed report on banks which had arrears in balancing of books at branches account for more than 40 percent of business are reviewed at periodical intervals. There has been a considerable improvement in balancing of books in public sector banks since June 1997 in as much as the total number of branches where books were not balanced came down from 4245 as on June 30, 1997 to 1356 branches as on June 30, 2000. Further the number of branches with balancing arrears for more than two years had also come down from 1650 to 630 branches during the above period.

**(iv) Reconciliation of Nostro Accounts:**

A Working Group consisting of three bankers and a chartered accountant, (besides RBI officials) had gone into the system of accounting of Nostro accounts transactions by banks and proposed solutions for speedy reconciliation of Nostro accounts entries in public sector banks. Top Management of banks which reported high pendency in this area are called for a monitoring discussion by the Deputy Governor and Executive Director. The number of entries pending for reconciliation in public sector banks had come down from 14.68 lakh entries (Rs. 224539 crore) as on March 31, 1996 to 8.60 lakh entries (Rs. 83491 crore) as on March 31, 2000.

**(v) Strengthening of Internal Audit / Control System**

Banks were advised to reconstitute the Audit Committee of the Board (ACB) with a view to making them more independent and with larger representation of non-executive directors. The ACBs are to be invariably headed by a Director who is a chartered accountant from among the non-executive directors of the bank. The minutes of ACB are to be placed before the Board of Directors on an ongoing basis to serve as a link between their functioning.

All public sector banks were advised to appoint a senior officer of the bank as Compliance Officer who should act as a nodal agency to ensure compliance of internal management controls as well as regulatory and guidance.

**(vi) Audit System in Banks:**

The Banks has evolved systems and norms of empanelment and appointment and remuneration of statutory auditors in banks and payments for special validation audit and provided guidance on accountability aspects under statutory audit of banks, quality and coverage in banks.

Further, the banks were advised to review the present system of concurrent audit immediately and incorporate necessary changes therein based on the guidelines of RBI. The banks are also to review once in a year the effectiveness of the system and take necessary measures to correct the lacunae in implementation.

**(vii) Fraud Monitoring:**

The system of internal control and follow-up in respect of cases of large frauds of Rs. 1 crore and above reported to the RBI is reviewed periodically. The emphasis of house keeping aspects has helped in detecting large frauds and instituting fraud prevention measures.

Banks are cautioned about the details of individuals / companies / proprietary concerns involved in perpetration of frauds, furnishing details of their directors / partners / guarantors / associates. In addition, *modus operandi* of new types of frauds is also circulated among banks and financial institutions, to put them on guard. RBI also conducts special scrutiny in respect of large value frauds at the branch – controlling office level to find out lapses contributing to the frauds.

All cases of frauds involving large amounts are analysed to identify the contributory factors and taken up with the banks concerned for remedial measures. The aspects relating to recovery, staff accountability and improvement in internal control are also pursued with the banks which are advised in the process to report the fraud cases to Police / Central Bureau of Intelligence (CBI), if not already done. Detailed instructions have been issued by Reserve Bank of India towards streamlining fraud prevention and control/ monitoring system.

With a view to expediting the investigation of fraud cases, RBI reports cases involving Rs. 1 crore and above as also those revealing inter-state ramifications irrespective of the amounts to CBI. The banks are advised to examine staff accountability aspect in all cases. Obtaining photographs of accountholders while opening accounts is one of the measures introduced to control frauds.

In-depth examination of large value frauds reported by commercial banks was conducted by a Study Group under the Chairmanship of CMD of a public sector bank. The group indicated common types of frauds by giving the *modus operandi* thereof and recommended several measures for early detection and prevention of frauds including recommendations for improvement in internal control, house-keeping, vigilance, management, etc. Apart from implementing the recommendations the banks were advised to adopt certain measures to avoid delay in reporting. It has also been decided that if large value of frauds were due to non-observance of prescribed internal control system, certain restrictions are to be placed on opening of new branches by these banks. The banks have been advised to scrupulously follow the time limit laid down by Chief Vigilance Commissioner (CVC) and the position of adherence to CVC guidelines reviewed by their board on a quarterly basis. If these guidelines are not strictly followed the concerned banks should furnish a report to the CVC.

An advisory Board on bank frauds was set up by the Governor, RBI with effect from March 1, 1997 under the Chairmanship of Shri S.S. Tarapore, former Member of BFS and Deputy Governor of RBI and five members drawn from areas such as law, administration, police, professional accounting and commercial banking. The Board has since covered as Central Advisory Board on Bank Frauds and functions as part of the Central Bureau of Investigation (CBI) of Government of India. The Board advises on the cases referred by the CBI either directly or through the Ministry of Finance for investigation/registration of cases against bank officers of the rank of General Manager and above. The Department of Banking Supervision is providing the secretarial assistance and RBI meets the cost of the functioning of the Board.

## Internet Banking in India: RBI Guidelines

Reserve Bank of India has set up a 'Working Group on Internet Banking' to examine different aspects of Internet Banking. The Group had focused on three major areas of Internet-banking, i.e., (i) technology and security issues, (ii) legal issues and (iii) regulatory and supervisory issues. RBI accepted the recommendations of the Group to be implemented in a phased manner. Following recommendations are to be adopted by all banks offering Internet banking services, with immediate effect. These recommendations are applicable, in general, to all forms of electronic banking.

**I. Technology and Security Standard:** Banks should designate a network and database administrator with clearly defined roles. Banks should have a security policy duly approved by the Board of Directors. There should be a segregation of duty of Security Officer / Group dealing exclusively with information system security and Information Technology Division, which actually implemented the computer systems. Further, Information Systems Auditor will audit the information systems

Banks should introduce logical access controls to data, systems, application software, utilities, telecommunication lines, libraries, system software, etc., Logical access control technique may include user-ids, passwords, smart cards or other biometric technologies. At the minimum, banks should use the proxy server type of firewall so that there is no direct connection between the Internet and the banks system. It facilitates a high level of control and in-depth and in-depth monitoring using logging and auditing tools. For sensitive systems, a stateful inspection firewall is recommended which thoroughly inspect all packets of information, and past and present transactions are compared. These generally include a real time security alert.

All the systems supporting dial up services through modem on the same LAN as the application server should be isolated to prevent intrusions into the network as this may bypass the proxy server. PKI (Public Key Infrastructure) is the most favored technology for secure Internet banking services. However, as it is not yet commonly available, banks should use the following alternative system during the transition, until the PKI is put in place:

Usage of SSL (Secured Socket Layer) which ensures server authentication and use of client side certificates issued by the banks themselves using a Certificate Server.

There should be use of at least 128-bit SSL for security browser to web server communications and, in addition, encryption of sensitive data like passwords in transit within the enterprise itself.

All unnecessary services on the application server such as FTP (File Transfer Protocol), telnet should be disabled. The application server should be isolated from the e-mail server.

All computer accesses, including messages received, should be logged. Security violations (suspected or attempted) should be reported and follow up action taken should be kept in mind while framing future policy. Banks should acquire tools for monitoring systems and the networks against intrusions and attacks. These tools should be used regularly to avoid security breaches. The banks should review their security infrastructure and security policies regularly and optimize them in the light of their own experiences and changing technologies. They should educate their security personnel and also the end-users on a continuous basis.

The information security officer and the information system auditor should undertake periodic penetration tests of the system, which should include:

Attempting to guess passwords using password-cracking tools.

Search for back door traps in the programs. Attempt to overload the system using DDoS (Distributed Denial of Service) & DoS (Denial of Service) attacks.

Check if commonly known holes in the software, especially the browser and the e-mail software exist.

The penetration testing may also be carried out by engaging outsides experts (often called 'Ethical Hackers')

Physical access controls should be strictly enforced. Physical security should cover all the information systems and sites where they are housed, both against internal and external threats.

Banks should have proper infrastructure and schedules for backing up data. The backed up data should be periodically tested to ensure recovery without loss of transactions in a time frame as given out in the bank's security policy. Business continuity should be ensured by setting up disaster recovery sites. These facilities should also be tested periodically.

All applications of banks should have proper record keeping facilities for legal purposes, it may be necessary to keep all received and sent messages both in encrypted and decrypted form.

Security infrastructure should be properly tested before using the systems and applications for normal operations. Banks should upgrade the systems by installing patches released by developers to remove bugs and loopholes, and upgrade to newer versions, which give better security and control.

# CHAPTER 5

## Origins of Urban Co-oprative Credit Institutions

The Urban Co-operative Credit movement originated in Germany, when Mr. Herman Schultz started such societies for the benefit of the artisans in the cities. Mr. Schulze found a friendly society in 1849 for relief in sickness. For provision of credit he founded in his native town the first loan society in 1850 and Hog originated the Dairy Co-operative Banking for the development of the dairy enterprise.

Dr. Hog's banks improved dairymen's life in the rural and suburban part of Germany and Schulze's model was designed to improve the social and economic life of urban part of Germany. The attractive business of co-operative banks in Germany created an ideal situation for the development of co-operative banking at an international level in the ear of 1849 to 1890.[3]

In Italy, the credit of originating of such societies goes to Luigi Luzzatti. Encouraged by the success of the urban credit institutions in those countries, social workers in India began to think in terms of co-operative as a means of bringing success to the middle classes as early as the close of nineteenth century.[4]

The Idea of co-operative bank was first discussed in Great Britain in the year of 1870, and at a conference on banking at Bury; Mr. Ludlow said that he saw no reason why there should not be a bank "in a for closest possible connection with the wholesale society".[5] This opinion had been sharply accepted and the co-operative wholesale society decided in May 1872, to undertake the business of banking as a separate department of co-operative wholesale society. This new department had been named as, "The Loan and Deposit Department" and the name of this department had not been changed till the year 1876. During the period, India too initiated the process of forming the urban credit society and the successful experiment had been done by some of the Maharashtrians in Vadoodara City in 1889.

### Origins of Urban Co-operative Credit Movement in India

The last two decades of the nineteenth century was stable for the establishment of voluntary organization linked with co-operative methods, which had the Indian Philosophy as the base and the European experience for guidance. The Madras Presidency had developed indigenous societies as NIDHIS, analogous the friendly and building societies in Britain, while Western India preferred mutual aid societies.

As early as in 1883, Sir Henry Stark had advocated the introduction of the co-operative credit system in India according to the European model and after four years, Sir Raymond West had renewed the plea. The Government of Madras was the first to grasp the possibilities of the co-operative movement in India. Considering the need in 1892, the Government had appointed, Mr. F.H. Nicholson as the Special Officer to study the theory and practice of the co-operative movement in Europe, with special reference to the organization of co-operative credit in Germany, and to suggest means for its introduction in India. In this two report as issued in the years 1895 and 1897, he gave exhaustive information about the development in Europe, and recommended the model of Reiffeisen Societies. His emphasis was, however, on the man whom they had discovered and not on the system, and, therefore, had found Raiffeisen who was the crux of his advice.

The Madras Government decided to set up two village banks as an experiment which had not shown much interest in the same recommendations. At the same time the states like Bengal, Uttar Pradesh and Punjab started co-operative societies on the Italian model. Those were registered in the absence of special legislation, either under the Societies Registration Act or the Company Act.

The origin of the urban co-operative credit movement in India can be traced to the close of the nineteenth century. Following the success of the urban credit institutions organized by Herman Schultz in Germany and Luigi Luzzatti in Italy during those period in 1855-85, some middle class Maharashtrian families who were settled in the erstwhile princely State of Baroda started a mutual aid society in Baroda on 5th February, 1889 under the guidance of Prof. (Vitthal Laxman) alias (Bhausaheb Kavathekar), who inspired with the experiments in the Vadodara state, such voluntary associations, for the twin purposes, were set up in the Bombay Presidency by public, spirited men with some Government assistance. At this juncture, Indian opinion had been impressed by the success of small village bank in Germany and Italy.

The enactment of Co-operative Credit Societies in the Act of 1904 conferred legal status on credit societies, and the first Urban Co-operative Credit Society was registered in 1904 at (Congeeveram) in Madras Province. Subsequently, the Bategari Co-operative Credit Society in Dharwar district in undivided Bombay province and the Bangalore city, the co-operative credit societies, in the erstwhile Mysore State were registered in October 1905 respectively. However, the real beginning was after the amendment in 1911, enhancing its scope to the formation of non-agricultural credit societies.

Co-operative endeavour is not an alien phenomenon to India. Kautilya in his Arthashastra described, 'Guilds of workmen as well as those who carry on any co-operative work shall divide their earnings either equally, or as agreed among themselves". The Co-operative Credit Movement in modern India, curiously, is a state initiated movement. Then state regime, as though it had an unbenign political dispensation towards native subjects, which had taken a lead to create an institutional credit structure essentially to cater to the needs of the farmers and lower income groups. It is further interesting to note that co-operative initiative as so taken was perhaps the first ever attempt at micro credit dispensation in India. Briefly outlining the theory of Cooperation, the Report of Maclagan Committee on Cooperation with the seminal document on co-operative credit movement in India, graphically describes:

"....that an isolated and powerless individual can, by association with others and by moral development and mutual support can obtain in his own degree the material advantages available to wealthy or powerful persons, and thereby develop himself to the fullest extent of his natural abilities. By union of forces material advancement was secured, and by united action self reliance was fostered, and it is from the interaction of these influences that was hoped to attain the effective realization of the higher and more prosperous standard, of life which has been characterised as better business than better farming and better living".

**Co-operative Banking in India – A Brief Review**

Co-operation emphasizes the idea of voluntary association of individual for the achievement of the common goods. The co-operative movement had a long history of nearly 150 years or more. The first co-operative organization was started in 1844 by ROBERT OWEN in the Northern part of England at Toad Line, Rochadal was the idea of a voluntary association of individual for the achievement of the common goods. Rochadal as the name of the co-operative organization was Equitable Pioneers Society, which was a co-operative consumer society covering 28 workers as members. The idea of using the 'co-operation' in India as a means to comet indebtedness as was suggested by Fredrik Nicholson in 1890. However no action was taken on this suggestion. The co-operative movement started in India in a real sense in 1904 when the co-operative credit societies Act of 1904 was passed which was allowed to establish credit society at Vadodara (Baroda) in 1889 which is being considered as first Urban co-op Bank in India. The Act provided scope for registration and controlling of co-operative credit societies. The objective of this Act, was to encourage thrift habits among people and to reduce dependence over the money lenders. Lacunas in the above mention act were removed by another act viz., the co-operative societies as in 1912, viz., establishment of non-credit co-operative societies as well as registration of co-operative Apex Banks/Federations of co-operative banks. In addition to that this act provided scope for regulation and development of co-operative credit / co-operative banking institution in India. The movement got momentum with the enactment of the act of 1919 under which 'co-operation' became a provincial state subject. The Act 1912 was replaced by provincial /state in Mumbai and Madras provinces in 1925 and 1931 respectively. The government of India appointed the royal commission on Agriculture 1927 and the co-operative banking enquiry committee in 1929 was to suggest the ways and means of reconstructing the co-operative credit movement in India. In 1934 the RBI was established and after that the RBI lead important part in strengthening the co-operative credit movement in India.

A major development in the co-operative sector since 1947 was appointment to Rural Credit Survey Committee in 1951. In the report, the committee has made several recommendations that brought following benefits in the sector, viz, state participation at different level, etc.

**Structure of Co-operative Credit Societies**

**The structure of co-operative credit societies is as follows:**

1. Urban Area :
    (a) Urban Co-operative Banks
    (b) Salary Earner' Credit Societies

2. Rural Area :
   (a) State level
      (1) State Co-operative Banks
      (2) State Land Development Bank
   (b) District Level
      (1) District Central Co-operative Banks
      (2) District Level Land Development Banks
   (c) Primary Level or Village Level
      (1) Primary Agricultural Credit Societies (PACs)
      (2) Farmer Server Societies
      (3) Large sized Adivasi Multi Purpose Co-operative Societies

It may be noted that at village level, the branches of district Central Co-operative Banks or District Level Development banks may be functioning. The Structure of co-operative institutions can be visualized as

1. Short term lending oriented co-op, banks/credit institutions
2. Long term lending oriented co-op, banks/credit institutions

**Primary Agricultural Credit Societies**

Primary Agricultural Credit Societies such as (PACs) are associates of borrowers and non-borrowers, who are residing in one locality. They know about each other and take interest in one and the other's affairs. Membership is open to any inhabitant of the same locality. This brings together persons of difference status into a common organization and promoted a true spirit of co-operation and brotherhood. Such societies are to be registered with Registrar. Operations of such societies are restricted to a particular area. Working funds of these organizations comprise (i) Owned Funds, (ii) Deposit from member and non-member, (iii) Loans from district central Co-operative banks including the government etc. The primary Agricultural credit societies such as (PACs) deal directly with the farmer. They give loans to their member against persons as well as mortgaged securities. Important function of PACs are summarized as follows: (a) To provide short term and medium term credit to farmer (b) To supply inputs needed by farming activity (c) To supply essential commodities (d) To supervise use of credit and recover the same punctually (e) To encourage thrift habit among the members and last, to associate itself with the programmes of economic welfare of the people.

**District Central Co-operative Banks**

The Central Co-operative Bank is a federation of primary agricultural credit societies located in a specific area, viz., one or more talukas or district. Normally the head quarter of such a bank is located at the district or town or an important town of the district. The central co-operative banks may have some branches also within the respective districts. Central co-operative banks play an important role in the Indian currency market. The organizations are linking point between primary co-op, Agricultural credit societies and state co-operative banks.

These central co-operative banks have undertaken banking related activities, viz., they are accepting deposit of different kinds. Resources of these organizations comprise (i) Share capital and reserve funds (ii) Deposits of different kinds (iii) Reserve funds of primary Agricultural Credit Societies are affiliated to them, (iv) Funds borrowed from various organization like state co-operative banks, commercial banks (v) Surplus funds deposited with them by organization like universities, municipalities and local boards etc.

These banks lend funds to Primary Agricultural Credit societies (PACs). These banks also undertake inspection of affiliated agricultural co-operative credit societies. These district central co-operative banks also grant credit to customer on the basis of first class gilt securities and gold etc., they also provide remittance related facilities to their customers. The important function of central co-operative banks are summarized as follows (i) to meet the credit requirement of primary level and co-operative credit societies for production supply and marketing products (ii) to act as the balancing center for adjusting the surplus and deficiency of funds of primary credit societies (iii) to undertake supply of seeds or fertilizers and other inputs which are likely to be used by the farmer (iv) to supervise, inspect the PACs which comes under its jurisdiction and at last to provide all Primary agricultural co-operative credit societies. Co-operative banks are being managed by board of director's.

**State Co-operative Banks**

They are the apex level banks viz., State Level, which undertake activities like mobilization of resources and to deploy them. They assume a key position in the co-operative credit structure. The (RBI) reaches to the cultivator only through the medium of state Co-operative banks. These banks also act as intermediaries between the central co-operative banks on one hand, and money market on the other. The share capital of state co-operative banks is contributed partly by central co-operative banks and partly by the individual, who plays an important part in the management of the bank. State co-operative banks also play a role of central co-operative in some places where central co-operative banks are not present of resources of such state level, co-operative banks comprises share capital. Reserves fund of various kinds of deposits, loans and overdrafts including borrowings, and surplus funds of central co-operative banks were affiliated to the respective bank. These banks lend to affiliate Central co-operative banks. The RBI also provides support to such state co-operative banks and in case of their needs. Deposits in co-operative banks such as the state co-operative banks and Central co-operative banks. The primary Agricultural credit societies, primarily the urban co-operative banks are covered by deposit insurance facility of DICGCI. The main function of state co-operative banks are summarized as follows : (i) it acts as bankers' for central co-operative banks (ii) it connects co-operative credit societies with co-operative banks for central co-operative banks with money market in the country (iii) It supervises, control and renders guidance to the central co-operative banks (iv) it also performs functions like issuing drafts, cheques and letters of credit etc. (v) it assist the state government in drawing up co-operative development related plans for the state.

# CHAPTER 6

# Urban Co-operative Banks

Evolution of urban co-operative banking movement in India can be traced through 3 distinct phases which are discussed in the succeeding paragraphs.

**Phase I (1904-1966)**

Inspired by the success of urban co-operative credit movement in Germany and Italy, the first mutual aid society 'Anyonya Sahakari Mandal' was organised in the princely State of Baroda in 1889 under the guidance of Late Shri Vithal Laxman Kavthekar. The enactment of Co-operative Credit Societies Act, 1904, however, gave the real impetus to the movement as the first urban co-operative credit society was registered in Canjeevaram town in the Madras province in October, 1904. Thereafter, few more societies were organised in Madras and Bombay provinces.

In 1912, some major amendments were brought in the Act with view to broadeing the base and to enable organization of non-credit societies. The Maclagan Committee's recommendations, as mentioned earlier, had much to contribute in evolving the urban co-operative credit movement. With the transfer of the subject of "Cooperation" from Central to Provincial Governments, as a sequel to the constitutional reforms popularly known as "Montague Chelmsford Reforms" and passing of the Act of 1919, was then provincial Government of Bombay which passed the first State Co-operative Societies Act in 1925" which not only gave the movement its size and shape but also considered as a pace setter of co-operative activities, and stressed the basic concept of thrift, self held and mutual aid.

In the formative phase, urban co-operative credit societies came to be organised on community basis and their lending operations was confined to meet the consumption oriented credit needs of their members. The term 'bank' was very much loosely used by many societies in the initial phase. Many urban banks which were organised in the early as a part of this century were essentially credit societies but later converted themselves into UCBs. Many urban credit societies which are not engaged in any other banking functions, also used the word 'bank' or 'banker'. There was no well defined concept of urban co-operative bank. It was just the Joint Reorganization Committee popularly known as Mehta Bhansali Committee (1939) in Bombay province, which was for the first time, made as an attempt to define an urban co-operative bank. It defined as a credit society as an Urban Co-operative Bank (UCB) whose paid up share capital was Rs. 20,000 or more and were accepting the deposits of money on current accounts or otherwise subject to withdrawals by cheques, drafts of order. In Madras province, urban co-operative credit societies were accepting current account deposits and maintaining credit amount of liquid resources, as prescribed by Registrar of Co-operative Societies, had come to be known as Urban Co-operative Banks (UCBs), irrespective of the size of their share capital. Subsequently, in 1966, when banking laws where made applicable to co-operative banks, provisions of section 5 (CCV) of Banking Regulation Act, 1949 [As Applicable to Co-operative Societies (ARCS)] was defined an Urban Co-operative Bank, or as a primary co-operative bank other then a primary agricultural credit society.

1. The primary object was the transaction of banking business;
2. The paid up share capital and reserves of which are not less than Rs. 1 lakh and
3. The by-laws of which do not permit admission of any other co-operative society as a member.

With the economic boom created by IInd World War, the urban banking sector received tremendous impetus and started diversifying its credit portfolio and branching out from meeting traditional consumption oriented credit needs into catering to the needs of artisans, small businessmen and small markets.

Various Committees and Study Groups, like the Central banking Enquiry Committee (1931), the Co-operative Planning Committee (1946) popularly known as Saraiya Committee, Varde Committee (1963), and the Study Group on Credit Co-operatives in Non-Agricultural sector (1963), and Working Group on Industrial Financing through Co-operative banks (1968) have commended the working of UCBs in extending support to the micro agencies, to whom the commercial banking sector was quite wary of lending. Interestingly, the survey made by RBI in 1958-59, for assessing the financial pattern of UCBs and their role in financing Small Scale Industries, revealed that notwithstanding absence of the state support to urban banking sector (unlike its counterpart viz., in the Agricultural Co-operative Credit Sector), the UCB sector, as a whole registered a fairly good rate of progress.

Data prior to 1948 about the urban co-operative banking sector was, unfortunately, not available. As at the end of financial year 1948-49, the number of UCBs stood at 815 and rose to become 1106 by the end of financial year 1966-67. During this period, the deposits held by UCB sector rose from Rs. 17 crores to Rs. 153 crores, registering a growth of 800 percent [Urban Co-operative banks were brought under the purview of B.R. Act, effective from 1 March, 1966]. An interesting feature of urban co-operative credit movement in the early part of this century was that the public confidence in urban co-operative credit sector, particularly the lower and middle income groups, was unshaken notwithstanding the collapse of joint stock banks. It is indeed interesting to note that during the year of 1913 and 1914, in Bombay Presidency and United Provinces of Punjab, where banking crisis led to the collapse of none of fewer than 57 joint stock banks, there was a flight of deposits from the joint stock banks, in where to co-operative urban banks. The Maclagan Committee graphically chronicled the phenomenon.

"As a matter of fact, the crisis had a contrary effect, and in most of the provinces, there was a movement to withdraw deposits from non-co-operative institutions, the distinction between two classes of security being well appreciated and a preference being given to the latter owing partly to the local character and publicity of co-operative institutions, but mainly, we think, to the connection of Government with Co-operative movement".

Similarly, between 1939-1949, when 588 joint stock banks failed in various states eroding public deposits to the tune of Rs. 26 crores, there was an even miniscule impact on urban co-operative banks, presumably due to the fact that co-operative institutions were subjected to stringent regulation as compared to a lax supervision over commercial banks. It is indeed strange to note that commercial banks were governed by the Company Law, applicable to ordinary non-banking companies. Very aptly, the Central Banking Enquiry Committee in 1931, had come to the conclusion that the provisions of Indian Companies Act were inadequate to deal effectively with banking malpractices and recommended comprehensive legislation. Although Companies Act was amended in 1936 and a separate Chapter relating to Banking Companies was added, the provisions therein were still found to be ineffective. This was a classic era of laissez faire banking and was a perfect Hobbesian state of nature. Shri B. Ram Rau, was then the Governor, RBI, succinctly described the scenario "Any financial adventurer who required money for a speculative venture or for financing a business, in which he was interested, started a bank with many branches and collected deposits by the offer of high rates of interest and by lavish advertisement".

Compared to the above scenario, the segment of urban co-operative banks was fairly better regulated and UCBs did not reflect any symptom of systemic failure.

**Phase II (1966-93)**

During this period, the demand for extension of deposit insurance was gaining momentum on account of significant increase in the operations of Urban Co-operative Banks and their volume of deposits and more particularly in the context of sad experience of Palai Central Bank failure. As an extension of deposit insurance to co-operative banking sector presupposes some semblance of Reserve Bank control over them, some provisions of B.R. Act, 1949 were made applicable to Urban Co-operative banks in 1966, after an intense debate among State Governments, Government of India and RBI. This was a landmark in the evolution of urban banking movement in India. Consequently, the co-operative banks came under duality of control.

The banking related functions such as licensing, area of operation, exposure norms, interest rates etc. were governed by RBI directives and regulations, incorporation and registration of co-operative banks, audit, management, liquidation, winding up, amalgamation etc., these functions are governed by the State Governments by virtue of powers conferred on them by the respective State Co-operative Societies Acts. Ironically, irritants thrown up by this dual control regime, had become one of the most vexations issues before the UCBs and cooperators. It is interesting to note that the Banking Regulation Act does not recognize the term 'urban co-operative bank' and defines it as a primary co-operative bank. The word "primary" is used to denote that the bank performs the role of a primary unit in a 3-tier co-operative credit structure. By this definition, the Urban Co-operative Banks were made an integral part of the well developed 3-tier co-operative credit structure which was developed to cater to the needs of rural India. The Urban Co-operative Banks, by implications, had to be affiliated to District Central Co-operative Bank (DCCB) at district level to State Co-operative Bank (SCB) at apex level and these banks, in turn, were supposed to help, nurse and guide the UCBs. Historically, UCBs were organised in semi-urban, urban and metropolitan centers. This was the reason why they came to popularly known as urban co-operative banks. However, the cooperators, UCBs and their federations have strongly pleaded for deleting the word 'primary' from the statute in view of phenomenal increase in their size and operations surpassing even District Central Co-operative Banks (DCCBs).

Between 1966-93, the resources mobilized by way of deposits by the UCBs had registered a phenomenal growth. From a meager Rs. 153 crores, as at the end of June 1967, they rose to Rs. 13,531 crores by the end of March 1993. The credit base surged from Rs. 167 crores to Rs. 10,132 crores during this period. The annualized average growth of deposits and advances was found to be quite impressive. The number of urban co-operative banks had grown from 1106 to 1399 during the corresponding period.

A class of urban co-operative banks, which are popularly called, Salary Earners Banks also emerged as a matter of course and had their own place in the urban co-operative banking system over the years. These banks are essentially thrift societies set up by employees of governmental departments/PSUs/large establishments for mutual help on the principles of cooperation. These societies also started using the word 'bank' and were accepting deposits from members of public. Since Reserve Bank of India did not find any rational for their continuing as banking entities, as they were essentially thrift societies, they were advised to go out of the purview of the B.R. Act, after returning the deposits to non-members. As a result, 599 salary earners banks went outside the purview of the B.R. Act, during the period 1 March, 1966 to 30 June, 1977 by converting themselves into co-operative credit societies. Marathe Committee had also endorsed this view. As on 31 March 1999, they were 90 salary earners banks.

Yet another interesting feature of the history of urban co-operative banking movement is that despite the exist of so many salary earner banks from the ambit of B.R. Act, the number of UCBs increased from 403 (excluding salary earners banks) to 1023 during 1 March 1966 and 30 June 1977. This increase in number of UCBs was not an account of a liberal licensing policy stance of RBI but an offshoot of statute indeed expansion i.e., automatic conversion of Primary Credit Societies in to USBs. The only difference between a primary credit society and an urban co-operative bank is the level of owned funds. If the owned funds of primary credit societies reaches Rs. 1 lakh, automatically, it has to apply to RBI for a licence to carry on banking business. If a primary credit society, after attaining Rs. 1 lakh of owned funds, does not meet the criteria laid down by the RBI, it can carry on banking business till its licence application is rejected by RBI. Due to this peculiar statutory dispensation, a large number of primary credit societies had necessarily had to be brought under the ambit of B.R. Act.

RBI has therefore decided, in 1978 that Registrar of Co-operative Societies should not register any new primary credit society of the object of which to carry on banking business. Because of this automatic entry of PCBs into the banking sector, today, there are as many as 181 unlicensed banks under RBI jurisdiction.

The period between 1966-1993 can be termed as an over regulated regime. The licensing policy of RBI was too restrictive as it was governed by the dictum "one district" – one bank notwithstanding the co-operative initiative demonstrated by the cooperators. Urban Co-operative Banks were also not allowed to expand beyond municipal limits. There was an embargo on their entry into rural areas and financing of agricultural operations. Branch licensing policy was linked to the "planned expansion of branches". There was also restrictions of deployment of UCB's surplus resources outside the co-operative fold. Growth of urban banking sector was confined to the states of Maharashtra, Karnataka, Gujarat and Tamil Nadu, where the co-operative movement had already taken strong roots. The regional disparities in the growth of urban co-operative movement was mostly due to strong co-operative initiative exhibited in these states and absence of similar co-operative leadership in other states.

**Phase III : Post 1993 – Scenario**

The year 1993 was a watershed in the annals of urban co-operative banking movement. After Narasimham Committee (Report I) addressed the ills of banking system in 1991, and suggested a road map for the banking sector, a similar need was also felt to look denovo at the regulatory issues relating to UCBs. Accordingly, RBI appointed the Marathe Committee in 1991 to address these issues. Recommendations of this Committee were quire far reaching, particularly, in the realm of new bank licensing, branch licensing and area of operation etc. Essentially, Marathe Committee, suggested to dispense with the "one-district-one bank" licensing policy. It also felt that existence of commercial banking network should not prevent the co-operative initiative. RBI accepted these recommendations and had come out with its new policy approach in May 1993, Between May 1993, when the revised policy was put in place and 31 March 1999, RBI had issued as many as 537 licenses for setting up new banks. The Oeager Clizat branch licensing policy's stress was more on bank's inherent financial strength rather than assessing the need for a branch and its viability in a given Meager. As a result, the branch network of UCBs had increased from 3691 as at the end of March 1993, to 6619 by 31st March 1999. Urban Co-operative banks were also allowed to extend their area of operation to the entire district without specific approval from RBI and banks, with deposits of Rs. 50 crores and above, which were permitted to cross the borders of the States of their registration. Banks complying with certain norms can now also open extension counters without RBI permission.

RBI had also appointed a Working Group under the Chairmanship of (Shri Uday M. Chitale) in December 1995 to review the existing audit systems of UCBs. With a view to instill professionalism in the audit of UCBs, the Working Group suggested that audit of UCBs, with deposits of Rs. 25 crores and above to be conducted by Chartered Accountants, thus, ending the monopoly of State Government's audit of USBc. It has suggested a standard format of audit for all the states. The Working Group also suggested revised audit rating model for USBs. Regrettably, other than Maharashtra, no other co-operatively advanced state, has implemented the recommendations of Chitale Working Group.

Besides, easing regulatory restrictions, a number of policy pronouncements were made in the operational sphere too. UCBs can now invest 10 percent of their surplus funds outside co-operative fold. Ceiling on quantum of advances to nominal members has been increased substantially and scheduled that UCBs have been allowed to do merchant banking/forex operations. Effective from November 1996, urban co-operative banks have been given freedom to finance direct agricultural operations. The interest rates on deposits of urban banks have been deregulated from 21 October 1977. They can also install ATMs without prior approval of RBI.

Thus, in the post Marathe Committee dispensation, there was a paradigm shift in RBI's regulatory approach. An excessively controlled regime gave way to a thoroughly Oeager Dizat dispensation. The shift in RBI policy on UCBs was a natural corollary of its policy stance on financial sector. Strangely, State Government who are co-regulators, have now brought out any significant parallel reforms in tune with Deager Eization process set in by RBI.

**Aggressive Marketing & Innovative Banking Need of the Hour**

The coming years will see banking gradually lose its standardization. Services and products will be priced to suit customer needs and each bank's ability to deliver. To provide both mass and class banking, public sector banks will have to adopt discriminatory pricing. A differentiated scheme of service charges, with a minimum charge levied on all customer and higher charge levied or more demanding clients could be a workable alternative. But higher service charges can be justified only if quality of the service in the banks improves, and, more important if it is allowed to reflect the differentiated rate structure. In the same way that rail travel is open to all, but a differentiated rate structure ensures a varying level of access to various amenities, similarly banks will need to keep access to banking services open to all, but use a differentiated service charges structure and varying minimum balance stipulation to ensure both profits for themselves as also qualitatively better service to the selected clients. For example foreign banks offer variety of services like credit cards, ATM cards, Club-membership, making arrangements for travel etc. For customers who keep certain balance varying from Rs. 50,000 to Rs. 5 lacs and levy extra service charges for various services are being provided to such customers. Customers don't mind paying for such services in case their needs are looked after efficiently by the banks.

Despite globalization, several banks will remain domestic in their orientation and focus. The ones that do seek to be global level players will compete with foreign banks, the new private banks and the investment banks. The recent influx of foreign banks is a challenge for the new private sector banks more than to public sector banks, as target group of class customers for both are the same.

For the globally-oriented banks, the reform process holds out both threat and opportunity. With full convertibility of rupee reality in the near future, their abilities to assess and quantify cross-border and exchange risks will be severely tested.

As already stated, traditional banking which basically concentrated deposit mobilization and lending activities will not be as important or as dominant as it used to be. Banks are diversifying in to new areas including merchant banking, leasing investment and international banking and different types of services like custody services, advisory services etc. Each bank will try to identify its own niche and strive to specialize and grow in that sector. In the changing scenario of their intermediation and liberalization, banks will face competition both on liability and assets sides. To ensure success, banks will have to pay attention to market segmentation and greater specialization in different niches of the market.

Another threat is the deregulation of interest rates announced by Reserve Bank of India on 17 October 1994. The first phase of deregulation of interest rate has been successful. RBI had abolished minimum lending rate and let the banks fixed their own deposit rates for term deposits of maturity for more than two years. The RBI also freed rates on deposits of over one year against two years earlier with effect from July 1996. However, banks have been asked to offer 'not exceeding 11 percent' on deposits of one year against 'not exceeding 12 percent' in the case of deposits up to two years earlier. It has also reduced the minimum period of deposit from 46 days to 30 days. In the monetary policy for the second half 1996-1997 announced by RBI on 19 October 1996, maximum permissible interest rates for deposit having maturity of 30 days and up to one year have been further reduced to 10 percent from the existing 11 percent in a bid to pull down short term deposit rates. With effect from 26 June 1997, maximum interest rate on Fixed Deposit upto one year is 8 percent as against 9 percent earlier. With effect from 21 October 1997, deposit rates were completely freed. Interest rates will be used more pro-actively to manage monetary conditions. The changes in deposit rates and lending rates were in response to RBI's decision to bring down the Bank Rate by 1 percent from 11 to 10 percent and 9 percent w.e.f. 30 April 1998. While the co-operative banks lending and deposit rates had been totally deregulated subject to minimum lending rate (MLR) of 12 percent, the minimum deposit rate for term deposit up to 1 year and concessional lending rates the priority sector and loans upto Rs. 25,000 and over Rs. 25,000 to Rs. 2 lakh of commercial banks have still remained with the Reserve Bank, RBI's next step would be to link the concessional rates to banks prime lending rates (PLR) and there after completely deregulate deposit rates w.e.f. 9 May 1998, interest on loans below Rs. 2 lakh capped at PLR.

Under next phase of financial sector reform, there may be a virtual dismantling of the administered interest rate regime, barring perhaps rates for very small loans. While the RBI may move away from prescribing interest rate, it would, however, use its own interest rates to influence the rates in the market. Interest rate movement will be more responsive to for evolving global situations as the domestic market integrate with the global economy. A deregulated environment would also require banks, financial institutions and non-bank finance companies willing to pay greater attention to asset-liability maturity mis-matches. All banks, irrespective of whether they are strong or weak, face a squeeze on their profit margins due to de-regulation of interest rates. Some banks will find an ideal opportunity to grow but for many others, it may mean a desperate struggle to survive. Interest rate risk has never been factored into the Indian Banking psyche in all these years, and is relatively new phenomenon. The banks will have to learn to manage under fear interest rate, which means they really have to look at each of their lending propositions. They have to restructure the mix of deposits in favour of low cost deposit. With deregulation of lending rates on a major chunk of banks advances, banks will be compelled to price their products to reflect their cost of operation. And as in the case of other markets, more efficient banks will be able to offer their products at a lower price and thereby grab a larger share of the market.

The less efficient banks will, meanwhile, be compelled to either spruce up their operations and cut costs or else close to shop. As long as Indian Banks do not improve their technology, they will be handicapped. Foreign banks have the crucial advantage of technology that has always kept them ahead of profitability. There will be a realm of 'triple future shocks" to the banking sector namely, the need for increased capital, increased competition and the impact of global information technology. The existing banking scenario may undergo a major change in the second phase of the financial sector deregulation. This is mainly because of India's commitment to WTO, which would force us to open parts of banking system to foreign entry and rapid advancement of global banking technology. Indian banks will have to merge in order to match global competitiveness. Over a period of time the structure and nature of banking is going to witness a sea of change. Through strategic amalgamations and merges, 7 to 8 large-sized, all India banks will emerge who will have the potential to become globalized banks. There will be different types of specialized banks operating at localize and limited scale of catering to niche markets. The Reserve Banks of India has recommended alliances and joint ventures between private and public sector banks to improve the profitability as well as accountability of the latter. The RBI has also recommended that banks will increasingly acquire expertise in pricing of heterogeneous risks to enable themselves in managing and modifying such exposures. This can be done through operational autonomy in strategic alliances with private sector banks. In the deregulated climate there will be an increased need for self-regulation among banks, as they will be under scrutiny from various regulatory bodies, auditors, stake-holders and the public.

## RBI's Vision Document for UCBs

The Vision Document for UCBs envisaged signing of MoU with the State and Central Governments for harmonization of dual regulation and supervision of UCBs and setting up of Task Force on Urban Co-operative Banks (TAFCUB) for identification of viable UCBs for their rehabilitation and non-viable UCBs for their non-disruptive exit.

## State-specific Strategy

The strategy to deal with the UCBs may need to be state specific, one that involves the concerned State Government, RBI and the UCBs operating in the state. A State level Task Force on Co-operative Urban Banks (TAFCUB) comprising the Regional Director (RD) of the RBI for the concerned state, Registrar of Cooperative Societies, an official from Central Office of Urban Banks Department (UBD), in-charge of UBD of the concerned Regional Office of RBI and a representative each from NAFCUB and the State Federation of the UCBs, could be set up, in each of the 5 states with high concentration of UCBs and in a few other states having, say, more than 50 banks to explore viable state specific solutions, including, on the future set up of the existing unlicensed banks whose license applications are pending with the RBI. Similar approaches may be considered for other states in a second phase after assessing the working of the state specific approach in the five states and in states with more than 50 UCBs.

## MoUs with States

Subsequent to the release of the Vision Document in public domain in March 2005, the Reserve Bank has entered into MoUs with 25 State Governments (nine entered during April 2008 to March 2009). As of date, 99 per cent of UCBs and 99 per cent of deposits of the UCB sector are covered under MoU arrangements. The number of UCBs in Grade III and IV, signifying various degrees of sickness, has since declined to 496 as on March 31, 2008 from 725 as on March 31, 2005. Till March 31, 2009 licences had been cancelled or rejected in respect of 85 banks and 31 unlicensed banks in MoU States have been issued banking licences.

Since the recommencement of new branch authorisation, 232 licences have been issued for opening of branches by UCBs in MoU States. The initiatives for voluntary mergers and amalgamations of weak UCBs for bringing consolidation in the sector were also carried forward and new policy guidelines on mergers were announced. Sixty-eight mergers between healthy and weak banks have been effected so far. In view of the improved financial condition and enhanced regulatory and supervisory jurisdiction of the Reserve Bank, additional business opportunities were opened up for well-functioning multi-state UCBs and UCBs in MoU States.

## Information Technology Support to UCBs

Based on the recommendations of the Working Group which looked into ways of supporting IT initiatives of the UCBs, IDRBT is being asked to facilitate UCBs availing of Core Banking Platform on an Application Service Provider (ASP) model. With this, the UCBs will be able to put in place cost-effective, modern technology so as to render better customer service and sound regulatory compliance.

# CHAPTER 7

## Emerging Banking Scenario – Challenges & Opportunities

In the recent past, the banking industry had undergone the following Major changes:

1. Financial sophistication
2. Deregulation / Decontrol / Liberalization of control in trade foreign Exchange / Industry to improve efficiency
3. Diversification in products / services

The forces which are significantly affecting financial serves are:

1. Deregulation (which is nothing but a passage to market driven financial forces)
2. Technology
3. Globalization

Due to liberalization and deregulation, banks and financial institutions will be free to choose (a) their segment (b) products / services (c) customers. Similarly, customers will also be free to choose products and services from the alternative sources. This will lead to increase competition and more risk for effectively dealing with which banks or financial institutions that will have to be highly innovated, as a result there will be more of reliance on price banking than relationship banking. The share of non-interest revenue will also increase. The banks may also have to diversify into non-traditional areas like

1. Asset-based finance
2. Mutual fund Banking
3. Electronic Banking Products and Services, Office banking, and house banking,
4. Other non-banking services – Travel related services, Securities Management, Debenture trustee business
5. Insurance linked services – Insurance brokerage and underwriting
6. Larger entry of non-banking organization into the business
7. Larger and more direct participation in capital and money market

The impact of these changes will be

a) Increased Marketing orientation.

b) Change from "order-taking" environment and administrative oriented banking to customer-oriented culture.

c) Product diversification and deeper market penetration with financial innovation.

d) Sector consolidation with increased competition.

e) Increased price competition.

f) Move to a cost conscious and customer-based organization structure.

g) High-Tech environment and information technology will lead to competitive alliances and competitive arenas.

h) A thinner spread / margin.

i) A shorter asset-liability management time frame.

j) Concern for fee-based income opportunities.

k) Plastic branching through credit card and easy credit nation-wide.

**Co-operative Banks: An RBI Perspective**

"RBI has decided not to allow urban co-operative banks (UCBs) with less than Rs. 50 crore net worth to spread their operations outside their state of jurisdiction. The main risk exposure of UCBs was not credit risk but interest rate risk. As interest rates paid by these banks, particularly on deposits, were out of sync with the rest of the banking sector. The sheer number of weak UCBs, which is well over 200, is a cause for concern for the RBI.

Rehabilitation of these banks may involve strategies such as the registrars directing banks and special recovery officers for speedy recovery process and execution for decrees, unviable branches being either relocated or closed down, exploring avenues for getting additional capital and merge with a well managed bank.

RBI is in favour of ending dual control for UCBs. Therefore, demarcation of banking related functions and those that warrant only state government action were required. According to Mr. Jagdish Kapoor, Deputy Governor of RBI issued that of dual control could be resolved in three ways.

"The first approach is by bringing the subject of co-operation under the concurrent list so as to enable the Union Government to legislate in matters pertaining to co-operative banking. But such a move will involve constitutional amendments. The second approach would be for the states to enact progressive legislations thereby making the registrars confine their functions only to registration and acceptance by law. This will lead to the dual command over UCB ending automatically. The last approach would be to demarcate the regulatory roles of state governments and RBI in the state acts, as suggested by the Madhava Rao Committee 'Mr Kapoor favours the third approach."

Government is considering incorporating amendments to the Banking Regulations Act to empower the Reserve bank of India to change the management and chief executive officer (CEO) of urban co-operative banks (UCBs).

Meanwhile, the RBI had mooted a proposal to set up a separate supervising and regulatory body for UCBs in its recent Credit Policy".

**Technology & Co-operative Banking Industry**

Technology plays an pivotal role in providing efficient customer service and creation of management information systems required at all levels of management hierarchy and assist in the decision making. In the present competitive environment, to withstand competition and also to cater to wider and expanding service areas of its customers, the use of technology definitely gives an edge over others. Realizing this, some of the Urban Co-operative Banks have fully computerized its operations way back in 1992, and more and more banks are falling in line. Various Co-operative Banks continue to upgrade the branches with latest technology and offer customer friendly facilities at all the branches which include services like tele-banking, Internet-banking, dmat services, ATM (both in Branches and Off-line) etc.

**Table No. 7.1 : Share of Co-operatives in National Economy**

| Sr.No. | | |
|---|---|---|
| 1 | Rural Network Villages Covered | 100 |
| 2 | Agricultural Credit Disbursed by Coops | 46.31 |
| 3 | Fertilizer disbursed (6.10-3 million Ton) | 36.30 |
| 4 | Fertilizer Produced (For Nitrogen-N) | 147.80 |
| 5 | Fertilizer Produced (For Phosphorus-P) | 23.5 |
| 6 | Sugar Produced (7.062 million tones) | 54.95 |
| 7 | Capacity utilization of sugar mills | 85.70 |
| 8 | Wheat Procurement | 27.80 |
| 9 | Jute Procurement (1997-1998) | 21.50 |
| 10 | Retail fair price shop (1,25,200) | 28.00 |
| 11 | Milk Procurement to total production | 6.70 |
| 12 | Milk Procurement to Marketable surplus | 10.00 |
| 13 | Oil Marketed/Procurement | 51.00 |
| 14 | Spindleage in Coop (3.313 million) | 10.00 |
| 15 | Cotton Marketed / Fabrics Production | 67.50 |
| 16 | Cotton Yarn / Fabrics Production | 22.00 |
| 17 | Handlooms in Co-operatives | 55.00 |
| 18 | Fisherman in Co-operatives (Active) | 21.00 |
| 19 | Storage facility (Village level PACs) | 62.50 |
| 20 | Soya Bean Production | 7.50 |
| 21 | Self Employment Generated for person (mini) | 12.50 |
| 22 | Salt Manufactured | 7.40 |

**Source:** Compiled & Computed by the researcher.

## UCBs: The Current Scenario

In the aftermath of the recent scams that are involving in co-operative banks, the image of the co-operative banking sector certainly seems to have taken a beating, but there is another side to co-operative banking, particularly in the urban segment, namely the emergence of the urban co-operative banks (UCBs) as the competitors to be reckoned with and seeking a change of image in a liberalized economy. With the local networks already in place, and the perils of the recession filtering out sick banks and leaving only the stronger ones to face the competition and globalization, the urban co-operative banks represent a potential peculiar to the Indian Banking sector, especially considering the co-operative bank accounts of the country's banking business. Moreover, out of 2085 urban banks, 52 scheduled urban banks have35 percent of the sector's total deposits, indicating the emergence of large and powerful banks. The management of the urban co-operative bank is aware of the competition lying ahead. D. Shirodkar, MD of Saraswat Co-operative Bank, Mumbai, explains that banks are not only facing competition from the nationalized banks but also from private banks and co-operative credit societies also. The structure and the customers of the bank are totally different. He maintains "the lower middle class, cobbler, taxi driver and shop keeper to continue to come to them for their banking needs. No other bank entertains the small loan requirements. The UCBs has also the advantage still there forever. Satish Marathe, former MD of Janakalyan Bank Mumbai says, "The competitive advantage of UCB over a commercial bank in the days to come will be thrust from the common man. Adding to the segment advantage, Shirodkar says that its the sheer variety of loans. "For the instance he explain a flat mortgage customer at our bank will also get an 11 percent loans for furnishing the flat, which he can repay over five years with no extra collateral. Such services are offered only for co-op banks.

"Only a part of the ceremony of layer of loan accounts has shifted to private banks, not everybody", says Marathe., "The nationalized banks have lost some business to the private sector, but private banks pose a threat neither to co-op nor nationalized banks today – they are small in size and net worth-wise. In a country the size of India, if you don't have a wide enough network, you can't go too far".[7]

The local reach of Co-op., made possible by their branch network, could turn out to be their biggest advantage yet. "I foresee a scenario in another 5 year where banks from other sector will approach a Co-op bank for strategy alliance. It could be with a sound financial institution even foreign bank. For eg., a co-op. bank like ours, with 25 branch network in Mumbai, Navi Mumbai and Thane, would be ideal for any bank, foreign or private, to strike an alliance for expanding business in the city".

Before that happens though the Co-op banking movement will have to get to act together. "Co-op banks as a corporate entities possess certain unique characteristics. Paradoxical as it may sound, evolution of co-op in India as people's organization rather than business enterprise adopting professional managerial system has hindered growth of professionalism in Co-op and proved to be neglected in areas of the evolution", said Vepa Kamesan Deputy Governor of RBI, at the inaugural address at the National Convention of Urban Co-op Banks some time back.

Kamesan suggested training programme encompassing skill up gradation and aptitude development, periodic job rotation, job enrichment and recognition of performance. "The Co-op banks should work like professional organization on sound managerial system intone with the need of the time, taking care of future projection of requirement to retain and improve their market share and identity in long run. It is in this context that professionalism and accountability of the banks boards assume such critical significance", he said.

Few industry representatives deny that internal administration and the quality of human resource in many Co-op banks needs some improvement. "In co-operation like in most modern set-ups" Marathe predicts, "Demutualization – separation of ownership and management – will eventually arrive. It is only a question of time. Once the operation are professionalised, the risk we face today will be sharply reduce".

Co-operative banks also have to deal with what they call step-motherly treatment from the RBI. "Because of aberration in the system caused by a few player". Complains an industry source who did not wish to be named, at the insistence of the finance ministry, the regulators have issued an unofficial circular stating. Don't accept Cheque issued on Co-op banks for acceptance of Income-tax, excise and custom, and more recently, at the insistence of the ministry, the petroleum ministry has stopped accepting cheques issued on co-op banks. This truly is unfair and unwarranted. The role of Co-op banks in addressing the priority sector needs to be doing away with money lenders who cannot be underestimated, but the road ahead would have to involve much modernization and image building. According to Thomas, "To modernize, UCBs it should would have to adopt e-banking, not only as mere technology solution, but also to deepen their market penetration, enhance their corporate image and support of new level of consumer expectations".

He adds, "The progressive figures registered by co-op banks shown that some of the UCBs have even bigger and certain commercial banks. With support from its customers, the co-operative banking movement can scale new height".

# CHAPTER 8

## Growth & Development of UCBs in India

The development of urban co-operative credit societies did not receive much attention until 1915 when the Mac-lagan Committee referred to the potentialities for the organization of such societies as a means of training the upper and middle urban classes in ordinary banking principles. The failure of local joint-stock bank in the country at that time gave an impetus to the growth of urban co-operative credit societies. It was then realized that urban credit societies were eminently suitable institutional agencies for collecting local savings and to provide relief to those who were in the clutches of moneylenders by providing them with financial accommodation. Many urban credit societies were organized in Bombay and Madras province during the period (1919-38). The urban credit societies which came into being in Bombay confined their activities mostly to the members of particular communities and their lending operations were also primarily with a view to meet the consumption needs of their members. The great depression of the thirties did not have any visible impact on the development of co-operative credit movement in country, because the fall in urban incomes was not as steep as the fall in rural income.

Later, the economic boom created by the Second World War (1935-45) provided a stimulus to the growth of urban co-operative banks in India. They grew not only in numbers but also in size, diversifying their activities considerably. Urban co-operative credit societies which had hitherto largely confined their loaning operations to provisions of the consumption credit needs of the members were called upon to take up new avenues such as financing to artisans, small businessmen and small traders for productive purpose, in the context of the hesitancy of commercial banks at that time to meet the credit needs of these classes due to the high cost of servicing of loans.

The usefulness of urban co-operative banks in financing artisans, small traders, factory workers and urban middle classes were recognized by various committees and working groups such as the Central Banking Enquiry Committee (1931), the Co-operative Planning Committee (1946), the Study Group on Credit Co-operative in the Non-Agricultural Sector (1963), and the Working Group on Industrial Financing through co-operative banks (1968).

An important development in urban co-operative banking was the survey undertaken by the Reserve Bank of India in 1958-59 with the objective of studying the pattern of financial resources of urban banks, part played by them in financial small scale industries, the outlets for their investments and the factors underline the success or failure in their working.

The most significant development relating to urban co-operative banks in recent years has been as an extension to co-operative banks of certain provision of Banking Regulation Act of 1949, from 1st March 1966. Earlier, the Banking companies Act of 1949 which came into force from 16th March 1949 had specifically excluded co-operative banks, including urban co-operative banks, from the purview of the Act, as co-operative banks were registered under the

Co-operative Societies Act of the respective state and such as could not be classified as 'companies'. Since 1966, the urban co-operative banks had over termed as "primary co-operative banks".

The co-operative movement in India started a century ago with the enactment of Co-operative Societies Act in 1904. Interestingly, legal status was conferred on credit societies keeping in view, in particular, the needs of the agricultural sector. Nevertheless, Sir Ibbetson, who piloted the legislation observed: "We recognize that artisans, employees on small pay and other persons in towns may very properly be admitted to the benefits of our legislation".

Although joint stock banks opened branches in urban and semi-urban areas, they did not find it advantageous to cater to the banking and credit requirements of the urban middle/lower class comprising of small businessmen, artisans, factory workers, salaried persons with limited incomes etc. The inability of joint stock banks to appreciate and cater to the needs of this class of clientele with limited means effectively drove them to money-lenders and similar agencies for loans at exorbitant rates of interest – this situation was the prime mover for non-agricultural credit co-operatives coming into being in India. The main objectives of such co-operatives were to meet the banking and the credit requirements of this section of people and protect them from exploitation. Thus, urban co-operative banks' emergence was a result of local response to enable legislative environment, unlike rural co-operative movement that was largely State-driven. The origin of co-operative banks can be traced in a small town in South India, called Conjivaram, where in 1904, the Conjivaram Urban Co-operative bank was set up, to cater to the needs of small businessmen as an alternative to moneylenders.

Little attention had been paid to the development of the urban credit movement until the Maclagan Committee (1914) drew attention to its potentials. Interestingly, a banking crisis in India in (1913-14), when no fewer than 57 joint stock banks collapsed, led to a flight of deposits from joint stock banks to urban co-operative banks. The 'Maclagan' Committee investigating the crisis stated 'As a matter of fact, the crisis had a contrary effect and in most provinces there was a movement to withdraw deposits from non-co-operatives and place them in co-operative institutions, the distinction between the two classes of security being appreciated and preference being given to latter, owing partly to the local character and publicity of co-operative institutions.

**Scheduled Status of Urban Co-operative Banks:**

The *Banking Commission (1972)* recommended that the establishment of urban co-operative banks should be encouraged by such means as according to the status of a *'scheduled'* bank to the well-managed Urban Co-operative banks if they desire. The *Government of India* by their Notification No., 15/10/87 BO.II Ministry of Finance, Department of Economic Affairs (Banking Division) dated 5th April 1988, (*notified the primary co-operative banks which are licensed and whose minimum demand and time liabilities*) *are not less than Rs. 50 Crores as financial institutions* for the purposes of sub-clause (iii) of clause (a) of Sub-Section (6) of Section 42 of the RBI Act 1934. Consequently, the RBI, by their Notification No. UBD.BR.94/9/88-89 dated 18th August 1988 (*directed the inclusion in second schedule to the RBI Act*) *1934*

*11 (eleven)* Urban Co-operative Banks (8 from Maharashtra and 3 from (Gujarat) *w.e.f. 1st September 1988*. By another Notification No. UBD.BR.106/A 90/91 dated 1st November 1990, three banks viz., Bassein, Cosmos and New India were given scheduled status w.e.f. 1st December 1990.

*Scheduling confers certain positive advantages which most of the commercial banks enjoy*. For example, it will enable them:

*(i)* *to have direct access to the Reserve Bank of India for availing themselves of refinance facilities* under Section 17(2) (bb) of RBI Act 1934;

*(ii)* *extension of the facilities under the Refinance and Bills Rediscounting Schemes operate by the Industrial Development* Bank of India;

*(iii)* *to access deposits from local bodies, quasi-governmental organizations, religious and charitable institutions* etc.;

*(iv)* *to issue guarantees* to central and state government departments;

(v) to *become members of the Clearing Houses* managed by the Reserve Bank and the State Bank of India;

(vi) to *enter the call money market* which provides and avenue for the investment of surplus funds at profitable rates for short-term periods; and

(vii) to *avail themselves of RBI Remittance Facilities Scheme 1975* for the purposes of remitting funds by telegraphic transfer, mail transfer of drafts through offices of the BRI and SBI and its associate banks.

At the same time, the *conferment of scheduled status imposes certain conditions and obligations on the banks* in the maintenance of books of accounts and submission of returns:

(i) Hitherto the banks are allowed to keep statutory cash reserve with themselves or in current account with state/central co-operative banks or Nationalised banks. Now *under Section 42 (1) of the RBI Act, banks are required to maintain with RBI an average of daily balance*, the amount of which shall not be less than 3 percent of total DTL subject to a maximum of 15 percent of total DTL in India of such banks as per the fortnightly return to be submitted to RBI. For this purpose, such banks are required to maintain the required minimum balance, the penal interest from 3 percent to 5 percent above the bank rate is recoverable from the banks depending on the length of the period for such violation.

(ii) Presently, the banks are required to submit the return in Form I indicating once in a month. *Now, under Section 42 of the RBI Act 1934, the banks are required to submit fortnightly returns* indicating the position of DTL on alternate Fridays within 7 days from the close of the fortnight. If the alternate Friday is not the last Friday of the month, the banks are required to submit an additional return on the last Friday of the month within 7 days.

**Audit, Supervision and Inspection :**

The mechanism regulating the affairs or Urban Co-operative banks is operated by three agencies viz., *Reserve Bank of India, Co-operation Department* of the State concerned and the *financing bank*. Control is broadly exercised through a system of returns, inspection and audit. *While inspections are carried out by all the three agencies* at different periodicity, *annual audit is conducted by the Co-operation Department* and in certain status by Chartered Accountants approved by the Registrars of Co-operative Societies. Inspection by financing banks is conducted mainly to ensure the safety of funds lent and fulfillment of the terms and conditions attached to the sanction of credit limits including the proper utilization of funds. The *supervision over the working of Urban Co-operative banks is exercised by the Urban Banks Department of the Reserve Bank of India* through a system of (i) statutory and other returns, (ii) periodical inspections including compliance and post-inspection compliance, discussions with Chairman and a few Directors of the concerned bank, and (iii) Special investigation/ visits/follow-up of frauds, complaints etc. The main objective of RBI inspection is to safeguard the interests of the depositors and to build-up and maintain a sound banking system in conformity with the banking laws and regulations, and also to look into the development role played by the banks in keeping with country's socio-economic objectives.

**Standing Advisory Committee**

*The Reserve Bank in January 1983 has constituted a Standing Advisory Committee for Urban Co-operative Banks* under the chairmanship of its Deputy Governor in-charge of Urban Banks Department *to advise the Reserve Bank of various aspects* pertaining to the Urban co-operative banks such as organizational matters, mobilization of resources and their deployment in various sectors including the priority sectors, coordinating with other institutions such as IDBI, DICGC etc., modalities on rehabilitation of weak banks, introduction of professional management, training and education of personnel of Urban Co-operative banks. *The membership of the Advisory Committee includes representatives of Government of India (Ministries of Finance and Agriculture), NABARD, State Governments, Urban Banks Federations / Associations, Urban Co-operative Banks and other Co-operative and Commercial Banks.* The Chief General Manager of Urban Banks Department is the ex-officio Member Secretary and the Urban Banks Department acts as its Secretariat.

**UCBs – An Advantage Over Commercial Banks :**

Urban Co-operative banks are not mere lending agencies set up as substitutes for private money-lender who used to resort to usurious practices, or for the commercial banks which have been by and large inaccessible to the people of small means and small needs. *Urban Co-operative banks are better substitutes with a noble mission to promote the thrift and savings to rehabilitate the precarious economy of the weaker sections. Their primary object, unlike commercial banks, is service and the profit motive in incidental.* Being local institutions, Urban Co-operative banks, unlike commercial banks are vitally interested in local development. Further, they are not to operate as just purveyors of finance but to function as friendly guides to their clients helping them to adopt better production techniques, sound financing and accounting systems. Since Urban Co-operative banks have the local feel, as they are *compared to Commercial banks, in a better position to appreciate the needs of the members and to adjust their policies and procedures to such needs with a greater degree of flexibility.* They transact their banking business according to the language and region of the people, fix their office hours either in the morning or evening and thereby rendering service at a time convenient to the people. This has motivated house-wives, office-going people, artisan class, laborers and others to open saving bank accounts with these banks and thereby fostering the habit of banking, savings and thrift among them. *They have thus promoted 'mass banking' as distinguished from 'class banking' by commercial banks.* As compared to commercial banks, the balance sheet and profit and loss account of an Urban Co-operative bank is more transparent. Unlike commercial banks, it show bad debts and reserves. *In Indian banking system, Urban Co-operative bank is the pioneer in acknowledging the common man as its clientele whom is to be services and commercial bank has realized this truth only after nationalization.*

*Now if we compare the actual performances of both types of banks on the basis of two important parameters viz., deposit mobilization and deployment of credit for the year 1993 and 1994, we observe that Urban Co-operative banks far excel the commercial banks.* The growth rates of deposits, achieved by Urban Co-operative banks during the year 1993 and 1994 were impressive at 21.8 percent and 23.9 percent respectively as compared to the growth rates achieved by commercial banks at 16.4 percent and 17.3 percent respectively. As regards to loans and advances, the growth rates achieved by Urban Co-operative banks during the years 1993 and1994 worked were out of 22.1 percent and 22.4 percent respectively, as compared to the growth rates achieved by commercial banks at 21.0 percent and 8.2 percent respectively, although the share of deposits of Urban Co-operative banks constitutes around 4.0 percent of the total resources from the banking system, *the mystery behind their better performance lies in their familiarity with the members, democratic management, local feel, personalized service, compactness in the area of operations, close supervisions over the end-use of credit and prompt recovery of dues from their member-borrowers.* All these characteristics inherent in Urban Co-operative banks act as a catalyst for their speedy and sustained growth, not withstanding the presence of commercial banks and financial intermediaries.

## Growth & Development Prior to March 1966

The development of the Urban Co-operative Credit Societies did not receive much attention until 1915 when the *Maclagan Committee on Co-operation* pointed out the potentialities for the organization of such societies: 'Urban Credit Societies might serve as a useful purpose in training the upper and middle urban classes to understand ordinary banking principles'. The *Central Banking Enquiry Committee (1931)* also felt that 'the duty of these urban banks should be to try to do for the small traders, the small merchants and the middle class population of what the commercial banks are doing for the big traders and big merchants'. The *Varde Committee* (1963) pointed out 'the failure of the Swadeshi Joint-Stock banks, created an opportunity for co-operative banking to develop as a medium for mobilising the savings of the persons who were modest means and helping those whom financial distress caused by high living costs and unemployment had driven into the clutches of money-lenders'.

*The inter-war period did not affect the Urban Credit movement as adversely as it affected the agricultural credit movement.* This might be due to the fact that during the depression the fall in urban incomes was not as steep as the fall in rural incomes. Another contributory factor to the stability of the movement in urban areas was the comparatively of high standard of the managerial efficiency available in urban areas of which the Urban co-operatives could afford on account of their larger resources. *The progress of urban co-operative credit societies and banks can be assessed from the following observations of the Reserve Bank;* 'Urban Credit societies and banks are the most important features of the Urban Co-operative movement in India, and make up to some extent for the absence of joint-stock banking facilities in smaller towns'.

Statistics regarding the progress of urban co-operative banks are not available on an all-India basis for the period prior to 1948-49. Data on all-India basis are presented in the *Review of the Co-operative Movement in India,* published by the *Reserve Bank of India*, from the year 1948-49 onwards. 'Even these data suffer from various limitation as no uniform definition of an urban bank was adopted by the different states. For instance, while in *Bombay* all urban credit societies having a paid-up share capital of Rs. 20,000 and above, and accepting any type of deposits were classified as urban banks, in *Madras,* all urban credit societies accepting deposits on current account and maintaining fluid resources according to the standards prescribed by the Registrar of Co-operative Societies were defined as urban banks. Further, *in some states,* salary earners' societies, Mill-hands, Societies etc., were classified as urban banks. The data published in the Reviews of the Co-operative Movement in India, though defective from the above points, however, provided a rough idea about the trends in the growth of urban banks'.

The figures relating to the working of these urban co-operative banks on the basis of these data presented in Table 8.1 for the period 1948-49 to 1959-60 are as follows.

**Table 8.1 : Progress of Urban Co-operative Banks in India from1948-49 to 1959-60**

(Rs. In Crores)

| Indicators of Progress | 1948-49 | 1949-50 | 1954-55 | 1959-60% | increase of (5) over (2) |
|---|---|---|---|---|---|
| (1) | (2) | (3) | (4) | (5) | (6) |
| Number | 815 | 776 | 1469 | 1242 | 52.39 |
| Membership in (000s) | 535 | 580 | 1044 | 1797 | 235.89 |
| Owned Funds | 4 | 5 | 8 | 17 | 325.00 |
| Deposits | 17 | 18 | 29 | 61 | 258.82 |
| Working Capital | 22 | 24 | 40 | 82 | 272.72 |
| Advances | 19 | 20 | 24 | 65 | 242.11 |
| Advances Outstanding | 12 | 13 | 20 | 58 | 383.33 |
| Overdues | 1 | 2 | 3 | 4 | 300.00 |

**Source:** Review of the Co-operative Movement in India-various years, RBI, Bombay

Data for the period (1960-61) to (1965-66) are not available separately for urban banks, either in the *Statistical Statements Relating to the Co-operative Movement in India or in the Reviews of the Co-operative Movement in India* published by the Reserve Bank, *as the statistic presented in these publications, include all non-agricultural credit societies together.*

**Growth and Development as on March 1966:**

As on 1st March 1966, i.e., *the date of extension of the B.R. Act of 1949 to Co-operative banks,* there were 1091 primary (urban) co-operative banks in the country. This number is not strictly comparable with the number of banks in 1959-60 at 1242, because it represented only those urban banks whose paid-up share-capital and reserves were Rs. 1 lakh and more consequently came under the statutory control of the Reserve Bank. *Of 1091 banks as on 1st March 1966, 4043 were Urban banks and 688 were salary earners' classified as primary co-operative banks, and their deposits and advances aggregated to Rs. 153 crores and to Rs. 167 crores respectively.* The state-wise position of urban banks is presented in Table 8.2

**Table 8.2 : Statements showing the number of Urban Co-operative Banks as on 1.3.1966**

| No. | State/Union Territories | Total | @Urban Co-operative Banks | *SESs Classified as Urban Co-operative Banks |
|---|---|---|---|---|
| 1 | 2 | 3 | 4 | 5 |
| 1 | Maharashtra | 382 | 84 | 298 |
| 2 | Gujarat | 154 | 62 | 92 |
| 3 | Tamil Nadu | 146 | 87 | 59 |
| 4 | West Bengal | 123 | 21 | 102 |
| 5 | Karnataka | 98 | 64 | 34 |
| 6 | Andhra Pradesh | 50 | 34 | 16 |
| 7 | Rajasthan | 9 | 4 | 5 |
| 8-12 | Bihar, Kerala, Madhya Pradesh, Orissa, Punjab | 74 | 37 | 37 |
| 13-15 | Assam, Himachal Pradesh, Uttar Pradesh | 28 | NIL | 28 |
| 16-17 | Delhi, Pondicherry | 27 | 10 | 17 |
| 18-21 | Haryana, Manipur, Meghalaya, Goa-Daman & Diu | NIL | NIL | NIL |
| | Total | 1091 | 403 | 688 |

**Source:** Researcher's Compilation from the records of UBD, CO, Bombay
**Note:** @ Urban Co-operative Banks.
* Salary Earners'/Employees' Societies

**Growth & Development of UCBs After March 1966**

The performance of urban banks during the period 1966-67 to 1983-84 is shown in Table 8.3. A care perusal of the data furnished, in the said table indicates the spectacular growth of the urban co-operative credit movement in India in terms of, inter alia, owned funds, deposits, loans, advances and profit earnings. The total number of urban banks has gone up from 1106

**Table 8.3 : Performance of Urban Co-operative Banks from 1966-67 to 1983-84 Trends in Progress**

| Indicators of progress | Co-operative Year | | | | | |
|---|---|---|---|---|---|---|
| | 1966-67 | 1969-70 | 1975-76 | 1978-79 | 1981-82 | 1983-84 |
| 1 | 2 | 3 | 4 | 5 | 6 | 7 |
| No. of Reporting Banks | 1106 | *989 | *1142 | $1194 | 1236 | 1309 |
| Membership (in lakhs) | 36.32 | 37.17 | 46.59 | 27.69 | 74.79 | 89.92 |
| Owned Funds | 58 | 52 | 108 | 167 | 290 | 403 |
| Deposits | 153 | 179 | 468 | 839 | 1667 | 2585 |
| Borrowings | 11 | 10 | 20 | 33 | 115 | 174 |
| Working Capital | 222 | 264 | 662 | 1148 | 2330 | 3608 |
| Investments | 38 | 44 | 42 | 121 | 230 | 321 |
| Loans Outstanding | 167 | 177 | 393 | 641 | 1412 | 2137 |
| Profit | 4 | 3 | 12 | 23 | 67 | 89 |

**Source:** Review of the Co-operative Movement in India – Various years, RBI-Bombay

**Note:** 1. * Includes particulars for certain primary credit societies also governed by the Banking Regulation Act, 1949

2. $ Excludes data in respect of 45 Primary Co-operative Banks.
(Cf. Page 201 of statistical statements etc., 1978-79, RBI, Bombay

as on 30 June 1967 to 1309 as on 30th June 1984, percentage growth rate being 18.35 percent. Similarly, the member-ship of these banks has risen from 36.32 lakh in (1966-67) to 89.92 lakh in 1983-84, recording a percentage growth of 147.58 percent. The owned fund i.e., share – capital and reserves have increased from a low level of Rs. 58 crores in (1966-67) to Rs. 403 crores in (1983-84) establishing a percentage increase of 594.83. Both the deposits and the loan components have registered a significant increase from Rs. 153 crores and Rs. 167 crores as on 30th June 1967 to Rs. 2585 crores, and Rs. 2137 crores as on 30th June 1984, the percentage increase was computed in respect of each component being 1589.54 and 1179.64. During the same period, the over-all net operating results of urban co-operative banks in India recorded profits, the percentage growth worked out to 2125.

## Growth & Development During the Period Under Study (1985-94)

Statistics relating to the growth and operations or urban co-operative banks form 1985 to 1994 (i.e., covering the 10 year period of the present research study) are furnished in Table 8.4. The Table indicates that urban co-operative banks continue to register a steady increase in respect of owned funds, deposits, loans and advances over the years. Percentages of growth in respect of owned funds, deposits, loans and advances and also of working capital have been incorporated in the table itself to have a comparative view of those selected indicators at a glance. *Incidentally, mentioned may be made that the number of urban co-operative banks which stands at 1400 as the end of March 1994, includes, inter alia, 48 Mahila Banks, 91 Salary Earners' types of societies classified as urban co-operative banks and also 51 urban co-operative banks under liquidation.* Besides out of the total 1400 urban co-operative banks, the number of licensed banks in 1045 as against 1039 and 1038 as on 31st March 1992 and 1993 respectively.

**Table 8.4 : Consolidated statement showing Operations of Urban Co-operative banks in India (1984-85 to 1993-94)**

| Co-operative year ended | Total No. of Banks | Owned Funds | Deposits | Loans & Advances | Working Capital |
|---|---|---|---|---|---|
| 1 | 2 | 3 | 4 | 5 | 6 |
| June 1985 | 1331(1321) | 478.66(18.8) | 3131.90(21.2) | 2536.39(18.7) | 4342.93(20.4) |
| June 1986 | 1346(1314) | 57007(19.1) | 3941.50(25.8) | 3059.33(20.6) | 5337.92(22.9) |
| June 1987 | 1359(1321) | 693.35(21.6) | 4883.08(23.9) | 3638.65(18.9) | 6502.80(19.4) |
| June 1988 | 1380(1308) | 886.01(27.8) | 5789.51(18.6) | 4635.90(27.4) | 7761.17(20.8) |
| June 1989 | 1378(1324) | 1082.43(22.2) | 7231.93(24.9) | 5819.51(25.5) | 9760.27(23.1) |
| June 1990 | 1390(1307) | 1256.30(16.1) | 8660.16(19.7) | 6802.46(16.9) | 11400.29(19.2) |
| June 1991 | 1397(1306) | 1480.84(17.9) | 10156.89(17.3) | 8003.14(17.7) | 13389.52(17.4) |
| June 1992 | 1401(1311) | 1765.55(19.2) | 11107.94(9.4) | 8712.52(8.9) | 14742.39(10.1) |
| June 1993 | 1399(1306) | 2223.93(26.0) | 13530.68(21.8) | 10132.14(16.3) | 18006.77(22.1) |
| June 1994 | 1400(1301) | 2722.75(22.4) | 16768.83(23.9) | 12172.34(20.1) | 22037.26(22.4) |

**Source:** Statistical statements relating to the co-operative Movement in India, various years, RBI/NABARD, Bombay.

**Note:** 1. Figs. In parentheses at Column 2 indicate total number of Reporting banks.
2. Figs in parentheses at Column 3 to 6 indicate percent of growth.

**Table 8.5 : State-wise details of Urban Co-operatives Banks as on 31st March 1994**

| No. | States/Union Territories | No. of Banks | Owned Funds | Deposits | Loans & Advances | Working Capital |
|---|---|---|---|---|---|---|
| 1 | 2 | 3 | 4 | 5 | 6 | 7 |
| 1 | Andhra Pradesh | 66 (121) | 52.34 | 439.41 | 328.14 | 596.42 |
| 2 | Assam | 8 (12) | 18.83 | 44.77 | 36.35 | 72.27 |
| 3 | Bihar | 5 (4) | 1.08 | 2.96 | 1.84 | 4.52 |
| 4 | Delhi | 17 (49) | 21.31 | 122.85 | 69.83 | 163.74 |
| 5 | Goa | 6 (42) | 35.18 | 251.57 | 184.84 | 334.30 |
| 6 | Gujarat | 293 (606) | 856.70 | 3737.95 | 2782.72 | 5211.57 |
| 7 | Haryana | 8 (12) | 3.722 | 21.87 | 17.64 | 33.64 |
| 8 | Himachal Pradesh | 4 (4) | 1.57 | 16.62 | 15.29 | 22.51 |
| 9 | Jammu & Kashmir | 3 (9) | 1.63 | 24.76 | 13.04 | 27.61 |
| 10 | Karnataka | 213 (445) | 187.24 | 979.09 | 791.21 | 1319.46 |
| 11 | Kerala | 59 (184) | 39.59 | 343.47 | 230.98 | 414.50 |
| 12 | Madhya Pradesh | 42 (65) | 24.90 | 156.45 | 100.34 | 205.59 |
| 13 | Maharashtra | 387 (1810) | 1242.77 | 9245.82 | 6512.52 | 11698.49 |
| 14 | Manipur | 5 (10) | 3.03 | 14.02 | 9.60 | 20.94 |
| 15 | Meghalaya | 2 (2) | 0.44 | 1.63 | 0.89 | 2.35 |
| 16 | Mizoram | 1 (1) | 0.86 | 4.39 | 7.714 | 10.68 |
| 17 | Orissa | 14 (28) | 15.35 | 110.25 | 84.62 | 149.44 |
| 18 | Pondicherry | 2 (5) | 1.20 | 8.99 | 6.37 | 11.29 |
| 19 | Punjab | 6 (10) | 4.04 | 34.68 | 24.07 | 42.21 |
| 20 | Rajasthan | 26 (63) | 16.40 | 103.67 | 64.38 | 133.69 |
| 21 | Tamil Nadu | 137 (203) | 108.75 | 632.42 | 522.6 | 843.48 |
| 22 | Tripura | 1 (1) | 0.60 | 2.02 | 1.47 | 3.28 |
| 23 | Uttar Pradesh | 47 (83) | 31.49 | 1293.92 | 129.43 | 285.10 |
| 24 | West Bengal | 48 (82) | 55.73 | 275.25 | 236.46 | 430.18 |
| | | 1400 (3851) | 2722.75 | 167568.83 | 12172.34 | 22037.26 |

**Source:** Statistical Statements relating to the Co-operative Movement in India, NABARD, Bombay.

**Note:** Figs. In Parantheses at Column 2 denote number of Offices.

A statement showing state-wise position of number of urban co-operative banks, their owned funds, deposits, loans and advances as on 31st March 1994 is given in Table 8.5. It will be seen there, from that out of the 1400 urban co-operative banks in the country as many as 1030 banks (i.e., 73.6 percent) are located in four states viz., Maharashtra, Gujarat, Karnataka and Tamil Nadu. The rest of the states/union territories could be considered more or less as *co-operative deserts / semi deserts. In terms of resources and outstanding loans and advances, urban co-operative banks in these four states account for 88 percent of owned funds, 87 percent of deposits, and 87.2 percent of loans and advances of all the urban co-operative banks in the country*. In terms of branch network, these four states have as many as 3064 branches forming 79.6 percent of the total number of branches in the entire country. Thus the urban co-operative banking movement in the country is characterised by *regional disparities*.

Another striking feature of the urban co-operative banking is its *heterogeneous character*. The number of banks according to the size of deposits, loans and advances as on 31 March 1994 is furnished in Table 8.6.

**Table 8.6 : Number of Reporting Urban Co-operative Banks according to size of Deposits and Advances as on 31st March 1994**

| Category | Deposits | | Advances | |
|---|---|---|---|---|
| | No. of Banks | Amounts | No. of Banks | Amount |
| 1 | 2 | 3 | 4 | 5 |
| 1. Upto Rs. 10 Crores | 966 | 3462.14 (20.6) | 1021 | 3323.02 (27.3) |
| 2. Rs. 10 Crores & Rs. 25 Crores | 215 | 3382.11 (20.2) | 198 | 3063.23 (25.2) |
| 3. Rs. 25 Crores & Rs. 50 Crores | 75 | 2503.52 (14.9) | 53 | 1828.35 (15.0) |
| 4. Above Rs. 50 Crores | 45 | 7421.06 (44.3) | 29 | 3957.74 (32.5) |
| Total | 1301 | 16768.83 (100.0) | 1301 | 12172.34 (100.0) |

**Source:** Researcher's Compilation from the records of UBD, CO, Bombay
**Note:** Figs. in parentheses denote percentage ( percent) of total deposits/Advances

Of the 1301 reporting urban co-operative banks, as many as 1181 banks (90.8 percent), having less than Rs. 25 crores of deposits, account for Rs. 6844 crores (or 40.8 percent) of aggregate deposits and the remaining 120 urban co-operative banks (9.2 percent) account for Rs. 9924 crores (or 59.2 percent) of the total deposits. *Such heterogeneity is also discernible in the advance portfolio*. As many as 1219 banks having less than 25 crores of advances account's for Rs. 6386 crores (or 52.5 percent) of the aggregate advances and the remaining 82 urban co-operative banks account for Rs. 5786 crores (or 47.5 percent) of the total loans and advances.

Again, according to the number of branches, urban co-operatives banks can be broadly classified into four categories (cf. Table 8.7). Unitary banks operate within the limits of a town

**Table 8.7 : Number of Urban Co-operative Banks according to Number of Branches**

| Sr.No. | Types of USBs as per number of Branches | Actual No. of Branches |
|---|---|---|
| 1 | 2 | 3 |
| 1 | No. of unitary banks | 741 |
| 2 | No. of banks having less than 5 branches | 462 |
| 3 | No. of banks having branches between 5 and 10 | 121 |
| 4 | No. of banks having above 10 branches | 47 |
| | Total | 1381* |

**Source:** Researcher's compilation from the records of UBD, CO, Bombay.
**Note:** * Data not available in respect of the remaining banks

or a few towns and generally cater to the needs of small borrowers engaged in retail trade, cottage and SSI units, and persons engaged in small avocation in semi-urban/small urban centers. Seven urban co-operative banks are operating banks, operating beyond their State of registration and are governed by the *Multi-State Co-operative Societies Act of 1984*. Urban co-operatives banks operating in metropolitan cities and larger urban centers, in addition to their traditional retail banking business, have also taken up diversified activities like stock-invest scheme, opening and maintenance of Non-Resident (External) and Ordinary Rupee accounts, investments in Certificates of Deposits and Commercial Papers, Bankers to Issue and Merchant Banking business etc. As at the end of March 1994, 67 urban co-operative banks each having a working capital or above Rs. 10 crores are authorized to open NRE and NRO accounts. Of the 14 scheduled urban co-operative banks, two banks are authorized dealers in *foreign exchange business*. Three scheduled urban co-operative banks have been permitted to as *"Bankers to Issue"* while other two scheduled urban co-operative banks have been authorized to conduct merchant *banking business* subject to the approval of Securities and Exchange Board of India (SEBI).

## Growth and Development of Scheduled Urban Co-operative Banks as on March 1994:

As on 31 March 1994, there were 14 scheduled urban co-operative banks of which 11 (eleven) pertain to the state of Maharashtra and the remaining 3 (three) belong to the state of Gujarat. *Urban co-operative banks which are licensed and whose demand and time liabilities (DTL) are not less than Rs. 100 crores (as against Rs. 50 crores earlier) will now qualify to be treated as 'financial institutions' eligible for inclusion in the second schedule of Reserve Bank of India.* The enhancement in DTL was made on the basis of the recommendation of the Marathe Committee (on Licensing of New Urban Co-operative Banks). A notification enhancing the DTL limit for according 'scheduled' status was issued by the Government of India on 24 September 1993 which was published in the official Gazette on 16 October 1993. Names of the scheduled urban co-operatives banks and their deposits and advances as on 31 March 1994 are detailed in Table 8.8.

**Table 8.8 : Scheduled Urban Co-operative Banks as on 31 March 1994**

| Sr. | Name | Deposits | Advances |
|---|---|---|---|
| 1 | 2 | 3 | 4 |
| | [A] Maharashtra | | |
| 1 | Abhyudaya Co-op Bank Ltd. Bombay | 469.38 | 216.52 |
| 2 | Bassein Cathalic Co-op Bank Ltd., Vasai | 136.37 | 59.82 |
| 3 | Bombay Mercantile Co-op Bank Ltd., Bombay | 893.97 | 494.29 |
| 4 | Cosmos Co-op. Urban Bank Ltd., Pune | 237.77 | 130.16 |
| 5 | Development Co-op Bank Ltd., Bombay | 466.32 | 246.42 |
| 6 | Janata Sahakari Bank Ltd., Pune | 500.59 | 368.10 |
| 7 | New India Co-op. Bank Ltd., Bombay | 131.67 | 70.14 |
| 8 | Rupee Co-op. Bank Ltd., Pune | 250.27 | 180.00 |
| 9 | Sangli UCB Ltd., Sangli | 215.70 | 141.67 |
| 10 | Saraswat Co-op. Bank Ltd., Bombay | 767.51 | 454.67 |
| 11 | Sharao Vithal Co-op Bank Ltd., Bombay | 271.45 | 147.87 |
| | Total [A] | 4341.00 | 2509.93 |
| | [B] | | |
| 12 | Kalupur Coml. Co-op. Bank Ltd., Ahmedabad | 303.13 | 171.12 |
| 13 | Rajkot NSB Ltd., Rajkot | 212.72 | 169.17 |
| 14 | Surat People's Co-op Bank Ltd., Surat | 159.87 | 88.11 |
| | Total [B] | 675.74 | 428.40 |
| | Grand Total [A + B] | 5016.74 | 2938.33 |

**Source:** Researcher's compilation from the records of UBD, CO, Bombay

It is interesting to note that out of 22 states in India, urban co-operative banks have achieved scheduled status only in the above two states. The share of deposits and advances of those scheduled urban co-operative banks, from 29.9 percent and 24.1 percent respectively to the total deposits and advances of the entire urban co-operative banking system in the country as on 31st March 1994.

### Position of the Weak Urban Co-operative Banks during the period of Study (1985-94):

Though urban co-operative banks have registered a tremendous growth in the fields of deposits mobilization, credit expansion and diversified business activities, there is a growing incidence of sickness among urban co-operative banks, which is the matter of serious concern. *The main causes of weakness are 'defective loan policy and procedure of the bank concerned such as predominance of loans for unproductive purposes which do not generate income and necessary repaying capacity, .... Concentration of loans to a few directors / preferred borrowers, .....' injudicious management of resources, lack of professional management and training staff, political interference, duality of control between Reserve Bank of India and the Co-operation Department inhibiting quick process of rehabilitation etc.* The year-wise position of weak urban co-operative banks from 1985 to 1994 is tabulated in Table 8.9.

**Table 8.9 : Position of weak Urban Co-operative Banks for a period of 10 years (1985-94)**

| As at the end of | Total No. of Urban Co-operative Banks | Not Complying With Sec.11 (1) | Under Rehabili-tation | Under Observa-tion | Nonviable | Total No. of Weak Urban Co-operative Banks |
|---|---|---|---|---|---|---|
| 1 | 2 | 3 | 4 | 5 | 6 | 7 |
| June 1985 | 1331 | NA | NA | NA | NA | NA |
| June 1986 | 1345 | 30 | 74 | 36 | 188 | 328 |
| June 1987 | 1358 | 31 | 72 | 42 | 143 | 288 |
| June 1988 | 1370 | 24 | 93 | 28 | 122 | 267 |
| June 1989 | 1378 | 25 | 86 | 28 | 118 | 257 |
| June 1990 | 1390 | 25 | 96 | 33 | 82 | 236 |
| June 1991 | 1397 | 24 | 111 | 32 | 63 | 230 |
| March 1992 | 1401 | 25 | 99 | 35 | 48 | 217 |
| March 1993 | 1399 | 58 | 94 | 29 | 43 | 224 |
| March 1994 | 1400 | 80 | 84 | 33 | 36 | 233 |

**Source :** Statistical Statements relating to Co-operative Movement in India (various years) as also records available with the Rehabilitation Section, UBD, CO, Bombay

The state-wise position of weak urban co-operative banks as at the end of March 1994 reveals that weak urban co-operative banks in *numerical terms* are more in Maharashtra (69), followed by Gujarat (44), Karnataka (27), Madhya Pradesh (16), Uttar Pradesh (16), and Andhra Pradesh (11); whereas *percentage-wise* Madhya Pradesh comes first (16 out of total 42 forming 38.1 percent) followed by Orissa (5 out of 14 consisting 35.7 percent), Uttar Pradesh (16 out of total 47 comprising 34 percent), Delhi (4 out of total 17 recording 23.5 percent) and Bihar (1 out of total 5 working out at 20 percent). The Big Fours viz., Maharashtra, Gujarat, Karnataka, Tamil Nadu, where concentration of urban co-operative banks are more as compared to the rest of India, percentage wise weak urban co-operative banks' position stand at 17.8 percent , 15 percent, 12.7 percent and 3.7 percent respectively.

Persistence of weak and non-viable units is contra indicated in a system which has to be dovetailed with one emerging economic scenario rooted in productivity, efficiency and competitiveness. In the context of cast changing financial scenario, including the entry of new private sector banks, urban co-operative banks have to face many challenges to effectively compete with the other components of the banking system and increase their productivity and efficiency. *The main challenges for urban co-operative banks are development of skills and expertise to cope with the diverse banking operations, professionalsiation and depoliticalisation of management, reorientation of banking policies and procedures, effective participation of dedicated co-operators and up gradation of technology by introduction of computerization and mechanization., It is, however, heartening to note that many urban co-operative banks have initiated measures towards the aforesaid end in order to improve their operational efficiency, productivity and competitiveness and in addition to their social responsibilities.*

The following three reforms are suggested.

1. Staff deployment is necessary
   (a) Clerical Staff should have responsibility to do their work accurately and correctly and checking should be to some extent done by them.
   (b) 80 percent of Officer's time in checking of books must be saved and diverted to supervision of credit.
   (c) Team work and group norms should be evolved and enforced.
2. A ceiling on operational expenses of bank should be fixed.
3. Simplification of systems, procedures and form designing will save paper and printing costs.
4. Better management of cash flow and investments.
5. Credit management and administration should be supervised closely.
6. Share capital of bank should be increased to increase own funds.

A programmer of revitalization of bank alone can strengthen Bank's profitability and viability and give us enough resources and capacity to continue to meet our social obligations.

## Operations & Financial Performance of Urban Co-operative Banks: A Profile

The urban co-operative banking sector comprises of a number of institutions with vary in terms of their size, nature of business and their geographical spread. The deposit size of most of Urban Co-operative Banks, barring a few, is small and most of them have only a single branch. As at end – March 2006, 1,423 Urban Co-operative Banks out of 1,853 (76.8 percent) had a deposit base of less than Rs. 50 crore and 1,633 (88.1 percent) less than Rs. 100 crore. The share of these two categories in total deposits held was 19.0 percent and 32.5 percent, respectively. On the other hand, 14 Urban Co-operative Banks with deposit base of above Rs. 1,000 crore accounted for about one fourth of deposits of all Urban Co-operative Banks (Table 8.10).

## Griwth and Development of Urban Co-operative Banks AFTER 1996:

In 1966 when the Banking Regulation Act was made applicable to Urban Co-operative Banks, there were about 1100 Urban Co-operative Banks with deposits and advances of Rs. 167 crores and Rs. 153 crore respectively. As at the of 1996, the number of Urban Co-operative Banks increased to 1501 and their deposits and advance rose significantly to Rs. 24,161 crore and Rs. 17,927 crore. The Urban Co-operative Banks continued to grow at a fast pace till 2003, when their number increased to 1941 and their deposits and advances to Rs. 1,01,546 crore's and Rs. 64,880 crore's respectively. Subsequently, the number of Urban Co-operative Banks declined in 2006 to 1853 with total deposits of Rs. 1,12,237 crore and advances of Rs. 70,379 crore. An overview of their growth since the 1990s is given in Table 8.10.

| Table 8.10 : Growth of Urban Co-operative Banks (Urban Co-operative Banks) (1996 to 2006) | | | | | |
|---|---|---|---|---|---|
| **Year Ended March 31** | **Number of Urban Co-operative Banks** | **Deposits in Crore** | **% Growth** | **Advances in Crore** | **% Growth** |
| 1 | 2 | 3 | 4 | 5 | 6 |
| 1996 | 1501 | 24161 | | 17927 | |
| 1998 | 1502 | 40692 | 68.4 | 27807 | 55.1 |
| 2001 | 1618 | 80840 | 98.7 | 54389 | 95.6 |
| 2002 | 1854 | 93069 | 15.1 | 62060 | 14.1 |
| 2003 | 1941 | 101546 | 9.1 | 64880 | 4.5 |
| 2004 | 1926 | 110256 | 8.6 | 67930 | 4.7 |
| 2005 | 1872 | 105021 | -4.7 | 66874 | -1.6 |
| 2006 | 1853 | 112237 | 6.9 | 70379 | 5.2 |
| **Source:** Statistical Statements relating to the Co-operative Movement In India, NABARD, Bombay | | | | | |

The spectacular growth of Urban Co-operative Banks in the late nineties and up to 2003, which had resulted in increasing their penetration, ironically, also led to certain weaknesses in the sector that adversely affected public perception and thereby, their competitiveness. A major reason for the decline in public confidence was the crisis faced in 2001 by a large multi-state bank in the state of Gujarat, when the bank witnessed a sudden 'run' on its branches, following rumors of its large exposure to a leading broker who had suffered huge losses in the share market. The large-scale withdrawal of deposits within short time and resulted in severe liquidity problems for the bank. The bank was also holding about Rs. 800 crore of inter-bank deposits from a large number of Urban Co-operative Banks in the state and form other States, which posed a systemic risk. In order to protect the interest of the general public and also that of the other co-operative banks, RBI had issued directions to the bank restricting certain operations (acceptance of fresh deposits, restricting payment to any single depositor to Rs. 1000 and ban on fresh lending) and requisitioned the Central Registrar of Co-operative Societies, New Delhi to supersede the Board of Directors and appoint an administrator. An order of moratorium was also enforced on the bank by the Central Government for a short period. The bank was subsequently placed under a scheme of reconstruction with the approval of Reserve Bank of India.

**Market Share of Urban Co-operative Banks:**

Urban Co-operative Banking sector is characterised by heterogeneity in terms of size, spread, profitability and professionalism. As on March 31 2006, there were 1853 Urban Co-operative Banks, 84 scheduled commercial banks, 133 Regional Rural Banks (RRBs) and 398 Rural Co-operative Banks (including 31 State Co-operative Banks and 367 District Co-operative Banks) in India. An analysis of market share of various banks groups indicates that the share grew steadily from 3.3 percent in 1990-91 to a high of 6.6 percent in 1999-2000, but thereafter gradually declined to 4.8 percent (provisional) in 2005-06, as shown in the following Table 8.11.

**Table 8.11: Market share of deposits of all banks groups to total deposits**

| Year ended March 31 | Urban Co-op Banks (Urban Co-operative Banks) | Rural Co-op Banks (RCBs) | Regional Rural Banks (RRBs) | Commercial Banks |
|---|---|---|---|---|
| 1 | 2 | 3 | 4 | 5 |
| 1996 | 4.5 | 7.2 | 2.5 | 85.8 |
| 1997 | 4.9 | 7.6 | 2.6 | 84.9 |
| 1998 | 5.3 | 7.7 | 2.8 | 84.2 |
| 1999 | 5.6 | 7.8 | 2.8 | 83.8 |
| 2000 | 6.6 | 7.7 | 2.8 | 82.9 |
| 2001 | 6.3 | 7.2 | 2.9 | 83.6 |
| 2002 | 6.4 | 7.2 | 3.0 | 83.4 |
| 2003 | 6.3 | 7.0 | 3.0 | 83.7 |
| 2004* | 5.8 | 6.6 | 3.1 | 84.5 |
| 2005* | 5.3 | 6.3 | 3.1 | 85.3 |
| 2006* | 4.8 | 5.5 | 3.0 | 86.7 |

**Source:** Co-operative Movement in India, NABARD, Bombay

**Table 8.12: A profile of Urban Co-operative Banks (As at end-March 2006)**

| | Item | No. of Urban Co-operative Banks | Assets | Deposits | Investments | Loans & Advances |
|---|---|---|---|---|---|---|
| | 1 | 2 | 3 | 4 | 5 | 6 |
| | All Urban Co-operative Banks (1+2) | 1853 | 1,40,432 (100.0) | 1,12,237 (100.0) | 48,472 (100.0) | 70,379 (100.0) |
| 1. | Scheduled Urban Co-operative Banks | 55 | 61,832 (40.0) | 45,285 (40.3) | 18,216 (37.6) | 28.022 (39.8) |
| 2. | Non-Scheduled Urban Co-operative Banks | 1798 | 78,600 (56.0) | 66,952 (59.7) | 30,256 (62.4) | 42,357 (60.2) |
| | of which:Non-Scheduled Urban Co-operative BanksWith Deposit Size of Rs. 100Crore and Above | 191 | 39,657 (28.2) | 31,479 (28.0) | 9,112 (18.8) | 19,489 (27.7) |

**Source:** Co-operative Movement in India, NABARD, Bombay.

**Note:** Figures in brackets are percentages to total of all Urban Co-operative Banks

## Operations, Financial Performance & Asset Quality of UCBs:

### Operations

As at end - March 2006, total assets/liabilities of Urban Co-operative Banks constituted about 5.0 percent of assets of scheduled commercial banks. Business operations of Urban Co-operative Banks grew by 6.3 percent during 2005-06. The broad composition of the assets and liabilities of Urban Co-operative Banks remained the same in the previous year. Deposits continued to be the mainstay of resources for Urban Co-operative Banks, accounting for 79.9 percent of total resources. During 2005-06, deposits and capital increased, while statutory reserved declined, albeit marginally. On the asset wide, nearly one half of the assets of Urban Co-operative Banks were deployed in the form of loans and advances, while investment constituted the second major avenue of development of funds. During 2005-06, while loans and advances, and investment grew at a moderate rate, cash in hand and balances in the call/ notice money market increased sharply (Table 8.13).

**Table 8.13: Liabilities and Assets of Urban Co-operative Banks**

| | Item | As at end-March | | Percentage Variations |
|---|---|---|---|---|
| | | 2005 | 2006 | 2005-06 |
| | 1 | 2 | 3 | 4 |
| | **Liabilities** | | | |
| 1 | Capital | 3,221(2.4) | 3,479(2.5) | 8.0 |
| 2 | Statutory Reserves | 10,383(7.9) | 10,161(7.2) | -2.1 |
| 3 | Deposits | 1,05,021(79.5) | 1,12,237(79.9) | 6.9 |
| 4 | Borrowings | 1,782(1.3) | 1,799(1.3) | 1.0 |
| 5 | Other Liabilities | 11,738(8.9) | 12,756(9.1) | 8.7 |
| | **Total Liabilities/Assets** | **1,32,145(100.0)** | **1,40,432(100.0)** | **6.3** |
| | **Assets** | | | |
| 1 | Cash in Hand | 937(0.7) | 1,539(1.1) | 64.0 |
| 2 | Balances with Banks | 7,136(5.4) | 8,227(5.9) | 15.3 |
| 3 | Money at Call & Short Notice | 1,139(0.9) | 1,996(1.4) | 75.2 |
| 4 | Investments | 46,872(35.5) | 48.472(34.5) | 3.4 |
| 5 | Loans and Advances | 66,874(50.6) | 70,379(50.1) | 5.2 |
| 6 | Other Assets | 9,185(7.0) | 9,819(7.0) | 6.9 |

**Source:** Balance Sheets of respective Urban Co-operative Banks.
**Note:** Figures in brackets are percentages of total liabilities/assets

### Priority Sector Lending

Urban co-operative banks are required to lend 60.0 percent of their total loans and advances to the priority sector and 25.0 percent of priority sector lending should go towards weaker sections. Credit extended by Urban Co-operative Banks to the priority sector and weaker sections increased significantly in recent years. A significant amount of credit was extended to cottage and small scale industries for housing loans (Table 8.14)

| | Table 8.14 : Priority Sector and Weaker Section Advances by Urban Co-operative Banks 2005-06 | | | | |
|---|---|---|---|---|---|
| | Segment | Priority Sector | | Weaker Sections | |
| | | Amount (Rs.Crore) | Share in Total Advances (Percent) | Amount (Rs. Crores) | Share in Total Advances (Percent) |
| | 1 | 2 | 3 | 4 | 5 |
| 1 | Agricultural And Allied Activities | 3007 | 4.3 | 1409 | 2.1 |
| 2 | Cottage and Small Scale Industries | 9817 | 13.9 | 1042 | 1.5 |
| 3 | Road and Water Transport Operators | 1819 | 2.6 | 655 | 0.9 |
| 4 | Private Retail Trade (Essential Commodities) | 1850 | 2.6 | 876 | 1.2 |
| 5 | Private Retail Trade (Others) | 3323 | 4.7 | 858 | 1.2 |
| 6 | Small Business Enterprises | 5456 | 7.8 | 1725 | 2.5 |
| 7 | Professional and Self Employed | 2165 | 3.1 | 864 | 1.2 |
| 8 | Educational Loans | 710 | 1.0 | 290 | 0.4 |
| 9 | Housing Loans | 9056 | 12.9 | 2773 | 3.9 |
| 10 | Consumption Loans | 456 | 0.6 | 173 | 0.2 |
| 11 | Software Industry | 55 | 0.1 | 6 | 0.0 |
| | Total 1 to 11) | 37714 | 53.6 | 10762 | 15.3 |

**Source:** Balance Sheets of Respective Urban Co-operative Banks

SLR investment constituted a bulk of investment (94.4 percent) of Urban Co-operative Banks at end-March 2006. While SLR investment, on the whole, grew moderately upto 92.1 percent) during 2005-06, investments in other approved securities (non-Government) and term – deposits with the State co-operative banks (STCBs) increased sharply. However, term deposits with district central co-operative banks (DCCDs) declined. Non-SLR investments comprising bonds of public sector institutions/AIFIs, shares of AIFIs and units of UTI witnessed a sharp growth during 2005-06 (Table 8.15).

**Table 8.15: Investment by Urban-Co-operative Banks**

(Amount in Rs. Crores)

| | Items | As at end-March | | Percentage variations |
|---|---|---|---|---|
| | | 2005 | 2006 | 2005-06 |
| | 1 | 2 | 3 | 4 |
| | **Total Investments (A+B)** | **46872(100.0)** | **48472(100.0)** | **3.4** |
| **A.** | **SLR Investments (I to v)** | **44817(95.6)** | **45740(94.4)** | **2.1** |
| (i) | Central Government Securities | 27147(57.9) | 28119(58.0) | 3.6 |
| (ii) | State Government Securities | 3883(8.3) | 3922(8.1) | 1.0 |
| (iii) | Other Approved Securities | 848(1.8) | 1107(2.3) | 30.6 |
| (iv) | Term deposits with StCBS) | 4257(9.1) | 4745(9.8) | 11.5 |
| (v) | Term deposits with DCCBs | 8683(18.5) | 7847(16.2) | -9.6 |
| **B.** | **Non-SLR Investments** (in bonds of public sector institutions/ AIFIs, shares of AIFI's and units of UTI) | **2055(4.4)** | **2732(5.6)** | **32.9** |

**Source:** Balance Sheets of Respective Urban Co-operative Banks
**Note:** Figures in brackets are percentages of total investments.

**Asset Quality:**

The asset quality of Urban Co-operative Banks improved significantly during the year. This was reflected in sharp decline in NPAs (gross and net) in absolute as well as percentage terms. However, NPAs of Urban Co-operative Banks at 19.7 percent (gross) and 9.6 percent (net) at end-March 2006 were high compared to the level at end-March 2001 (16.1 percent gross NPAs) and in comparison with scheduled commercial banks (3.3 percent gross and 1.2 percent net NPAs) (Table 8.16). The high level of gross NPAs of Urban Co-operative Banks was, to an extent, on account of burdensome procedure for write-off of loans.

**Table 7.16: Non-Performing Assets of Urban Co-operative Banks**

(Amount in Rs. Crores)

| End-March | No.of reporting Urban Co-operative Banks | Gross NP As | Gross NP As as percentage of total Advances | Net NP As | Net NP As as percentage of total Advances |
|---|---|---|---|---|---|
| 1 | 2 | 3 | 4 | 5 | 6 |
| 2001 | 1942 | 9245 | 16.1 | – | – |
| 2002 | 1937 | 13706 | 21.9 | – | – |
| 2003 | 1941 | 12509 | 19.0 | 6428 | 13.0 |
| 2004 | 1926 | 15406 | 22.7 | 8242 | 12.1 |
| 2005 | 1872 | 15486 | 23.4 | 8257 | 12.5 |
| 2006 P | 1853 | 13871 | 19.7 | 6718 | 9.6 |

**Source:** Balance Sheets of Respective Urban Co-operative Banks
P: Provisional

**Operations and Performance of Scheduled UCBs :**
**Operations**

Continuing the growth momentum, liabilities/assets of scheduled Urban Co-operative Banks expanded at a healthy rate during 2005-06. Deposits of scheduled Urban Co-operative Banks grew at a higher rate in comparison with the previous year. On the asset side, while loans and advances portfolio witnessed an accelerated growth, investments slowed down in sync with the trend witnessed in the commercial banking sector in recent years (Table 8.17)

**Financial Performance:**

Net interest income of scheduled Urban Co-operative Banks increased by Rs. 1721 crore during 2005-06 as compared with Rs. 999 crores in the previous year. This combined with reduction in banks' burden (excess of operating expenditure over non-interest income) resulted in an increase in the operating profits, in contrast to a decline in the previous year. Nearly same level of provisions and contingencies in comparison with the previous level resulted in higher net profit during the year (Table 8.18). Although, the number of banks suffering losses increased to eight from seven during the previous year, total losses incurred by the loss making scheduled Urban Co-operative Banks declined.

**Table 8.17: Liabilities and Assets of Scheduled Urban Co-operative Banks**

(Amount in Rs. Crores)

| 1 | Item | As at end-March | | Percentage Variations | |
|---|---|---|---|---|---|
| | | **2005** | **2006** | **2004-05** | **2005-06** |
| 1 | 2 | 3 | 4 | 5 | |
| | **Liabilities** | | | | |
| | Capital | 782(1.4) | 899(1.5) | 16.6 | 15.0 |
| 2 | Reserves | 6927(12.3) | 6594(10.7) | 182.0 | -4.8 |
| 3 | Deposits | 40950(72.8) | 45285(73.2) | 7.8 | 10.6 |
| 4 | Borrowings | 890(1.6) | 970(1.6) | 50.8 | 9.0 |
| 5 | Other Liabilities | 6668(11.9) | 8083(13.1) | -31.6 | 21.2 |
| | **Total Liabilities/Assets** | **56217(100.0)** | **61832(100.0)** | **9.2** | **10.0** |
| | **Assets** | | | | |
| 1 | Cash in Hand | 303(0.5) | 348(0.6) | -4.9 | 14.8 |
| 2 | Balances with Banks | 4975(8.5) | 4973(8.0) | -11.7 | 3.7 |
| 3 | Money at Call & Short Notice | 517(0.9) | 581(0.9) | 20.9 | 12.3 |
| 4 | Investments | 17094(30.4) | 18216(29.5) | 14.1 | 6.6 |
| 5 | Loans and Advances | 25061(44.6) | 28022(45.3) | 8.2 | 11.8 |
| 6 | Other Assets | 8447(15.0) | 9692(15.7) | 18.0 | 14.7 |

**Source:** Balance Sheets of respective Urban Co-operative Banks.
**Note:** Figures in brackets are percentages of total liabilities/assets

**Table 8.18: Financial Performance of Scheduled Urban Co-operative Banks**

(Amount in Rs. Crores)

| 1 | Item | As at end-March | | Percentage Variations | |
|---|---|---|---|---|---|
| | | **2004-05** | **2005-06** | **2004-05** | **2005-06** |
| | 1 | 2 | 3 | 4 | 5 |
| **A.** | **Income (i+ii)** | **3735(100.)** | **3951(100.0)** | **-6.0** | **5.8** |
| (i) | Interest Income | 3322(88.9) | 3458(87.5) | 4.5 | 4.1 |
| (ii) | Other Income | 413(11.1) | 494(12.5) | -48.1 | 19.6 |
| **B.** | **Expenditure (i+ii)** | **3598(100.)** | **3617(100.0)** | **-4.4** | **0.5** |
| (i) | Interest Expended | 2323(64.6) | 2287(63.2) | -1.2 | -1.5 |
| (ii) | Provision and Contingencies | 335(9.3) | 348(9.6) | -36.9 | 3.9 |
| (iii) | Operating Expenses of which | 940(26.1) | 982(27.2) | 6.6 | 4.5 |
| | Wage Bill | 508(14.1) | 521(14.4) | 2.2 | 2.6 |
| **C.** | **Profit** | | | | |
| (i) | Operating Profit | 472 | 682 | -36.3 | 44.5 |
| (ii) | Net Profit | 137 | 335 | -34.9 | 144.5 |
| **D.** | **Total Assets** | **56217** | **61832** | **9.2** | **10.0** |

**Source:** Balance Sheets of respective Urban Co-operative Banks
**Note:** Figures in brackets are percentages to respective totals

**Operations and Performance of Non-Scheduled UCBs with Deposits of Rs. 100 crore and Above:**

**Operations**

The non-scheduled Urban Co-operative Banks, deposit size of Rs. 100 crore and above (numbering 191) were brought under the closer scrutiny of off-site surveillance in view of their large deposit holdings and systemic importance. Total assets/liabilities of these non-scheduled Urban Co-operative Banks were Rs. 39,657 crore at end March 2006, constituting 64.1 percent of assets of scheduled Urban Co-operative Banks and 28.2 percent of total assets of all Urban Co-operative Banks (scheduled and non-scheduled). The major source of funds for non-scheduled Urban Co-operative Banks was deposits, accounting for 79.4 percent of total assets at end-March 2006. Most of the assets were held in the form of loans and advances (49.1 percent) and investment (23.0) percent. These banks also held a significant part of their assets in the form of balances with banks (16.0 percent) at end-March 2006 (Table 8.19)

**Table 8.19: Liabilities and Assets of Non-Scheduled Urban Co-operative Banks with Deposits of Rs. 100 Crore and Above**

| | Item | Amount (Rs.Crores) | Share in Total Assets (percent) |
|---|---|---|---|
| 1 | 2 | 3 | 4 |
| | **Liabilities** | | |
| 1 | Paid-up Capital | 1020 | 2.6 |
| 2 | Reserve Fund and Other Reserve | 2507 | 6.3 |
| 3 | Deposits | 31479 | 79.4 |
| 4 | Borrowings | 275 | 0.7 |
| 5 | Other Liabilities | 4377 | 11.0 |
| | **Total Liabilities/Assets** | 39657 | 100.0 |
| | **Assets** | | |
| 1 | Cash in hand | 484 | 1.2 |
| 2 | Balances with Banks | 6348 | 16.0 |
| 3 | Money at Call and Short Notice | 295 | 0.7 |
| 4 | Investments | 9112 | 23.0 |
| 5 | Loans and Advances | 19489 | 49.1 |
| 6 | Other Assets | 3929 | 9.9 |

**Source:** Balance Sheets of respective Urban Co-operative Banks

**Financial Performance:**

Net interest income of non-scheduled Urban Co-operative Banks of Deposits of Rs. 100 crore and above was Rs. 1046 crore during 2005-06. The wage bill constituted 14.6 percent of total expenses. As a result, their operating profits were significantly lower than their net interest income. Return on assets of non-scheduled Urban Co-operative Banks at 0.76 percent during (2005-06) was higher than that of scheduled Urban Co-operative Banks at 0.54 percent (Table 8.20)

| | Table 8.20: Financial Performa nce of Non-Scheduled Urban Co-operative Banks with Deposits of Rs. 100 Crore and Above 2005-06 | | |
|---|---|---|---|
| | **Item** | **Amount (Rs.Crore)** | **Share in Respective Total (percent)** |
| | 1 | 2 | 3 |
| **A.** | **Income (i+ii)** | **3072** | **100.0** |
| | (i) Interest Income | 2936 | 95.6 |
| | (ii) Other Income | 136 | 4.4 |
| **B.** | **Expenditure (i+ii+iii)** | **2772** | **100.0** |
| | (i) Interest Expenses | 1890 | 68.2 |
| | (ii) Provision Against Risks/Contingencies | 195 | 7.0 |
| | (iii) Other Operating Expenses | 687 | 24.8 |
| | of which: Wage Bill | 404 | 14.6 |
| **C.** | **Profit** | | |
| | (i) Operating Profit | 495 | |
| | (ii) Net Profit | 300 | |
| **D.** | **Total Assets (as at end-March)** | **39657** | |
| **Source:** Balance Sheets of Urban Co-operative Banks | | | |

## UCBs – Regional Operation:

The spatial distribution of Urban Co-operative Banks is highly skewed as they are concentrated mainly in five States/Union Territories, viz., Andhra Pradesh, Gujarat, Karnataka, Maharashtra and Tamil Nadu. Kerala was also well covered in terms of number of branches of Urban Co-operative Banks. As at the end – March 2006, two-thirds of total Urban Co-operative Banks with four – fifth of total branches operated in Maharashtra and Goa, Karnataka and Gujarat. Maharashtra and Goa alone accounted for 58.8 percent of total branches of Urban Co-operative Banks. 7217 branches of Urban Co-operative Banks 914 were unit banks, i.e., banks which function as head office-cum-branch. Maharashtra and Goa. Karnataka and Gujarat had the highest number (59.5 percent) of unit banks (Table 8.21)

Of 55 scheduled Urban Co-operative Banks at end-March 2006, 39 were located in Maharashtra, 9 in Gujarat, 3 in Andhra Pradesh, 2 in Goa and 1 each in Karnataka and Uttar Pradesh. Maharashtra and Goa accounted for 85.8 percent of total deposits and 84.9 percent of all loans and advances of all scheduled Urban Co-operative Banks (Table 8.22)

Non-scheduled Urban Co-operative Banks in five centers viz., Ahmedabad, Bangalore, Chennai, Mumbai and Nagpur accounted for more than three-fourth of capital and reserves and about four-fifth of deposits, advances, and demand plus time liabilities of all non-scheduled Urban Co-operative Banks at end-March 2006, Wide variations were also observed in the C-D ratio. Chennai had the highest C-D ratio (69.8 percent), while New Delhi the lowest (38.0

| | Table 8.21: Distribution of Urban Co-operative Banks – State-wise (As an end-March 2006) | | | | | |
|---|---|---|---|---|---|---|
| | **State** | **No. of Banks** | **Share In Total (Percent)** | **No. of Unit Banks** | **No. of Branches** | **No. of Extension Counters** |
| | **1** | **2** | **3** | **4** | **5** | **6** |
| 1 | Andhra Pradesh | 124 | 6.7 | 95 | 310 | 5 |
| 2 | Assam/Manipur/ Meghalaya/ Mizoram/ Nagaland/Sikkim/ Tripura/Arunachal Pradesh | 18 | 1.0 | 15 | 11 | – |
| 3 | Bihar-Jharkhand | 5 | 0.3 | 4 | 1 | 1 |
| 4 | Gujarat | 2996 | 16.0 | 151 | 637 | 3 |
| 5 | Jammu & Kashmir | 4 | 0.2 | 1 | 16 | 4 |
| 6 | Karnataka | 297 | 16.0 | 153 | 885 | 18 |
| 7 | Kerala | 60 | 3.2 | 17 | 325 | – |
| 8 | Madhya Pradesh/ Chhattishgarh | 75 | 4.0 | 58 | 45 | 4 |
| 9 | Maharashtra and Goa | 630 | 34.0 | 240 | 4423 | 23 |
| 10 | New Delhi | 15 | 0.8 | – | 60 | 1 |
| 11 | Orissa | 14 | 0.8 | 5 | 50 | 4 |
| 12 | Punjab/Hariyana/Himachal Pradesh | 16 | 0.9 | 10 | 39 | 3 |
| 13 | Rajasthan | 39 | 2.1 | 19 | 142 | 7 |
| 14 | Tamil Nadu and Pondicharry | 132 | 7.1 | 62 | 180 | 0 |
| 15 | Uttar Pradesh/ Uttaranchal | 77 | 4.2 | 53 | 219 | 28 |
| 16 | West Bengal | 51 | 2.8 | 31 | 54 | 0 |
| | **Total 1 to 16)** | **1853** | **100.0** | **914** | **7217** | **101** |

**Source:** Balance Sheet of Urban Co-operative Banks

| | Table 8.22: Select Indicators of Scheduled Urban Co-operative Banks-Center-wise (As at end-March 2006)s | | | | | |
|---|---|---|---|---|---|---|
| | **Centre** | **Paid-up Capital** | **Free Reserves** | **Deposits** | **Loans & Advances** | **Demand and Time Liabilities** | **C-D Ratio (percent)** |
| | 1 | 2 | 3 | 4 | 5 | 6 | 7 |
| 1 | Ahmedabad | 93 | 3680 | 51925 | 3441 | 5491 | 66.3 |
| 2 | Bangalore | 6 | 44 | 349 | 213 | 477 | 61.0 |
| 3 | Hyderabad | 32 | 437 | 709 | 458 | 741 | 64.6 |
| 4 | Lukhnow | 5 | 18 | 185 | 125 | 193 | 67.6 |
| 5 | Mumbai | 686 | 2324 | 35752 | 21717 | 35294 | 60.7 |
| 6 | Nagpur | 78 | 91 | 3097 | 2067 | 2098 | 66.7 |
| | Total (1 to 6) | 899 | 6594 | 45285 | 28022 | 44295 | 61.9 |

**Source:** Balance Sheet of Urban Co-operative Banks

percent) which incidentally was the only center with C-D ratio of less than 50 percent. C.D. ratio for other centers remained within the large of 51.8 percent and 67.4 percent (Table 8.23).

| | Table 8.23: Select Indicators of Non-Scheduled Urban Co-operative Banks – Center – Wise (As at end March 2006) | | | | | | |
|---|---|---|---|---|---|---|---|
| | Centre | Share Capital | Free Reserves | Deposits | Advances | Demand And Time Liabilities | C-D Ratio (percent) |
| | 1 | 2 | 3 | 4 | 5 | 6 | 7 |
| 1 | Ahmedabad | 239 | 778 | 6632 | 3717 | 6802 | 56.1 |
| 2 | Bangalore | 375 | 527 | 7952 | 5129 | 7300 | 645 |
| 3 | Bhopal | 48 | 71 | 1071 | 570 | 1094 | 53.3 |
| 4 | Bhubaneshwar | 25 | 28 | 591 | 389 | 594 | 65.8 |
| 5 | Chandigarh | 30 | 46 | 648 | 336 | 628 | 51.8 |
| 6 | Chennai | 153 | 124 | 2941 | 2054 | 3163 | 69.8 |
| 7 | Guwahati | 12 | 19 | 334 | 182 | 378 | 54.5 |
| 8 | Hyderabad | 81 | 108 | 1318 | 832 | 1210 | 63.1 |
| 9 | Jaipur | 72 | 99 | 1348 | 782 | 1313 | |
| 10 | Jammu | 4 | 6 | 194 | 109 | 197 | 56.1 |
| 11 | Kolkata | 123 | 132 | 1856 | 1108 | 197 | 59.7 |
| 12 | Lukhnow | 122 | 125 | 2015 | 1262 | 2472 | 62.6 |
| 13 | Mumbai | 941 | 900 | 27779 | 18714 | 28490 | 67.4 |
| 14 | Nagpur | 228 | 399 | 8611 | 5070 | 4018 | 58.9 |
| 15 | New Delhi | 40 | 82 | 898 | 341 | 928 | 38.0 |
| 16 | Patna | 3 | 7 | 30 | 19 | 31 | 62.9 |
| 17 | Thiruvananthapuram | 83 | 117 | 2734 | 1743 | 2873 | 63.8 |
| **Total (1 to 17)** | | **2580** | **3567** | **66952** | **42357** | **63469** | **63.3** |
| ***Memo Item :*** Share of Ahmedabad, Bangalore, Chennai Mumbai & Nagpur in total | | 75.0 | 76.5 | 80.5 | 81.9 | 78.4 | |
| **Source:** Balance Sheet of Urban Co-operative Banks | | | | | | | |

Co-operative banking has passed through many phases since the enactment of the Agricultural Credit Co-operative Societies Act in 1904. Co-operative banks, developed largely as an offshoot policy, expanded rapidly in the post-independence era and played an important role in implantation of various Government schemes. Their business is now being re-engineering to strengthen their role in co-distributing to financial inclusion and deepening banking penetration in an increasingly competitive financial landscape.

The co-operative banking structure in India is complex. It comprises of urban co-operative banks and rural co-operative credit institutions. Urban co-operative financial institutions consists of a single tier, viz., primary co-operative banks, commonly referred to as urban co-operative banks (Urban Co-operative Banks). However, they are classified according to their scheduled status, operational outreach and purpose/clientele. Out of the 1853 Urban Co-operative Banks, 55 enjoyed scheduled status, of which 24 had multi-State presence as on March 31[st] 2006. Of the non-scheduled Urban Co-operative Banks, 117 were *Mahila* (women) Urban Co-operative Banks and another 7 were Scheduled Caste (SC) / Scheduled Tribes (ST) banks. In addition, there were 79 salary earner's Urban Co-operative Banks. Out of 1853 banks, Urban Co-operative Banks were unit i.e., having a single Head office/ branch set up.

Historically, rural co-operative credit institutions had plated an important role in providing institutional credit to the agricultural and the rural sectors. These credit institutions have

| Table 8.24: Select Financial Sector Indicators: 2005-06 | | | | | |
|---|---|---|---|---|---|
| | **Category** | | **Indicator** | **2004-05** | **2005-06** |
| | **1** | **2** | **3** | **4** | **5** |
| 1 | Schedule Commercial Banks | (a) | Growth in Major Aggregates (percent)<br>Aggregate Deposits<br>Loans and Advances<br>Investment in Government Securities | 16.6<br>33.2<br>9.4 | 17.8<br>31.8<br>-1.0 |
| | | (b) | Financial Indicators (as percentage of total assets<br>Operating Profits<br>Net Profits<br>Spread | <br>2.2<br>0.9<br>2.8 | <br>2.0<br>0.9<br>2.8 |
| | | (c) | Non-Performing Assets<br>(aspercentages of advancesGross NPAs<br>Net NPAs | <br>5.2<br>2.2 | <br>3.3<br>1.2 |
| 2 | Urban Co-Operative Banks | (a) | Growth in Major Aggregated (percent) Deposits<br>Credit | -4.7<br>-1.6 | 6.9<br>5.2 |
| | | (b) | Financial Indicators (as percentages of total assets)@<br>Operating Profits<br>Net Profits<br>Spread | <br>0.8<br>0.2<br>1.8 | <br>1.1<br>0.5<br>1.9 |
| | | (c) | Non-Performing Assets (as percentages of advances<br>Gross NPAs<br>Net NPAs | <br>23.4<br>12.5 | <br>19.7<br>9.6 |
| 3 | Rural Co-operative Banks | (a) | Number | 109924 | – |
| | | (b) | Growth in Major Aggregates (percent)<br>Deposits<br>Credit | <br>3.3<br>9.0 | <br>–<br>– |
| | | (c) | Financial Indicators (as percentage of Total assets)@<br>Societies in Profit (Number)<br>Societies in Loss (Number)<br>Overall Profit/Loss (Rs. Crore) | <br>47610<br>61872<br>232 | <br>–<br>–<br> |
| | | (d) | Non-Performing Assets (as percentage Of advances* | 24.4 | – |
| 4 | All-India Financial Institutions | (a) | Growth in Major Aggregates (percent)# Sanctions<br>Disbursements | -45.1<br>-37.0 | 383.9<br>33.9 |
| | | (b) | Financial Indicators (as percentage ofTotal assets)**<br>Operating Profits<br>Net Profits<br>Spread | <br>1.2<br>0.8<br>1.6 | <br>1.4<br>1.0<br>1.8 |
| | | (c) | Non-Performing Assets (as percentageOf advances** | 4.0 | 1.1 |
| 5 | Non-banking Financial Companies (excluding RNBCs) | (a) | Growth in Major Aggregates (percent)<br>Public Deposits | <br>-9.1 | <br>-32.1 |
| | | (b) | Financial Indicators (as percentageof total assets<br>Net Profits | <br>1.6 | <br>0.4 |
| | | (c) | Non-Performing Assets (as percentageOf adbvances)##<br>Net NPAs | <br>2.5 | <br>0.4 |
| 6 | Residuary Non | (a) | Growth in Major Aggregates (percent | | |
| **Source :** Report on trend on progress of banking in India 2005-06 | | | | | |

| Table 8.25: Progress of Co-operative Credit Movement in India | | | | | | |
|---|---|---|---|---|---|---|
| **Sr. No.** | **Type of Institution** | **Item** | **2002-03** | **2003-04** | **2004-05** | **2005-06** |
| | **1** | **2** | **3** | **4** | **5** | **6** |
| 1 | Urban Co-operative Banks (Urban Co-operative Banks) | Number | 1941 | 1926 | 1872 | 1853 |
| | | Owned Funds | 9830 | 12348 | 13604 | 13640 |
| | | Deposits | 101546 | 110256 | 105021 | 112237 |
| | | Borrowings | 1590 | 1474 | 1782 | 1799 |
| | | Working Capital | 11746 | N.A. | N.A. | N.A. |
| | | Loans Outstanding | 64880 | 67930 | 66874 | 70379 |
| | | C-D Ratio | 64 | 62 | 65 | 64 |
| 2 | State Co-Operative Banks (StCBs) | Number | 30 | 31 | 31 | 31 |
| | | Owned Funds | 7540 | 8473 | 9495 | N.A. |
| | | Deposits | 39384 | 43586 | 44316 | 45833 |
| | | Borrowings | 13374 | 12457 | 14608 | 17054 |
| | | Working Capital | 57134 | 57936 | 65879 | N.A. |
| | | Loans Issued | 38534 | 33961 | 44452 | 43837 |
| | | Loans Outstanding | 34754 | 35105 | 37346 | 39967 |
| | | Recovery Performance (as per percent to demand) | 80 | 83 | 84 | N.A. |
| | | C-D Ratio | 88 | 81 | 84 | 87 |
| 3 | District Central Co-operative Banks (DCCBs)* | Number | 367 | 365 | 367 | 365 |
| | | Owned Funds | 14695 | 19131 | 20495 | N.A. |
| | | Deposits | 73858 | 79153 | 80298 | 86855 |
| | | Borrowings | 19641 | 20256 | 22568 | 24622 |
| | | Working Capital | 106187 | 114702 | 111970 | N.A. |
| | | Loans Issued | 58802 | 58708 | 66266 | 64276 |
| | | Loans Outstanding | 64126 | 67152 | 73091 | 80090 |
| | | Recovery Performance (as percent to demand) | 61 | 63 | 71 | N.A. |
| | | C-D Ratio | 87 | 85 | 89 | 92 |
| 4 | State Co-operative Agriculture And Rural Development Banks (SCARDBs)@ | Number | 20 | 20 | 20 | 20 |
| | | Owned Funds | 3199 | 4403 | 5022 | N.A. |
| | | Deposits# | 501 | 524 | 566 | 502 |
| | | Borrowings | 15904 | 16933 | 17118 | 16964 |
| | | Working Capital | 20473 | 22038 | 23187 | N.A. |
| | | Loans Issued | 2959 | 2837 | 3292 | 2819 |
| | | Loans Outstanding | 15365 | 16263 | 17425 | 17895 |
| | | Recovery Performance (as percent to demand) | 49 | 44 | 44 | N.A. |
| 5 | Primary Co-operative Development Banks (PCARDBs) | Number | 768 | 768 | 727 | 697 |
| | | Owned Funds | 2729 | 3856 | 3494 | N.A. |
| | | Deposits# | 254 | 395 | 365 | 298 |
| | | Borrowings | 11235 | 11879 | 12873 | 13238 |
| | | Working Capital | 15352 | 15812 | 17143 | N.A. |
| | | Loans Issued | 2177 | 2164 | 2569 | 2184 |
| | | Loans Outstanding | 10814 | 11311 | 12763 | 12792 |
| | | Recovery Performance (as percent todemand) | 44 | 44 | 51 | N.A. |

**Source:** Report on trend and progress of banking in India.

typically been divided in two distinct structures, commonly known as the short-term co-operative credit structure (STCCS) and the long-term co-operative credit structure (LTCCS). The STCCS, comparing primary agricultural credit societies (PACS) at the village level, district central co-operative banks (DCCBs) at the intermediate level, and the state co-operative banks (STCBs) at the apex level, provides crop and other working capital loans primarily for short-term purpose to farmers and rural artisans. The LTCCS, comprising state co-operative agriculture and rural development banks (SCARDBs) at the State level and primary co-operative agriculture and rural development banks (PCARDBs) at the district or block level, has been providing typically medium and long-term loans for making investments in agriculture, rural industries and, in the recent period, housing. However, the structure of rural co-operative banks is not uniform across all States of the country. Some States have a unitary structure with the State level banks operating through their own branches, while others have a mixed structure incorporating both unitary and federal system.

The regional concentration of UCB is reflected by the fact that 4 large MOU states, viz., Maharashtra, Gujarat, Andhra Pradesh and Karnataka, account for 72 percent of total number of Urban Co-operative Banks. Analysis of Urban Co-operative Banks in terms of number of branches, which has a bearing on the acquisition of IT infrastructure, shows a similar characteristics as given below:

| **No. of Branches** | **No. of Banks ( percent of total)** |
|---|---|
| Unit bank | 894 |
| 2 to 10 | 656 |
| 11 – 25 | 135 |
| > 25 | 29 |
| Total | 1714 |

Almost 50 percent of Urban Co-operative Banks are Unit Banks i.e., having single head office/branch. It is evident that the smaller banks, i.e., unit banks and those banks having upto 10 branch compromise an overwhelming majority of Urban Co-operative Banks in terms of numbers only a small number of banks had more than 25 branches. These banks mostly have their own computing systems including (CBS) Core Banking Solutions. This group, considering size, spread and nature of operations does not need high-end facilities for computerizing their operations.

Distribution of banks in terms of their size is tabulated below:

| **Deposits (Rs. Cores)** | **No. of Banks** | **No. of Unit Banks** | **percent of Unit Bank to total** |
|---|---|---|---|
| 0 < 5 272 | 260 | 95.6 percent | |
| 5 < 10309 | 73 | 23.6 percent | |
| 10 < 25 | 451 | 255 | 56.5 percent |
| 25 < 50 | 274 | 256 | 93.4 percent |
| 50 < 100 | 184 | 34 | 18.5 percent |
| 100 < 500 | 190 | 16 | 8.4 percent |
| 500 < 1000 | 19 | 0 | 0 |
| 1000 and above | 15 | 0 | 0 |
| **Total** | **1714** | **894** | |

# CHAPTER 9

## Human Resource Development and Management in Co-operatives

In the broadest term, cooperation is basically an economic system with social content and outlook. The concept of human resource development (HRD) in co-operative sectors is a recent phenomenon. Hence, it has remained neglected in the national psyche. Generally, co-operative institutions constitute to organizational elements namely business enterprise and social institutions signifying associations of persons. The growth of non-agricultural co-operative sectors consists of two parts (a) State Co-operative Bank (b) State Industrial Co-operative Bank.

**Mahatma Gandhi,** once mentioned that India lies in her rural sides. In other words, a huge portion of Indian population comes from rural areas. Hence, having recognized co-operative organization as principle agencies promoting economic development in the country. Government of India launched a scheme of social and economic justice with a view of uplifting the weaker sections of the community and other group such as farmers, artisans, craftsman, consumers, women and other casts, oppressed socially and economically. That alone formed the core motive of the scheme. Political freedom without socio-economic freedom is meaningless. Hence, assurance of a reasonable degree of socio-economic development to these people and their participation in the development process remains the soil of these co-operative undertakings. That in it becomes a hallmark of conditions leading to human millennium. Hence, providing necessary resources and organizational framework for the weaker sections of the community becomes the sole motto of every co-operative system.

Human Resource Management (HRM) and Human Resource Development (HRD) has been the most talked about subject in the last few years. The importance of HRM needs no special emphasis today since it constitutes the most valuable resource of any co-operative enterprises big or small. The mission of HRM is to assure a stead source of sound people that can contribute to the success of co-operative organization. The co-operative at all levels have to effect operational efficiency, improvement in quality of products and services, developing managerial and technological excellence, developing strong financial and human resource based with full autonomy and adequate infrastructure facilities. In the new economic environment, an important area which needs serious and continuous attention related to HRM and HRD. Human Resource is unpredictable and also dynamic. No one can predict how an individual will respond to a particular situation. Thus, factfully handling of personnel becomes very important. The importance of HRM is felt in co-operatives in recent times.

**Definition of HRM:**

Although often used synonymously with personnel management, Human Resource Management transcends traditional personnel concerns, taking the most expensive view of the personnel department's mandate. Instead of viewing the personnel function as simply that collection of desperate duties necessary to recruit pay, and discharge employees, a Human

Resource Management approach assumes that personnel's appropriate mission is the maximum utilization of its organization's human resources.

**Objectives of HRM:**

1. To secure and maintain a satisfactory and satisfied working group.
2. To attain with welfare of an employee as an individual in the organization so that he may give his best to the enterprise.
3. To enable each person to make his maximum personal contribution and thereby promote productive efficiency of the organization; and
4. To maintain good human relations within the organization.

On the whole the objective of HRM must be to evolve an effective system to attain the top most efficiency standard by the co-operatives. The human resource is a co-operative enterprise that coordinates all other factors to achieve the highest efficiency.

**Importance of HRM in Co-operatives:**

Co-operatives are essentially an economic institution though it is formed and managed by members. Resources like buildings, machines and material can be purchased as one's wish but the people part of co-operative is the most elusive and difficult resource to get and manage. Money may come and go but men can always go with the enterprise. Such as goods and services are produced, products are sold and profit and surpluses are availed by people. Co-operatives whether big or small cannot exist without individuals and the quality and effectiveness of the co-operative is depends on the people. Therefore seen very clear that the management of human resource is of prime importance.

HRM practices are inevitable for co-operative organization. Co-operatives are considered as an important tool in the overall development of the society by promoting individual initiative for common welfare. With the rapid expansion and diversification of the co-operative enterprise and its integration into the mainstream of economic planning, Co-operatives are expected to attain higher norms of economic efficiency and achieve results for achieving such goals, there is an imperative need for proper man power planning and recruitment of personnel in the co-operatives.

**Manpower Planning:**

Man power planning calls for systematic and comprehensive inventory of existing human resources and aims at forecasting personnel needs for the future. In the co-operative sector, broad details of personnel employed, category wise and sector wise may be available but the estimate of manpower requirements in terms of sector wise may be available but the estimate of manpower requirements in terms of anticipated growth of each segments of co-operative movement is not readily available. In view of large number of units undertaking diversified activities and operations at different levels of viability, it is extremely difficult to have such micro level estimates of the requirements of manpower. However, it could be possible to arrive at micro level estimates of manpower requirements in respect of the identified co-operative sectors at state and national levels. Forecasting of manpower requirements could be made at the macro level through the parameters like level of anticipated investments in the perspective period and the level and pattern on technology choice applicable to these sub – segments of the co-operative movement.

**Recruitment of Personnel:**

Regarding the tentative manpower plan, recruitment of right type of people for specific jobs is an important issue that needs almost some consideration. In this connection, the co-operatives face a number of constraints in the form of absence of well defined personnel policies, absence of better service conditions, and absence of promotion of career development opportunities. To get over these constraints, it is necessary to streamline the recruitment policies and systems in the co-operative movement so that right type of people are attracted and retained in the co-operatives.

**HRD in Co-operatives:**

Human Resource Development (HRD) is the process of increasing knowledge, skills and capabilities of all the people in a society. It is development process with an organizational base, within the framework or organizational development and industrial growth and individual growth, HRD embraces all facts of the system. In co-operatives, as people's enterprise, the process comprises.

- Member's needs and objectives,
- Organisational aims and objectives, in tune with community needs and member's interest.
- Job requirement and manpower audit,
- A well designed election and selection system,
- A well organised induction, education and training programme
- Leadership and promotion programme
- Job/role appraisal system,
- Methodology of inter-personnel/public and industrial relations.

HRD in Co-operative means all the planned information education, training, mobilization and manpower development activities are undertaken by the co-operatives, so as to create economically efficient organizations, capable of providing services rendered by their members.

**Concept of HRD in Co-operatives:**

The International Co-operative Alliance (ICA) has promoted and organised co-operative education and training programmes for a long time in accordance with its principle on co-operative education and its development policy. Socio-economic changes affecting co-operatives demand that ICA redefine the concept of HRD in order to better respond to the aspirations of cooperators. The ICA executive committee has formulated the policy on HRD in co-operative way to prepare the co-operative for the challenges of the 21st century. The concept of HRD in co-operatives is defined as follows.

"The concept of HRD in co-operatives means all the planned information, education, training, mobilization and manpower development activities undertaken by co-operatives so as to create economically efficient organizations capable of providing services required by the members".

The overall aim of the ICA policy of HRD is effective implementation of the ICA policy for co-operative development. Members and personnel of co-operative to realize their potential and enrich their lives materially, socially and culturally.

**Members Education:**

The raison d'etre for the co-operative movement are the members. Its strength lies in the quality of its membership and its ability to mobilize men and women. Thus, it is essential that:

- The members have an awareness and understanding of the co-operative principles, practices and values.
- Women and young people are included in co-operative activities at all levels and sufficient resources are made available for appropriate programmes.

The National Council for Co-operative Training (NCCT) set up under the aegis of National Co-operative Union of India (NCUI) is over all responsibilities for formulation policies and management of co-operative Education programmes in the country. The co-operative education of members has been the major thrust areas of NCUI. The overall objectives of co-operative education programme is to bring about improvement in the working and management of co-operative societies through motivation of membership and leadership at grass root besides creation of awareness among masses about cooperation. Two approach of education programmes have been implemented. The member Education Programme for Industrial Co-operatives, Education-cum-Development Programme for handloom co-operatives. The Leadership Development Programmes for Co-operatives are being conducted by the NCUI and also the State Co-operative Unions. A detailed institutional arrangements for co-operative education and training chart is given in the next page.

**Training of Personnel:**

Employees of co-operative organizations have a vital role to play in the establishment and management of economically efficient co-operative organizations. It is therefore essential that:

- Modern personnel policies are applied, they have an awareness and understanding of the co-operative principles, practices and values; and
- They be professionally qualified and given required training.

Training is a vital aspect of the Human Resource Development system in organizations, as an instrument for building up a competent work force. It helps, if properly imparted, the personnel to perform their job more efficiently and prepare them for holding higher responsibilities in future. The training facilities have been diversified during the last few years. Every year, Vaikunth Mehta National Institute of Co-operative Management (VAMNICOM) at Pune offers as many as 70 programmes with an overall capacity to train more than 1400 personnel. The Institutes of Co-operative Management (ICM) also organize various programmes including diploma courses and provide training to middle level executives of co-operative sector. The Institutional arrangement for Co-operative Education and Training depicted in the chart in the next page.

**Co-operative Education & Training**

Human Resource Management has assumed great important and significance in the process of management and decision. Making in co-operatives, HRM is a wide area and covers a broad spectrum of activities of the employee welfare, personnel administrational and industrial relations. Human Resource Management is to keep an efficient manpower to run the co-operatives successfully.

Human Resource Development is a process aimed mainly at performance improvement in an organization. Co-operative organizations in a developing country like India, urgently needs to adopt HRD approach to usher in an era of effective management and development at all levels. Planning in human resource development can give optimum results when it is undertaken as an integral part of organizational development.

**HRD's Rapid Progress:**

Urban co-operative credit institutions have made a rapid progress during last three decades. The total number of urban co-operative banks (1400) and co-operative credit societies (520) has made a remarkable increase at the end of the year 1994. Urban co-operative banks deposits have grown to the extent of Rs. 17,348 crores from Rs. 520.67 crores during the period between 1977 to 1994. The rate of loans and advances of these banks has also increase to Rs. 12,346 crores from Rs. 507 crores during the same period. Their own funds and working capital amounted to Rs. 2,691.81 crores and Rs. 22,924 crores respectively during the year 1994. Urban co-operative banks thus have emerged radiantly as full-fledged banking institutions in the country.

Credit deployment is the prime function of economic development system in India. For effective and efficient functioning, banks to have mobilized adequate resources in order to raise their own funds and borrowed funds. Credit deployment of these banks extends to cottage and small scale industries, trade and commerce, transport operators, exporters, self-employed or allied agricultural activities, powerlooms, consumption loans, housing loans and also loans for acquiring domestic articles required by middle class persons. Hence, professionalization of management becomes important for urban co-operative banks.

**Fig. 8.1 : Co-operative Education & Training**

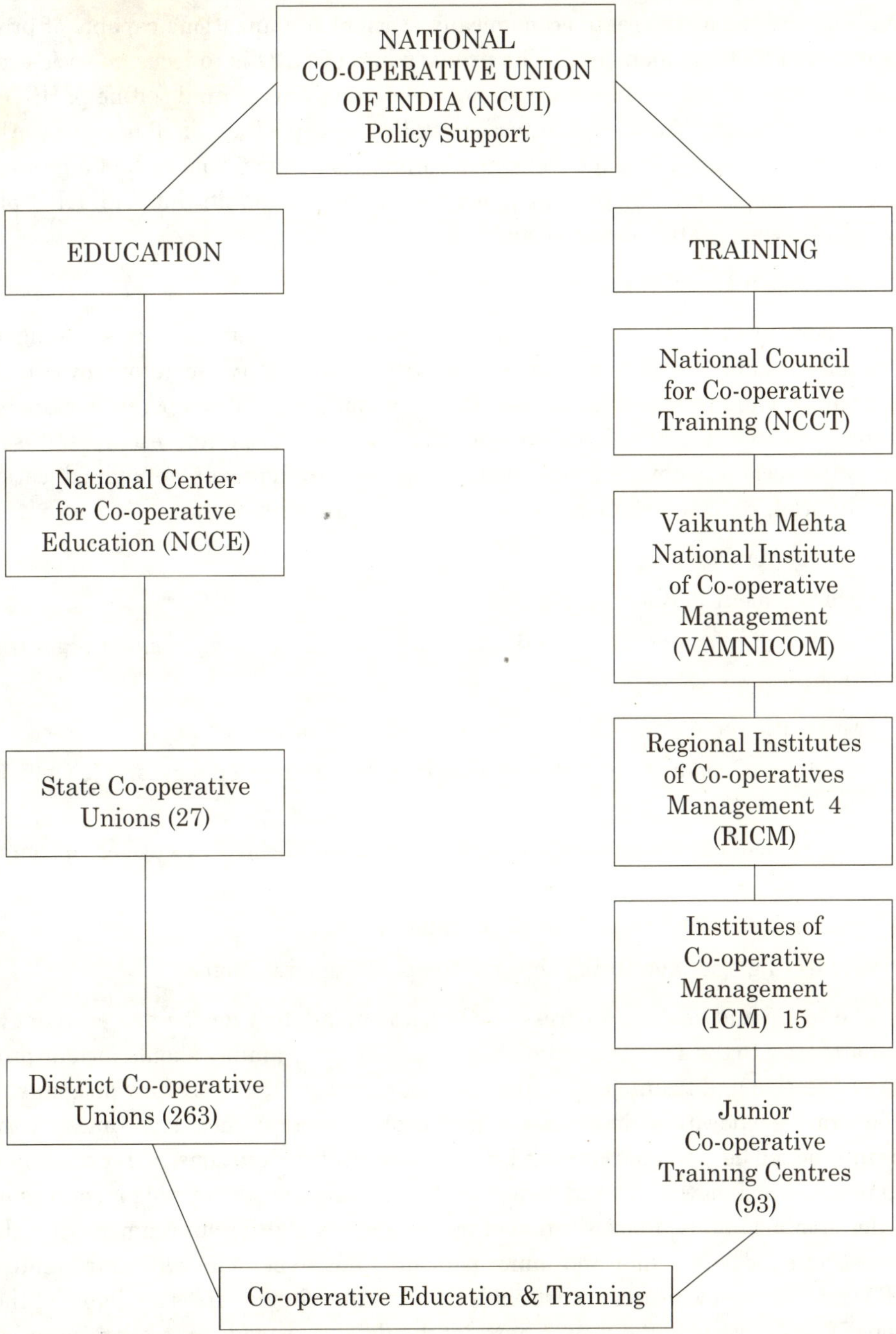

The concept of HRD in the co-operative sector means "All the planned information, education, training, mobilization and manpower development activities undertaken by co-operative societies, so as to create economically efficient organizations capable of providing services required by their members". The primary aim of HRD is to focus on socio-economic goals and co-operative values like socio-economic equality and mutual self-help. HRD trusts the process of increasing Knowledge, interests, skills and capacities, of all persons working in co-operative organizations. It is a developmental process in the framework of organizational and sectoral development. The present paper focuses on the significant role, HRD plays in non-agricultural co-operative credit sectors.

**Aspects of Human Development:**

The important of HRD in the urban co-operative credit systems excels management's considerations. It aims at evolving devices to preserve and identify the autonomy of urban co-operative banks. Human resources become the very foundation of co-operative management emphasizing economic activities and development of natural and capital resources. It is mainly "Related to the socio-economic activities and manpower development through education and training". In brief, HRD in urban co-operative banks deals with –

a) Manpower Planning
b) Management development policies
c) Review of roles of different officials / executives in the management organizations.
d) Recruitment, selection, induction and placement
e) Evaluation and appraisal of the role of different officials
f) Creation of conductive work environment for self-development and job satisfaction of official.
g) Evolvement efficient schemes, career planning for officials / executives and employees of urban co-operative banks.
h) Identification and evaluation of training needs.
i) Educating and monitoring through co-operative education.

For the sound and healthy progress of HRD, it is mandatory for the management to play sufficient attention to the aspects mentioned above. HRD programmes should include problems related to education and training. It is high time now for the HRD to review present status of state co-operative federations in co-operative education programmes. It is time for them to enhance interaction between national and state co-operative federations. So far as co-operative training is concerned, new ways and means for fuller utilization of training resources need to be considered immediately. Identification of training needs of different segments in urban co-operative sectors for both senior and junior personnel has to be made with immediate effect. The HRD training review process must not ignore the human resources available in the form of women. Effective use of audio-visual material should also be made in co-operative education and training programmes. Improvements in co-operative organization, planning of manpower also constitute the integral parts or organizational development.

**HRD and Organizational Groups :**

HRD in urban co-operative banking sector, generally consist of three different group.

(I) Member group

(II) Group of board of directors

(III) Personnel group

These groups need to have an awareness and understanding of the co-operative principles, practices and values. Manpower planning requires scientific, consistent and comprehensive inventory of existent human resources. Forecasting personnel need for future becomes equally necessary. In order to bring necessary awareness, social and political environment also should be taken in to account so that proper perception and motivation can be provided to the members. Members placed in hierarchical structure of HRD should be made aware of their duties and responsibilities while conducting the business in the co-operative sectors.

**Members:**

Members have vital role to play in the growth and development of human resources in co-operative sectors. Particularly, their awareness is essential to achieve desired aims and objectives of the co-operative systems. A member should be vigilant and fully involved in the entire management process of urban co-operative banks. Every member is generally given to elect leaders or board of members possessing abilities and dynamism necessary for growth., development and success. Every member should, therefore, be trained through proper exposure for meeting, seminars, workshops, camps and conferences. Members, so trained should be allowed to hold the office for a longer period so that smooth and effective functioning of the urban co-operative banks becomes much easier. Literature related to co-operative ideology, saving schemes, credit deployment programs, loan utilization aspects should be circulated in the form of magazines and pamphlets so that the enlightenment of the member becomes possible.

**Directors:**

The failure or success of banks depends on the character and dynamism of the board of directors. As a vigilant guardian of urban co-operative banks, they are actively involved in the functioning of the banks. Framing of the plans and policies, formulating of the banks, formulating aims and objectives becomes major responsibility of the directors. Hence, directors must be equipped with knowledge, education, training and managerial skills so as to become the torchbearers to executives and personnel in the bank. These directors can be trained through workshops, seminars, and short-term orientation courses through their exposure to functioning of banking in the country and abroad. This will enhance the quality of urban cooperating banking industry.

**Personnel:**

It is the chief executive who is responsible for effective and day-to-day working of the bank. He is the key figure in the conduct of banking system. He has to transact the business according to framework by-laws, Acts and policies laid down by the board. Both executives and managerial staff are accountable to co-operative principles and values. To achieve success, harmony and coordination it is necessary for them to consider the members as owners of the urban co-operative banks. Seminars, conference, workshops and trainings contribute to the efficiency of banking personnel's. Banking success depends on making these personnel dynamic through training aids such as film, job studies, case studies, study tours, audio-video equipments and so on.

# CHAPTER 10

## Progeress of Urban Co-operative Banks in Maharashtra

Before going to the present position of Urban Co-operative Banks in Maharashtra, it is necessary to know the geographical features, population and other related data of Maharashtra. The following table gives the data for the year 2001, in comparison with India.

**Table 10.1: Progress of Urban Co-operative Banks in Maharashtra**

| Sr. No. | Particulars | India | Maharashtra | Percen-tage |
|---|---|---|---|---|
| | 1 | 2 | 3 | 4 |
| 1 | Geographical area (lakh Sq.Kms) | 32.87 | 3.08 | 9.4% |
| 2 | Total population (lakh) | 10100.35 | 967.52 | 9.57% |
| 3 | of which Rural population (lakh) | 7287.00 | 557.32 | 7.2% |
| 4 | of which Urban population (lakh) | 2813.35 | 410.2 | 13.0% |
| 5 | of which Male population (lakh) | 5230.00 | 503.34 | 10.0% |
| 6 | Female population (lakh) | 4900.35 | 464.18 | 9% |
| 7 | of which Scheduled Castes (lakh) | | 88.60 | |
| 8 | of which Scheduled tribes (lakh) | 2266.0 | 74.30 | 7.25% |
| 9 | Literacy rate | 56% | 77% | |
| 10 | No of Banking offices | 79799* | 13838* | |
| 11 | No of Banking offices per lakh population | 8 | 14 | |
| 12 | Deposits per Capita (Rs.) | 12655 | 31387 | |
| 13 | Loan per Capita (Rs.) | 7436 | 26829 | |

* This does now include Co-operative Banks.

It would be seen from the above that the banking development in Maharashtra is far above that of all India average.

**Source:** Co-operative Movement at a Glance - Maharashtra.

**Table 10.2: Co-operative Movement in Maharashtra**

| Sr. No. | Particulats | Year | India | Maharashtra |
|---|---|---|---|---|
| | 1 | 2 | 3 | 4 |
| 1 | No. of Co-operative Societies | (1995) | 4.10.863 | 1,34,338 |
| 2 | No. of Co-operative Societies | (2000) | NA | 1,52,745 |

**Source:** Co-operative Movement at a Glance - Maharashtra

It will be seen from the above figures that Maharashtra has made a spectacular progress in the growth of Co-operative Societies as a whole.

Maclagan Committee had reported in 1915. that total number of Co-operative Societies all over India was then 14881 of while in Bombay had only 719 Co-operative Societies, which include one provincial Co-operative Bank, three District Co-operative Banks and the rest 715 were other primary Co-operative Societies. The percentage of Societies in erstwhile Bombay province then was only 4.8 percent in comparison with India. In 1995, there were 4,10,863 Co-operative Societies in India of which 1,34,338 Co-operative Societies were in Maharashtra, which comes to 33 percent of the total Co-operative Societies in India. Maharashtra has

| **Table 10.3: Salient features of Co-operative Societies in Maharashtra as on 31.03.2002** | | |
|---|---|---|
| **Sr. No.** | **Particulars** | |
| | **1** | **2** |
| 1 | No. of Co-operative Societies | 165789 |
| 2 | No. of Members (in lakhs) | 439 |
| 3 | Paid up Share Capital (Rs. in Crores) | 10677 |
| 4 | Owned funds (Rs. in Crores) | 21827 |
| 5 | Deposits (Rs. in Crores) | 83334 |
| 6 | Loans Advanced (Rs. in Crores) | 58724 |

(**Source:** Co-operative Movement at a glance – Maharashtra 2002 published by Commissioner for Coopn. & Registrar of Co-operative Societies, Maharashtra State. Pune-I).

| **Table 10.4: Comparative position of Urban Co-operative Banks in Maharashtra – *vis-à-vis* India 31.03.1999** | | | | |
|---|---|---|---|---|
| **Sr. No.** | **Particulars** | **India 1999** | **Maharashtra** | |
| | | | **1999** | **2002** |
| | **1** | **2** | **3** | **4** |
| 1 | No. of Urban Co-operative Banks | 1936 | 632 | 657 |
| 2 | No. of Members (in '000) | N.A. | 7757 | 8186 |
| 3 | Share Capital (Rs. in lakhs) | N.A. | 48944 | 105544 |
| 4 | Deposits (Rs. in lakhs) | 5054000 | 2652300 | 4569095 |
| 5 | Loans | 3265000 | 1517700 | 2696671 |

(**Source:** Co-operative movement at a glance by 2002; CC & RCS, M.S. Pune)

continued to be leading in Co-operative Movement in India. It has maintained accelerated growth of the Co-operative Movement as compared to other States.

It is seen that as on 31 March 1990 there were 632 Urban Co-operative Banks in Maharashtra as against 1936 Banks in India, (which include Urban Co-operative Banks in Maharashtra),Urban Co-operative banks in Maharashtra constituted 33 percent of the total number of Urban Co-operative Banks whole of India in the year 1998-99. As regards to deposit mobilization and loans advanced and outstanding as on 31 March 1999, the share of Urban Co-operative Banks in Maharashtra was 52 percent and 46 percent respectively of the total deposits and loans granted by all the Urban Co-operative Banks in India, in the year 1998-99. Thus as far as the position of Urban Co-operative Banks is concerned, Maharashtra has made outstanding progress as compared to other States.

The following table will indicate State-wise position of No. of Urban Co-operative Banks and their branches in India as on 31 March 1999.

It is seen from the above statement that there is regional imbalance in the growth of Urban Co-operative Banks in the country. Maharashtra, Gujarat, Tamilnadu, Andhra Pradesh and Karnataka account for 1523 Urban Co-operative Banks out of 1936 Banks in the country.

**Table 10.5: State-wise Position of No. of Urban Co-operative Banks and their Branches**

| Sr. No. | State | No. of Urban Co-operative Banks | No. of branches |
|---|---|---|---|
| 1 | Andhra Pradesh | 137 | 257 |
| 2 | Assam | 11 | 12 |
| 3 | Bihar | 8 | 8 |
| 4 | Goa | 7 | 72 |
| 5 | Gujarat | 341 | 958 |
| 6 | Himachal Pradesh | 5 | 5 |
| 7 | Jammu & Kashmir | 4 | 15 |
| 8 | Karnataka | 299 | 723 |
| 9 | Kerala | 63 | 302 |
| 10 | Madhya Pradesh | 82 | 103 |
| 11 | Maharashtra | 616 | 3336 |
| 12 | Manipur | 5 | 10 |
| 13 | Meghalaya | 2 | 2 |
| 14 | Mizoram | 1 | 1 |
| 15 | Nagaland | 1 | 1 |
| 16 | New Delhi | 19 | 63 |
| 17 | Orissa | 14 | 47 |
| 18 | Pondicherry | 2 | 5 |
| 19 | Punjab | 6 | 17 |
| 20 | Rajasthan | 40 | 115 |
| 21 | Tamilnadu | 136 | 225 |
| 22 | Tripura | 1 | 1 |
| 23 | Uttar Pradesh | 73 | 161 |
| 24 | West Bengal | 55 | 104 |
| | Total for India | 1936 | 6619 |

(Source: Report of the High Power Committee on Urban Co-operative Banks published by Reserve Bank of India)

The Northeastern part of the country (i.e., Manipur, Mizoram, Meghalaya, Nagaland and Tripura) account for 10 Urban Co-operative Banks only. Haryana and Punjab are well-developed states in agriculture, but they have hardly 14 Urban Co-operative Banks. Himachal Pradesh 5 and Jammu & Kashmir 4, account for 9 Urban Co-operative Banks only. Sikkim, Daman & Diu an Andaman Nicobar (under Union Territory) have not a single Co-operative Urban Bank. The Reserve Bank of India with the help of concerned States, Union Territory Government and with local Co-operative leadership need to make efforts to organize Urban Co-operative Banks in these areas, so that the entire country will have Urban Co-operative Banks in all the states.

## District-wise Progress of UCBs in Maharashtra

The following table will indicate the District-wise comparative position or Urban Co-operative banks in Maharashtra in 1990 and 2000.

| Table 10.6:District-wise progress of Urban Co-operative Banks in Maharashtra | | | | | | | | | |
|---|---|---|---|---|---|---|---|---|---|
| | | Position on 30.06.1991 | | | | Position as on 30.03.2000 | | | |
| Sr. No. | District | No. of Banks | Mem Errs (000) | Deposits Rs in lakhs | Loans Rs. in lakhs | No. of Banks | Members (000) | Deposits Rs. in lakhs | Loans Rs. on lakhs |
| | 1 | 2 | 3 | 4 | 5 | 6 | 7 | 8 | 9 |
| 1 | Mumbai | 93 | 1600 | 181797 | 144056 | 84 | 1560 | 1308909 | 800729 |
| | Total | 93 | 1600 | 181797 | 144056 | 84 | 1560 | 1308909 | 800729 |
| 2 | Thane | 18 | 197 | 35425 | 25466 | 19 | 256 | 223769 | 124433 |
| 3 | Raigad | 7 | 83 | 5231 | 4637 | 10 | 122 | 37245 | 29820 |
| 4 | Sindhudurga | 2 | 9 | 374 | 381 | 2 | 19 | 2996 | 2163 |
| 5 | Ratnagiri | 4 | 44 | 1900 | 1531 | 5 | 53 | 9681 | 7298 |
| | Total | 31 | 333 | 42930 | 32015 | 36 | 450 | 273691 | 163714 |
| 6 | Nasik | 24 | 241 | 17941 | 14923 | 49 | 297 | 144435 | 99173 |
| 7 | Dhule | 13 | 82 | 6347 | 6822 | 18 | 121 | 43756 | 32904 |
| 8 | Jalgaon | 14 | 128 | 9806 | 8371 | 21 | 186 | 37381 | 23469 |
| 9 | Ahmednagar | 15 | 147 | 12041 | 10493 | 22 | 186 | 81215 | 63187 |
| | Total | 66 | 598 | 46135 | 40609 | 110 | 790 | 306787 | 218733 |
| 10 | Pune | 42 | 329 | 74980 | 45928 | 61 | 414 | 509773 | 335383 |
| 11 | Satara | 16 | 125 | 13584 | 12296 | 32 | 189 | 100679 | 76411 |
| 12 | Sangli | 23 | 597 | 23131 | 17925 | 32 | 177 | 127988 | 86491 |
| 13 | Solapur | 39 | 110 | 15750 | 12747 | 41 | 164 | 54976 | 66589 |
| 14 | Kolhapur | 37 | 423 | 37132 | 31370 | 63 | 555 | 178067 | 120611 |
| | Total | 137 | 1584 | 164587 | 120266 | 229 | 1499 | 1011483 | 685485 |
| 15 | Aurangabad | 5 | 16 | 1309 | 1077 | 14 | 37 | 17010 | 11906 |
| 16 | Jalna | 2 | 10 | 1185 | 1699 | 7 | 26 | 4155 | 3473 |
| 17 | Parbhani | 4 | 6 | 1789 | 805 | 26 | 56 | 27749 | 18041 |
| 18 | Beed | 3 | 18 | 1435 | 944 | 16 | 58 | 30442 | 20271 |
| 19 | Nanded | 2 | 6 | 661 | 606 | 10 | 33 | 10477 | 7216 |
| 20 | Osmanabad | 1 | 24 | 1965 | 1307 | 12 | 41 | 21577 | 15518 |
| 21 | Latur | 2 | 15 | 1109 | 800 | 18 | 43 | 6687 | 4997 |
| | Total | 19 | 95 | 9453 | 7238 | 103 | 294 | 110097 | 81422 |
| 22 | Amaravati | 6 | 28 | 1899 | 1508 | 12 | 70 | 21144 | 13840 |
| 23 | Akola | 5 | 50 | 4048 | 3813 | 9 | 124 | 73793 | 55164 |
| 24 | Buldana | 7 | 34 | 4145 | 4346 | 9 | 69 | 53349 | 37113 |
| 25 | Yeotmal | 2 | 12 | 683 | 528 | 4 | 59 | 22564 | 15491 |
| | Total | 20 | 124 | 10775 | 10195 | 34 | 222 | 170850 | 121608 |
| 26 | Nagpur | 11 | 89 | 7982 | 6593 | 20 | 144 | 53375 | 37099 |
| 27 | Wardha | 2 | 17 | 1137 | 1090 | 5 | 29 | 12945 | 8861 |
| 28 | Bhandara | 2 | 24 | 1496 | 841 | 3 | 37 | 16188 | 9554 |
| 29 | Chandrapur | | | | | 4 | 12 | 4399 | 2799 |
| 30 | Gadchiroli | | | | | 2 | 2 | 163 | 98 |
| | Total | 15 | 130 | 10615 | 8524 | 34 | 1224 | 87070 | 58411 |
| | Gr. Total | 381 | 4464 | 466292 | 362903 | 630 | 5039 | 3276887 | 2130102 |

**Source:** Report of the High Power Committee on Urban Co-operative Banks

It is seen from the progress made by Co-operative Banks in Maharashtra state, that in Mumbai Region there were 93 Co-operative Banks on 30.6.91. This number has come down to 84 in 2000, due to amalgamation and liquidation of weak banks. One urban Co-operative bank has gone out of Co-operative fold in to the Private Sector. Konkan Region had 31 banks in 1991. This increased to 36 in the year 1999-2000. Though satisfactory, the progress is not comparable with other regions. Western Maharashtra had 203 banks in 1991, which rose to 339 banks in 2000. Western Maharashtra continues to lead in the number of Banks as compared to other regions. Marathwada had 19 banks in the year 1990-91. Then it increased to 103 in 1999-2000. Vidarbha had 35 banks in 1991 which had gone up to 68 in 2000. This is satisfactory progress, but not as good as progress made in Marathwada region.

Within 10 years the numbers of co-operative Banks in Maharashtra has increased from 381 to 630. Maharashtra thus continues to lead in India as compared to other States. It is seen from the above figures that during the last 10 years Maharashtra recorded the growth as shown under:-

1. No. of Urban Banks 165%
2. No. of members 115%
3. Deposits 703%
4. Loans 587%

The present Maharashtra State came into existence following reorganization of erstwhile Bombay State excluding Gujarat and Karnataka areas while new territories of Marathwada and Vidarbha were included in Maharashtra. Maharashtra is now (as in 2002) divided in to 6 Revenue Divisions of 35 Districts having 326 Talukas. There are 41251 villages and 336 towns. The Co-operative Department has however 9 Divisions for administrative purposes. Geographically; Maharashtra is divided in to 5 Zones as under:

1. Mumbai Zone : Mumbai and Mumbai Suburban District
2. Western Maharashtra : Pune, Satara, Sangli, Solapur, Kolhapur, Nasik, Jalgaon, Dhule, Ahmednagar and Nandurbar.
3. Konkan : Thane, Raigad, Ratnagiri and Sindhudurg, Districts.
4. Marathwada : Aurangabad, Beed, Jalna, Parabhani, Nanded, Osmanabad, Latur and Hingoli.
5. Vidarbha : Amaravarti, Akola, Buldhana, Yavatmal, Nagpur, Wardha, Chandrapur, Gadchirolui, Washim and Gondia.

The following table will indicate the growth of Urban Co-operative Banks in the present Maharashtra State from 1961 to 2000:

It is seen from the above that since 1960 when Maharashtra State came into existence, the progress made by the Urban Co-operative banks thereafter from 1961 onwards is really remarkable. This can also be attributed to the change in policy for registration of Urban Co-operative Banks on the part of the Reserve Bank of India. The Urban Co-operative Banks were brought into the ambit of Banking Regulation Act in 1966. Insurance cover for the deposits

**Table 10.7: Growth and Development of Urban Co-operative banks in Maharashtra State from 1961 to 2000**

| Sr. No. | Particulars | 61-62 | 71-72 | 81-82 | 91.92 | 99-2000 |
|---|---|---|---|---|---|---|
| | 1 | 2 | 3 | 4 | 5 | 6 |
| 1 | No. of Urban Co-operative Banks | 149 | 265 | 345 | 381 | 630 |
| 2 | No. of Members ('000) | 433 | 883 | 1618 | 4464 | 7782 |
| 3 | Share Capital (Rs. in lakh) | 284 | 987 | 4201 | 18692 | 57032 |
| 4 | Deposits (Rs. in lakh) | 1243 | 6832 | 65779 | 466298 | 350193 |
| 5 | Loans Outstanding (Rs. in lakh) | 1671 | 5007 | 48003 | 322718 | 1691398 |
| 6 | Overdue (Rs. in lakh) | N.A. | 364 | 3752 | 45735 | 103108 |

**Source:** Co-operative Movement at a Glance - Maharashtra

of Co-operative banks was also extended. These limits of insurance cover were increased from time to time. The present limit of insurance cover for deposits is Rs. 1 lakh. These are also some of the reasons for the rapid growth and development of Urban Co-operative Banks.

From the above statistics it would be seen that during the past forty years, Urban Co-operative Banks in Maharashtra have registered all-round progress in respect of various indicators like number, membership, share capital, deposits and loan outstanding. The District wise population and number of Urban Co-operative Banks as on 31.3.2001 is given in the following table.

Till 1991, the Reserve Bank of India had restrictive policy, in respect of registration, area of operation and expansion of branches of Urban Co-operative banks. New registration was allowed in unbanked and undeveloped areas only. However following the recommendations of Marathe Committee Report 1992 and liberalized economic policy of the Government of India in respect of financial sector, Reserve Bank of India also followed the policy of liberalization in regard to registration, expansion of branches of banks, area of operation of Urban Co-opeartive Banks etc. The Reserve Bank of India prescribed only entry point norms about share capital, membership and social standing of promoters. This liberalization policy of Reserve Bank of India concerning Urban Co-operative Banks resulted in the growth of Urban Co-operative Banks. This is revealed from the above figures.

Moreover, Deposit Insurance and Credit Guarantee Corporation Act, 1961 was also extended to the deposits of urban Co-operative Banks. This gave further impetus to the growth of deposits, Loans, and Advances of Urban Co-operative Banks. Besides this the Urban Co-operative Banks are also allowed to lend finance for agriculture and allied activities, which was the monopoly of District Central Co-operative Banks and RRBs in the past.

The following table will indicate the position of Urban Co-operative Banks as on 31.3.2000, according to the geographical divisions of Maharashtra.

The following table will show the average amount of Deposits and Loans Outstanding per 1000 population.

**Table 10.8: Statement showing the District-wise number of Urban Co-op Banks in Maharashtra State as on 31.3.2001**

**(Population in '000)**

| Sr. No | District | Population | No. of Banks |
|---|---|---|---|
| | 1 | 2 | 3 |
| 1 | Mumbai | 11814 | 84 |
| | Total | 11814 | 84 |
| 2 | Thana | 8129 | 19 |
| 3 | Raigad | 2206 | 10 |
| 4 | Ratnagiri | 1696 | 5 |
| 5 | Sindhudurg | 862 | 2 |
| | Total | 12893 | 21 |
| 6 | Nasik | 4988 | 49 |
| 7 | Jalgaon | 3680 | 21 |
| 8 | Dhule | 3018 | 18 |
| 9 | Ahmednagar | 4088 | 22 |
| | Total | 15774 | 110 |
| 10 | Pune | 7224 | 61 |
| 11 | Kolhapur | 3515 | 63 |
| 12 | Solapur | 3855 | 41 |
| 13 | Satara | 2797 | 32 |
| 14 | Sangali | 2582 | 32 |
| | Total | 19973 | 229 |
| 15 | Aurangabad | 2921 | 14 |
| 16 | Nanded | 3855 | 10 |
| 17 | Jalna | 1612 | 7 |
| 18 | Parbhani | 1491 | 26 |
| 19 | Beed | 2160 | 16 |
| 20 | Osmanabad | 1472 | 12 |
| 21 | Latur | 2078 | 18 |
| | Total | 15589 | 103 |
| 22 | Nagpur | 4051 | 20 |
| 23 | Bhandara | 1136 | 3 |
| 24 | Chandrapur | 2078 | 4 |
| 25 | Wardha | 1231 | 5 |
| 26 | Gadchiroli | 2170 | 2 |
| | Total | 1066 | 34 |
| 27 | Amaravati | 2606 | 12 |
| 28 | Akola | 2649 | 9 |
| 29 | Yeotmal | 2226 | 9 |
| | Total | 9941 | 34 |
| | **Total** | **96650** | **630** |

**Source:** Co-operative Movement at a Glance-Maharashtra

**Table 10.9: Geographical Divisions of Maharashtra**

(Rs. in Lakhs)

| Sr. No. | Region | No. of Banks | No. of Members ('000) | Owned Funds | Deposits | Loans out-standing |
|---|---|---|---|---|---|---|
| | 1 | 2 | 3 | 4 | 5 | 6 |
| 1 | Mumbai | 84 | 1560 | 158669 | 1308909 | 800729 |
| 2 | Konkan | 36 | 450 | 32380 | 273691 | 163714 |
| 3 | Western Maharashtra | 339 | 2289 | 125014 | 1318270 | 904218 |
| 4 | Marathwada | 103 | 294 | 12592 | 118097 | 81422 |
| 5 | Vidarbha | 68 | 546 | 16724 | 257920 | 179919 |
| | Total | 630 | 5139 | 345379 | 3276887 | 2130002 |

**Source**: Co-operative Movement at a Glance - Maharashtra

**Table 10.10: Urban Co-operative Banks – Regionwise percentage for Maharashtra**

| Sr No | Region | Membership | Owned Funds | Deposits | Loan out-standing |
|---|---|---|---|---|---|
| | 1 | 2 | 3 | 4 | 5 |
| 1 | Mumbai | 30% | 46% | 40% | 38% |
| 2 | Konkan | 9% | 9% | 8% | 8% |
| 3 | Western Maharashtra | 45% | 36% | 40% | 42% |
| 4 | Marathwada | 6% | 4% | 4% | 4% |
| 5 | Vidarbha | 10% | 5% | 8% | 8% |
| | Total | 100% | 100% | 100% | 100 |

**Source:** Co-operative Movement at a Glance - Maharashtra

**Table 10.11: Deposits and Loans Outstanding per 1000 population**

| Sr.No. | Region | Deposits per 1000 population (Rs. in lakhs) | Loan Outstanding per 1000 population (Rs. in lakhs) |
|---|---|---|---|
| | 1 | 2 | 3 |
| 1 | Mumbai | 111 | 68 |
| 2 | Konkan | 21 | 13 |
| 3 | Western Maharashtra | 37 | 25 |
| 4 | Marathwada | 8 | 5 |
| 5 | Vidarbha | 13 | 9 |

**Source:** Co-operative Movement at a Glance - Maharashtra

It is further seen from the above table that Konkan, Marathwada and Vidarbha regions continue to lag behind in comparison with Western Maharashtra and Mumbai regions, in respect of no. of Urban Co-operative Banks, their membership, deposits and loans outstanding. Konkan, Marathwada and Vidarbha Regions have average deposits per 1000 population to the tine of Rs. 21 lakhs, Rs. 8 lakhs and Rs. 13 lakhs respectively, whereas loans outstanding per 1000 population amounted to Rs. 13 lakhs, Rs. 5 lakhs and Rs. 9 lakhs respectively. This is far below average as compared to Western Maharashtra and Mumbai Regions, which are relatively economically developed due to industrialization and development of Trade and Commerce in these two regions.

**Urban Co-operative Banks : Part of Three-Tier Structure:**

Consequent upon recommendations of Gorwala Committee, Co-operative movement all over India accepted three tier structure for Co-operative Credit Institutions, i.e., primary Co-operative Societies at the village level or primary level, District Central Co-operative Banks [D.C.C. Banks] at the District level and State Co-operative Bank at the State level. Maharashtra has also adopted this three tier structure. 630 primary Urban Co-operative Banks are affiliated to 30 District Central Co-operative Banks and these District Central Co-operative Banks are affiliated to the Maharashtra State Co-operative Bank (M.S.C.B.) Thus the Urban Co-operative Banks are a part of three tier structure, as mentioned above.

In the Co-operative Banking sector, there are two types of Co-operative Banks. The first type is the primary bank, which are popularly known as Urban Co-operative Banks which draw their membership generally from the individuals, firms and are not allowed to extend loans to Co-operative Societies. The second type of banks is Federal Banks (i.e., D.C.C. Banks and S.C.Bs). The Co-operative Societies including Urban Co-operative Banks are, by law expected to open their accounts and invest their funds with the Central Co-operative Banks or State Co-operative Bank. Further Zilla Parishads are also by law, required to keep their funds with District Central Co-operative Banks. Naturally these Federal Co-operative Banks have an inbuilt system of collection of funds from the primary Co-operative Societies. Zilla Parishads, trust etc. including the primary Co-operative banks, which are required to deposit their surplus funds with District Central Co-operative banks or M.S.C. Bank. These federal Co-operative Banks also collect deposits from individuals and firms. The statement below will indicate the no. of banking offices, deposits and loans outstanding of primary Co-operative Banks, District Central Co-operative banks and the M.S.C. bank as on 31 Marh 2000

**Table 10.12: Performance of Urban Co-operative Banks**

| Sr No. | Type of Banks | No. of Banks | No. of Banking Offices | Members ('000) | Deposits (Rs. in Lakhs) | Loan Out-standing (Rs. in Lakhs) |
|---|---|---|---|---|---|---|
| | 1 | 2 | 3 | 4 | 5 | 6 |
| 1 | M.S.C. Bank | 1 | 52 | 35 | 809980 | 67004 |
| 2 | D.C.C. Banks | 30 | 3657 | 105 | 1523163 | 538600 |
| 3 | Urban Co-operative Banks | 650 | 3336 | 7782 | 3500193 | 1691398 |
| | Total | 681 | 7045 | 7920 | 583336 | 2904002 |

**Source:** Co-operative Movement at a Glance - Maharashtra

It would be clear from above that the performance of primary Urban Co-operative Banks in respect of collection of deposits, disbursement of Loans is far better as compared to the District Central co-operative Banks, which enjoy exclusive advantages like Government Share Capital, Government Guarantees, etc.

In fact better performance of Urban Co-operative Banks can be attributed to their non-dependence on Government. Excessive dependence on Government help has brought in weakness in higher Co-operative Banking sector. These banks should be free to do the banking business without being loaded with Government favours and the consequential liabilities like financing Government aided projects at times over-looking financial norms due to political pressure; Now that Co-operative Banking sector in particular and cooperation in general has developed fairly in Maharashtra, there is a demand from the Urban Co-operative Banking sector that Maharashtra is Self Reliant and Autonomous Co-operative. Societies Act on the lines of Andhra Pradesh Legislation be passed and banks allowed to go under the preview of the said Act or in the alternative separate Co-operative societies Act may be passed for Urban Co-operative Banks removing unnecessary restrictions.

The following table will indicate the deposit-wise position of Urban Co-operative Banks as on 31.3.2000

| | | |
|---|---|---|
| 1. | Deposits above Rs. 100 crores | 34 |
| 2. | Deposits between Rs. 50 to 100 crores | 128 |
| 3. | Deposits between Rs. 25 to 50 crores | 72 |
| 4. | Deposits between Rs. 10 to 25 crores | 92 |
| 5. | Deposits below Rs. 10 crores | 304 |
| | Total | 630 |

**Weak/Sick Banks**

The following table will indicate the position of weak banks as on 31.03.1998.

**Table 10.13: Positions of Weak Urban Co-operative Banks**

| Sr No. | India/Maharashtra | No. of weak/sick banks | Reasons for Non-comp of (s.11 91) of B.R. Act | Non-viable | Other Reasons | Under Observation |
|---|---|---|---|---|---|---|
| | 1 | 2 | 3 | 4 | 5 | 6 |
| 1 | India | 293 | 112 | 90 | 71 | 20 |
| 2 | Maharashtra | 77 | 24 | 27 | 22 | 4 |

**Source:** Report of the High Power Committee on Urban Co-operative banks 1999

It is seen from above that Maharashtra is also leading in the number of Weak/sick banks in comparison with other States. Out of 293 weak-sick banks at all India level, Maharashtra had 77 weak/sick banks, which accounts for 27 percent.

| **Reserve Bank of India identified weak/sick Banks considering the norms prescribed by it. They are as follows:** | | |
|---|---|---|
| **Parameter** | **Weak Banks** | **Sick Banks** |
| CRAR | Less than 75% of minimum prescription OR | Less than 50% of minimum prescription AND OR |
| Net NPA | 10% or more but less than 15% of Loans outstanding as on 31st March OR | 15% or more of Loans outstanding as on 31st March |
| History of losses | Net losses for two years out of lass three consecutive years | Net losses for last three consecutive years |

Recently the reserve bank of India has changed the nomenclature of weak/sick banks following representations made by federations of Urban Co-operative Banks to the Reserve Bank of India, stating that such nomenclature induced the depositors to take away their deposits from weak and sick banks making it difficult for them to recover from bad financial position. Revised system of classification of Urban Co-operative Banks classified them in 4 categories i.e., Grade I/II/III and IV. Nomenclature of weak banks and sick banks is now changed to Gr. III and Gr. IV category banks respectively. Presently Maharashtra has 78 such banks.

**UCBs in Liquidation:**

There are 31 Urban Co-operative Banks in liquidation as on 31/3/2000 in Maharashtra. The following table will indicate Divisions wise position of Urban Co-operative Banks declared as weak-sick and in Liquidation conditions.

| **Sr No.** | **Region** | **Urban Banks Weak/Sick** | **Urban Co-operative banks in Liquidation** |
|---|---|---|---|
| | **1** | **2** | **3** |
| 1 | Mumbai | 17 | 14 |
| 2 | Kokan | 5 | 3 |
| 3 | Western Maharashtra | 37 | 8 |
| 4 | Marathwada | 11 | 4 |
| 5 | Vidarbha | 8 | 2 |
| | Total | 78 | 31 |

The registrar of Co-operative Societies for Maharashtra has also classified the banks in to A, B, C, D categories. As on 31. March 2003 there were 333 banks in A Grade, 173 banks in B Grae, 103 Banks in C Grade, and 22 Banks in D Grade. The Division wise break-up of these banks was under. The table below gives the no. of banks in profit/loss and the no. of banks having over-dues exceeding 20 percent.

| Sr. No. | Division | No. of Banks in | | | | Banks in Liquidation | Banks in Profit | Banks in loss | Banks having over-due over 20% |
|---|---|---|---|---|---|---|---|---|---|
| | 1 | | | | 2 | 3 | 4 | 5 | 6 |
| | | A Gr | B Gr | C Gr | D GR | | | | |
| 1 | Mumbai | 30 | 27 | 16 | 7 | 14 | 49 | 10 | 12 |
| 2 | Kokan | 13 | 12 | 7 | - | 3 | 32 | 2 | 4 |
| 3 | Kolhapur | 68 | 34 | 17 | 7 | 2 | 116 | 10 | 13 |
| 4 | Pune | 63 | 24 | 14 | 2 | 4 | 98 | 6 | 11 |
| 5 | Nasik | 58 | 38 | 17 | 2 | 2 | 103 | 13 | 17 |
| 6 | Aurangabad | 32 | 7 | 10 | 1 | 3 | 42 | 8 | 5 |
| 57 | Latur | 36 | 13 | 6 | - | 1 | 52 | 3 | 6 |
| 8 | Amaravati | 21 | 6 | 8 | - | 2 | 27 | 8 | - |
| 9 | Nagpur | 12 | 12 | 8 | 3 | - | 30 | 5 | 4 |
| | Total | 333 | 173 | 103 | 22 | 31 | 569 | 65 | 72 |

It is seen from the above statement that the position of Urban Co-operative Banks in Maharashtra as on 31/3/2003 was quite satisfactory. Out of 630 Urban Banks, 569 banks are in profit. However there were certain areas, which needed more attention of Reserve Bank of India as well as the Co-operative Department of the State. There were 65 banks in losses, 72 banks are having overdues exceeding 20 percent. Moreover there are 103 banks in 'C' category and 22 banks in 'D' category. These banks required close supervision and a time bound programme for improving their financial position.

The classification developed by Co-operative department is based on few selected indicators monitored regularly at the district and the state Level. This helps in initiating timely action to safeguard the interest of the Urban Co-operative Banking movement. Besides, strict action taken by the Co-operative department inspite of pressures from outside agencies, has been helping to improve the health of this sector.

**Growth and Development of Co-operative Socieites in Maharashtra:**

Cooperation plays an important role in safeguarding the vulnerable unorganized sections of the people engaged in various economic activities. The co-operative movement has been in existence for nearly a century and faced so many critics. Still it has helped preventing exploitation of the rural masses from capitalists and in raising the economic condition of small farmers, village artisans, and landless labors. It has developed growth centers in the rural area generating new employment opportunities, augmenting productive capacity and enhancing the competitive ability of weaker sections. In its initial era, the co-operative movement in Maharashtra was confined mainly to the field of agricultural credit. It rapidly spread in other fields like agro processing, agro marketing, rural industries, consumer stores, social services. This resulted in considerable beneficial impact in raising the standard of living of the people. However, suitable strategies need to be adopted in order that the co-operative movement competes in the new economic scenario and market trends.

## Number of Co-operative Societies:

The data in respect of the number of various co-operative societies from (1960-61) to (2004-05) are presented in Table 10.14.

**Table 10.14: Number of Co-operative Societies in Maharashtra**

| Year | Apex & Central Agricultural & Non-Agricultural Institutions | PACS | Non-Agricultural Credit Societies | Marketing Societies | Productive Enterprises | Social Services & Other Co-operatives | Total |
|---|---|---|---|---|---|---|---|
| 1 | 2 | 3 | 4 | 5 | 6 | 7 | 8 |
| 1960-1961 | 39<br>(0.12) | 21400<br>(67.80) | 1630<br>(5.16) | 344<br>(1.09) | 4306<br>(13.64) | 3846<br>(12.18) | 31565<br>(100) |
| 1970-1971 | 29<br>(0.07) | 20420<br>(47.94) | 2964<br>(6.96) | 410<br>(0.96) | 6810<br>(15.99) | 11964<br>(28.09) | 42597<br>(100) |
| 1980-1981 | 31<br>(0.05) | 18577<br>(30.58) | 5474<br>(9.01) | 423<br>(0.70) | 14327<br>(23.58) | 21915<br>(36.08) | 60747<br>(100) |
| 1990-1991 | 34<br>(0.03) | 19565<br>(18.70) | 11291<br>(10.79) | 931<br>(0.89) | 28954<br>(27.68) | 43845<br>(41.91) | 104620<br>(100) |
| 2000-2001 | 34<br>(0.02) | 20551<br>(13.01) | 22014<br>(13.93) | 1115<br>(0.71) | 39070<br>(24.73) | 75232<br>(47.61) | 158016<br>(100) |
| 2002-2003 | 34<br>(0.02) | 20839<br>(12.02) | 25107<br>(14.48) | 1252<br>(0.72) | 40171<br>(23.17) | 82999<br>(49.60) | 173402<br>(100) |
| 2003-2004 | 34<br>(0.02) | 21000<br>(11.74) | 25664<br>(14.35) | 1222<br>(0.68) | 40885<br>(22.8) | 90049<br>(50.35) | 178854<br>(100) |
| 2004-2005 | 35<br>(0.02) | 21091<br>(11.44) | 26145<br>(14.18) | 1314<br>(0.71) | 41699<br>(22.61) | 94106<br>(51.04) | 184390<br>(100) |
| % Change over 1960-1961 | -10.26 | -1.44 | 1503.99 | 281.98 | 868.39 | 2346.85 | 484.16 |

**Source:** Co-operative Movement inIndia – NABARD, Bombay
Figures in parentheses are the percentages to the total)

It was revealed from the data presented in Table 10.14 that the total number of all the co-operative societies in Maharashtra was 31,565 in the year 1960-61 and had increased to 1,84,390 by the end of March 2005. This resulted in 484 percent changes over the base year (1960-61). Among the different categories of co-operative societies the proportionate number of the apex and central institutions was very less and it was declined by 10 percent over the entire period under study. The proportion of number of PACs in the total number of co-operative societies was continuously showed declining trend over a period of time. There was marginal decrease in the number of PACS by 1.44 percent in the year 2004-05 over the year 1960-61. During the period up to early seventies the number of PACs was higher than the other co-operative societies in Maharashtra. The rapid increase in the number of rest of the co-operative societies was noticed. This change over maximum to the extent of 2347 percent in case of social societies and other co-operatives. This was followed by non-agricultural credit societies (1504 percent), productive co-operatives (868 percent and marketing societies (282 percent). At the end of 2004-05 more than 50 percent co-operative societies were under the category of social societies and other co-operatives.

**Members of Co-operative Societies:**

Table 10.15 represents the information regarding number of members of different co-operative societies. According to Table 27 the total number of members under all the categories of co-operative societies was 41.91 lakhs in 1960-61 was shown a change over by 993 percent in the year 2004-05. The proportion of number of members in the total members was more under PACs up to the period of early eighties. This proportion later on was more under non-agricultural credit societies. Almost all the categories of co-operative societies had shown a positive over in the year 2004-05 as compared to the year 1960-61. This change over was maximum incase of productive enterprises followed by non-agricultural credit societies.

**Table 10.15: Number of members of the Co-operative Societies (in thousands)**

| Year | Apex & Central Agricultural & Non-Agricultural Institutions | PACS | Non-Agricultural Credit Societies | Marketing Societies | Productive Enterprises | Social Services & Other Co-operatives | Total |
|---|---|---|---|---|---|---|---|
| 1 | 2 | 3 | 4 | 5 | 6 | 7 | 8 |
| 1960-1961 | 76<br>(1.81) | 2170<br>(51.78) | 1087<br>(25.94) | 141<br>(3.36) | 323<br>(7.71) | 3946<br>(9.40) | 4191<br>(100) |
| 1970-1971 | 70<br>(0.82) | 3794<br>(44.21) | 2438<br>(28.41) | 282<br>(3.29) | 959<br>(11.18) | 1038<br>(12.10) | 8581<br>(100) |
| 1980-1981 | 1041<br>(6.86) | 5416<br>(36.64) | 3759<br>(25.43) | 471<br>(3.19) | 2124<br>(14.37) | 1999<br>(13.52) | 14783<br>(100) |
| 1990-1991 | 1485<br>(5.52) | 7942<br>(29.72) | 9302<br>(34.58) | 745<br>(2.77) | 3974<br>(14.77) | 3455<br>(12.84) | 26903<br>(100) |
| 2000-2001 | 1371<br>(3.19) | 10125<br>(23.53) | 18467<br>(42.92) | 840 5<br>(1.95) | 6339<br>(14.73) | 5880<br>(13.67) | 43022<br>(100) |
| 2002-2003 | 177<br>(0.37) | 11500<br>(24.17) | 19818<br>(41.64) | 903<br>(1.90) | 8722<br>(18.33) | 6468<br>(13.59) | 47588<br>(100) |
| 2003-2004 | 186<br>(0.41) | 11629<br>(25.78) | 19547<br>(43.34) | 917<br>(2.03) | 6695<br>(14.84) | 6127<br>(13.59) | 45101<br>(100) |
| 2004-2005 | 185<br>(0.40) | 11840<br>(25.85) | 19841<br>(43.32) | 930<br>(2.03) | 6790<br>(14.82) | 6214<br>(13.58) | 45804<br>(100) |
| % Change over 1960-1961 | 143.42 | 445.62 | 1725.30 | 559.57 | 2002.17 | 1478.17 | 992.91 |

**Source:** Co-operative Movement in India, NABARD, Bombay
Figures in parentheses are the percentages to the total)

## Working Capital:

Quite a significant and sizable increases in the working capital was observed at the total level as well as at the level of individual co-operative societies (Table 10.16). A continuous increasing trend in the working capital of non-agricultural credit societies was noticed over a entire period under study excepting the period of early seventies. Both increasing and decreasing trend in the working capital was found in rest of the co-operative societies during the period under study. At the end period of study, out of the total working capital of all the co-operatives societies more than 50 percent was alone shared by non-agricultural credit societies followed by apex and central credit institutions (30.64 percent). This proportion of working capital was ranged between 0.69 to 5.99 percent incase of rest of the co-operative societies.

**Table 10.16: Working capital of the Co-operative Societies**

**(Rs. Lakh)**

| Year | Apex & Central Agricultural & Non-Agricultural Institutions | PACS | Non-Agricultural Credit Societies | Marketing Societies | Productive Enterprises | Social Services & Other Co-operatives | Total |
|---|---|---|---|---|---|---|---|
| 1 | 2 | 3 | 4 | 5 | 6 | 7 | 8 |
| 1960-1961 | 11907 (40.92) | 5812 (19.98) | 4593 (15.79) | 592 (2.03) | 4132 (14.20) | 2060 (7.08) | 29096 (100) |
| 1970-1971 | 61317 (41.14) | 43329 (23.03) | 16806 (11.28) | 3910 (2.62) | 21920 (14.71) | 10749 (7.219) | 149031 (100) |
| 1980-1981 | 183052 (35.13) | 52746 (10.12) | 120881 (23.20) | 18822 (3.61) | 102945 (19.76) | 42591 (8.17) | 521037 (100) |
| 1990-1991 | 880554 (36.26) | 185100 (7.62) | 750784 (30.92) | 33960 (1.40) | 458810 (18.89) | 119137 (4.91) | 2428345 (100) |
| 2000-2001 | 3926678 (29.21) | 698824 (5.20) | 6688685 (49.75) | 151791 (1.13) | 1328835 (9.88) | 649249 (4.83) | 13444062 (100) |
| 2002-2003 | 4678195 (27.06) | 971670 (5.62) | 8531976 (49.36) | 12204 (0.71) | 2584302 (14.95) | 398256 (2.30) | 17286423 (100) |
| 2003-2004 | 5232214 (30.69) | 1046727 (6.14) | 9184721 (53.88) | 121727 (0.71) | 1042940 (6.12) | 418311 (2.45) | 17046640 (100) |
| 2004-2005 | 5437595 (30.64) | 1062366 (5.99) | 9643957 (54.34) | 122919 (0.69) | 1055480 (5.95) | 42644 (2.04) | 17748961 (100) |
| % Change over 1960-1961 | 45567.21 | 1178.84 | 209870.76 | 20663.34 | 25444.05 | 20610.87 | 60901.38 |

**Source:** Co-operative Movement in India, NABARD, Bombay
Figures in parentheses are the percentages to the total)

## Disbursement of Loan:

Tremendous increase in the quantum of loan disbursed by all the co-operative societies was observed over the period under study except the marketing societies (Table 10.17). The proportion of loan advanced in the total loan disbursed by all the societies was more the case of apex and central co-operative societies up to the period of early nineties, later on this proportion was maximum in case of non-agricultural credit societies. The PACS, a major source of providing agricultural credit ranked third in the total quantum of loan advances by these societies. At the end of the study period the non-agricultural credit societies had advanced more than 7 percent out of the total disbursement.

**Table 10.17: Loan disbursed by different Co-operative Societies**

| Year | Apex & Central Agricultural & Non-Agricultural Institutions | PACS | Non-Agricultural Credit Societies | Marketing Societies | Productive Enterprises | Social Services & Other Co-operatives | Total |
|---|---|---|---|---|---|---|---|
| 1 | 2 | 3 | 4 | 5 | 6 | 7 | 8 |
| 1960-1961 | 17538 (64.97) | 4252 (15.75) | 4703 (17.42) | 347 (1.29) | 71 (0.26) | 84 (0.31) | 26995 (100) |
| 1970-1971 | 75103 (68.35) | 13296 (12.10) | 20443 (18.61) | 327 (0.30) | 328 (0.30) | 377 (0.34) | 109874 (100) |
| 1980-1981 | 152751 (52.05) | 24999 (8.52) | 112948 (34.49) | 349 (0.12) | 1208 (0.41) | 12185 (0.42) | 293473 (100) |
| 1990-1991 | 908475 (59.97) | 79966 (5.28) | 517816 (34.18) | 845 (0.06) | 1678 (0.11) | 60295 (0.40) | 1514809 (100) |
| 2000-2001 | 2870373 (39.83) | 373413 (5.18) | 3926791 (54.49) | 1815 (0.03) | 10273 (0.14) | 23476 (0.3) | 7206141 (100) |
| 2002-2003 | 2680617 (32.72) | 382462 (4.67) | 5098643 (62.24) | 351 (0.04) | 8307 (0.10) | 21719 (0.27) | 8192099 (100) |
| 2003-2004 | 1948336 (25.27) | 404991 (5.25) | 5325248 (69.07) | 358 (0.04) | 8696 (0.11) | 22390 (0.29) | 7710019 (100) |
| 2004-2005 | 1933614 (23.95) | 411497 (5.10) | 5696511 (70.56) | 366 (0.04) | 88709 (0.11) | 22614 (0.28) | 8073472 (100) |
| % Change over 1960-1961 | 10925.28 | 9577.73 | 121025.50 | 5.48 | 12392.96 | 26821.43 | 29807.29 |

**Source:** Co-operative Movement in India, NABARD, Bombay

## Overdues:

The data on outstanding loan of the various types of co-operative societies are exhibited in Table 10.18. Overdues means non-payment of loan within stipulated period of Time. This resulted in accumulation of loan with the borrowers. The quantum of outstanding loan is associated with the quantum of loan disbursed. The proportionate change over in 1960-61 showed the non-agricultural credit societies were at the top so far overdues are concerned. Prima-facie it is noted that all the credit co-operatives are facing the problem of overdues of loan.

**Growth of the co-operative societies:**

The compound growth rates (CGR) were worked out for the numbers, members working capital advances and outstanding of loan in respect of all the co-operative societies for the period 1960-61 to 200-01. These CGRs are presented in Table 10.18

**Table 10.18: Outstanding Loans of the Co-operative Societies (Rs. Lakh)**

| Year | Apex & Central Agricultural & Non-Agricultural Institutions | PACS | Non-Agricultural Credit Societies | Marketing Societies | Productive Enterprises | Social Services & Other Co-operatives | Total |
|---|---|---|---|---|---|---|---|
| 1 | 2 | 3 | 4 | 5 | 6 | 7 | 8 |
| 1960-196 | 8714 (51.13) | 4788 (28.10) | 3185 (18.69) | 80 (0.47) | 57 (0.33) | 218 (1.28) | 17042 (100) |
| 1970-1971 | 47803 (54.14) | 28410 (32.18) | 10506 (11.90) | 182 (0.21) | 607 (0.69) | 785 (0.89) | 882934 (100) |
| 1980-1981 | 113677 (49.19) | 36367 (16.60) | 73089 (31.63) | 387 (0.17) | 3033 (1.31) | 2533 (1.10) | 231086 (100) |
| 1990-1991 | 588901 (48.82) | 131021 (10.86) | 459440 (38.09) | 935 (0.08) | 6884 (0.57) | 19101 (1.58) | 1206282 (100) |
| 2000-2001 | 2312013 (34.17) | 530833 (7.85) | 3590811 (53.08) | 18174 (0.27) | 23559 (0.35) | 289949 (4.29) | 6765339 (100) |
| 2002-2003 | 2617031 (31.31) | 700361 (8.38) | 4952200 (59.24) | 4683 (0.06) | 25416 (0.30) | 59300 (0.71) | 8358991 (100) |
| 2003-2004 | 2606451 (29.93) | 743755 (8.54) | 5256134 (60.36) | 6218 (0.07) | 22554 (0.26) | 72801 (0.84) | 8707913 (100) |
| 2004-2005 | 2602250 (29.16) | 815126 (9.14) | 5399101 (60.51) | 6529 (0.07) | 23641 (0.26) | 76441 (0.86) | 8923088 (100) |
| % Change over 1960-1961 | 29762.86 | 16924.35 | 169416.51 | 8061.25 | 41375.44 | 34964.68 | 52259.39 |

**Source:** Co-operative Movement in India – NABARD, Bombay
(Figures in parentheses are the percentages to the total)

The data on CGRs presented in Table 10.20 indicated the positive and significant growth of all the parameters in all the types of co-operative societies over the entire period of time. At

| Table 10.20: Compound Growth Rates | | | | | | | |
|---|---|---|---|---|---|---|---|
| **Year** | **Apex & Central Agricultural & Non-Agricultural Institutions** | **PACS** | **Non-Agricultural Credit Societies** | **Marketing Societies** | **Productive Enterprises** | **Social Services & Other Co-operatives** | **Total** |
| 1 | 2 | 3 | 4 | 5 | 6 | 7 | 8 |
| 2000-01 | 0.99* | 0.99* | 1.06* | 1.03* | 1.06* | 1.07* | 1.04* |
| 2001-02 | 1.09* | 1.03* | 1.07* | 1.04* | 1.07* | 1.06* | 1.05* |
| 2002-03 | 1.15* | 1.11* | 1.20* | 1.14* | 1.15* | 1.14* | 1.16* |
| 2003-04 | 1.13* | 1.11* | 1.18* | 1.04* | 1.12* | 1.15* | 1.14* |
| 2004-05 | 1.14* | 1.11* | 1.19* | 1.13* | 1.15* | 1.19* | 1.15* |

**Source:** Co-operative Movement in India – NABARD, Bombay
* Indicates 5% level of significance

the total level the values of CGR were ranged between 1.04 and 1.16 indicated on an average per annum increase. This increase was observed to be 1.16, 1.15 and 1.14 percent in case of working capital, outstanding of loan and advances respectively, which was by and large the same. The per annum change was maximum for working capital (1.20 percent), advances (1.18 percent) and overdues (1.19 percent) under non-agricultural co-operatives societies.

It concludes that co-operative movement in Maharashtra showed satisfactory performance though the working of the different co-operative credit societies. Rapid changes in the development and growth of non-agricultural credit societies were also noticed. Efforts are needed to minimize the quantum of overdues.

Overall, UCBs have played an important role in the development of the State of Maharashtra. Their success is attributed to zeal an interest of the local level shareholders, directors and high degree of commitment on the part of the employees along with quick decision making and prompt implementation of the ideas as well as the support of the general public. As a part of the competitive race in the banking sector, UCBs have accepted the challenges and adopted the new technology to extend quicker service to the customers. The need of the hour is better NPA management in the co-operative sector by taking some right decisions. The sector can do this with help of comparatively more committed stakeholders. Therefore there is an increase of competition among the services of the UCB and Nationalised Banks.

# CHAPTER 11

# Future of Urban Co-operative Banks - Bharat

There is an all pervasive sense of crises in the UCB sector in spite of the fact that a spectacular growth has been achieved in the last decade. Regulators are concerned at the erosion of public confidence. Crises of confidence in the Urban Co-operative Banks seems the order of the day. The need of the hour is to remedy the situation and not only because of the economic implications and financial considerations, but for the values, the ideals and philosophy of life that we as Bharatiyas cherish from the time immemorial.

Bharat has a unique distinctions of organizing first ever co-operative effort in human history – it was termed as 'Yagnam". The Bharatiya socio-economic order is baseed on co-operation and not competition.

At a conference in January 1978 – Ministers for Co-operation from the States made a resolution envisaging co-operative movement to be autonomous politically neutral, self reliant, free from outside interference and excessive control which is in tune with the Bharatiya socio-economic order.

If we take stock of the situation of this co-operative movement, by and large the performance will be satisfactory, the philosophy and objectives have been achieved to a larger extent but the perceptions in some cases seems to have drifted for a personal gain or a political benefit and position.

Urban Co-operative Banks shall have to work with a concept of Unit Banking, and not to go in for a financial empire, catering to the needs of urban areas only. We should have a targeted class of citizens for their better economic upliftment, a self-employed and self sustained common man.

- Δ 44.4 million Non-Agricultural Enterprises employ 79.7 million persons without any hired worker.
- Δ 17.02 million enterprises are working in organized manufacturing sector having one hired person.
- Δ 9.15 million SSI units are in unregistered sector.
- Δ 97% of the above units have no access to institutional credit. Low productivity, and sub-standard quality is seen in many units. The average capital employed in these unit is Rs. 68,000/- only.
- Δ Only 3% of the above have a credit facility from Banks.

The Banking Sector – Public – Private or foreign is still shy of lending to these units inspite of the emphasis on lending to priority sector for over 35 years. Here is the role of Urban Co-operative Banks to bridge the credit gap.

Share of SSI Credit in Bank credit flow has declined from 17.3% in 1998 to 10.5% in 2003.

Increase in the net bank credit to SSTs which was Rs. 7909 Crores in 1998 has come down to Rs. 737 Crores in 2003 with in over 68000 branches and 400 SSI branches as this is the situation.

The Urban Co-operative Banks have a role to have to find out the credit gap – credit requirement in these units also.

Bank credit is getting skewed towards larger loans. CMIE showed steadily rising share of loans above Rs. 10 crore category from 20% to 41% during 1996-2003.

Credit shyness syndrome can be overcome by UCBs. UCBs should adhere to mutual co-operation, local feel and personal rapport and devise schemes and structures for that area of operation which will provide common infrastructure facilities, develop selected trade, industry or occupation and protect and patronage identical and opted activities.

For efficient and effective economic activities of targeted areas and groups members, UCBs should work as a catalytic agent.

Looking to the above special tasks the former Governor of RBI and Member of Parliament (Dr. Bimal Jalan) in his speech on Banking regulation and amendment and miscellaneous Provision Bill in 2004 in parliament observed, "I think we have to be absolutely sure that you regard the co-operative Banks to be different from say commercial banks. They are more local and they are more self governed. The prudential regime, the owned capital to asset capital ratio should be much softer. But the whole idea is that in the co-operative banking structure, the approach should be much more oriented towards the smaller persons as so on and so forth. It is exactly right and that is what they are supposed to do, if that is to be so sir, it will surprise you to know that I feel that Right Institutions should be the regulator for this agency".

That it is much better to give responsibility of regulating this institution, supervising this institution to those who are actually managing or running it. Supervising guidelines can be laid down but actual inspection, supervision etc. should be entrusted to some other apex institutions.

Prudential standards and norms and NPA norms, licensing CRAR norms or any other rules and regulations should be framed for the UCBs distinctively.

Co-operative bank oin India have been registered, but licence is not being given for a defective provision in Section 56 B of the Act. The act should be amended to pave the way for some other Apex Institution as suggested by Dr. Jalan.

In UCBs that we are charged of a breakdown of corporate governance – what has happened to Global Trust Bank, Centurion Bank is known to all of us. Is it not a fact that Capital support by budgetary means to Public Sector Banks had to be given? Is it not a fact that an amount of Rs. 96,080/- crore are termed as NPAs of these Public Sector Banks, even today.

Of Rs. 17,76,250 crores of Deposits only Rs. 11,41,701 have been given as advances but the lions share goes to metropolitan cities where C/D ratio is 76 to 92% but in small towns it is as low at 20 to 30%.

Another disturbing feature of allowing foreign capital upto 74% in Private Sector banks which comes to nearly 25,000 crores shall give entire Control over deposits of Rs. 3,00,000 crores to foreigners, whose sole aim is to earn profits. Depositors money in some of the UCBs could not be repaid after the Madhavpura scam, scam by Home Trade etc., but if depositors money are lost in these Banks who should be blamed and Entire sector of someone who manages for self-interests.

If this is the case with private Sector Banks then by blame UCBs as a whole and tighten the control by making norms, rules, regulations should not be expected for this sector.

The charge that of political interference can be overcome by not allowing office bearers – Chairman, Vice-Chairman, MD to contest election of any other body, restricting term of office bears and Directors, by providing for direct election and imposing borrowing restrictions for Board Members and relations, simplifying Act and rules to minimize interference by bureaucrats and politicians.

Dual control by RBI and State or Central Government should not be a problem. For organizing, forming and administering let us go by respective State Co-op Act. And rules, but for Financial operations, Monetary management, norms for lending and investment, RBI should prevail till the co-op Bank of India is given the status of a separate Apex body for UCBs.

RBI should see that stringent regulatory measures are in what way stringent for an UCB. Analyse inabilities, then Practical, modified and simplified mandates by given in consonance with co-operative spirit, co-operative philosophy and target group in the area of operation of UCBs.

Natural calamities, down turn in business cycles, recessionary trends in economy adversely affect UCBs and its loanees. This should be looked upon to. Banks are required to reschedule payment, and moratorium on installments and interests, to take relief measures for members to arrange for a seed capital or venture capital at concessional rates to help sustained the economic activity of the members.

In the last 13-14 years of liberalization a sea change is seen in Financial Service Industry. Technology is a threat and opportunity too. Existing Services can be offered more efficiently and New Services can also be offered. Credit risk can be lessoned by the use of technology.

Banking has become a buyers market now in place of a sellers market, the retail customer is important and should be so.

If we look at the domestic loan to GDP ratio, it is only 62.4%, while it is 166.3% in China and 104.5% Indonesia.

Consumer Credit in India is only 7% of GDP, while it is 22% in Indonesia and 70% in U.S.A. Home Loan in India is only 3% of GDP, while it is 44% in Australia and 23% in Malaysia.

This shows a very wide scope of retail Banking which in turn will strengthen the purchasing Power of those who are in need to purchase goods and services. Thereby it will accelerate economic activity and Economic development of the society and country at large.

Private sector banks, public sector banks and foreign banks can do a little. By making the UCB sector only more effective we can achieve these results and therefore Urban Co-operative Banking should spread in every nook and corner of the country. Urban co-operative Banks in India have a strong social content. This apparently, appears at a variance with the basic principles of Market driven economy where maximizing profits is the basic goal. Private sector and multi-nationals are targeting the richer and upper middle class to earn more profit only. Unorganized sector, retail trade, self employed sector of India require uninterrupted credit which is the life line of any economy. Unconfirmed findings show that funds requirement for microfinance in the informal sector of urban areas is in the order of Rs. 1,00,000/- crores per annum.

A huge business Potential for UCBs is available. Let the Reserve Bank of India, Government of India and State Governments respond of the needs, difficulties, requirements and aspirations of UCB's.

**Use of Core Banking Solutions**

UCBs in India cater to the needs of common public as well as business community at large. The structure of these banks is very well defined and one can see variety of composition which vary from one bank to other like membership, shareholders, depositors, creditors etc.

The effect that will take urban co-operative banks to even greater heights will be by utilizing effectively the modules of Information Technology.

The use of core banking can be of immense help and they can curb the operating costs lower, they can also enhance profits by controlling revenue leakages. The members and shareholders of the bank who are Technology savvy can get 24 hours access to their account in any branch of the bank through Internet and Tele-banking.

If core banking is implemented, following things can be done at the earliest:

- The consolidated MIS will be available on line.
- Decisions will be taken on the basis of real time MIC
- Focus on erring branches from audit/vigilance perspective.
- Monitoring ALM especially in the 0-14 day ...... which is typically the most valuable.
- Performances of branches will be monitored on regular basis.
- Head office will have direct control of the branches.

## Conclusions

Evolution of Urban Co-operative Banking movement in India can be traced through three distinct phases which are discussed in the point no. 1.16, i.e., Urban Co-operative Banking Movement concerned with three phases, Phase I 1904-1906, Phase-II 1966-1993 and Phase-III, Post 1993 onwards. Urban Co-operative Banks have played an important role in the development of the State of Maharashtra. The achievement of the Urban Co-operative Banks (UCBs) in Maharashtra is quite admirable. The Urban Co-operative Banking Industry today is in the midst of an IT revolution. A combination of regulatory and competitive reasons have led to increasing importance of total banking automation in the banking industry.

Deregulation and demands of the globalized economy is transforming the banking industry, in this metamorphosis technology, customer service and consolidation have emerged as the key parameters for defining performance and progress of the banks. The growing competition growing expectations led to increased awareness amongst banks on the role and importance of technology in banking. Technology has enabled banks to manage operations without increasing staff strength.

The Information Technology (IT) is also helping a cutting costs by providing cheaper ways of delivering products to customers. Technology has enabled banks to minimize frauds. ATM transactions have facilitated withdrawal of cash by customers. It is unlikely that customers PIN would be traced even in cases where card is lost. Technology has facilitated banks for having built in checks to prevent misuse and or committing of frauds by customers and or in collusion with the staff members of the Bank.

## The Madhavpura Bank Scan

It is relevent to mention the Madhavpura Mercantile Co-operative Bank scam in this chapter. The Bank was established on October 10, 1968 with the primary objective to cater to the banking needs of wholesale grocery traders of Madhavpura area in Ahmedabad. Two years ago, the bank got the status of scheduled bank from Reserve Bank of India, which permitted the bank to expand its banking activities outside Gujarat.

Before RBI superceded the bank's board on March 15, Madhavpura Bank had 12 directors on its board including chairman Ramesh Parikh, CEO and managing director Devendra B Pandya, Ramanlal M Parikh, Natverlal V Desai, Manilal G Shah, Prabhudas Kothari, Natverlal Thakkar, Purshottamdas Shah, Pravinchandra Shah, Dinesh Majumdar, Sevantilal Shah and Pravinchandra Patel.

## Madhavpura Bank before the scam

Madhavpura Bank was conducting normal banking activities with a deposit base of Rs 12 billion, of which Rs 6 billion was from other co-operative banks and organisations, while the rest is from the public. Depositors had put huge deposits after the bank had received scheduled bank status from RBI.

**When did the trouble start?**

RBI restricts co-operative banks from capital market activities. Scheduled co-operative banks are allowed to invest 10 per cent of their net worth in capital markets and allied activities.

Madhavpura's cash reserve ratio (CRR) and statutory liquidity ratio (SLR) were in line with RBI norms in the third quarter ended on December 31, 2000. It is believed that in the last two months, the bank has made extensive and imprudent advances.

Madhavpura Bank chairman Ramesh Parikh had accommodated big bull Ketan Parekh, with whom he had business dealings. It is believed that advances to the tune of Rs 2 billion have been given by Ramesh Parikh to big bull Ketan Parekh.

If this was not sufficient, there are other allegations. Ramesh Parikh's son Vinit Parikh runs a company called Madhur Capital and Finstock Limited, which deals in shares. Parikh is alleged to have paid off his son's dues at the stock market through Madhavpura Bank's fund. According to market sources, Vinit Parikh incurred losses of Rs 500 million in the recent stock market crash.

**The run on the bank**

On March 8, residents of Ahmedabad heard rumours of the bank having granted a bank guarantee of Rs 1.5 billion to Ketan Parekh. This resulted in panic among the depositors who started withdrawing deposits. The next day the bank faced a liquidity crisis and since then the bank has been in trouble.

**Why did RBI supercede the bank board?**

Faced with acute liquidity crisis, Madhavpura Bank has been forced to pull down the shutters of its branches in Ahmedabad and Bombay.

Preliminary inquiry conducted by RBI revealed that the bank's liquidity position was precarious after it issued pay-orders of Rs 650 million to the depositors. However, the bank was not in a position to honour pay-orders amounting to Rs 650 million, which was issued by the bank. This situation forced RBI to recommend Central Registrar of Co-operative Banks to supercede the board of the bank and appoint an Administrator.

**How is Bank of India involved?**

Bank of India is the worst hit in the pay-order scam from Madhavpura Mercantile Co-operative Bank. Madhavpura Bank had issued pay-orders worth Rs 1.2 billion to Ketan Parekh. In turn, Parekh had discounted these pay-orders, which bounced later.

A pay-order is similar to a demand draft but is valid only in the same centre. The issuing bank is required to debit the account of the person who takes the pay-order. Thus the other bank, that receives the instrument, safely presumes that the money has already been recovered by the issuing bank and the instrument is secured. The difference in case of Madhavpura Bank was that the money was not debited, and Vinit Parikh's company Madhur Capital was instrumental in the issuance of large number of pay-orders, that were dishonoured.

# A CASE STUDY

## A Review of Literature

### Introduction

It is a generic term covering computers, broadcasting, telecommunications, data networks and smart components which are being increasingly applied in diverse uses. It can be defined as a total of the electronic means to collect, store, process and present information to the end users in support of their activities, and consists of computer systems, data communication systems, knowledge systems, office systems and consumer electronics. As new forms of IT function inter-dependently , the assembly of IT is an intelligent information network. For example, the merging of communication, home electronics, broadcasting and publishing into all-in-one computer implies that most of the personal computers will come with voice and fax facilities, making telephones and fax machines redundant. Similarly, as digitalization makes compression and decompression of images very easy, communication and broadcasting are becoming integrated digital devices. This is leading to the information super-highway or an electronic communication network which provides connectivity for any conceivable transaction, including trading, banking and financial transactions, organization of production, delivery of services such as airline tickets, books and newspapers, including software and music compact discs (CDs), and home shopping also Internet is one of such a network which provides connectivity between more points than any other, and at a comparatively low cost. Network service providers are available in many developing economies of the ESCAP region, including Bangladesh; China; Guam; Hong Kong, China; India; Indonesia; Malaysia; Pakistan; Philippines; Republic of Korea; Singapore; Taiwan Province of China; and Thailand.

In the 1990s, the commercial dimension of the Internet emerged form is growing business networks. The cohabitant of non-commercial and commercial sectors on the Internet is current reality. This has led to several concerns: there is no governing body or agency, there is no service quality guarantees; there is no security of transactions; information is often unstructured, unsorted and difficult to find; operations that are often unstable; and there are no agreed payment schemes for access. These issues will have to be solved before as Internet can become a real information as a superhighway.

Banking system in modern times has become a part and parcel of life and one cannot do anything without banking. In the age of information technology, the banking systems has reengineered and have changed its total functioning. The use of information technology therefore is seen as a boost for other service sectors like Insurance, Hospitals, postal services, Income tax and other tax payments etc. The banking sector of all type viz., private, public, co-operative have all been in the race for deployment of latest technology solutions. Though, in comparison to other sector banks, co-operative banks are slow in IT deployment, the decision makers are serious on this issue. There is a need to evaluate the technology to use in the individual! Co-operative banks. To begin with the exercise, may need to be divided into three phases, viz., the co-operative banks with computerization of all its branches and head office, the co-operative banks with computerization of selected branches only and co-operative banks with little or no computerization and intending to spread the computerization in their branches and head office activities. The study with defined parameters in terms of Hardware, Application Software, System Software, infrastructure and manpower employed will give an overview of computerization status, and future scope for improvement, and will also help to arrive at conclusion to find out the investment made and the success achieved through computerization. Such exercise will also guide for co-operative banks on the required investments for upgrading them within a set period.

However the exact status on computerization is not easily available in the desired format either at Reserve Bank of India or at Department of cooperation of the respective States. Moreover the co-operative banks do not communicate what their targets for IT are and the actions they have taken to realize them. The RBI also do not maintain details of the information about IT investments made by the co-operative banks. The partial information on investment are made on computerization through yearly balance – sheets of these banks. This can provide expenditure incurred on computerization and information technology including those relating to network associations but such spending often includes investments as well as operational expenditure. IT is not as easy to check whether the investment outlays, where they can be identified are in line with the targets for the periods.

Most of the data about co-operative banking sector in India emanates from the Reserve Bank of India because most of co-operative banks do not have their own Web sites for disseminating information. There is however, no doubt that the expenditure of the banking sector in general on IT has increased in decade or sc in particular after the scare in the year 2000. A number of co-operative banks used the opportunity which afforded by the Y2K scare to update their computerization systems, procure new Y2K compliant computers to extend computerization to cover some front – and back – office operations.

### The Technology Implementation in Co-operative Banks

Customers are demanding access to sophisticated products and services through multiple channels like the telephone, Internet, cellular phones and the ATM. Today, the top managements of several Indian banks are viewing IT as a business enabler and a vital part of their strategy. Banks are revisiting their technology architecture. Even at the risk of being labeled as gross generalizations, it is useful to appreciate at the outset, that in the decade of considerable number of co-operative banks have increased their computerization base by adding Any Branch Banking, Tele Banking and ATM interface each other wherever required. This has facilitated the Co-operative banks to provide efficient and effective customer services and has resulted in economizing on the costs per transaction. Apart from computerization of basis operational systems, the co-operative banks especially the Urban Co-operative banks have also computerized major loan accounts, the investment operations and the clearing system has also been computerized at the head office levels. However still there are gaps in technology of up gradation in the Co-operative banks. The new private sector banks and also the commercial banks have moved their technology base to integrate the information systems and provide bank banking though the core banking solution which is also referred as Centralized banking. There is however no such gap that which is worth noticing between the new private banks and foreign banks in India. It is true that a majority of co-operative banks especially the customers of co-operative banks located in rural and semi-urban areas are not comfortable with computers. There is no reason why technologically laggard banks should impose on their customers high transaction costs in terms of the time and money spent on visits to the branch office and in terms of the delays in completing their transactions. It is also true that a majority of co-operative banks, especially the customers of co-operative banks located in rural and semi-urban areas are not comfortable with computers. There is no reason why technologically laggard banks should impose on their customers high transaction costs in terms of the time and money spent on visits to branch offices and in terms of the delays in completing their transactions. It is also true that the staff of the co-operative banks at operational, middle and top level are not very keen in making use of the information technology to it's fullest extent in their day to day activities which is also one of the main reason for the gap in implementation of information technology.

The technologically laggard Co-operative banks should realize that the economic class and age composition of their customers are already not favourable. Most young professionals, irrespective of their economic class, prefer to do business with technologically advanced banks. It would obviously be difficult for laggard co-operative banks to attract new young customers if they do not increase their investments on IT in right direction with cautious approach.

It is now high time for the decision makers in co-operative banks to realize the need to enlarge the base of computerization and see that the real benefits are delivered at all the levels, customers and stakeholders of the bank. The decision makers have to work out in a definitive time frame for technological advancement in their respective banks with complete involvement in monitoring, controlling and evaluating the progress with set parameters. In the present context these things are missing and therefore every co-operative banks are baring few exceptions needs to give serious thought on this aspect.

**Factors Influencing Technology Initiatives in the Banking Sector**

- Heightened competition, a persistent bearish market, and a general erosion of consumers confidence continue to influence bank's IT decisions.
- Increasing number of banks are looking at IT deployment as a part of a comprehensive IT strategy, rather than as fragmented investments.
- Offering of allied products such as insurance and investment products will drive the growth for total automation.
- In wholesale banking banks will further harness Internet – enabled technologies to improve customers offerings and service.

- New initiatives by the RBI, such as data warehousing, Real Time Gross Settlement, Cheque Truncation will open a lot of new avenues.
- Payment and settlement systems and computerization of the government securities, money market and foreign exchange operations in the banking sector as a whole.

Co-operative movement in India was introduced by enactment of co-operative societies act, 1904. Now the movement crossed a hundred years. There are 5.45 lakh co-operative functioning at various levels with 236.23 million membership and covering 100% villages and 75% rural households. Co-operative banks have emerged as a vital segment of economy in our country. Total deposits in all the co-operative banks were Rs. 17,75,211.30 millions.

The co-operative banking sector in India has recorded a fast growth since 1954. The co-operative credit structure consists of two wings namely short term (ST), and long term (LT). ST credit structure deals with medium term (MT) credit and also for agricultural purposes. It is mostly based on a three tier pattern with state co-operative banks (SCBs) at the apex, district central co-operative banks (DCCDs) at the intermediate, and primary agricultural co-operative societies (PACSs) at village level.

Computerization of co-operative banks in all states is a very difficult task. Very few states like Maharashtra, Karnataka, Gujarat and Goa are leading in computerization. Computerized urban co-operative banks have on-line branches and have succeeded in taking almost all operational activities. Urban co-operative banks are leading in information technology implementation but in state and district co-operative banks are still lagging in computerization drive and are still in infancy stage. Urban co-operative banks in Maharashtra have started their customer services through tele-banking, inter branch transaction and providing 24 hours services through ATM (automated teller machine).

If information technology is used in a scientific manner, following benefits are to be earned by co-operative banks :

⇨ Offering new and innovative financial products,

⇨ Get accurate information which will help in time effectively,

⇨ Maintain good management information system (MIS) and

⇨ Improve head office improvement and reconciliation to improve customer services.

Measuring productivity of emerging information technology in co-operative banking sector is difficult to assess. It is due to difficulty of measuring output accurately when quality of service is changing as a result of such factors as greater convenience, speed, and lower risk. We can identify three reasons for co-operative banks to make an investment in information technology.

- Co-operative banks anticipate reduction in operation costs through such efficiencies as streamlining back office processing and eliminating errors prone to manual input of data.

- They have to see opportunities to serve their existing customers by offering new services, and
- Co-operative banks are able to develop and implement sophisticated risk, information management system and techniques with more powerful data storage and analysis technologies.

Information technology has a significant influence on co-operative banking sector. In fact, it started a new era in banking operation. The emerging super power of information technology reduced the scope of conventional banking with manual operation. Co-operative banking sector is still under-going changes with innovation. It seems several lessons have been emerged in banking on account of this powerful technology.

***Review of Literature***

During the period of research various libraries/ institutions in India were visited. The available related literature in these libraries / institutions was studied which proved to be very useful in getting an insight into the main objective of the study and in finalizing the methodology. Some relevant abstracts from these studies are briefly discussed below:

**B. Janki, (2002)**[1], analyzed in his article that how technology has affected employee's productivity. There is no doubt, in India particularly PSBs will need to use technology to improve operating efficiency and customer services. Harnessing employee technology synergy is crucial for unleashing productivity and reaching out to the huge base of retail customers, who are also dispersed in rural and semi-urban areas. Banks can use technology to address customers needs and improve their interaction with customers keeping in touch through telephone and Internet. The focus on technology will increase like never before to add value to customer service, develop new products, strengthen risk management, and asset liability management and improve profitability. However technology is only an enabling tool and whether banks actually achieve what they want to achieve will be determined by the drive and motivation of their work force and response of the staff.

**Bajaj, (2000)**,[2] highlighted e-commerce related issues due to the adoption of recent IT. In all over the world banks traditional business of taking advances and leading out the proceeds is in terminal decline. The spread of IT and the dramatic advances in financial theory have made it cheaper for big companies to raise the capital markets than from banks. IT is also helping in cutting the costs by providing cheaper ways of delivery products to the customers. ATMs, telephone banking and now the Internet banking. He also explained e-commerce, payment systems as a smart card and electronic cheque etc. He concluded that electronic payment systems are emerging and are getting accepted in the market place. They need to gain both consumer and business acceptance. But the major point emerges from the above discussion that banking stands to radically change. It remains to be seen whether banks use e-commerce and other IT systems to reinvest themselves and gain access to new markets or become extinct as dinosaurs whether advances in technology to create new opportunities for banks or they become extinct.

**Bajaj, (1999),**[3] Information and IT are the key drivers of the Information Age, also referred to as the post industrial society. The Information Age has ushered in a knowledge-based industrial revolution. The business in this era is networked and uses IT to survive in a highly competitive environment. The relationship between IT and business are discussed in this article and it is explained that how IT is affecting business.

**Benton, (1990),**[4] no doubt, with the introduction of IT, it has positively affected the productivity, profitability and efficiency of banks. But many bank frauds are also taking place. They are the hidden threat to financial institutions. He analysed the mechanism that how bank frauds are taking place and how to tackle with them. Dealing with frauds, impact on banking productivity as on-line banking need to invest into resources that manually, scrutinize orders tack down, bad transactions and negotiate in case of trouble with the bank.

**Bhasin, (2001),**[5] he analysed the impact of IT on banking sector. The IT has revolutionized various aspects of our life. It has transformed the repetitive and overlapping systems and procedures, into simple single key pressing technology resulting in speed, accuracy and efficiency of conducting business. The computerization of banks has provided a major push for enabling them to enter into the newer activities. The banking industry has itself prepared, and is strongly emerging to play a major supplementary role in nurturing e-commerce applications which is still in the infancy stage in India. While few of the new generation private banks have taken an early initiative in these innovative areas, other banks are gradually catching up. The author feels that utmost importance is proper security infrastructure should be in place for routing seemed transactions through the public network.

**Bhattacharya (1997),**[6] studied the impact of the limited liberalization initiated before the deregulation of the nineties on the performance of the different categories of banks, using Data Development analysis. Their study covered 70 banks in the period 1986-91. They constructed one grand frontier for the entire period and measured technical efficiency of banks under study. They found PSBs had the highest efficiency among the three categories with foreign and private bank having much lower efficiencies. However PSBs started showing a decline in efficiency after 1987, private banks showed no change and foreign banks showed sharp rise in efficiency. The main results accord with the general perception that in the nationalized era, public sector banks were successful in achieving their principle objective of deposit for loan expansion.

**Birla Institute of Scientific Research,**[7] conducted a study to evaluate performance of nationalized banks I comparison with that of banks in private sector. The emphasis of the study was on the objective of nationalization and their achievements, relative performance of private sector banks and nationalized banks since 1969 and the effect of nationalization on rest of the banking sector. The study reveals that the growth and development in banking after nationalization was not just because of transfer of ownership. It was rather because various incentives and punitive measures were implemented with more vigilance and care after 1969 by the government and the Reserve Bank of India to makes bank fulfill their social responsibilities. Similarly in same spheres even better results were achieved by non-nationalized banks. The performance of private sector banks in the post nationalization period was notworthy, especially because of the odds they faced in securing the growth of the business. The achievement of significantly high growth in deposits, advances and branches etc. clearly showed the high quality of entrepreneur-ship and management of these banks.

**Clifford, (1996)**,[8] studied the impact of IT on the financial services. Due to the introduction of IT, the role of banks, mutual funds and insurance companies were changing. The banks will never be the same again. The dimensions of banking business were changing in the new economy.

**Federick & Phil. (2000)**,[9] analyzed the E-Loyalty. With the introduction of IT, it had created many doubts and questions. In the rush to build Internet business, many executives concentrate all their attention on attracting customers rather than retaining them. According to them, the unique economics of e-business make customer loyalty more important than ever.

**Hussain, (1988)**,[10] also highlighted the importance of IT in various sectors. In the introduction of any new technology or system various organizational, financial and functional problems are faced in the initial stages. People are generally reluctant to accept new system, howsoever beneficial it may be. Such various issues which were involved in computerization have been critically and vividly discussed.

**Johri & Jauhari, (1994)**,[11] also analyzed the importance of computers in banking industry. He also analyzed various issues related to computerization in banks in India. Whether banks use e-commerce or other IT systems to invest themselves, gain access to new markets or become extinct as dinosaurs whether advances in technology create new opportunities for banks, or they become extinct.

**Kaveri, (2001)**,[12] this study attempts to extend the study conducted by the Varma Committee more specifically to ascertain whether enough signals of weakness were indicated much before the event. The present study considers 1998-99 as the years of even when the Varma Committee identified weak banks strong banks and potential weak banks. This study considers nine efficiency parameters which are computed, based on the data collected from the Reserve Bank of India Publications. The parameters include :

- Capital Adequacy Ratio.
- Net Non-Performance Assets/Net Adequacy.
- Net profit/Total Assets.
- Gross Profit/Working Funds.
- Net Interest Income/Total Assets.
- Interest Expended/Total Assets.
- Intermediation Cost/Total Assets.
- Provisions and Contingencies/Total Assets.

The above parameters focus on two major concern of banks, i.e., loan default and profitability whereas the Varma Committee covered all aspects of financial health. This article has given some evidence to indicate that no bank can be weak or potentially weak all of a sudden. There is a gradual deterioration in the position of loan default and profitability. Hence it is suggested to develop a ratio model to arrive at a single score to classify banks into three categories i.e., weak, strong and potentially weak.

**Nair, (2000)**,[13] the technological advancements achieved very recently in the field of computerization have unfolded many areas of innovations in our living styles. The world of banking is fast shedding its ancient image and entering from 'brick-and mortar' model to 'click' model. The virtual banking is rising in a total revolution in the banking transactions.

The author realized that those banking and financial services provider, who switch over to the electronic environment in the quickest possible time frame alone will be able to survive. The introduction of Cyber Law is also expected to boost the E-Commerce and E-Banking further in the days to come. And the writing on the wall rather on the net is clear for the Indian Banking Industry : E-Banking has come to stay.

**Niranjan, (2000)**,[14] studied the changing business dimensions of banks due to the introduction of IT. Internet is also taking banks in directions other than loans and deposits. Banking in India will never be the same again. E-Banks have started E-Commerce and many banks are entering in insurance sector.

**Pathrose, (2001)**,[15] banking the world over is undergoing a rapid and radical transformation due to the all – pervasive influence of It and breath taking developments in the technology of telecommunications and electronic data processing. The winds of change are blowing in India too which implies the integration of information system with communication technology which has radically altered the traditional ways of doing banking business and allowed banks to wipe out the difference in time as well as distance. It is in this context his article an attempt to trace the present status of hi-tech banking in India, visualize its prospects and look at the challenges and problems in the tracks to be traversed. He concludes that in the scenario of severe competition and escalation expectation of customers for newer products and alternative delivery channels, the contours of banking are being redefined. The key to the survival of banks, therefore is retention of customers loyalty by providing them with value added services tailored to their needs, using state-of-the-art of IT. There is no way a bank can remain lukewarm to hi-tech and yet hope to grow. It is a choice between survival and extinction.

**Rangarajan, (2000)**,[16] in his inaugural address at the 4$^{th}$ Bank Educationists Conference on March 6, 2000 at Hyderabad, explained the importance of IT in the financial sector. At a time when banking the world over is under going a radical transformation due to all pervasive influence of IT. Banking education and training must not only respond to the fast changing needs of the financial system but also become proactive, and play the role of a 'Change agent' and bring about a 'skills revolution' in the banking industry. Banks will begin to function increasingly under competitive pressures. In meeting the new challenges, the use of computer, Internet and communication technology will assume a critical role. Bank customers are also becoming very demanding, and it's extensive use of technology that will enable banks to satisfy adequately the requirements of customers. The use of technology is also improving the availability of information for management decision and for monitoring operations.

**Rao, (2002)**,[17] analyzed the impact of new technology on banking sector. The advent of technology both in terms of computers and communication has been changing totally the ways, and doing banking business. Technology has also opened new vistas, and in turn brought new possibilities every day for doing the same work differently and in most cost-effective manner. Tele-banking and Internet banking are making forays such that branch banking may give to home banking. In order to protect their profitability, the banks need to address urgently the following emerging areas :

- Product development and marketing skills.
- Modern credit management skills.
- New risk management practices.
- Skills for operating in electronic environment.
- New internal audit skills in a changing business environment.
- New focus on customers and his needs.

**Rao, (1999)**,[18] explained the role of IT in the financial service industries. Technology is bringing about important evolutionary changes in the investment industry, giving portfolio managers greater control for their activities and even more time to spend on developing insights into the stock they own.

**Sabnani, (2000)**,[19] analyzed the importance of "Universal Banking" in India. Globalization, Liberalization and Deregulation of financial markets in many developed and developing countries have resulted in increased disinter-mediation and have made commercial banks vulnerable to interest rate risk. Relaxing exchange controls, adopting uniform accounting practices in regard to income recognition, assets classification and provisioning norms and prescribing capital adequacy norms has further aggravated the position. Now the developments in IT and telecommunications are allowing international pooling of financial resources thereby spreading the risk across more than one market.

**Sarkar and Das, (1997)**,[20] compare performance public, private and foreign banks for the year 1994-95 by using measures of profitability, productivity and financial management. They find PSBs comparing poorly with the other two categories. However, they are cautious that no firm inferences can be derived from a comparison done for a single year.

**Saxena, (2000)**,[21] also analyzed the importance of IT in the banking sector. According to him, the future promises will be even more exciting, interesting and challenging. The Internet has enabled us to talk to each customer as an individual, with different needs and requirements. IT will affect the productivity and profitability of the banks.

**Shah, (1977)**,[22] in his various papers discussed bank profitability and productivity. He expressed concern about increased expenses and overhead. Slow growth in productivity and efficiency is wasteful work of banks, that higher profitability can result from increased spread and that innovations have a limited role. He favored written job descriptions for improvement of staff productivity. He also emphasized reduction of costs, creation of a team spirit improvement in the management for improving bank profitability and productivity.

**Shanti, (1984)**,[23] has made a pioneering attempt to examine the issues relating delivery of customer services in Indian Banks as against the backdrop of a sound conceptual framework. She was provided with empirical analysis of bank employees job behaviour and its relationship with bank services delivery. She has found that lack of job motivation, lack of freedom at branch level, lack of leadership qualities among bank managers, job security etc. have resulted in poor of quality customer services in Indian banks.

**Shapiro, (2000)**,[24] studied the affects of cyberspace which are evolving in ways that threaten privacy and other constitutional rights. It's eroding the liberty. The character of cyberspace is still up for grabs and different user environments yield widely difference experience. The nature of cyberspace may flip instead of promoting free and open exchange. It may end up controlling our lives in ways we have never imagined.

**Shastri, (2001)**,[25] analyzed the effect and challenges of new technology for banks. Technology has brought a sea of change in the functioning of the banks. The earlier manual system of preparation of voucher, etc. is slowly being automated thereby saving a lot of time and effort. The use of ATMs and introduction of more than in the past, especially in the Post – VRS Scenario.

**Singhal's (1987)**,[26] is yet another important study about customer services in Indian banks. This study is based on a research project of Sushila Singhal's, sponsored by Shri Ram's enter for Industrial Relations in New Delhi. The study itself has two objectives : (a) "An adequate and systematic descriptive analysis and explanation of customer services". This study is based on a broad sample of 528 bank employees (both officers and clerks) and 1,427 customers selected by a purpose – wise procedure. She had adopted a stage – wise methodology to select banks for the case study. In this first stage, she has chosen six banks and in the second stage five branches of the six banks for a more intensive study. The most important findings of this study are :

- There are considerable differences between different banks in regard to employees job involvement and motivation, customer loyalty and identification of banks and branches employe attitudes towards bank customers and colleagues, etc.
- The demographic and psychological variables were identified and their relationship with employees job performance and customer service is explained.
- It is also found that there is no correlation ship between service efficiency and customers satisfaction; further she has also not found any systematic relationship between the size of bank branch and customer satisfaction. She has also elaborately discusses the

implications of her findings for efficient bank management. The important merit of her study is that it is based on multi-method and multi-variable approach to explain the bank employees job behavior.

Swami, (2001),[27] studied the comparative performance of different bank groups since 1995-96 to 1999-2000. During that period, IT was new competition and deregulation took place. He studied three important aspects :

- What has been the impact of financial sector reforms on the structure of the Indian banking system?
- What are the advantages reaped by some of the new Indian private and foreign banks vis-à-vis PSBs?
- Whether new competition has enhanced the overall efficiency of the bank system?

An attempt is made in this paper, in the context of financial sector reforms, to identify factors which could have led to changes in the position of individual banks in terms of their share in the overall banking industry. He analyzed the share of rural branches, average branch size, trends in bank's profitability, share of PSAs, share of wages in expenditure provision and contingencies, net not performance asset in net advances, spread, has been calculated. He concludes that in many respect NPSCs is much better than PSBs even though they are better than foreign sector banks.

**Vegesh, (2000)**,[28] highly appreciated the NPSBs which have adopted IT. The NPSBs, with their state-of-the-art technology and grandiose plans to make in-roads into e-banking, are now darlings of the stock markets. Banks like HDFC and ICICI are foraying into net banking which offers great convenience to the customers on one hand and results in lower transaction costs for the banks on the other hand.

**Vijay, K. & S. Annamalai, (2002)**,[29] they considered that human resources is considered to be the most valuable asset of any organization. It is essential to ensure that the human resource is utilized to a maximum level in order to realize the organizational goals. These articles deals with the crucial area of HRD/HRM under the had 'job satisfaction' and its significance in banking sector, factors associated with job satisfaction and dissatisfaction, present level of job satisfaction in different banking sectors etc. It also includes a measurement study conducted by the author and tries to provide some useful practical suggestions to improve the level of job satisfaction in banking sector in order to enhance the higher level of productivity. In this study out of 100 represents in SBI and its associate banks only 25% of them have higher level of job satisfaction, 52% of them have medium level of job satisfaction and 23% of them have low level of job satisfaction. In nationalized banks out of 100 represents only 27% of them have higher level of job satisfaction 48% of them have medium level of job satisfaction and 25% of them have low level of job satisfaction. The study also reveals that out of 100 represents in private sector banks only 28% of them have high level of job satisfaction, 22% of them have medium level of job satisfaction. It could be observed from the study, that the higher level of job satisfaction ratio is 25% in SBI and its associate banks, 27% in nationalized banks and 28% in private sector banks. Hence this study confirms that the level of job satisfaction ratio is higher in the private sector banks than nationalized banks and SBI and its associate banks.

**Verghese, (1983)**,[30] considered that the work on profits and profitability of Indian commercial banks in the seventies was a comprehensive study on bank's profitability. It provided a useful analysis of the income statements of commercial banks during 1970-1979 but cost of usable funds, the author used the absolute amount of establishment cost, and otherwise expenses instead of proportionate amounts. But while calculating the net yield on advances the author has taken into account the cost of servicing of loans and advances.

**Varma, (2000)**,[31]analysed the impact of IT on PSBs and NPSBs in her article 'Banking on Change'. The IT is a threat for the PSBs. It has to be a complete face off for the PSBs. With the business per employee, even for the front-run PSBs, a mere fraction of that of NPSBs, the PSBs have to do a lot on improving their productivity and efficiency. NPSBs are fully computerized and providing services on Internet. Especially, ICICI Bank, HDFC bank is very active on this front and is concentrating on Internet and e-commerce to offer their clientele a whole range of products under one roof. New banks like GTB., BOP, IDBI and UTI bank are not lagging behind. While some of them are concentrating on expansion and modernization, some are focusing on mergers and acquisitions for their growth.

**Wadikar, (1980)**,[32] conducted a study of private sector banking in India since 1969. He discussed bank profitability in terms of assets and liability portfolio management and touched upon the trends in income and expenses of the private sector banks. The study revealed that performance of private sector scheduled commercial banks was better than public sector during 1969-76. The branch expansion was at a higher rate in private sector than in public sector banks and their spread in semi-urban and rural areas was also better.

**Zahir, (1980)**,[33] recommended transfer of pricing as one of the important parameter for evaluating branch level performance of commercial banks. The determination of transfer price for branches should be based on the concept of opportunity cost. The application of the concept of transfer price mechanism for valuation of the branch level performance will give more meaning to profit statement of branches.

**Patil, (2006)**,[34] observed that the IT based solutions for any business has become a common phenomenon in today's age of computers. The banking sector has emerged as one of the leading sector in computerization and co-operative banks are no exception to this. Even for this matter the primary credit societies have also shown a remarkable progress in introducing computerization for their various activities in some of the States like (Kerala) and (Maharashtra). The co-operative banks in Maharashtra, Gujarat, Karnataka, and Goa are leading in computerization. The success of computerization in Urban Co-operative banks in these is on the higher side than the State level and District level co-operative banks. The co-operative banks have dual control of Reserve Bank of India / NABARD and Co-operative Department.

The banking sector has seen major changes in the recent past, and this has resulted in large number of new foreign and private banks competing in the Indian market place with both the Public Sector banks and co-operative banks. The main difference between the co-operative banks and these banks is Branch automation vs. Bank automation. Banking technology, the world over has concentrated on deployment of applications and services on their corporate network with the primary objective of providing state of the art customer services.

**Patil, (2000)**,[35] highlighted the light of the liberalization policy of the government unleashing many forces of competition, the Co-operative Banks cannot afford to ignore computer technology and must adapt to the use of computers in order to modernize themselves and prepare to face the future challenges. Computerization is of paramount importance and computers are being increasingly used in all walks of life.

In order to computerize, it is essential to develop an integrated computerized system. This integrated system will consist of many sub-systems, all of them sharing data as per requirements and the sub-systems will be independent systems by themselves. This led to a inter-linking between various sub-systems. The banks need to follow a pattern of computerizing one sub-systems at a time and ensure the desired results with the facility for future changes as per the user requirements with scalability and upgradability to the possible extent.

**Kulkarni, (2006)**,[36] observed that banks in India have appreciated and have realized the power of Information Technology and are fast gearing up to build business activities around it. Bank Wide Automation or Total bank Automation has become a buzzword from IT and banking point of view. In India, only few banks have gone ahead and successfully implemented the Bank Wide Automation, consisting of retails branches, head office, service branch, foreign exchange branch, DP branch automation etc. While majority of the banks have completed the first phase of Bank Wide Automation by computerizing their large to medium size branches, there are still some banks that have yet to start the Branch Automation. Nevertheless, it is also important to note that the current computerization level is not sufficient to be compared to the international market.

The author also highlighted the importance of computerization in banking industry and difficulties being faced by individual banks in choosing software as also vendors. The author is of the opinion that success of bank computerization lay in right selection of software products, setting up a dedicated I.T. team, effective liasioning with vendor and keeping I.T. team updated on the latest technologies.

**1**,[37] observed that co-operative banking system in India consists of Rural and Urban Co-operative banks. Rural banking system has got a hierarchical structure like State Co-operative Banks, District Central Co-operative banks and Primary Agricultural Credit Societies. Urban co-operative banks for that matter are independent entities. In recent past Government has opened sectors like Banking and Insurance to private sector companies as well. In such a scenario co-operative banks have to compete with these private sector banks in addition to public sector banks. This competition is mostly going to be based on providing better customer service and increase the reputation of bank. Customer services has gained such a importance which was never before so much considered. For providing better customer service, Information Technology plays an important role. Private sector banks are very aggressive in adopting and implementing new technology. It is because of technology that they are able to give services like 24 x 7 days banking through ATM, Any where in banking, Internet Banking and most latest Mobile banking is available. In order to be a competitor in such a situation Co-operative banks also have to think on same line.

**Bakshi, (2006)**,[38] observed that the increasing use of computers prompted by phenomenal development Information and related technology during last four decades, has also changed the references of organizational security aspects. Today, it has become essential to have a reference framework for the seem, and control for Information, and related Technology. Managers, controllers, regulators, Government authorities, law makers, users and service providers should understand and implement the controls to assure security organizational assets that uses Information Technology.

Effective management of Information Technology (IT) is foremost and critical for the success and survival of any organization. This criticality arises from :

- Changing role of Information technology in conducting business operations.
- The increasing dependence on information systems.
- The increasing vulnerabilities and a wide spectrum of cyber threats.
- The scale and cost of the current and future investments in information technology.
- The potential for technologies to change organizations' business processes procedures and practices.
- Probability that technology can create new business opportunities at reduced costs.
- Information travels through cyberspace without the constraints of time, distance and speed.

For a successful organization, to understand and manage the risks associated with implementing new technologies is essential. Thus, management needs to have an appreciation for and a basic understanding of the risks and constraints of IT in order to provide effective direction and adequate controls. While information systems security and control helps manage risks, it does not eliminate them.

**Velanganni, (2005)**[39], observed that the silent introduction of LPG policies have agreeably impressed and affected functions, objectives, and operations of many co-operative organizations including co-operative banking sector (system). Information systems and communication or information technology enabled services (ITES) play a very crucial role for organizational adaptability to accept emerging changes and modify their strategies, inputs, communication, planning, organizing, control, coordination, and technologies as required by dynamic global changes exacerbated by new economic milieu. Only viable option for co-operative banking organizations is to computerize and capture benefits of new centenary by offering high quality services and products. Therefore, modernization and upgradation of technology through domestic research and development for continuous improvement in the quality of products/services becomes critical at this juncture. By installing e-governance structures such as internet and information technology, co-operative sector can effectively and efficiently handle operations of functional areas of management, materials management, human resource management, personnel management, office management, MIS and IT. The banks can provide on-line services because of dynamic revolution in information technology and communication system which have made everything possible in e-banking world. Even purchase (e-purchase), payment (e-payment) customers transactions, operations of all types, etc. are made electronically with complete uses of latest methods of ICT. Moreover, through e-governance mechanization and computerization process, performance of co-operative banking organizations will be made effective and efficient in 21st century.

**Edwinraj, (2005)**,[40] observed that the co-operative movement in India has crossed a hundred years, a milestone and it is largest movement in the world. Among various sectors of co-operative movement, banking has recorded fast growth since submission of All India Rural Credit Survey Committee (AIRCSC) report (1954). The role of information technology in co-operative banks is significant in establishing and maintaining contact with potential customers. It can be harnessed to great advantage of banks. Rapid developments in communication and network system is set to change operational environment of co-operative banks. An effective and efficient management information system (MIS) can make a major impact on deposits, loans, and other services provided by co-operative banks. Technological innovations, both internal and external, brought about changes in co-operative banks. Its adoption has resulted in development of e-banking, on-line banking, internet banking, telephone banking, and automated teller machine. Co-operative banks shall have to change their vision, mission, strategy, and governance in the context of information technology. It has a lot of influence on co-operative banking transactions, and ensures quick service with low transaction cost to the customers. Adoption of information technology in co-operative banks will help them to face competition and new challenges to meet customers expectations in the context of globalization and structural readjustment.

**Gulati, (2005)**,[41] analysed that with the fast prevalence of the World Wide Web, the deployment of information systems on to the World Wide Web especially in banks in order to employ the WWW as a strategic tool to support business operations is becoming indispensable. In this paper, we have discussed the concept of web based information systems as applicable to banks, and also provided a WIS model as well as a structured methodology for the implementation of web based information systems in banks.

There are a number of issues involved that need to be taken into consideration to ensure a smooth and successful implementation of the model:

- The branch being the originator of the major chunk of the information required for WIS, it is necessary to conduct a detailed study of the precise items of information to be transmitted. After the field-level study is made, it is necessary to map this information to those departments.
- Integration – the integration of the Web based information systems with the transaction processing systems and other systems and databases needs to be smooth.
- As WIS handles huge amount of sensitive information that support critical functions apart from decision support and other managerial activities, the threat of risk security breach needs to be mitigated by incorporating a robust security framework.
- Ensuring the basic prerequisite of proper connectivity in the branches of the banks is crucial to implement the web based information systems. The computerization of all the branches of the bank is a gargantuan task and yet essential.
- Change management and culture management are necessary for educating the organization and various users to cope with change and make the transition to the new systems smooth as possible.

The analysis of the development of WWW based information systems within the bank's context has exposed many implementation issues resulting from the complex interaction of technology at organizational culture. A strategic approach required to ensure the smooth implementation WIS and thereby enhance effective functional toward becoming information oriented at a intelligent organizations. The authors are currently involved with one of the leading public sector banks to implement this model.

**Das, (2007)**,[42] observed that Agriculture continued to be the bulwark of Indian economy and also a decisive drive of GDP growth. It is playing the central role in all strategies for planned socio-economic development of the country. Rapid growth in agriculture is essential not only to achieve self-reliance at national level but also for household food security and to bring about equity in distribution of income and wealth resulting in rapid reduction in poverty. Credit is one of the key factors in agricultural development. In the context of technological upgradation and commercialization of agriculture, which is envisaged for the coming years, it is necessary that credit support to agricultural sector be stepped up considerably.

On the other hand Information and Communication Technology (ICT) has emerged as an effective facilitator in the development of any society and is a prime driving force in the growth of economies worldwide. In a vibrant democracy like India, which is marked by plethora of languages and diverse cultures, ICT assumes greater significance in delivery of credit to the farm sector cutting across various linguistic barriers.

Though the government as well as the banks has in a big way tried to orient various practices to reach the farmers through numerous activities, there still exists gaps and extensive work needs to be done to achieve progressive development in agriculture. The one major area that needs to be emphasized is the application of information and Communication Technology (ICT) and IT Enabled Services (ITES) as the improvised delivery channel to finance agriculture. These initiatives could bring a change in the systems of lending to this important sector of the economy by the banks with better efficiency and at a lesser cost.

This article reviews the state of existing delivery channels of the Commercial Banks, discusses the impact of new information and communication technology on the lending process and proposes models to improve efficiency of the delivery channels for better credit dispensation to agriculture sector.

**Kakkad, (2006),**[43] analyzed that the trend of Non-Branch Service Delivery in banking started with the growth popularity of electronic payment services in the 1970s in the US. It was a technology push, which enabled banking services to be started with Electronic Funds Transfer (EFT). Then came credit cards, ATMs and smart cards which were next in the evolutionary history, gradually, with the advance of computing technology, telephone banking and Computer Technology Integration (CTI) has become a powerful medium of delivering banking services. The newest product is Internet banking, where the technology and other issues are still under evolution. All this technology is now finding widespread use and acceptance in India.

These new technologies have broken the paradigm of branch-banking. Customers, whether individuals or corporate, no longer have to go to the bank to do their business. It can be done from home, using the PC or the telephone, or at the shopping markets, using plastic money. Most of the progressive players in this industry have invested in setting up state-of-the-art computer networks, along with satellite communication links. This has enabled these players to get all their bank branches connected together. As a result, fund transfers have become instantaneous within the branches of the same bank, moreover to do his/her banking at any branches, irrespective of which branch the customer may have opened his/her own accounts. This is the flexible financial supply chain.

**Patil, (2007),**[44] observed that to achieve proper automation, banks will have to create adequate infrastructure and keep themselves abreast of development in the field of information technology and integration of various communication networks. They would also have to undertake periodical review of development and upgradation of various communication systems ad introduce appropriate technologies suiting to their requirements. Simultaneously, they would have to make arrangement for educating and training the bank staff and also the customers so as to enable them to adapt to changes on the technology front. It would also be desirable to draw up another perspective plan of computerization of banking industry after the current plan comes to an end in 1994. This should, inter alia, consider all other relevant and allied issues.

**Bakshi, (1999),**[45] observed that Electronic commerce (besides its technological dimensions) raises legal issues of practical importance for the commercial world. These legal issues arise mainly because traditional legal phraseology does not expressly address itself to matter which is transmitted invisibly and intangibly. The law of contracts particularly needs attention in this context. It is probable that its present language will receive liberal interpretation, so as to recognize electronic commerce. At the same time, legislative clarification will be desirable.

**Naik, (2007)**,[46] observed that the business continuity is so vital to business success now that it can no longer remain a concern of the IT/IS department alone. The time, money and customer confidence that can be lost due to downtime or business interruption can seriously damage a company of any size – and the reputation of its key executives – both short and long term.

The risk are even greater for e-Business and companies that operate in 24 x 7 x 12 mode. To assure survival, companies must adopt proven business strategies to protect both business processes and vital information and implement corporate-wide programs for continuity and recovery management.

Today's businesses face risks from multiple sources due to its very nature of operation. Risks can be managed, but even the best-designed system may be a victim of a natural or a man-made disaster. Every organization should have a contingency planning process and a formal disaster recovery plan. The critical business operations need to survive a disaster or the firm itself may be causality.

**Kakkad, (2006)**,[47] observed that the internet is truly a revolutionary medium that exceeds the capabilities of other media. It is already being adopted at a rate that far outpaces any other channel that has preceded it.

Without question, companies ignore the Internet at their peril. The Internet effectively lowers the barriers to entry by virtue of its low cost, convenience, and ubiquity. Thus, new competitors enter various segments.

E-Commerce has enabled Microsoft, an operating-system vendor only five years ago, to also deal in automobiles and travel services. Similarly, Amazon.com, a company that did not exist until just a few years ago, is the leader in the online book retailing segment. Major Booksellers have thus been compelled to follow with e-commerce solutions. Companies in industries vulnerable to e-commerce alternatives simply cannot afford to ignore the Internet.

The growth of Web users is exponential globally, due to the comparable growth in bandwidth and ebbing security concerns. E-commerce is bound to be the mainstream of business, worldwide.

A review of the literature on the subject indicated that the introduction of IT is very vital for the present banking system. The concept of IT in its present form, is new, no comprehensive study has yet been made regarding the impact of IT on Co-operative banking industry. No doubt some articles in the leading newspapers, magazines and journals have highlighted the importance of IT in banking industry, especially in Co-operative banking.

Hence there is a need to examine the impact of IT on the growth and performance of Urban Co-operative Banks on one hand and on the other hand, it is equally important to assess the customers satisfaction levels in the Urban Co-operative Banks where this IT is used. Therefore this used is concerned with mainly two aspects (i.e., performance of these banks and customers in these banks).

# Research & Methodology

## Introduction

The Information technology revolution has brought about a fundamental transformation in financial and banking sector. It has become the most important factor for dealing with the intensifying competition and the rapid proliferation of financial innovations. It has rising volumes of transactions, falling margins and more empowered customer expectations. In particular, there are four key areas in which the financial system has experienced the benefits of the technology revolution, viz., product development, market infrastructure, risk control and market reach (Jalan Bimal 2002).

The Urban Co-operative Banks (Urban Co-operative Banks), an important component of the banking system in the country has been able to remain insulated from the consequences of banking sector reforms. The challenges thrown up by the reforms in the banking sector, in a way, forces Urban Co-operative Banks to re-position themselves in the increasingly competitive environment. It needs no emphasis that only well managed Urban Co-operative Banks will be able to withstand the onslaught of the competition. In their strategies for survival and growth, Urban Co-operative Banks must place weight on information technology for better banking business and enhanced customer satisfaction (Remesha K, 2001). However, many Urban Co-operative Banks are lagging behind in this regard and thus, not in a position to even retain their market share. Further, the entry of Public Sector Banks (PSBs) and newly established Private Sector Banks to the foray of Urban Co-operative Banks i.e., retail segment, has put the latter in a very tight position. While the newly established Private Sector Banks have entered the market with the state of art technology, the PSBs with their size advantages have threatened the very existence of Urban Co-operative Banks. The ongoing reforms in the banking sector, particularly tightening prudential standards have only added to the woes of Urban Co-operative Banks. In view of this scenario, it is said that one of the methods of enhancing the competitiveness and also improve the efficiency of Urban Co-operative Banks, is to increasingly adopt information technology. Needless to mention, information technology in banking offers several advantages to Urban Co-operative Banks. On the one hand, application of information technology will improve the banking operations such as improved efficiency, profitability, productivity, higher levels of customer satisfaction, quick services etc. on the other, facilitates decision making at the branch and bank level through better Management Information System (MIS) and improved back-office operations.

## Review of Literature

During the period of research various libraries/ institutions in India were visited. The available related literature in these libraries / institutions was studied which proved to be very useful in getting an insight into the main objective of the study and in finalizing the methodology. Some relevant abstracts from these studies are briefly discussed below:

**Benton, (1990)**, no doubt, with the introduction of IT, it has positively affected the productivity, profitability and efficiency of banks. But many bank frauds are also taking place. They are the hidden threat to financial institutions. He analyzed the mechanism that how bank frauds are taking place and how to tackle with them. Dealing with frauds, impact on banking productivity as on-line banking need to invest into resources that manually, scrutinize orders tack down bad transactions and negotiate in case of trouble with the bank.

**Bhasin, (2001)**, has analyzed the impact of IT on banking sector. The IT has revolutionalised various aspects of our life. It has transformed the repetitive and overlapping systems and procedures, into simple single key pressing technology resulting in speed, accuracy and efficiency of conduction business. The computerization of banks has provided a major push for enabling them to enter into the newer activities. The banking industry has itself prepared and is strongly emerging to play a major supplementary role in nurturing e-commerce applications which is still in the infancy stage in India. While few of the new generation private banks have taken an early initiative in these innovative areas, other banks are gradually catching up.

**Birla Institute of Scientific Research**, conducted a study to evaluate performance of nationalized banks in comparison with those of banks in private sector. The emphasis of the study was on the objective of nationalization and their achievements, relative performance of private sector banks and nationalized banks since 1969 and the effect of nationalization on rest of challenges and problems in the tracks to be traversed. He concludes that in the scenario of severe competition and escalation expectation of customers for newer products and alternative delivery channels, the contours of banking are being redefined. The key to survival of banks therefore is retention of customers loyalty by providing them with value added services tailored to their needs, using state-of-the-art IT. There is no way a bank can remain lukewarm to hi-tech and yet hope to grow. It is a choice between survival and extinction.

**Rangarajan, (2000)**, in his inaugural address at the 4th Bank Educationists Conference on March 6, 2000 at Hyderabad, explained the importance of IT in the financial sector. At a time when banking the world over is under going a radical transformation due to the all pervasive influence of IT, Banking education and training must not only respond to the fast changing needs of the financial system but also become proactive and play the role of a 'Change agent' and bring about a 'skills revolution' in the banking industry. Banks will begin to function increasingly under competitive pressures. In meeting the new challenges, the use of computer, Internet and communication technology will assume a critical role. Bank customers are becoming very demanding and it is the extensive use of technology that will enable banks to satisfy adequately the requirements of customers. The use of technology would also improve availability of information for management decision and for monitoring operations.

**Rao, (2002)**, has analyzed the impact of new technology on banking sector. The advent of technology both in terms of computers and communication has been changing totally the ways of doing banking business. Technology has opened new vistas and in turn brought new possibilities every day for doing the same work differently and in most cost-effective manner. Tele-banking and Internet banking are making forays such that branch banking may give to home banking. In order to protect their profitability, the banks need to address urgently the following emerging areas :

- Product development and marketing skills.
- Modern credit management skills.
- New risk management practices.
- Skills for operating in electronic environment.
- New internal audit skills in a changing business environment.
- New focus on customers and his needs.

**Rao, (1999)**, has explained the role of IT in the financial services industry. Technology is bringing about important evolutionary changes in the investment industry, giving portfolio managers greater control for their activities and even more time to spend on developing insights into the stock they own.

**Kakkad, (2006)**, observed that the internet is truly a revolutionary medium that exceeds the capabilities of other media. It is already being adopted at a rate that far outpaces any other channel that has preceded it.

Without question, companies ignore the Internet at their peril. The Internet effectively lowers the barriers to entry by virtue of its low cost, convenience, and ubiquity. Thus, new competitors enter various segments.

E-Commerce has enabled Microsoft, an operating-system vendor only five years ago, to also deal in automobiles and travel services. Similarly, Amazon.com, a company that did not exist until just a few years ago, is the leader in the online book retailing segment. Major Booksellers have thus been compelled to follow with e-commerce solutions. Companies in industries vulnerable to e-commerce alternatives simply cannot afford to ignore the Internet.

**Problem Definition (Selection of Topic)**

The technology in banking has been changing a majority of Urban Co-operative Banks, however has not been able to keep pace with the changing technological advancements. In addition, the application of information technology is rather partial in the case of Urban Co-operative Banks and focusing mainly on automation of branches. Apart from these, there are several other constraints such as lack of skilled manpower, lack of vision / direction from the board of directors, obsolete hardware and software and other cultural factors encompassing customers and employees. Notwithstanding these limitations, Urban Co-operative Banks have been able to make a reasonable progress in the application of technology in their banking operations. While Urban Co-operative Banks are increasingly spending on information technology, interestingly, the literature / study on the impact of information technology is limited. Further, an analysis of the cost-benefit of the information technology would be not only beneficial to Urban Co-operative Banks but also serve as a blue print for future technology up-gradation. In view of this, in the present study an attempt have been made to study the **'Application of Information Technology in Co-operative Banking – A Comparative Analysis of Scheduled and Non-Scheduled Urban Co-operative Banks'.**

**Importance of the Study**

Information technology is entirely changing the way of banking business including Co-operative banking sector. Information technology have improved the urban co-operative banking operations. The manual process is being converted into computers for doing the transaction processing. The urban co-operative banking sector in Maharashtra is trying to take advantage of the revolution in information technology towards reducing the cost of operation, better efficiency and better service for customers.

Basically the applications of information technology in urban co-operative banks in Maharashtra is in younger stage but the overall impact of computerization in Urban Co-operative Banks is positive. Very few research studies have been done on the impact of IT on urban co-operative banking sector. The present study will be more helpful to evaluate and to measure the impact of information technology on profitability, productivity, customer satisfaction and operating expenses of Urban Co-operative Banks.

This analysis would not only be beneficial to Urban Co-operative Banks but the whole Co-operative, public and private banking sector also. This study will facilitate to RBI to frame the policies, to take initiatives for future technology upgradation.

**Objectives of the Study:**

A research study is usually formulated with certain objectives helpful to conduct the enquiry in given manner. These objectives guide the researcher to undertake the research activity in defined manner. They also help the researcher to avoid crowdy and other related consideration distorting the process of research, a well define set of objectives is a beacon for proper conduction of research activity. Because of this the researcher have identified the following objectives for the present research study.

1. To take a critical stock of the application of the information technology in banking operation of selected Urban Co-operative Banks.

   This has been helped to understand the applications of information technology in banking operations of Apna Sahakari Bank Ltd., Mumbai and Thane Janata Sahakari Bank Ltd., Thane.

2. To investigate the impact of information technology on business growth, profitability of selected Urban Co-operative Banks.

   This has been helped to evaluate and to measure the impact of information technology on business growth, profitability of Apna Sahakari Bank and Thane Janata Sahakar Bank.

Following was the indicators have been selected such as Net Profit, Income, Expenditure, Spread, Burden, net-worth and Operating Profits.

3. To analyse the impact of information technology on productivity of selected Urban Co-operative Banks.

The purpose of the productivity analysis was to assess the impact of information technology on productivity of employees. The productivity is analysed by the various parameters such as per-employee deposits, per employee loans and advances, per employee business, per employee earnings and per employee net profit.

4. To find out the impact of information technology on deposit mobilization of selected Urban Co-operative Banks.

Deposits constitutes the main product of the banking business. The size of the deposits that largely decides the lending activity of the bank. Mobilization of deposits helps to increase the banking business and therefore the role of information technology is important. Hence the objective has been assessed by certain parameters.

5. To investigate the customer satisfaction levels and operating expenses in selected URBAN COOPERATIVE BANKS.

Customer satisfaction is the feeling or attitude of a customer towards a product or service after it has been used. Customer Satisfaction is widely recognized as a key influence in the formation of customers. Future purchase intensions, Customer satisfaction level ahs been measures by certain parameters such as personnel factors, physical factors, service quality and social factor.

6. To offer suggestions to help Urban Co-operative Banks to optimally utilize the information technology.

Application of information technology in banking operations has positively influenced the performance of selected Apna Sahakari Bank and Thane Janata Sahakari Bank. Some major suggestions has been given to utilize the information technology for rapid progress of Urban Co-operative Banks.

**Hypothesis of the Study:**

1. Application of information technology to banking operations has positively influenced the performance of selected Urban Co-operative Banks in terms of business growth, profitability, productivity, deposit mobilization and customer satisfaction.
2. The Operating expenses in select Urban Co-operative Banks have been reduced on account of the application of information technology.
3. The adoptions of information technology in select Urban Co-operative Banks has resulted in improved MIS and facilitates decision making at various levels.

4. The adoption of information technology has enabled select Urban Co-operative Banks to comply with the requirements of RBI/Co-operative Department with in a given time frame.

## Research Design

### (A) Sampling Framework

In order to study the problem, the researcher has adopted the following sampling procedure.

Urban Co-operative banking sector is characterized by heterogeneity in terms of size, spread, profitability and professionalism. As at the end of March 31, 2006 in Maharashtra there were total 630 Urban co-operative banks, out of which 39 USBs were in scheduled status. Obviously the size, level of business and type and level of technology adoption differs

**Table : Classification of Customer in Apna Sahakari Bank Ltd. Mumbai (Non-Scheduled Bank)**

| No. of Customers | Total | Age Composition | | | Educational Qualifications | | | |
|---|---|---|---|---|---|---|---|---|
| | | 0-20 | 21-60 | Above 60 | Upto SSC | SSC – UG | UG – PG | Other Technical |
| 1 | 2 | 3 | 4 | 5 | 6 | 7 | 8 | 9 |
| Males | 90 (64.28%) | 02 | 65 | 07 | 30 | 23 | 14 | 12 |
| Females | 50 (35.72) | – | 62 | 04 | 22 | 17 | 11 | 11 |
| Total | 140 (100%) | 02 | 127 | 11 | 52 | 40 | 25 | 23 |

**Table : Classification of Customer in Thane Janata Sahakari Bank Ltd., Thane (Non-Scheduled Bank)**

| No. of Customers | Total | Age Composition | | | Educational Qualifications | | | |
|---|---|---|---|---|---|---|---|---|
| | | 0-20 | 21-60 | Above 60 | Upto SSC | SSC –UG | UG –PG | Other Technical |
| 1 | 2 | 3 | 4 | 5 | 6 | 7 | 8 | 9 |
| Males | 95 (59.37%) | – | 82 | 6 | 30 | 29 | 20 | 17 |
| Females | 65 (40.63%) | – | 65 | 7 | 25 | 16 | 12 | 11 |
| Total | 160 (100%) | – | 147 | 13 | 55 | 45 | 32 | 28 |

considerably within and between these becomes one of the most difficult tasks. In view of this the researcher has selected two Urban Co-operative Banks from Maharashtra, one from scheduled segment and another from non-scheduled segment for the study. Hence we adopted the case study method to investigate and assessing the impact of information technology on business growth, profitability, productivity, deposits mobilization, customer satisfaction and E-governance system. Following are the selected Urban Co-operative Banks for present research Study.

1. **Thane Janata Sahakari Bank Ltd., Thane (Scheduled Bank)**
2. **Apna Sahakari Bank Ltd., Mumbai (Non-Scheduled Bank).**

For the purpose of assessing the impact of information technology on customer satisfaction Total 300 sample respondents have been selected. Out of the 300 samples 140 (46.67%) sample from the Apna Sahakari Bank Ltd., Mumbai (ASB) and 160 (53.33%) samples from Thane Janata Sahakari Bank Ltd., Thane have been selected. Following table 4.1 shows the classification of customers in selected Urban Co-operative Banks.

**(B) Collection Analysis**

The information and the data required to carry out the present study has been collected from both primary and secondary sources of data.

**(i) Primary Data**

In order to obtain a clear picture and also supplement the quantitative data a detailed discussion has been made with the Board of Directors and top executives of the banks. In addition to this primary data has been collected through interview schedule. The researcher has also conducted pilot survey. Some minor changes were incorporated in the schedule after completing the pilot survey. All the schedules have been scrutinized so as to appraise the qualitative and quantitative aspects of the data. The analysis of the data has been made with reference to objective and hypothesis to be tested.

**(ii) Secondary Data**

The secondary data is collected from various annual reports of the banks, various committees reports, research reports, journals, books, various references, internet and various institutions. The researcher have approached aforesaid libraries and institutions for the present study such.

- Vaikunth Mehta National Institute of Co-operative Management – Pune
- National Institute of Bank Management – Pune
- Gokhale Institute of Economics and Politics – Pune
- Library of Pune University – Pune
- Tata Institute of Social Sciences – Mumbai
- Library of Mumbai University – Mumbai
- National Insurance Academy- Pune
- Reserve Bank of India - Mumbai

## Tools and Techniques used for Analysis

An analysis of the data was made with reference to the hypothesis to be tested. For the analysis and interpretation of data the researcher has used statistical tools such as :

- Growth rate
- Percentage change
- Frequency distribution
- Averages
- Mean
- Ratio Analysis etc.

## Use of Graphs and Charts

For the analysis and interpretation of data the researcher has used various graphs and charts such as bar diagram, pie charts, histograms, etc.

## Scheme of Chapterization

### Chapter – I – Introduction

This chapter explains the conceptual framework, examines the co-operative banking structure, deals with the origin of urban co-operative banks in the world and in India, a brief review of urban co-operative banking movement, co-operative banks and RBI perspectives, Emerging banking scenario challenges and opportunities, current scenario of Urban Co-operative Banks, the relationship of information technology and Urban Co-operative Banks and Future of Urban Co-operative banks.

Generally Four major objectives of Computerization in the Urban Co-operative Banks, i.e., improvement in customer service, Better house keeping, Faster decision making and increase in productivity and profitability. In view of this the discussion has made in the present chapter.

### Chapter – II – Growth and Development of Urban Co-Operative Banks in India and Maharashtra

The present chapter deals with the growth and development of urban co-operative banks prior to March 1966, after March 1966, 1985-94 and after 1996. It also deals with the progress of co-operative credit movement in India. The importance of human resource management needs special emphasis. It constitutes the most valuable resource of any co-operative banking. Hence it has been also focused in this chapter that how to utilize the proper manpower and national application of information technology. It also includes the emerging trends in banking technology.

### Chapter – III - Review of Literature

This chapter comprises of the available literature on urban co-operative banks and information technology, which is proved to be very useful in getting an insight into the main objective of the study and in finalizing the methodology. Near about 50 relevant reviews have been taken from the various journals, articles, books and other publications.

**Chapter – IV – Research Methodology**

The present chapter comprises of the important aspects like introduction, statement of the problem, objectives of the study, hypothesis, research design. The research design deals with the sampling framework, sample selection of Urban Co-operative Banks, sources of data, i.e., primary data and secondary data collection process, again statistical tools used in the study. Limitation of the study and Chapter Scheme of the Study.

**Chapter – V – Data Analysis and Interpretations**

This chapter comprises of two sections. Section First deals with the profile of selected Urban Co-operative Banks. The whole profile of the Apna Sahakari Bank Ltd., Mumbai and Thane Janata Sahakari Bank Ltd., Thane represented with a systematic manner e.g., History of banks, Board of Directors, Important Events of the Bank, Annual Financial Review and present Status of the IT in banks.

Section II deals with the data analysis and interpretation keeping in view the objectives of the present study. On the basis of certain parameters interpretation has been made, such as Profitability, trend analysis, ratio analysis, productivity, deposit mobilization, customer satisfaction etc.

**Chapter – VI – Findings and Recommendations**

In the earlier chapter various issues connected with selected Urban Co-operative Banks in Maharashtra have been dealt with in broad details on the basis of data collected from both primary and secondary sources. Therefore, this chapter highlights the major findings and recommendations drawn on the basis of present study.

**Period of the Study**

The period of the study has been selected on the basis of introduction of information technology in Apna Sahakari Bank and Thane Janata Sahakari Bank. The period of the study have been divided into two parts namely (1) Pre- IT Periods – This is called as the period of before application of information technology and (2) Post It period – This is called as the period of after the application of information technology. The pre IT period is same i.e., year 1999 in both the selected banks and post IT period started from year 2000-2009.

**Limitations of the Study :**

1. As the study is confined to two Urban Co-operative Banks, one from scheduled and another from non-scheduled UCB, the conclusion drawn may have their own limitations.
2. The impact of information technology may not be felt in the short-run and some of the intangible benefits of technology may now be easily captured.

# Data Analysis & Interpretations

## SECTION - I

## Profile of Apna Sahakari Bank Ltd., Mumbai

### Introduction :

A group, functioning since freedom struggle, belonging to 'Rashtra Seva Dal' and having socialistic ideology who competently runs a consumers co-operative society known as "APNA BAZAAR" decided to establish (Nagari Sahakari Bank) in the above Departmental Stores itself. In a very short time, share capital and necessary funds were raised and RBI Licence was obtained. In 1968, on the auspicious day of (Gudi Padwa), Apna Bank was inaugurated by then Speaker of Government of Maharashtra, (Shri Balasaheb Bharde). The function was presided by the eminent and bellowed socialist leader Hon'ble Shri Nanasaheb Gore. Till 1977, it had only one branch, admeasuring barely 150 square feet, wherein Head Office was also accommodated, at Lower Parel, second branch of Apna Sahakari Bank opened in 1978. During the last 40 years, Bank has maintained steady growth. Bank deposits crossed the level of Rs. 693 crores and Loan Outstanding stood at Rs. 468 crores. Business mix of the Bank is crossed over Rs. 1150 crores.

Apna Bank started the first "Night Bank" in Mumbai and teller system for speedy withdrawal of cash. Bank has 13 branches all over Mumbai which are fully computerized with ATM services at 9 branches. Bank is managed by 18 dedicated/devoted directors and more than 100 other co-operators selflessly. The branch advisory committees are also constituted for the improvement of customer services.

Apna Bank is pride of the excellent performance and service of its staff. Bank maintains very cordial relation with its employees. The Bank has started its own, well equipped training facilities at Kurla. The bank had also send its employees for training centers at RBI and also to other co-operative training centers. Bank always encourages sports, cultural and allied activities for the employees. Our bank is firmly in belief that technology is impacting on our every day life in different and profound way and banking is no exception at all. Keeping in view the new generation of customer's needs. Our bank is implementing Core Banking System (CBS) shortly.

In the year 2001-2002 Bank was the winner of "Padmabhushan Vasantdada Patil award for Best Urban Bank" honoured by the Maharashtra State Co-op Banks Association, Mumbai. In 2003-04 Bank was the winner of "Maharashtra Gourav Puraskar". In the year 2006-07 Brihanmumbai Co-op Bank's Association has awarded as <u>BEST CO-OP BANK</u> in Mumbai region. They have contributed Rs. 21 lacs to the Army Central Welfare fund for the rehabilitation of the soldier families and Rs. 21 lacs to the people, whose lives were affected due to earthquake in state of Gujarat. Bank has also given financial aid to Sane Guruji Rashtriya Smarak Trust, Matrumandir, Devrukh, Kustrog Niwaran Samiti and so on, whose motto is only to assist and help to the needy class of the society.

Apna Bank is team of more than 3,50,000 people, which includes share Holders, depositors, and borrowers etc. It is, a literally an "Apna Parivar".

**Present Board of Directors of Apna Bank Sahakari Bank Ltd. Mumbai**

**Branch Network of Apna Sahakari Bank Ltd. & Important Events of the Bank**

**Table : Annual Financial Review**

| | Particulars | 31.03.2004 | 31.03.2005 | 31.03.2006 | 31.03.2007 |
|---|---|---|---|---|---|
| 1 | Paid up Share Capital | 664.16 | 958.69 | 1313.19 | 1813.17 |
| 2 | Reserves | 7152.02 | 8189.29 | 9517.17 | 10751.85 |
| 3 | Own Funds | 8120.00 | 9147.98 | 10830.36 | 12565.02 |
| 4 | Gross Profit | 1080.60 | 1122.03 | 1483.06 | 1695.30 |
| 5 | Deposits | 428360.44 | 47978.74 | 55069.71 | 65184.90 |
| 6 | Total Investment | 21279.45 | 18720.72 | 22127.96 | 29767.37 |
| 7 | Total Loans and Advances | 27452.67 | 36268.31 | 41659.34 | 45849.61 |
| 8 | % of Net NPA to Net Loans and Advances | | 4.54 | 0.98 | 0.00 |
| 9 | Working Capital total Liabilities (-) Contra | 54703.48 | 61336.35 | 70233.68 | 82633.31 |
| 10 | Membership (Nos.) | 34031 | 35147 | 36278 | 37418 |
| 11 | CRAR % | 11.01 | 11.10 | 12.01 | 12.20 |
| 12 | Audit Classification | A | A | A | A |
| 13 | Dividend | 15 % | 15 % | 15 % | 15 % |

**Source :** Various Annual Reports of Apna Sahakari Bank

**Present Status of IT in Apna Sahakari Bank Ltd., Mumbai**

For taking the advantage of automation as well as to give prompt service to the customers, Apna Bank had decided to computerized its all branches spread over in Mumbai and its suburbs. To that effect firstly, Naigaon branch was made computerized in July 1993. All the branches was made computerized in 1999 on Lan environment.

Following are the specific activities of computerization undertaken in accordance with the Functional activities.

1. Deposits and Loan
2. Personnel
3. Word Processing
4. Monitoring and Evaluation of transaction
5. Servicing Monitoring
6. ATMs.

All hardware of the bank was replaced recently because that was not suitable for new window and CBS environments and also the hardware was used by the bank more than 6 to 7 years. The composition of computerization in APNA bank was home computer senior manager, System Analyst, Accountant and Computer Operator.

The APNA Bank has 60 Desktop, 22 Laptops, 140 Thine Client, 15 Server and 46 Printer.

The computer system are useful for all critical operations like calculation of interest, grouping of customer account for various purpose, money transfer from one place to any other place without any geographical hurdle, day to day balancing of account. Bank has also expanded its services using ATM, Cash Dispensing machine, utility service like bill payment junction, collection of cheques etc.

Bank used packaged software from the vendors. CBS software is procured from Infrasoft Technologies Ltd. All the software has been acquired legally and bank hold the license for the same. Bank has also selected vendor's for maintenance of banking software and hardware on annual contract basis.

Bank has given staff training for 2-3 days before the change of new software. Training includes what is the changes in the software, day to day functionality. Facility newly available

**Profile of the Thane Janata Sahakari Bank Ltd., Thane**

**Introduction**

The Thane Janata Sahakari Bank Ltd. was established in 1972, with an aim of serving common man's necessities. Thane Janata Sahakari Bank has made tremendous progress over last 36 years due to professional and visionary Board of Directors and resulted oriented management at the operational level. Absolute loyalty to the customers and committed staff has added feathers to the success of the bank. Thane Janata Sahakari Bank has the spread of

40 branches and 2 extension counters at Thane, Mumbai, Navi-Mumbai, Pune, Pimpri, Chinchwad and Nashik. With the recent takeover orders of two Pune based banks, there is a spread of 42 in totality. Bank has recently got license for 4 additional branches.

Thane Janata Sahakari Bank has been techno savvy in all the operations. It has changed with the time and has adapted to every demand of time on the technology front. Bank is on the Core Banking Solution (CBS) for all its operations and Any Branch Banking has been successfully completed. At e-lobby in Naupada Branch, there are 24X7 ATMs, Cheque Depository Machines and Cheque Dispensing Machine, which is unique in itself. All the branches have 24X7 ATMs and Cheque Depository Machines. Bank has its own Data Centre with the capacity to cater the network of 100 branches. Presently the same has been shared by one Co-operative bank. In a very near future, Thane Janata Sahakari Bank will get connected to more than 4500 locations all over India through BANCS network. Thane Janata Sahakari Bank web-site has been recognized as the best by National Frontier Magazine. Bank offers facilities under RTGS arrangement of fund transfer. The case study of the same has been placed on the international web site of HP.

Thane Janata Sahakari Bank has won the award of Best Co-operative bank declared by the Maharashtra State Urban Bank's Federation for the year 04-05. It has also won "Vasantdada Patil Utkarsha Nagri Sahakari Bank Award". First rank continuously for 2 years. The Kalupura Commercial Co-operative bank has rated Thane Janata Sahakari Bank within first 5 best co-operative banks.

Thane Janata Sahakari Bank has proactively implemented, right from inception, certain norms of financial discipline, now imposed by RBI. It has been a profit making Bank right from inception and has maintained audit Class "A". The total business mix of Thane Janata Sahakari Bank is Rs. 3324.53 crores. The gross NPA is 6.61% and net NPA is 0%. Net Owned Funds are Rs. 261.41 crores and CRAR is 13.85%.

Thane Janata Sahakari Bank has taken strategic steps since last 3 years to capitalize its financial strength for acquisition of running weak banks and spread its base. The recent takeover has been after s systematic due diligence study. The takeover process has been very smooth with very ambitious plans of growth. The acquired banks are operating as Strategic Business Units (SBU) and are expected to attain annualized profit of Rs. 15 crores and business growth of Rs. 250 crores in the existing levels in the first year of operations. The SBU has potential business growth of Rs. 3000 crores in the next three years. The SBU will be under CBS platform in next 3 months time and will be integrated in due course. Thane Janata Sahakari Bank has received NOC from R.B.I.,.Co-operative Department of Maharashtra State and Karnataka State to attain Multi-state status and will shortly be opening its branches out of State.

Thane Janata Sahakari Bank offers all types of Forex Services through its various correspondents, in the field of Import, Export, Remittances etc. At select 11 centres, Thane Janata Sahakari Bank offers money changing, facility. Under this all types of currencies are exchanged and Travellers cheques of American Express Bank are issued to all going on Business Tour and leisure Trips. As per revised R.B.I. guidelines, bank is eligible to operate as Authorised Dealer in Forex market and is expected to get license to that effect shortly. Bank has Corporate Agency under life and non-life insurance. The alliance with Max New York Life Insurance Company has been rated as one of the best Bank assurance tie up in the banking industry.

With strategies business plan Thane Janata Sahakari Bank aims to have the business mix of Rs. 10,000 crores and 2011 and emerge as the "STRONGEST REGIONAL BANK".

**Table 5.2.2: Present Board pf Directors of Thane Janata Sahakari Bank Ltd., Thane**

| Sr. No | Name | Qualification | Status |
|---|---|---|---|
| 1 | Shri Madhukar N. Bapat | M.E.F.I.E. | Retired |
| 2 | Shri Viresh B. Bhate | B.Com., CA, LLB | Practicing Chartered Accountant |
| 3 | Shri Bhalchandra W. Date | BSC, Paints, & Varnish Diploma | Industrialist |
| 4 | Shri Sharad N. Gangal | B.Com., LLB, MLS | General Manager HDFC Standard Life |
| 5 | Mrs. Padma B. Iyer | B.Com, ACA | Chartered Accountant |
| 6 | Shri Madhukar D. Khutade | | Agriculturist |
| 7 | Shri Manohar P. Kulkarni | Diploma in Electrical Communication Engineering | Industrialist |
| 8 | Shri Ramesh K. Kanani | Diploma in Mechanical Engineering | Industrialist |
| 9 | Shri N. Nandgopal Menon | BA, BGL | General Manager (Corporate) Natvar Parikh Industries Ltd. |
| 10 | Dr. Suvarna T. Raval | MSC, PHD | Professor, B.N.N. College, Bhivandi |
| 11 | Shri Pandharinath R. Rothe | | Retired Social Worker |
| 12 | Shri Jugalkishor Sharma | BE Mechanical | Retired |
| 13 | Shri Dilip A. Soman | BE Mechanical | Industrialist |
| 14 | Shri Pradeep D. Thakur | B Com., LLD | Practicing Advocate |
| 15 | Dr. Shri Vivekand S. Vadke | B.Tech, MSC, PHD | Process Engineering Consultant to Oil Industries |
| 16 | Shri Vidyadhar A. Vaishampayan | M.Tech, Chartered Engineer | Consultant |

**Table 5.2.3: Branch Network of Thane Janata Sahakari Bank Ltd., Thane**

| S.No. | Branch | Opening Date | Inaugurated by |
|---|---|---|---|
| 1 | Registered Office Deendayal Bhavan | 30.10.1977 | Mr. Atalbihari Vajpeyee–Ex. Foreign Minister |
| 2 | Administrative Sevadham | 10.01.1994 | |
| 3 | Naupada Branch | 05.02.1972 | Mr. Vashushri Shrishrimal |
| 4 | Main Branch | 30.10.1977 | |
| 5 | Wagle Estate | 23.09.1980 | |
| 6 | Rabodi Branch | 03.02.1984 | Smt. I.T. Vaz, RBI, GM |
| 7 | Thane East Branch | 07.07.1985 | Mr. Rambhau Kapse–MLAMr. Gulabrao Khapde–Co-op. Bank's Federation, Member |
| 8 | Vertaknagar Branch | 09.05.1986 | Mrs. Kamala Kapoor – Social Worker |
| 9 | Panchpakhadi Branch | 23.11.1988 | Mr. Chandrashekhar Wagh – News Reporter |
| 10 | Khopat Branch | 25.09.1995 | Mr. Arvind Reddy – Collector Thane District |
| 11 | Airoli Branch | 26.11.1996 | Mrs. Sushma Dande – Mayor,Navi Mumbai, Mr. Narayanrao Marathe – Chairman, Cidco |
| 12 | Shreenagar Branch | 06.05.1997 | Mrs. Vijaya Deshmukh- Mayor, Thane, Mr V.K. Kelkar (CA) Ex-Chairman THANE JANATA SAHAKARI BANK |
| 13 | Vashi Branch | 15.05.1997 | Mr. Jaganath Patil – MPMr. V. Ramdurai |
| 14 | Nasik Branch | 20.03.1999 | Mr. Damuanna Date – Social Worker |
| 15 | Kalwa Branch | 08.03.2000 | Smt. Ushatai Chati – Social Worker |
| 16 | Mulund Branch | 18.08.2000 | Mr. Sudhir Kumar Goyal – Commissioner of Co-operation |
| 17 | Pune Branch | 28.09.2000 | Mr. Anirudh Deshpande – Principal BMCC College, Pune |
| 18 | Ghatkopar Branch | 15.10.2000 | Mr. Pramod Mahajan, M.P. |
| 19 | Shifting of HO to Madhukar Bhavan | 18.03.2002 | |
| 20 | Vile Parle East Branch | 18.05.2003 | Mr. Madandas Devi – Social worker |
| 21 | Dombivali East Branch | 10.08.2003 | Mr. Vinay Sahastrabudhe – Social Worker |
| 22 | Wagle East Branch Shifting | 21.02.2005 | Mr. Jantre – Collector, Thane Mr. Prakash Paranjape, MP |
| 23 | Goregaon Branch | 08.03.2005 | Mr. Ram Naik – Ex Railway Minister |
| 24 | Borivali Branch | 13.03.2005 | Mr. R.R. patil, Home Minister, Maharashtra |
| 25 | Pune Extension 2 (Narhe Pune) | 10.08.2006 | Mr. Nawale Sir – Managing Director, Sinhagad Institute, Pune. |
| 26 | Vile Parle Extension | 09.04.2006 | Mr. Deepak Ghaisas–Chairman I Flex, Mumbai |
| 27 | Nashik Gangapur Road Branch | 30.12.2007 | Mr. Sachin Pilgaonkar - Brand Ambassador, THANE JANATA SAHAKARI BANK Mrs. Supriya Pilgaonkar - Brand Ambassadoir, THANE JANATA SAHAKARI BANK |
| 28 | Ghodbandar Road Branch | 27.01.08 | Mr. Sachin Pilgaonkar - Brand Ambassador, THANE JANATA SAHAKARI BANK Mrs. Supriya Pilgaonkar - Brand Ambassador, THANE JANATA SAHAKARI BANK Mr. Chandrashekhar Tilak, Economist |

| | Particulars | 31.03.2003 | 31.03.2004 | 31.03.2005 | 31.03.2006 | 31.03.2007 |
|---|---|---|---|---|---|---|
| 1 | Paid up Share Capital | 780.07 | 915.97 | 1071.89 | 1231.71 | 1447.84 |
| 2 | Reserves | 3442.19 | 4586.44 | 5458.05 | 6062.07 | 6678.36 |
| 3 | Own Funds | 10262.78 | 12459.78 | 15200.30 | 16950.09 | 19817.05 |
| 4 | Gross Profit | 2127.66 | 2400.43 | 2202.36 | 2563.49 | 4195.87 |
| 5 | Net Profit | 1519.66 | 1588.43 | 1594.31 | 2399.49 | 2518.95 |
| 6 | Deposits | 77630.57 | 87213.21 | 93881.97 | 107305.91 | 132852.18 |
| 7 | Total Investment | 35044.20 | 44178.92 | 47733.55 | 53023.52 | 60129.04 |
| 8 | Total Loan & Advances | 51130.84 | 54219.77 | 58247.44 | 68042.85 | 90292.63 |
| 9 | % of NPA | 1.75 | 0.46 | 0.80 | 0.00 | 0.00 |
| 10 | Working Capital (Total Liabilities – contra) | 96358.51 | 109392.48 | 117779.13 | 13412.40 | 166796.62 |
| 11 | Membership (No.s) | 19969.00 | 21409.00 | 22965.00 | 24569.00 | 26424.00 |
| 12 | CRAR | 20.22% | 20.22% | 20.29% | 20.01% | 18.41% |
| 13 | Audit Classification | A | A | A | A | A |
| 14 | Dividend % | 15.00% | 15.00% | 15.00% | 15.00% | 15.00% |
| 15 | Dividend (AMT) | 106.85 | 126.00 | 149.15 | 175.0 | 200.00 |

**Table 5.2.4: Annual Financial Review**

**Source:** Various Annual Reports of Thane Janata Sahakari Bank

**Specific Activities of Computerization Undertaken in Accordance with the Functional Activities**

- Deposits & Loans
- Personnel & Administration
- Credit Monitoring & Follow up
- ATM Switch controlling 28 ATM's of the Bank
- Centralized Recovery Management
- Centralized Recovery Management
- Specialized Credit Cell
- Centralized Credit Cell
- Centralized Processing Cell
- Centralized Management Information System
- Centralized ATM Card Management System
- Email Solution for all Employees of the Bank
- Intranet for the Employees of the Bank
- RTGS and NEFT Fund Transfer System
- Disaster Recovery System

- Data Center Sharing for KJSM Co-op Bank
- Cheque Book Dispensing Machine
- SMS & Internet Banking

**Present Status of IT in Thane Janata Sahakari Bank**

Bank has 540 Desktop Computers and over 75, Servers installed. All the Computers has operating system from Windows 98 to windows XP to Vista Business. All the computers are connected to Centralized Virus update system which updates Anti Virus definitions daily on all computers connected to the network. All the servers are having Windows Server 2003 as networking operating system.

No. of PCS, 540, Printers 120

IT Cell has 15, Staff as per the levels given below

Chief Information Officer

Chief Manager (2)

Managers M2 (5)

Officers M1 (1)

Officer MO (6)

Loan Originating System for sanctioning and disbursement of loans

Internet banking for customers

SMS banking for customers

RTGS / NEFT Fund Transfer system interface to Branches for funds transfer

Tie up with BANCS network for ATM sharing

Image base cheque depository machines

Call Center implementation

Steps for issue of VISA tie up for Debit Card

Knowledge portals for staff

**Awards for Thane Janata Sahakari Bank**

- For the second consecutive year Thane Janata Sahakari Bank was awarded 1st Prize for Best co-operative Bank in Maharashtra in November 2007, for Banks having deposit of over 500, crores.
- Thane Janata Sahakari Bank has been awarded Indian Bank Association's Special Jury Award for Outstanding Achievement in Banking Technology for the year (2007).

- ⇨ The Thane Janata Sahakari Bank Ltd., has won the award by 'Banking Frontiers for e-security implementation and best website in the category of big co-operative banks having business mix of more than 500 crores.
- ⇨ 1st Prize for Best Co-operative Bank in Maharashtra for the (year 2005) by Maharashtra Urban Co-operative Banks Federation.
- ⇨ In 2004 Thane Janata Sahakari Bank was recognized amongst top 5 Co-operative banks in the country, during centenary celebration of Co-operative movement by The Kalupur Commercial Co-operative Bank Ltd.

Thane Janata Sahakari Bank has ambitious plans for rapid inorganic growth through the M&A route and has already merged two Banks in Pune Region having Total Business Size of over 550 crores. THANE JANATA SAHAKARI BANK's strategic business direction is to achieve business target of Rs. 10,000/- crores by (2011) and emerge as strongest and most preferred regional Bank in the State of Maharashtra.

**Projects Implemented**

1. 24x7 Cheque Book Dispensing Machine
2. Data Center Sharing a Revenue Model
3. Core Banking Solution reaping the benefits
    a) Extending delivery channels for customers
    b) Formation of Centralized Processing Cell for back office
    c) Formation of Credit Monitoring Center for controlling the NPA and overdues
    d) Formation of Specialized Credit Cell for Small and Medium size customers
    e) Formation of Centralized Retail Business Cell for promoting the retail loans
    f) Formation of MIS Dept for internal and regulatory reporting
    g) Implementation of credit origination Inter Branch Reconciliation system

**Business Process Changes in CBS**

While drawing business strategy Thane Janata Sahakari Bank realized that simply implementing a core banking solution immediate results cannot be achieved as the truth is that CBS is only the foundation on which Banks have to build products, systems and processes which will help them meet their objectives.

Visible benefits by way of improvements in customer service and reduction in operational costs can only if a Bank changes its processes and practices to take advantage of the CBS.

Business Plan of Thane Janata Sahakari Bank thus laid the foundation for business process changes to be made while implementing CBS as for Thane Janata Sahakari Bank, it was a business transformation issue. Thane Janata Sahakari Bank reviewed its internal processes, systems and controls and replaced or modified the existing processes to take advantage of the new technology and make them quicker and more customer centric.

The benefits that can accrue out of exercise are:

- Value to the Thane Janata Sahakari Bank Customer
  - Quick and Efficient Service
  - East access to information
  - Innovative products
- Value to the Thane Janata Sahakari Bank
  - Optimum resource utilization
  - Reduced cost of operation
  - Timely and correct decision making / control
  - Branches focus on sales and service.

Case Studies attached distinctly shows the Thane Janata Sahakari Bank approach in adoption of new technology and the process changes made are unique and distinct in the sector in which banks operates. Bank has been consistently awarded and maintained its performance on financial and technological parameters and hence is an overall winner in the segment.

**Core Banking Solution**

Thane Janata Sahakari Bank started its CBS initiative, in the year (2002-03) with review of the existing infrastructure which indicated that from the long term perspective to improve the customer service and efficiency for the expansion of the Branches the optimization of resources and staff is necessary and there is need to centralize the basic operations which is possible by implementation of core banking solution.

In (2004-05) Banks started looking at newer ways to make a customer's banking experience more convenient, efficient, and effective. Centralized operations and process automation using core banking applications and IP-based networks, improve efficiency and productivity levels tremendously. Core banking applications help a bank to shift from 'branch banking' to 'bank banking'. The basically means that a customer will be treated as a bank's customer than just the customer of a particular branch which was the case earlier. Also, IP-based networks lets a bank offer multiple services over the same network, resulting in cost savings.

**Project Planning**

Having identified the need for implementation of the Core banking Solution the bank decided to adopt Project Planning Management approach with following steps.

- Understanding the Strategic direction of the bank for next 5 years
- Formation of project Steering Committee

- Drawing up of the requirement
- Formation of Core Team
- Communication of the message to all Staff of the bank

Understanding the Strategic direction of the bank for next 5 years and identification of business needs

By end of (2004) having achieved the Deposits of and Advances of the management of the bank has the target of achieving Business Mix of 5000, Crores by the year (2009). Bank had further focused an expansion of the Branch network by mergers of the other viable co-operative banks. Taking into consideration the impending CBS project.

**Formation of Functional Teams for Implementation**

IT Cell had prepared one important checklist that was to be addressed while conversion from Dos to Windows base software. Thereafter in co-ordination with M/s. Infrasoft Technologies Ltd., migration policies /activities were finalized. Migration tool / programmes of M/s. Intrasoft Technologies Ltd. were also checked by doing the pre-migration exercise on the test database of one branch and the migrated data was checked by generating various reports and the sampling of the data fields. The outputs were compared manually by the IT Cell and Audit and Inspection Department of the Bank. After satisfying about the migration tool the data conversion process were finalized and freezeed.

After putting the migration tool through rigorous test, I T Cell first migrated the flagship branch having more than 200 crores plus business mix successfully. This branch was selected keeping in mind that whatever issues that shall arise in this branch and that are properly handled then rest of the branches will not have any issues for migration and implementation. It was also evident that this shall considerably boost confidence of all the employees of the Bank towards the CBS project.

In the First phase all the Branches were converted from Legacy Dos based system to windows based system with Oracle 10g Database. The migration process was started on (23rd May 2005) and 16, branches of the bank were migrated by (31st August 2005).

**Training of the Implementation Teams**

Special emphasis was given on Training programme for creating the awareness on CBS among all the staff members and the training center was equipped with the entire infrastructure required. Windows base software functional training was also imparted to the branch staff before 2 days of converting the branch of new software.

**Customization**

Regular Review meetings were taken of the Branches migrated to the new software and based on the user feed back the customization issues were finalized with the Vendor and implementation of the same was carried out.

**Security Issues and Implementation**

Bank had identified and recognized the importance of information security considering the implementation of the CBS project wherein all the risks are concentrated at central place and operating environment and equipments are being specialized and the hardware too, system software and RDBMS configuration and implementation made by the vendor has to be counterchecked and security has to be built around these equipments.

It was therefore, imperative to classify the risks associated and take adequate counter measures to mitigate the risks. Considering this it was necessary to undertake detail security analysis and procedures for logical security of the Bank's Information System set up pre and post CBS implementation.

To safeguard the information system setup of the Bank and to have Information System Security Policy, Procedures were to implement the information security across the organization. To ensure the safety and security a Security Consulting company, having professionals with BS7799 Assessor, CISA, CISSP, CCNA and FCA qualifications and having expertise in Banking/ Finance domain was appointed to provide the services in the area of design, implementation ad audit of information systems security and networks. The activity was carried out based on BS 7799 and COBIT standards.

**Delivery Channels of the Bank**

**ATM's**

All the 28, ATM's of the bank are connected to Central ATM Switch and Customers are able to do all the transactions through any of the Branches of the bank.

With the relaxation in ATM related norms by Reserve Bank of India the bank is now in talks with other ATM switch providers for sharing of the ATM's which will enable the sharing of more than 3000 ATM's for the customers of the Bank across all over India.

**E-Lobby at Naupada Branch**

Customer Delight being focus the bank was implementing and focusing on creation of virtual service outlets operated through Customer Activated delivery channels. The E-Lobby of the Bank at Naupada is now equipped with 3 ATM's, Cheque Depository machinery and now Automated Cheque Book Dispenser machines.

**Cheque Depository Machines**

Branches of the Bank are fully equipped with Cheque depository machines giving the convenience to the customers to deposit the cheques 24X7X365. The printed acknowledgement is given to the Customers by the Cheque depository machine of Cheque being deposited in the machine.

**Automated Cheque Book Dispenser**

With Core banking solution in place the stress of the bank is now on providing the additional services to the customers which will be operational on 24X7X365. As part of this process, Bank is installing the Automated Cheque Depository Machine at its e-lobby at Naupada Branch.

Through Cheque Book Dispenser Machine by putting the Customer ID ad Pin Number the Customer will able to get personalized Cheque books without any manual intervention.

**SMS Banking**

SMS Banking will enable the customer of the banks to know the latest balances and last 5 transactions in their account using the SMS feature of the Mobile Phones. Apart from Customer pull operations Bank will be giving SMS alerts to the Customers for clearance of cheques, maturity of terms deposits, return of the cheques and host of other services.

**Specialized Credit Cell (SCC)**

It handles the Advances for 5 big size Branches of the bank and contribute 45% share in Bank's business and 54% share in total profit of branches. Implementation of Core Banking system has helped in

1. Master creation by SCC – For Cash Credit Accounts – Branches to issue the cheque books, - For Term Loans Branches to issue the pay orders.
2. Update the expiry dates of cash credit accounts on renewal.
3. Has reduced the credit delivery time by 3 days.
4. Avoids duplication of work.
5. Better Customer Service.
6. Has reduced the burden on branch for Loan Processing and follow up.
7. Simplified the procedure at Branch level for Staff and Customers with Improved turn around time.

Core Banking System has helped the Centralized SCC ell, in improving the performance which is evident from the figures given below:

- Staff Strength - 18
- Branches - 5
- Total Advances (as on 31.03.2007) Rs. 298.86 Cr
- The Gross NPA % of SCC Branches is 0.29%
- Per Employee Business Handled as on 31.03.05 – Rs. 908.13 Lakhs
- Per Employee Business Handled as on 31.03.06 - Rs.1190.93 Lakhs
- Per Employee Business Handled as on 31.03.07 - Rs.1449.48 Lakhs

## Cash Management

Bank has Centralized Currency Chest, which handles the cash requirement of the Branches. Prior to CBS the cash was given to Branches based on the demands placed. Branches were holding excess cash for customer withdrawals and ATM transactions resulting in overall excess cash holding bank wise and resulting in loss of revenue / opportunity cost on the excess cash held by the Bank.

Post CBS, Centralized Currency Chest was able to monitor online Cash Balances at Branches including denomination wise cash held by them, and the demand for cash was checked against the cash held by the Branches and only required cash is now given resulting in control on excess cash holding.

## Customer Data Updation and MIS generation

One of the prominent weaknesses of the Distributed system was incomplete data for Customer Information File and Loans Classification. As the data was inadequate and consolidation was not possible responding to business challenges was a big task.

With implementation of Core Banking System data updation was centralized. All the Customer Accounts forms are processed by Centralized Processing Cell and KYC compliance and audit is also done centrally.

Centralized MIS Department started controlling and completing the Loans Classification which was done at Branches. Accurate Classification and completion of data ensured generation of consolidated statements for Advances and Deposits without any time delay. Data consolidation process helped to take proactive decision on Interest rate management for Deposits and Advances. Internal and Statutory Return generation was facilitated and dependence on branches was eliminated. For the year ending (31st March 2007), all the closing relating work and MIS generation was completed by Branches and Centralized Dept. on 1st April 2007 only.

## Top Two New Controls Introduced by Core Banking

- **Inter-Branch Reconciliation**

Automated Inter Branch Transfer Accounting ensured that Reconciliation is on-line ensuring that no inter branch entries remain outstanding for more than 48 hours. Bank customized the IBT System to put in additional controls resulting in Branches generating only originating Credits and non-originating Debits allowed by the system. The process was made STP with Head Office vouchers being fired instantly on generation of IBT entries by the Branches.

Results –

- No outstanding entries over the period
- 3 person manpower saved in the process
- As originating Credits are only allowed stricter control on the system
- Instant identification of outstanding entries

**Centralized Credit Monitoring**

With Core Banking System in Place dedicated Centralized Credit monitoring Cell was established with Staff Strength of 3 persons. Centralized Credit Monitoring Cell monitors all schematic / retail advances of the Bank. Work process for Centralized Credit Monitoring was fully defined.

Centralized Credit monitoring cell uses the Core Banking System for follow-up of all the overdue loan accounts of the Bank. CBS system enables to identify the accounts which overdue for less than 2/3 installments. For all these accounts the customer contact is made for payment of defaulted amount. Customer is informed about the defaults and response / commitment received from the customers are entered in the Follow-up module of CBS.

Every Day follow-up schedule is generated from CBS system and customer's commitment for the day are verified and customer is reminded against about the commitment for payment of defaulted amount.

For all the defaulted Loan Accounts Notices are generated from CBS system centrally and are dispatched. This resulted in controlling and reducing Gross NPA of the Thane Janata Sahakari Bank from 7.06% as of 31st March 2006 to 4.52 % as on 31st March 2007.

**Data Center Sharing**

Having established the State of art data center Thane Janata Sahakari Bank felt the need for creating revenue model for the Data Center which can offset the running cost of managing data center.

Towards this end Thane Janata Sahakari Bank approached other small co-operative banks in the sector which were deciding on CBS project in their Bank. Bank has entered into Data Center Sharing Agreement with M/s Kalyan Janata Sahakari Bank. Thane Janata Sahakari Bank offered Total Solution to The Kalyan Janata Sahakari Bank Ltd., and the 8 branches of Kalyan Janata Sahakari Bank are on CBS platform of Thane Janata Sahakari Bank. Thane Janata Sahakari Bank gained by getting fixed annual revenue and one time fee for implementation of the project.

Data Center sharing model implemented by Thane Janata Sahakari Bank ensured following benefit to Kalyan Janata Sahakari Bank.

1. Reduction in Capital Cost Investment
2. Reduction in Total Cost of Ownership
3. No initial high cost and spread across the period
4. Implementation of the project in short time
5. No need of specialized Technical persons
6. Follow up with multiple vendors is reduced
7. No risk of technical obsolesce

8. IT Dept concentrated on Application
9. Reduction in Administrative cost of manning the data center 24x7x365
10. ATM Network / Tele-Banking sharing in future.

With this successful implementation Thane Janata Sahakari Bank has offered the solution to, 2 other co-operative banks which are in advance stage of finalizing the CBS plan.

**Migration** – The bank had distributed database with each branch having sizeable database size. Migrating all the customer related details to the perfection and generating Unified Customer Number without hampering the customer service was biggest challenge. IT Team developed standard checklist and made trial conversions and all the branch migrations were tested and verified with expected results of the Standard checklist. Deviations observed were rectified immediately.

**ATM** – The 28 ATM's of the bank were running with the Any Where banking transaction routed through ATM Switch. IT Team ensured the integration of transactions generated on ATM from CBS and Non CBS Branches on Centralized ATM Switch which ensured the uniform feel to the customers while doing the transaction on ATM's.

**Network Shifting** – The bank had the connectivity through 64 KBPS leased circuits at its Office at Deendayal Bhavan. For the CBS Data Center was established at other Office at Wagle Estate. IT Team planned the network shifting with the help of (MTNL/BSNL) and entire network was shifted from Deendayal Bhavan premises to Madhukar Bhavan premises at Wagle Estate at Thane without taking the down time and affecting customer service.

**Centralized Process Implementation** – Defining Centralize processes, policies and training the staff was implemented and started the process from Day 1.

**Training of Staff** – I T Team gave special emphasis on a Training programme for creating awareness on the CBS among all the staff members. Training center was equipped with the entire infrastructure required. Windows-based software functional training was also imparted to the branch staff two days before moving the branch on to the CBS new software.

IT team of Thane Janata Sahakari Bank not only migrated the Branches successfully to CBS platform but ensured uninterrupted service during the migration period concerning in Customer and employee satisfaction.

Implementation of the CBS enhanced the Business Volumes of the bank and in short span of 9 months posts CBS:

- Business volume increased by Rs. 450 Crores in 9 months period from (April 2006) which is more efficiently managed in existing staff strength.
- 9 % reduction in operating cost post implementation of CBS.
- Gross Profitability increased from Rs. 25 Crores at the end of March 2006 to Rs. 40 Crores projected annualized for March 2007 based on 9 months performance up to December 2006.

- With CBS in place and having the capacity a separate Revenue Model was created by IT Team with introduction of Data Centre Sharing Concept with other Banks which is expected to generated revenue of Rs. 30 Lacs per annum and inflow of Rs. 20 lacs towards consultancy fees.

IT Team of Thane Janata Sahakari Bank is headed by Chief Information Officer, and is supported by 3 Managers, 2 Officers and 2 Sr. Clerks.

IT Team has established helpdesk to give the support for CBS Application to Branch Users and all the calls for application support are handed by IT Team centrally. This ensures immediate resolution of the calls and calls do remain pending for more than 30 minutes.

Managers in the Team independent handles functions like Database and Server Administration, Delivery Channel Management, Application Support and release, Data Center Infrastructure management and control, Network Management etc.

Team has successfully migrated all the Branches of the Bank to CBS platform. Important functions like Customer Unification were handled by IT Team internally by writing in-house programme which simplified the task of customer unification.

IT Team has made the Asset's Classification with the risks associated and had take an adequate counter measures to mitigate the risks. IT Team has successfully implemented information system set up of the Bank and Information System Security Policy, Procedures to implement the information security across the organization. The activity was carried out based on BS 7799 and COBIT standards.

Thane Janata Sahakari Bank has set up its own data center with n+ redundancy and is comparable with Tier 3 data centers. Data Center infrastructure has the inbuilt capacity to take the load up to 100 branches. Thane Janata Sahakari Bank has plan to build the Data Center as revenue model and hence offered the data center sharing services to other banks with Total Solution Approach so as to reduce the CAPEX cost of the other smaller co-operative banks and bringing them in CBS mainstream at lesser OPEX cost.

Towards this Thane Janata Sahakari Bank entered into Data Center Sharing Agreement with M/s. Kalyan Janata Sahakari Bank. Thane Janata Sahakari Bank offered Total Solution to Kalyan Janata Sahakari Bank and the 8 branches of Kalyan Janata Sahakari Bank are on CBS platform of Thane Janata Sahakari Bank. Thane Janata Sahakari Bank gained by getting fixed annual revenue and one time fee for implementation of the project.

Data Center sharing model implemented by Thane Janata Sahakari Bank ensured following benefit to Kalyan Janata Sahakari Bank.

1. Reduction in Capital Cost Investment.
2. Reduction in Total Cost of Ownership.
3. No initial high cost and spread across the period.
4. Implementation of the project in short time.

5. No need of specialized Technical persons.
6. Follow up with multiple Vendors is reduced.
7. No risk of technical obsolesce
8. IT Dept concentrated on Application
9. Reduction in Administrative cost of manning the data center 24x7x365

IT Team studied the requirement of the KJSB Bank and ported the CBS database of the KJSB Bank on the same infrastructure used by the Thane Janata Sahakari Bank which includes network, firewall, routers, storage, and database servers. All the 14 branches of the Kalyan Janata Sahakari Bank are now on CBS platform of Thane Janata Sahakari Bank and IT Team of Thane Janata Sahakari Bank is managing all the infrastructure and has shifted the focus from cost center to revenue center.

The Bank's I T Team was small and was headed by newly appointed CIO, however the Team had a clear vision of implementing the Core Banking Solution in the Bank as per the deadline i.e., end of March 2006. To achieve this target the IT Team worked well with the vendor's Network provider agencies and the work profile was aligned with the team members under the overall supervision of the CIO. The IT team had regular meeting and knowledge sharing sessions, whereby any difficulties in the implementation was brought to the attention of the superiors and the solution to the problem were sought out immediately.

IT Team of the Thane Janata Sahakari Bank is the team of the year for reasons as under:

- Their skills required to complete the project and its tasks.
- Their ability to work by consensus
- Their ability to take challenges and executing it to satisfaction
- Their ability to complete the project in given time frame
- Their capacity to participate effectively with all the staff members
- Their ability to work well in a team environment
- Their access and cordial relation with vendor resources

## SECTION – II

This section deals with the data analysis and interpretation keeping in view the objectives of the present study. On the basis of certain parameters following interpretations have been made.

### Trend Analysis of Selected Urban Co-operative Banks

Trend Analysis becomes imperative to evaluate the profits and profitability performance of selected Urban Co-op Banks. It indicates the magnitude and direction of operations over a period of time, highlighting the trend pattern to identify the historical developments and helping in identifying certain banks in respect of their level of efficiency in operations. In order to workout the trends in the overall and profitability of the banks. Following indicators have been selected.

Net profit

Income

Expenditure

Spread

Burden

Net-Worth and

Operating Profits.

**Trends in Net Profit**

Profit is the renewal source of business activity. Without profit, ultimately there can be no continuity of operations. Growth with profit is an essential for continued success of a bank. Profit of the co-op bank represents the revenue in excess of its expenditure and hence is a result of two functions i.e., revenue function and cost function. The revenue function shows that the total income of a bank is derived from services rendered by, it while the cost function shows the total expenditure incurred on producing the services rendered by the Bank.

**Table 5.1: Trends in Net Profit of Apna Sahakari Bank Ltd. and Thane Janata Sahakari Bank Ltd.**

(in Lakhs)

| Year | Net Profit of Apna Sah. Bank in Lakhs | Percentage Growth | Net Profit of Thane Janata Sah. Bank in Lakhs | Percentage Growth |
|---|---|---|---|---|
| 1 | 2 | 3 | 4 | 5 |
| Pre IT Year 1999 | 132.96 | | 834.52 | |
| Post IT Years | | | | |
| 2000 | 312.13 | 234.75 | 943.73 | 113.08 |
| 2001 | 368.5 | 277.15 | 1359.12 | 162.86 |
| 2002 | 150.52 | 113.2 | 1405.99 | 168.47 |
| 2003 | 211.85 | 159.33 | 1519.66 | 182.09 |
| 2004 | 410.68 | 308.87 | 1588.43 | 190.34 |
| 2005 | 504.62 | 379.52 | 1594.32 | 191.04 |
| 2006 | 573.91 | 431.64 | 2399.49 | 287.52 |
| 2007 | 525.07 | 394.9 | 2518.88 | 301.83 |

**Source:** Annual Reports of Apna Sahakari Bank and Thane Janata Sahakari Bank Ltd.

**Fig 5.1: Trends in Net Profit of Apna Sahakari Bank Ltd. and Thane Janata Sahakari Bank Ltd.**

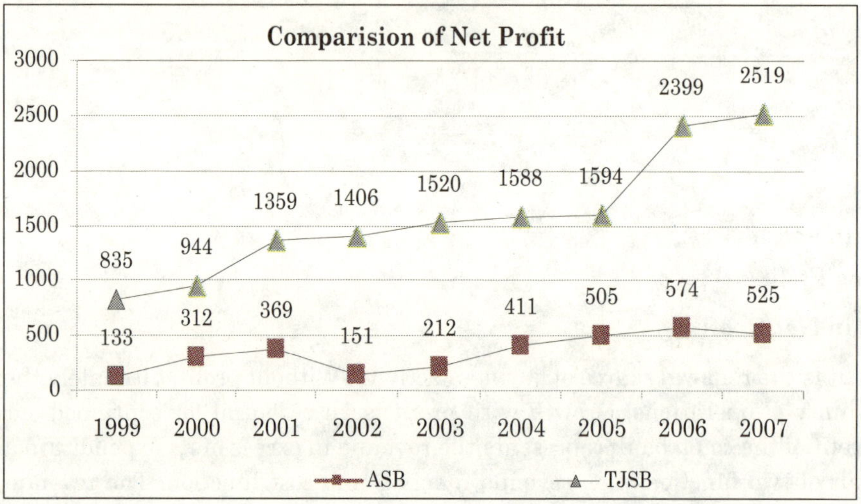


The table No. 5.1 reveals that the Net profit of Apna Sahakari Bank during the Pre-IT year of 1999 was Rs. 132.96 lakhs and it was Rs. 525.07 lakhs in year 2000. The year 2007 means the profit has increased more than 4 times during the period from 1999 to 2007. The percentage growth rate of Net Profit during the study period (i.e., 1999 to 2007) has increased from 234.75 in 2000 to 394.90 in 2007. It was lowest growth rate i.e. 113.20 during 2002 and highest in the period of 2006 i.e., 431.64 respectively.

The Net Profit of the Thane Janata sahakari Bank during the Pre IT year of 1999 was Rs. 834.52 lakhs and now it has increased upto Rs. 2518.88 lakhs in the year 2007. Means the Net Profit has increased more than 3 times during the period from 1999 to 2007. The percentage growth of net profit during the study period has increased from 113.08 in 2000 to 301.83 In 2007. It was the lowest percentage growth i.e., 113.08 during the year 2000 and highest in the period of 2007 i.e., 301.83 respectively.

It is reveals that the percentage growth has not steadily increased in the Apna Sahakari Bank. However Thane Janata Sahakari Bank's the growth rate has increased steadily during the Post IT period.

**Table No. 5.2: Trends in Income**

**(A) Apna Sahakari Bank, Mumbai**

| Year | Interest & Discount | Commission, Exchange & Brokerage | Other Earnings | Total Income | Percentage Growth |
|---|---|---|---|---|---|
| 1 | 2 | 3 | 4 | 5 | 6 |
| Pre IT Year 1999 | 2580.04 [97.06] | 8.8 [0.33] | 69.11 [2.7] | 2657.95 [100] | |
| Post IT Years | | | | | |
| 2000 | 3146 [97.14] | 9 [0.28] | 83.59 [2.58] | 3238.59 [100] | 121.84 |
| 2001 | 3953.37 [96.98] | 10.36 [0.25] | 113 [2.76] | 4076.41 [100] | 153.36 |
| 2002 | 4793.1 [97.65] | 7.36 [0.15] | 108.18 [2.20] | 4908.64 [100] | 184.67 |
| 2003 | 4953.16 [96.70] | 12.92 [0.25] | 155.93 [3.04] | 5122.01 [100] | 192.70 |
| 2004 | 5002.48 [95.33] | 15.62 [0.30] | 229.56 [4.37] | 5247.66 [100] | 197.43 |
| 2005 | 5087.35 [94.83] | 19.95 [0.37] | 257.65 [4.80] | 5364.95 [100] | 201.84 |
| 2006 | 5636.37 [95.12] | 23.65 [0.40] | 265.41 [4.48] | 5925.43 [100] | 222.93 |
| 2007 | 6441.97 [95.48] | 40.13 [0.59] | 264.88 [3.93] | 6746.98 [100] | 253.84 |

**Source:** Annual Reports of Apna Sah. Bank
Figures in parenthesis shows percentage to total income

**(B) Thane Janata Sahakari Bank Ltd.**

| Year | Interest & Discount | Commission, Exchange & Brokerage | Other Earnings | Total Income | Percentage Growth |
|---|---|---|---|---|---|
| 1 | 2 | 3 | 4 | 5 | 6 |
| Pre IT Year 1999 | 5030 [94.98] | 107.11 [2.02] | 158.56 [2.99] | 5295.67 [100] | |
| Post IT Years | | | | | |
| 2000 | 6056.35 [92.56] | 125.22 [1.91] | 361.68 [5.53] | 6543.25 [100] | 123.55 |
| 2001 | 7667.02 [94.08] | 127.75 [1.57] | 355 [4.35] | 8149.5 [100] | 153.88 |
| 2002 | 8780.44 [93.98] | 132.82 [1.42] | 429.5 [4.60] | 9342.76 [100] | 176.42 |
| 2003 | 9832.01 [92.79] | 164.24 [1.55] | 599.84 [5.66] | 10596.09 [100] | 200.08 |
| 2004 | 9883.73 [92.52] | 176.54 [1.65] | 622.71 [5.83] | 10682.98 [100] | 201.73 |
| 2005 | 9922.93 [95.56] | 207.57 [2.00] | 253.58 [2.44] | 10384.08 [100] | 196.08 |
| 2006 | 10799.42 [93.98] | 319.07 [2.78] | 372.19 [3.24] | 11490.68 [100] | 216.98 |
| 2007 | 12993.01 [92.82] | 371.35 [2.65] | 633.01 [4.52] | 13997.37 [100] | 264.31 |

**Source:** Annual Reports of Thane Janata Sah. Bank
Figures in parenthesis shows percentage to total income

**Fig. 5.2: Trends in Income of Apna Sahakari Bank Ltd. and Thane Janata Sahakari Bank Ltd.**

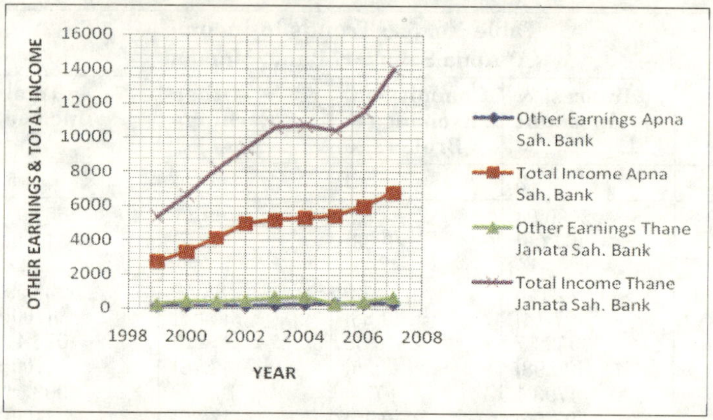


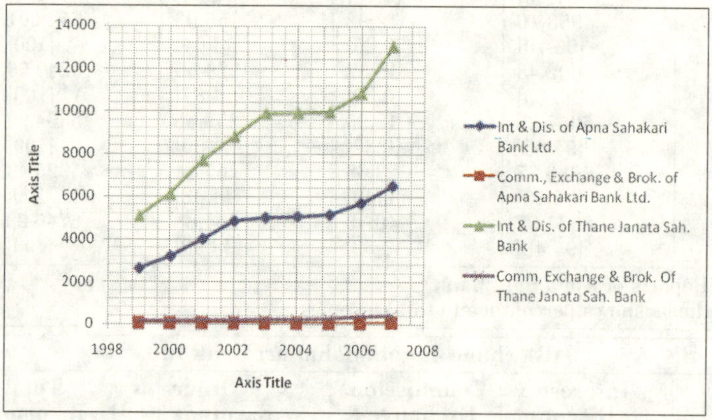


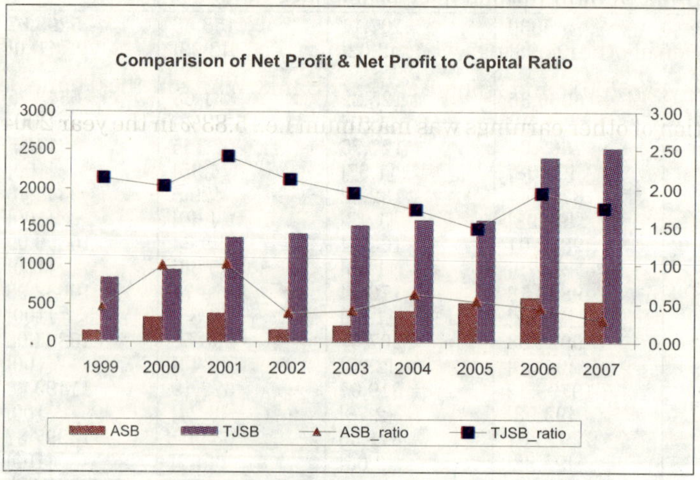

The income of the Urban Commercial Banks is the result of the size and types of assets held the return in these assets and the changes imposed for the performance of various services. Usually for the banks main source of the income as shown in profit and loss account include following:

Interest and Discount (I & D)

Commission, Exchange and Brokerage (CEB)

Other Earnings (OE)

**Interest and Discount (I & D)**

It is the major source of income to co-operative banks. Interest and Discounts of 'Apna Sahakari Bank' contributes the 95.48% in year 2007 the total earnings of the bank. The proportionate share of I & D income in the total was the maximum i.e., 97.65% in the year 2002 and minimum i.e., 95.12% in the year 2006. Interest and Discounts of Thane Janata Sahakari bank contributes 92.82% in 2007, in the total earnings of the bank. The proportionate share of I & D income in the total was the maximum i.e., 95.56% in the year 2005 and minimum i.e., 92.52% in the year 2004.

**Commission Exchange and Brokerage**

The contribution of this component is relatively less in both Apna Sahakari Bank and Thane Janata Sahakari bank. This component contributes nearly (0.15% to 0.59%) of the total income. The proportionate share of commission, exchange and brokerage in Apna bank was maximum upto 0.59% in the year 2007 and minimum i.e., 0.15% in the year 2002. While in the Thane Janata Sahakari bank the maximum proportion was 2.78% in the year 2006 and minimum 1.42% in the year 2002. It is observed that the ratio has increasing in some extent that the contribution to total income has become less.

The proportion of other earnings was maximum, i.e., 4.80% in the year 2005 and minimum i.e., 2.58% in the year 2000, and Apna Sahakari Bank. While in the Thane Janata Sahakari bank the proportion of other earnings was maximum i.e., 5.83% in the year 2004 and minimum, i.e., 2.44% in the year 2005.

The table reveals that the total income of Apna Sahakari bank was minimum in the year 1999 i.e., Rs. 2657.95 lakhs and the maximum i.e., Rs. 746.98 lakhs in the year 2007. While in the Thane Janata Sahakari bank also showing the same position. The total income was minimum in the year 1999 i.e., Rs. 5295.97 lakhs and maximum in the year 2007 i.e., Rs. 13997.37 lakhs. It is analysed that the total income of Apna Sahakari bank and Thane Janata Sahakari bank has continuously increasing after the application of Information technology.

**Table No. 5.3: Trends in Expenditure**
**(A) Apna Sahakari Bank Ltd., Mumbai**

| Year | Interest paid (Deposits & Borrowings) | Staff Expenses | Other establishment expenses | Other expenses | Total Expenses | Growth rate |
|---|---|---|---|---|---|---|
| 1 | 2 | 3 | 4 | 5 | 6 | 7 |
| Pre IT Year 1999 | 1574.79 [65.62] | 551.72 [22.99] | 73.92 [3.08] | 199.56 [8.32] | 2399.99 [100] | |
| Post IT Years | | | | | | |
| 2000 | 1809.89 [65.95] | 607.07 [22.12] | 88.83 [3.24] | 238.66 [8.70] | 2744.45 [100] | 114.35 |
| 2001 | 2145.01 [64.71] | 757.25 [22.85] | 103 [3.12] | 309.04 [9.32] | 3314.63 [100] | 138.11 |
| 2002 | 2437.88 [68.52] | 718.04 [20.18] | 124.14 [3.49] | 278.06 [7.81] | 3558.12 [100] | 148.25 |
| 2003 | 2659.79 [67.76] | 846.63 [21.57] | 129.57 [3.30] | 289.17 [7.37] | 3925.16 [100] | 163.54 |
| 2004 | 2781.48 [68.21] | 877.7 [21.52] | 127.82 [3.13] | 290.62 [7.13] | 4077.62 [100] | 169.90 |
| 2005 | 2908.59 [69.14] | 816.68 [19.41] | 124.17 [2.95] | 357.49 [8.50] | 4206.93 [100] | 175.28 |
| 2006 | 2930.98 [66.09] | 973.4 [21.95] | 136.91 [3.09] | 393.34 [8.87] | 4434.63 [100] | 184.77 |
| 2007 | 3418.08 [67.66] | 1056.72 [20.92] | 131.94 [2.61] | 444.94 [8.81] | 5051.68 [100] | 210.48 |

**Source:** Annual Reports of Apna Sahakari Bank Ltd.
Figures in parenthesis shows percentage

**(B) Thane Janata Sahakari Bank Ltd.**

| Year | Interest paid (Deposits & Borrowings) | Staff Expenses | Other establishment expenses | Other expenses | Total Expenses | Growth rate |
|---|---|---|---|---|---|---|
| 1 | 2 | 3 | 4 | 5 | 6 | 7 |
| Pre IT Year 1999 | 3080.87 [71.38] | 674.8 [15.63] | N.A. N.A. | 560.78 [12.99] | 4316.45 [100] | |
| Post IT Years | | | N.A. | | | |
| 2000 | 3825.83 [73.58] | 737.99 [14.19] | N.A. N.A. | 636 [12.23] | 5199.82 [100] | 120.46 |
| 2001 | 4810.18 [74.86] | 743.76 [11.58] | N.A. N.A. | 871.45 [13.56] | 6425.39 [100] | 148.85 |
| 2002 | 5694.69 [74.57] | 921.65 [12.07] | N.A. N.A. | 1020.43 [13.36] | 7636.77 [100] | 176.92 |
| 2003 | 6328.3 [74.73] | 995.53 [11.76] | N.A. N.A. | 1144.6 [13.52] | 8468.43 [100] | 196.18 |
| 2004 | 5878.28 [70.97] | 1037.05 [12.52] | N.A. N.A. | 1367.22 [16.51] | 8282.55 [100] | 191.88 |
| 2005 | 5455.54 [66.68] | 1269.73 [15.52] | N.A. N.A. | 1456.43 [17.80] | 8181.7 [100] | 189.54 |
| 2006 | 6003.69 [67.25] | 1284.37 [14.39] | N.A. N.A. | 1639.13 [18.36] | 8927.19 [100] | 206.81 |
| 2007 | 6470.75 [66.02] | 1580.36 [16.12] | N.A. N.A. | 1750.38 [17.86] | 9801.49 [100] | 227.07 |

**Source:** Annual Reports of Thane Janata Sahakari Bank Ltd., Thane
N.A. = Not Available
Figures in parenthesis shows percentage

**Fig 5.3: Trends in Expenditure of Apna Sahakari Bank Ltd. and Thane Janata Sahakari Bank Ltd.**

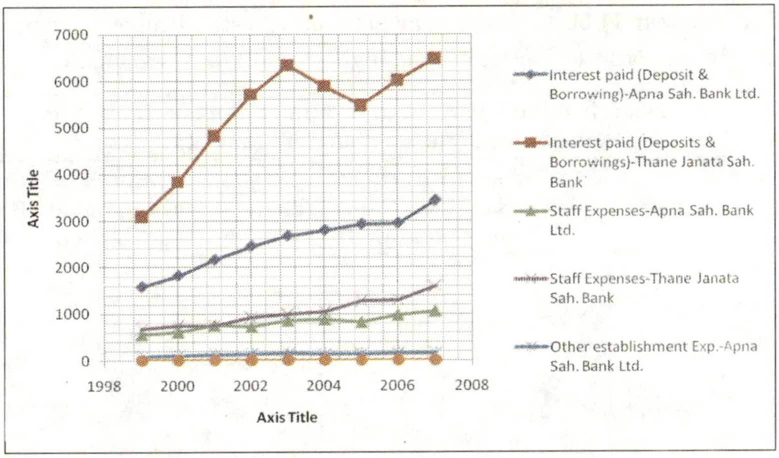


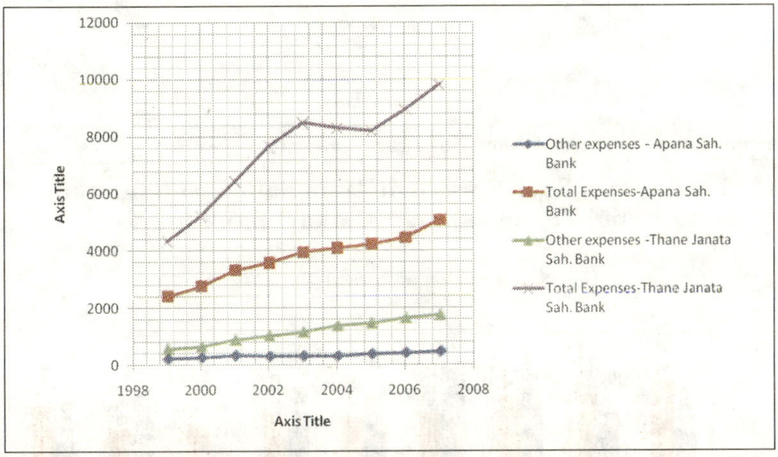


Banking is highly personalized service industry. In recent years, the managements of the bank have attempted to reduce their expenditure by introducing information technology and organizational structure. The expenses of a bank can be divided into four heads including

- Interest paid on deposits and borrowings
- Staff expenses including salaries, allowances, provident funds and bonus etc.
- Other established expenses
- Other expenses

**Interest paid**

It is the major source of expenditure to co-operative banks. Year-wise statistical analysis of Apna Sahakari bank showed that out of the total expenditure on interest paid was highest i.e., 69.14% in the year 2005 and lowest expenditure i.e., 64.71% in the year 2001. While interest paid expenditure of Thane Janata Sahakari bank was highest i.e., 74.86% in the year 2001 and lowest expenditure i.e.., 66.07% in the year 2007. Out of the total expenditure staff expenses of Apna Sahakari bank was highest i.e., 22.99% in the year 1999 and lowest 19.41%) in the year 2005. While the Thane Janata Sahakari bank staff expenses was highest 16.12%%) in year 2007 and lowest 11.50%) in the year 2001 other establishment expenses and other expenses showed same position regarding the highest and lowest expenses.

**Table No. 5.4: Trends in Spread of Apna Sahakari Bank Ltd. and Thane Janata Sahakari Bank Ltd.**

| Year | Spread Ratio of Apna Sahakari Bank (Non-Scheduled) | Spread Ratio of Thane Janata Sahakari Bank (Scheduled) |
|---|---|---|
| 1 | 2 | 3 |
| Pre IT Year 1999 | 3.95 | 5.3 |
| Post IT Years | | |
| 2000 | 4.44 | 5.14 |
| 2001 | 5.02 | 4.87 |
| 2002 | 5.82 | 4.4 |
| 2003 | 5 | 4.29 |
| 2004 | 4.06 | 4.39 |
| 2005 | 3.55 | 4.13 |
| 2006 | 3.85 | 3.98 |
| 2007 | 3.66 | 4.61 |

**Source:** Annual Reports of Apna Sahakari bank Ltd.

**Fig 5.4: Trends in Spread of Apna Sahakari Bank Ltd. and Thane Janata Sahakari Bank Ltd.**

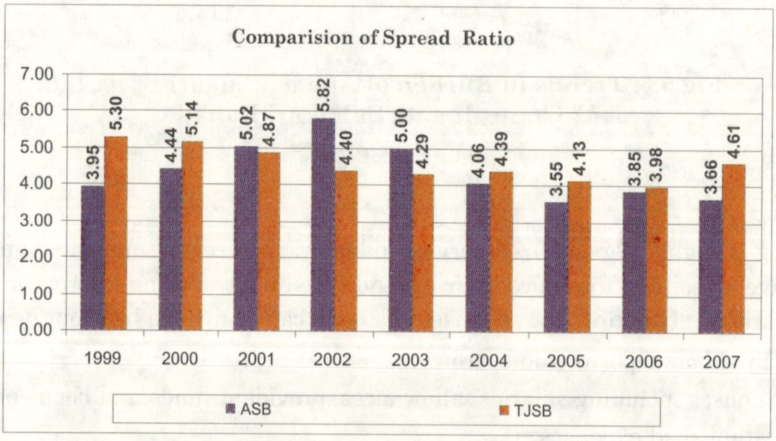


The trend of the spread earned is an important criterion to judge the profitability of Funds related to business of banks. Spread is the difference between interest carried and interest paid by the co-operative banks. Since money is the raw material of banks, banks must relate their performance and profitability to the net earnings from Funds spread that can be expressed in absolute amounts or as the percentage difference between the two variables viz., difference between interest income to working funds and interest spent to working funds.

The table 5.4 shows that the spread ratio of Apna Sahakari bank was 3.95 in the pre IT period and it went down to as 3.66 in the year 2007 i.e., post IT year. The ratio was variable the year by years. It was maximum in the year (2002 i.e., 5.82) and minimum in the year (2007 i.e. 3.66). There is no stability in the spread ratio of Apna bank.

Year wise statistical analysis of Thane Janata Sahakari bank shows that in the year 1999 it was 5.30, and it is decreased upto 4.61 in the year 2007. It was minimum spread ratio during the year 2006, i.e., 3.98 and maximum during the year 1999 i.e., 5.30.

**Table No. 5.5: Trends in Burden of Apna Sahakari Bank Ltd. and Thane Janata Sahakari Bank Ltd.**

| Year | Burden Ratio of Apna Sahakari Bank (Non-Scheduled) | Burden Ratio of Thane Janata Sahakari Bank (Scheduled) |
|---|---|---|
| 1 | 2 | 3 |
| Pre IT Year 1999 | 2.94 | 2.67 |
| Post IT Years | | |
| 2000 | 2.8 | 2.3 |
| 2001 | 2.91 | 2.05 |
| 2002 | 2.51 | 2.06 |
| 2003 | 2.39 | 1.87 |
| 2004 | 1.93 | 1.97 |
| 2005 | 1.66 | 2.1 |
| 2006 | 1.64 | 1.86 |
| 2007 | 1.6 | 1.61 |

**Source:** Annual Reports of Apna sahakari Bank and Thane Janata Sahakari Bank Ltd.

**Fig 5.5: Trends in Burden of Apna Sahakari Bank Ltd. and Thane Janata Sahakari Bank Ltd.**

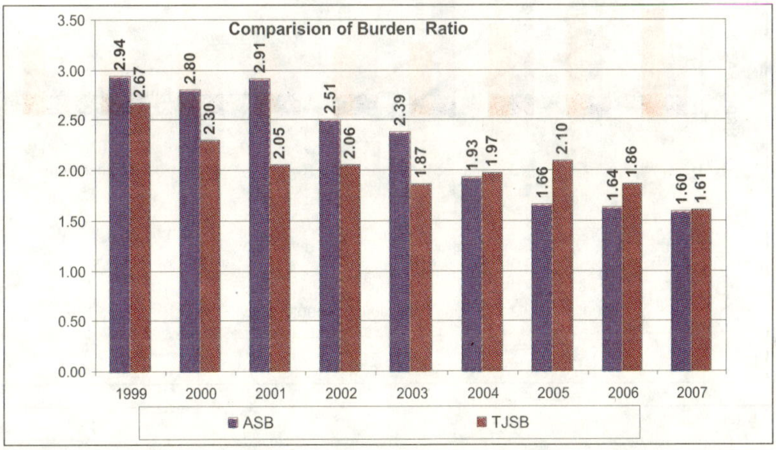

Burden means the difference between non-interest expenditure (comprising establishment expenditure and other expenditure of current and non-current nature) and non-interest income consisting of commission, exchange, brokerage and other miscellaneous receipts) of a bank and hence it represents the amount of non-interest expenditure which is not covered by non-interest income.

Table 5.5 shows that the Burden of Apna Sahakari bank and (Thane Janata Sahakari bank). The burden ratio of Apna Sahakari bank is highest in the year (2001 i.e., 2.91) and the lowest burden ratio in the year (2007 i.e., 1.60). There is a variations in the burden ratio was observed. However the trend in burden or Apna Sahakari bank is significantly and continuously declining.

The burden ratio of Thane Janta Sahakari bank was highest in the pre IT year 1999 i.e., 2.67. Followed by 2.30 (in 2000), 2.05 (2001), 2.06 (2002), 1.87 (2003), 1.97 (2004), 2.10 (2005), 1.86 (2006) and lowest i.e., 1.61 in the year (2007). It means the burden ratio of Thane Janata Sahakari bank is continuously declining after the application of Information Technology (IT).

**Table No. 5.6: Trends in Spread and Burden Ratio of Apna Sahakari Bank Ltd. and Thane Janata Sahakari Bank Ltd.**

| | Apna Sahakari Bank | | Thane Janata Sahakari Bank | |
|---|---|---|---|---|
| | **Spread Ratio** | **Burden Ratio** | **Spread Ratio** | **Burden Ratio** |
| 1 | 2 | 3 | 4 | 5 |
| Pre IT Year 1999 | 3.95 | 2.94 | 5.3 | 2.67 |
| Post IT Years | | | | |
| 2000 | 4.44 | 2.8 | 5.14 | 2.3 |
| 2001 | 5.02 | 2.91 | 4.87 | 2.05 |
| 2002 | 5.82 | 2.51 | 4.4 | 2.06 |
| 2003 | 5 | 2.39 | 4.29 | 1.87 |
| 2004 | 4.06 | 1.93 | 4.39 | 1.97 |
| 2005 | 3.55 | 1.66 | 4.13 | 2.1 |
| 2006 | 3.85 | 1.64 | 3.98 | 1.86 |
| 2007 | 3.66 | 1.6 | 4.61 | 1.61 |

**Source:** Annual Reports of Apna Sahakari Bank and Thane Janata sahakari Bank Ltd.

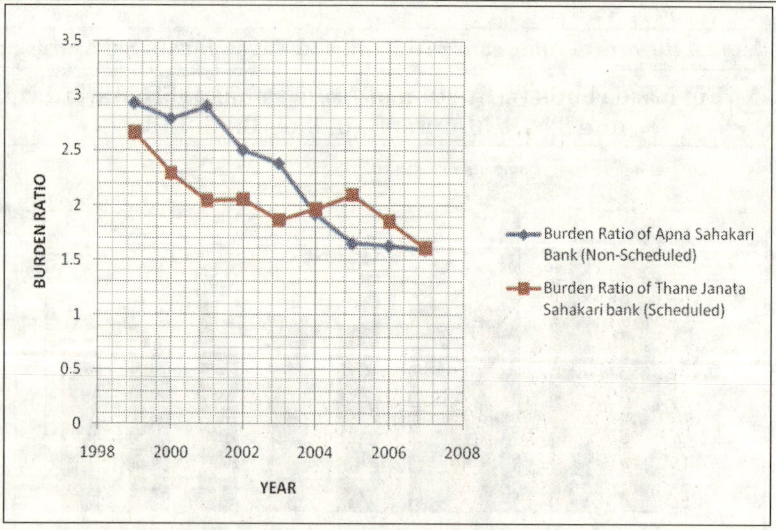

Table No. 5.6 shows that the trends in spread and Burden ratio of (Apna Sahakari Bank) and (Thane Janata Sahakari bank). Comparatively the spread ratio of Thane Janata Sahakari bank has more than the Apna Sahakari bank. The spread ratio of Thane Janata Sahakari bank was highest i.e., 5.30 in the year 1999 while in Apna Sahakari bank 5.82 in the year 2002. It reveals that the Thane Janata Sahakari bank spread ratio is continuously declining. From 5.30 to 4.61 while in the Apna bank spread ratio's are fluctuating but to some extent it has also declined.

Comparatively the burden ratio of Apna Sahakari bank and Thane Janata Sahakari bank has continuously declined after the application of Information Technology (IT). The burden ratio of Apna Sahakari bank has declined from 2.94 in 1999 to 1.60 in 2007 while it came down up to 1.61 in the year 2007.

**Table No. 5.7: Trends in Net worth**

**(A) Apna Sahakari Bank Ltd., Mumbai**

**(Rs. in Lakhs)**

| Year | Capital | Percentage Growth | Reserves | Percentage Growth | Surplus | Percentage Growth |
|---|---|---|---|---|---|---|
| 1 | 2 | 3 | 4 | 5 | 6 | 7 |
| Pre IT Year 1999 | 285.66 | | 2362.38 | | 132.99 | |
| Post IT Years | | | | | | |
| 2000 | 313.56 | 109.76 | 2673.89 | 113.18 | 312.17 | 234.73 |
| 2001 | 365.9 | 128.08 | 3432.89 | 145.31 | 368.55 | 277.12 |
| 2002 | 411.82 | 144.16 | 4967 | 210.25 | 150.58 | 113.22 |
| 2003 | 528.26 | 184.92 | 6152.07 | 260.41 | 211.85 | 159.29 |
| 2004 | 664.16 | 232.50 | 7125.02 | 301.60 | 410.68 | 308.80 |
| 2005 | 958.69 | 335.60 | 8156.29 | 345.25 | 504.62 | 379.44 |
| 2006 | 1313.19 | 459.70 | 9517.17 | 402.86 | 573.91 | 431.54 |
| 2007 | 1813.17 | 634.73 | 10751.85 | 455.12 | 888.29 | 667.93 |

**Source:** Annual Reports of Apna Sahakari Bank Ltd.

**(B) Thane Janata Sahakari Bank Ltd., Thane**

**(Rs. in Lakhs)**

| Year | Capital | Percentage Growth | Reserves | Percentage Growth | Surplus | Percentage Growth |
|---|---|---|---|---|---|---|
| 1 | 2 | 3 | 4 | 5 | 6 | 7 |
| Pre IT Year 1999 | 390.93 | | 520.08 | | 834.51 | |
| Post IT Years | | | | | | |
| 2000 | 465.54 | 119.08 | 6656.1 | 1279.82 | 943.73 | 113.08 |
| 2001 | 560.84 | 143.46 | 8214.19 | 1579.40 | 1359.11 | 162.86 |
| 2002 | 663.75 | 169.78 | 10243 | 1969.50 | 1405.99 | 168.48 |
| 2003 | 780.07 | 199.54 | 10262.78 | 1973.30 | 1519.66 | 182.10 |
| 2004 | 915.97 | 234.30 | 12459.78 | 2395.74 | 1588.43 | 190.34 |
| 2005 | 1071.89 | 274.18 | 14128.41 | 2716.58 | 1594.31 | 191.04 |
| 2006 | 1231.71 | 315.07 | 15718.4 | 3022.30 | 2399.49 | 287.53 |
| 2007 | 1447.84 | 370.35 | 18369.23 | 3532 | 3718.88 | 445.63 |

**Source:** Annual Reports of Thane Janata Sahakari Bank Ltd., Thane

Trends in net worth of Apna Sahakari bank and Thane Janata Sahakari bank includes the capital, reserves and surplus of the bank. The capital of the Apna Sahakari bank has increased from 285.66 to 1813.17 during the period 1999 to 2007. It means the capital has increased by more than 6 times during that period. The Reserves of Apna bank has increased by 2362.38 to 10751 lakh during 1999 to 2997 and the surplus of the Apna Sahakari bank has increased by 132.99 lakhs to 888.29 lakhs during 1999 to 2007. It is observed that the capital, Reserves and Surplus of Apna Sahakari bank has continuously increasing in other words growth rates are also continuously increasing in an increased rate.

The capital of the Thane Janata Sahakari bank has increased from 390.93 to 1447.84 lakhs during the period of 1999 to 2007. The Reserves of the Thane Janata Sahakari bank has increased from 52.08 to 18369.23 lakhs during the period from 1999 to 2007 and the surplus of the Thane Janata Sahakari bank has increased from 834.51 to 3718.88 lakhs during the period of 1999 to 2007. It is observed that the percentage growth of capital, reserves and surplus of Apna bank, and Thane Janata Sahakari bank, has continuously increasing trend. After the application of Information Technology both bank's have significantly positive impact.

**Table No. 5.8: Trends in Net Operating Profit of Apna Sahakari Bank Ltd. and Thane Janata Sahakari Bank Ltd.**

| Year | Net Operating Profit of Apna Sahakari Bank | Percentage Growth | Net Operating Profit of Thane Janata Sahakari Bank | Percentage Growth |
|---|---|---|---|---|
| 1 | 2 | 3 | 4 | 5 |
| Pre IT Year 1999 | 257.97 | | 834.51 | |
| Post IT Years | | | | |
| 2000 | 494.14 | 191.54 | 943.73 | 113.08 |
| 2001 | 761.78 | 295.29 | 1359.11 | 162.86 |
| 2002 | 1350.53 | 523.52 | 1406 | 168.48 |
| 2003 | 1196.85 | 460.07 | 1519.66 | 182.10 |
| 2004 | 1170.04 | 453.55 | 1588.43 | 190.34 |
| 2005 | 1158.02 | 448.89 | 1594.31 | 191.04 |
| 2006 | 1490.80 | 577.89 | 2399.49 | 287.53 |
| 2007 | 1695.29 | 657.16 | 2518.88 | 301.83 |

**Source:** Annual Reports of Apna Sahakari Bank Ltd. and Thane Janata Sahakari Bank Ltd.

The Table No. 5.8 reveals that the Net Operating Profit of Apna Sahakari bank and Thane Janata Sahakari bank shows significant effect. The net operating profit of the bank was 257.97 lakhs and it has increased upto 1695.29 lakhs during the year of 2007. While in the Thane Janata Sahakari bank it was 834.51 lakhs in the year 1999 and it was 2518.88 in the year 2007. Both the banks Net Operating Profit has continuously increased after the introduction of information technology. The percentage growth of Apna Sahakari bank was 191.54 in 2000 and it has increased upto 657.16. In 2007. While in the Thane Janata Sahakari bank the percentage growth was 113.08 in the year 2000 and it has increased upto 301.83 in 2007. Comparatively both the banks of the percentage growth have continuously increasing trend.

## Productivity Analysis of Selected Urban Co-operativer Banks

Productivity is related with the profitability. There is a direct relationship between productivity and profitability. An increase in productivity will increase the profitability and vice-versa. Productivity may be defined as the output per unit of a factor of production in a given period. Productivity index thus tells us something about the relationship between inputs and outputs in an enterprise. In a banking institution staff member's constitutes the most important input. Because of this fact, the concern's for improving productivity has to be focused on staff productivity alone.

Determinants of productivity include physical conditions of work such as lighting, ventilation, facilities for resting etc., social conditions of work such as personnel policies and practices, communications, interpersonal system, a managerial philosophy and styles, extent of humanization in the organization etc., and an individual needs, such as physical, social, egoistic and self actualization needs and perceived possibilities of need fulfillment. Now-a-days Information Technology is another powerful factor which is affecting productivity of banks.

Productivity is a ratio of input and output. When we talk of productivity, we enter into the area of employee efficiency, which is a definite bearing on profitability. As banking operations are influenced by government policy, RBI directives and various other socio-economic compulsions, are difficult to set fixed parameters for productivity in co-operative banks. The parameters keep's changing with the change in banking policy and differ according to the organizational structure. Productivity can reveal a great deal about the future course of improvement or deterioration. The purpose of the productivity analysis is to assess the impact of computerization on productivity of employees. The productivity is analysed by various parameters, such as per employee deposits, per employee loans and advances, per employee business, per employee earnings, and per employee net profit.

**Table No. 5.9: Per Employee Deposits of Apna Sahakari Bank Ltd. and Thane Janata Sahakari Bank Ltd.**

(Rs. in lakhs)

| Year | Apna Sahakari Bank | | Thane Janata Sahakari Bank | |
|---|---|---|---|---|
| | Total Deposits (Rs. in Lakhs) | Per Employee Deposits | Total Deposits (Rs. in Lakhs) | Per Employee Deposits (Rs. in Lakhs) |
| 1 | 2 | 3 | 4 | 5 |
| Pre IT Year 1999 | 20548.16 | 58.70 | 36833.95 | 83.90 |
| Post IT Year | | | | |
| 2000 | 24710.23 | 70.80 | 46730.61 | 103.38 |
| 2001 | 29477.54 | 85.19 | 59197.47 | 133.92 |
| 2002 | 32809.66 | 95.65 | 73388.76 | 165.66 |
| 2003 | 36422.23 | 106.8 | 77630.57 | 178.45 |
| 2004 | 42836.44 | 126.35 | 87213.21 | 202.82 |
| 2005 | 47978.74 | 145.82 | 93881.97 | 217.82 |
| 2006 | 55069.70 | 169.44 | 104305.91 | 243.13 |
| 2007 | 65184.99 | 201.18 | 132852.18 | 312.56 |

**Source:** Annual Reports of Apna Sahakari Bank and Thane Janata Sahakari Bank Ltd.

**Fig 5.6: Per Employee Deposits of Apna Sahakari Bank Ltd. and Thane Janata Sahakari Bank Ltd.**

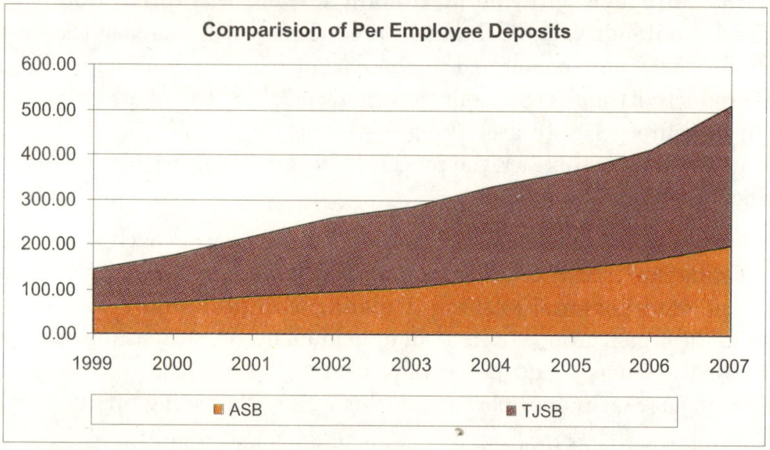


It is observed that the per employee deposits in Apna Sahakari Bank was Rs. 58.70 lakhs during the study period from 1999 to 2007. Whereas in Thane Janata Sahakari Bank Ltd the per employee deposits in 1999 was Rs. 83.90 lakhs and it has increased by Rs. 312.59 lakhs during the period from 1999 to 2007.

**Table No. 5.10: Per Employee Loans of Apna Sahakari Bank Ltd. and Thane Janata Sahakari Bank Ltd.**

| Year | Apna Sahakari Bank | | Thane Janata Sahakari Bank | |
|---|---|---|---|---|
| | Total Advances (Rs. in lakhs) | Per Employee Advances (Rs. in Lakhs) | Total Advances (Rs. in Lakhs) | Per Employee Advances (Rs. in Lakhs) |
| 1 | 2 | 3 | 4 | 5 |
| Pre IT Year 1999 | 11199.70 | 31.99 | 22191.24 | 50.54 |
| Post IT Year | | | | |
| 2000 | 13656.61 | 39.12 | 28040.93 | 62.03 |
| 2001 | 15718.13 | 45.42 | 37307.19 | 84.39 |
| 2002 | 18454.50 | 65.78 | 43368.26 | 97.89 |
| 2003 | 22433.15 | 80.97 | 51130.84 | 117.54 |
| 2004 | 27452.67 | 110.23 | 54219.77 | 126.09 |
| 2005 | 36268.30 | 128.18 | 58247.44 | 135.14 |
| 2006 | 41659.33 | 141.51 | 68042.85 | 158.60 |
| 2007 | 45849.61 | 141.51 | 90292.63 | 212.45 |

**Source:** Annual Reports of Apna Sahakari Bank Ltd. and Thane Janata Sahakari Bank Ltd.

**Table No. 5.11: Per Employee Business of Apna Sahakari Bank Ltd. and Thane Janata Sahakari Bank Ltd.**

| Year | Apna Sahakari Bank | | Thane Janata Sahakari Bank | |
|---|---|---|---|---|
| | Total Business (Deposits + Advances) | Per Employee Business | Total Business (Deposits+ Advances) | Per Employee Business |
| 1 | 2 | 3 | 4 | 5 |
| Pre IT Year 1999 | 31747.86 | 90.70 | 59025.19 | 134.45 |
| Post IT Year | | | | |
| 2000 | 38366.84 | 109.93 | 74771.54 | 165.42 |
| 2001 | 45195.67 | 130.62 | 96504.66 | 218.33 |
| 2002 | 51313.66 | 149.60 | 116757.02 | 263.55 |
| 2003 | 58855.38 | 172.59 | 128761.41 | 296.00 |
| 2004 | 70289.11 | 207.34 | 141432.98 | 328.91 |
| 2005 | 84247.04 | 256.06 | 152129.41 | 352.96 |
| 2006 | 96729.03 | 297.67 | 175348.76 | 408.73 |
| 2007 | 111034.60 | 342.69 | 223144.81 | 525.04 |

**Source:** Annual Reports of Apna Sahakari Bank and Thane Janata Sahakari Bank Ltd.

**Fig 5.7: Per Employee Business of Apna Sahakari Bank Ltd. and Thane Janata Sahakari Bank Ltd.**

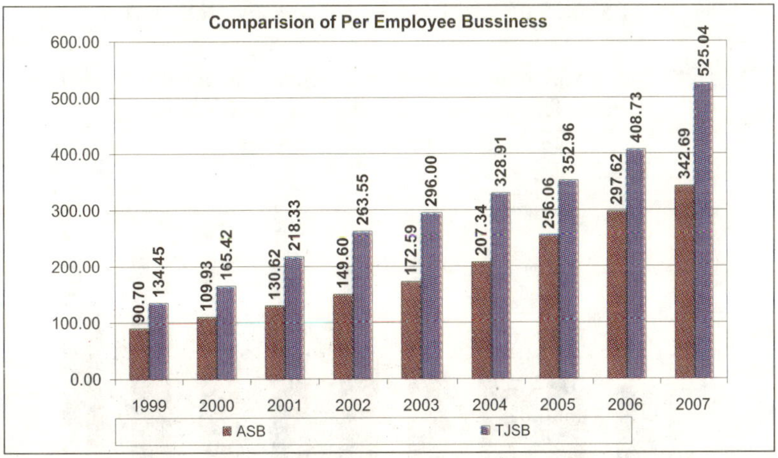


Per employee business (Deposits + Advances) of Apna Sahakari Bank was Rs. 90.70 lakhs and after application of information technology the per employee business has shows continuously an increasing trend and it has been Rs. 342.69 lakhs in the year 2007. The total growth of per employee business has been increased by 377.88 lakhs during the period from 1999 to 2007. However the same situation has showing in Thane Janata Sahakari Bank was Rs. 134.45 lakhs in the year 1999 and it has increased by Rs. 525.04 lakhs during 1999-2007. It means the growth of per employee business has been increased by 390.50 percent during the study period. The per employee business growth rate is slightly higher in Thane Janata Sahakari Bank than that of Apna Sahaakri Bank.

| Table No. 5.12: Per Employee Earnings of Apna Sahakari Bank Ltd. and Thane Janata Sahakari Bank Ltd. | | | | |
|---|---|---|---|---|
| **Year** | **Apna Sahakari Bank** | | **Thane Janata Sahakari Bank** | |
| | **Total Earnings (Rs. in Lakhs)** | **Per Employee Earnings (Rs in Lakhs)** | **Total Earnings (Rs. in Lakhs)** | **Per Employee Earnings (Rs. in Lakhs)** |
| **1** | **2** | **3** | **4** | **5** |
| Pre IT Year 1999 | 2657.95 | 7.59 | 5295.97 | 12.06 |
| Post IT Year | | | | |
| 2000 | 3238.59 | 9.27 | 6543.55 | 14.47 |
| 2001 | 4076.41 | 11.78 | 8149.50 | 18.43 |
| 2002 | 4908.64 | 14.29 | 9342.76 | 21.08 |
| 2003 | 5122.01 | 15.02 | 10596.09 | 24.35 |
| 2004 | 5247.66 | 15.47 | 10682.98 | 24.84 |
| 2005 | 5364.95 | 16.30 | 10384.08 | 24.09 |
| 2006 | 5925.43 | 18.23 | 11490.68 | 26.78 |
| 2007 | 6746.98 | 20.82 | 13997.37 | 32.93 |
| **Source:** Annual Reports of Apna Sahakari Bank and Thane Janata Sahakari Bank Ltd. | | | | |

**Fig 5.8: Per Employee Earnings of Apna Sahakari Bank Ltd. and Thane Janata Sahakari Bank Ltd.**

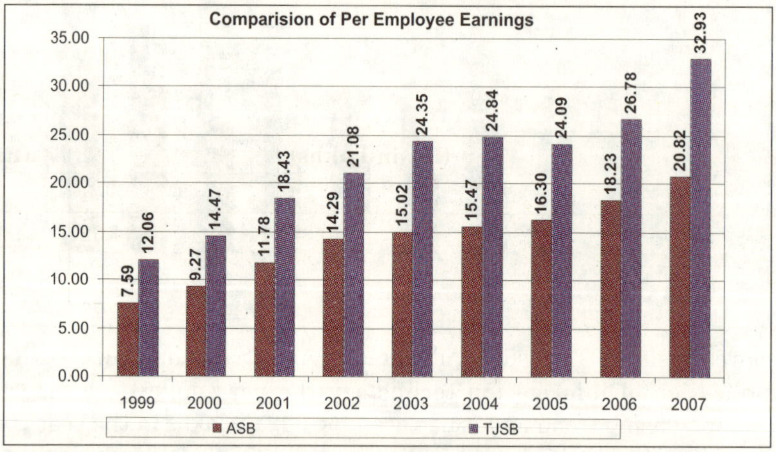


The per employee earnings in Apna Sahakari Bank has increased from Rs. 7.59 lakhs to rs. 20.82 lakhs during 1999 to 2007, While in Thane Janata Sahakari Bank per employee earnings has increased from Rs. 12.06 lakhs to Rs. 32.93 lakhs during 199 – 2007. It is also found that the growth rate of both the selected banks has shown as increasing trend.

| Table No. 5.13: Per Employee Staff Expenses of Apna Sahakari Bank Ltd. and Thane Janata Sahakari Bank Ltd. | | | | |
|---|---|---|---|---|
| **Year** | **Apna Sahakari Bank** | | **Thane Janata Sahakari Bank** | |
| | **Total Staff Expenses (Rs. in lakhs)** | **Per Employee Staff Expenses (Rs. in Lakhs)** | **Total Staff Expenses (Rs. in Lakhs)** | **Per Employee Staff Expenses (Rs. in Lakhs)** |
| 1 | 2 | 3 | 4 | 5 |
| Pre IT Year 1999 | 551.72 | 1.57 | 674.80 | 1.53 |
| Post IT Year | | | | |
| 2000 | 607.07 | 1.73 | 737.99 | 1.63 |
| 2001 | 757.25 | 2.18 | 743.76 | 1.68 |
| 2002 | 718.04 | 2.09 | 921.65 | 2.07 |
| 2003 | 846.63 | 2.48 | 995.53 | 2.28 |
| 2004 | 877.70 | 2.58 | 1037.05 | 2.41 |
| 2005 | 816.68 | 2.48 | 1269.73 | 2.94 |
| 2006 | 973.40 | 2.99 | 1284.37 | 2.99 |
| 2007 | 1056.72 | 3.26 | 1580.36 | 3.71 |

**Source:** Annual Reports of Apna Sahakari Bank and Thane Janata Sahakari Bank Ltd.

| Table No. 5.14: Per Employee Net Profit of Apna Sahakari Bank Ltd. and Thane Janata Sahakari Bank Ltd. | | | | |
|---|---|---|---|---|
| **Year** | **Apna Sahakari Bank** | | **Thane Janata Sahakari Bank** | |
| | **Net Profit (Rs. in Lakhs)** | **Per Employee Net Profit (Rs. in Lakhs)** | **Net Profit (Rs. in Lakhs)** | **Per Employee Net Profit (Rs. in Lakhs)** |
| 1 | 2 | 3 | 4 | 5 |
| Pre IT Year 1999 | 132.96 | 0.37 | 834.52 | 1.90 |
| Post IT Year | | | | |
| 2000 | 312.13 | 0.89 | 943.73 | 2.08 |
| 2001 | 368.50 | 1.06 | 1359.12 | 3.07 |
| 2002 | 150.52 | 0.43 | 1405.99 | 3.17 |
| 2003 | 211.85 | 0.61 | 1519.66 | 3.49 |
| 2004 | 410.68 | 1.20 | 1588.43 | 3.69 |
| 2005 | 504.62 | 1.53 | 1594.32 | 3.69 |
| 2006 | 573.91 | 1.76 | 2399.49 | 5.59 |
| 2007 | 525.07 | 1.62 | 2518.88 | 5.92 |

**Source:** Annual Reports of Apna Sahakari Bank and Thane Janata Sahakari Bank Ltd.

**Fig 5.9: Per Employee Net Profit of Apna Sahakari Bank Ltd. and Thane Janata Sahakari Bank Ltd.**

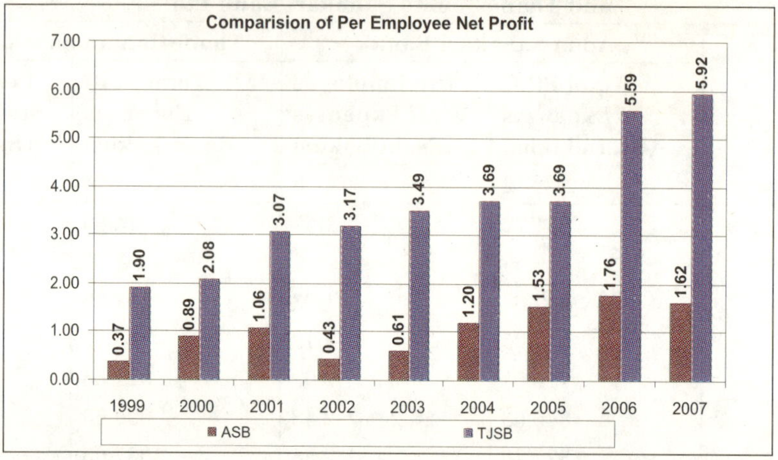


It is observed that the per employee Net profit has grew at the rate of 437.83 percent in Apna Sahakari Bank during the period from 1999 – 2007. Whereas in Thane Janata Sahakari Bank per employee net profit has grew at the rate of 311.57 percent. It is also found that the per employee net profit in Apna Sahakari Bank has increased from Rs. 0.37 lakhs to Rs. 1.62 lakhs during 1999 to 2007, while in Thane Janata Sahakari Bank it has increased from Rs. 1.90 lakh to rs. 5.92 lakhs during the said period. The growth rate of net profit in Apna Sahakari Bank is higher than the Thane Janata sahakari Bank after the application of information technology. It indicates that the impact of IT has positively significant in both the banks, but it is higher in Apna Sahakari Bank as compared to Thane Janata Sahakari Bank.

## Ratio Analysis of Selected Urban Co-operative Banks

The ratio analysis is one of the most widely used techniques of financial analysis of banks. It aims at making use of quantitative information for decision making and thus provides great help to the management in planning and control of their activities. For measuring the profitability of banks, analysis of relevant ratios is the best available method because of their consistencies, comparability and the direct relevance of the relationships established to the various earnings and capabilities of the banks. Ratio analysis also enables the management of banks to identify the causes of the changes in their profits and profitability over the period of time and thus helps in pin-pointing the direction of action required for altering the profitability prospects of the banks in future.

The Table No. 5.15 shows that the Income ratio of Apna Sahakari Bank and Thane Janata Sahakari Bank Ltd., Interest and discount as percentage to total income in Apna Sahakari Bank in the year 1999 was 97.06 whereas after that period no significant change has been observed, this ratio was slightly changed in 2007 i.e., it was 95.48% before.

**Table No. 5.15: Income Ratio of Apna Sahakari Bank Ltd. and Thane Janata Sahakari Bank Ltd.**

**(Rs. in lakhs)**

| **Apna Sahakari Bank** | | | |
|---|---|---|---|
| **Year** | **Interest & Discount as % to Total Income** | **Commission, Exchange and Brokerage as % to Total Income** | **Other Earnings as % to Total Income** |
| **1** | **2** | **3** | **4** |
| Pre IT Year 1999 | 97.06 | 0.33 | 2.7 |
| Post IT Year | | | |
| 2000 | 97.14 | 0.28 | 2.58 |
| 2001 | 96.98 | 0.25 | 2.76 |
| 2002 | 97.68 | 0.15 | 2.20 |
| 2003 | 96.70 | 6.25 | 3.04 |
| 2004 | 95.33 | 0.30 | 4.37 |
| 2005 | 94.83 | 0.37 | 4.80 |
| 2006 | 95.12 | 0.40 | 4.48 |
| 2007 | 95.48 | 0.59 | 3.93 |

**Source:** Annual Reports of Apna Sahakari Bank Ltd.

| **Thane Janata Sahakari Bank Ltd.** | | | |
|---|---|---|---|
| **Year** | **Interest & Discount as % to Total Income** | **Commission, Exchange and Brokerage as % to Total Income** | **Other Earnings as % to Total Income** |
| **1** | **2** | **3** | **4** |
| Pre IT Year 1999 | 94.98 | 2.02 | 2.99 |
| Post IT Year | | | |
| 2000 | 92.56 | 1.91 | 5.53 |
| 2001 | 94.08 | 1.57 | 4.35 |
| 2002 | 93.98 | 1.42 | 4.60 |
| 2003 | 92.79 | 1.55 | 5.66 |
| 2004 | 92.52 | 1.65 | 5.83 |
| 2005 | 95.56 | 2.00 | 2.44 |
| 2006 | 93.98 | 2.78 | 3.24 |
| 2007 | 92.82 | 2.65 | 4.52 |

**Source:** Annual Reports of Thana Janata Sahakari Bank

Whereas the ratio in Thane Janata Sahakari Bank of the year 1999 was 94.98% and onwards some fluctuations has been observed in the year 2007 this ratio is slightly declined i.e., 92.82%

The income from Commission, Exchange and brokerage as % to total income in Apna Sahakari Bank in the year 1999 was 0.33% and it has increased upto 0.59% in the year 2007. Whereas in Thane Janata Sahakari Bank the share of commission, exchange and brokerage as % to total income in the year 1999 was 2.02% and it has increased upto 2.65% in the year

2007. Again in the other earnings as % to total income in Apna Sahakari Bank in the year 1999 was 2.7 and it has increased upto 3.93%. Whereas in Thane Janata Sahakari bank the share of other earnings as % to total income in the year 1999 was 2.99% and it has increased upto 4.52 in the year 2007.

It is clearly indicated that in both the banks the ratio of interest and discount to total income is very high i.e., more than 92%. Hence it is a major source of income for both the banks.

**Table No. 5.16: Expenditure Ratio of Apna Sahakari Bank Ltd. and Thane Janata Sahakari Bank Ltd.**

**(Rs. in lakhs)**

**Apna Sahakari Bank**

| Year | Interest paid as % to Total Expenditure | Staff Expenses as % to Total Expenditure | Establishment expenses as % to Total Expenditure | Other Expenses as % to Total Expenditure |
|---|---|---|---|---|
| 1 | 2 | 3 | 4 | 5 |
| Pre IT Year 1999 | 65.62 | 22.99 | 3.08 | 8.32 |
| Post IT Year | | | | |
| 2000 | 65.95 | 22.12 | 3.24 | 8.70 |
| 2001 | 64.71 | 22.85 | 3.12 | 9.32 |
| 2002 | 68.52 | 20.18 | 3.49 | 7.81 |
| 2003 | 67.76 | 21.57 | 3.30 | 7.37 |
| 2004 | 68.21 | 21.52 | 3.13 | 7.13 |
| 2005 | 69.14 | 19.41 | 2.95 | 8.50 |
| 2006 | 66.09 | 21.95 | 3.09 | 8.87 |
| 2007 | 67.66 | 20.92 | 2.61 | 8.81 |

**Source:** Annual Reports of Apna Sahakari Bank Ltd.

**Thane Janata Sahakari Bank Ltd.**

| Year | Interest paid as % to Total Expenditure | Staff Expenses as % to Total Expenditure | Establishment expenses as % to Total Expenditure | Other Expenses as % to Total Expenditure |
|---|---|---|---|---|
| 1 | 2 | 3 | 4 | 5 |
| Pre IT Year 1999 | 71.38 | 15.63 | N.A. | 12.99 |
| Post IT Year | | | | |
| 2000 | 73.58 | 14.19 | - | 12.23 |
| 2001 | 74.86 | 11.88 | - | 13.56 |
| 2002 | 74.57 | 12.07 | - | 13.36 |
| 2003 | 74.73 | 11.76 | - | 13.52 |
| 2004 | 70.97 | 12.52 | - | 16.51 |
| 2005 | 66.68 | 18.52 | - | 17.80 |
| 2006 | 67.25 | 14.39 | - | 18.36 |
| 2007 | 66.02 | 14.12 | - | 17.86 |

**Note:** N.A. = Not Available
**Source:** Annual Reports of Thane Janata Sahakari Bank Ltd.

The Table 5.16 shows that the Expenditure ratio of Apna Sahakari Bank and Thane Janata Sahakari Bank Ltd. The ratio of interest paid to total expenditure in Apna Sahakari Bank was 65.62% in the year 1999 and it has increased upto 67.66% in the year 2007. Whereas in Thane Janata Sahakari Bank the ratio of interest paid to total expenditure was 71.38% in the year 1999 but it has slightly declined upto 66.02% in the year 2007. It reveals that there is a fluctuation over the period from 1999 to 2007.

The ratio of staff expenses to total expenditure in Apna Sahakari Bank in the year 1999 was 22.99% and it has reduced upto 20.92% in the year 2007. Whereas in Thane Janata Sahakari Bank the ratio of staff expenses was 15.63% in the year 1999 and went to 14.12% in the year 2007. It clearly indicates that after the bank automation in both the banks the staff expenses has been reducing but not in significant proportion.

**Table No. 5.17: Deposit Ratio of Apna Sahakari Bank Ltd. and Thane Janata Sahakari Bank Ltd.**

**Apna Sahakari Bank**

| Year | Fixed Deposit as % of Total Deposits | Saving Deposits as % of Total Deposits | Current Deposits as % of Total Deposits |
|---|---|---|---|
| 1 | 2 | 3 | 4 |
| Pre IT Year 1999 | 53.76 | 37.85 | 8.18 |
| Post IT Year | | | |
| 2000 | 55.53 | 37.87 | 6.60 |
| 2001 | 56.26 | 36.54 | 7.21 |
| 2002 | 59.25 | 35.13 | 5.62 |
| 2003 | 60.56 | 34.40 | 5.03 |
| 2004 | 61.16 | 33.49 | 5.35 |
| 2005 | 61.04 | 33.57 | 5.39 |
| 2006 | 61.13 | 32.75 | 6.13 |
| 2007 | 61.64 | 31.57 | 6.79 |

**Source:** Annual Reports of Apna Sahakari Bank

**Thane Janata Sahakari Bank**

| Year | Fixed Deposit as % of Total Deposits | Saving Deposits as % of Total Deposits | Current Deposits as % of Total Deposits |
|---|---|---|---|
| 1 | 2 | 3 | 4 |
| Pre IT Year 1999 | 64.57 | 28.50 | 6.93 |
| Post IT Year | | | |
| 2000 | 66.24 | 26.70 | 7.07 |
| 2001 | 68.13 | 26.13 | 5.73 |
| 2002 | 71.17 | 23.34 | 5.49 |
| 2003 | 68.28 | 25.55 | 6.17 |
| 2004 | 67.15 | 26.57 | 6.27 |
| 2005 | 65.72 | 27.66 | 6.62 |
| 2006 | 62.51 | 29.27 | 8.21 |
| 2007 | 65.08 | 26.75 | 8.17 |

**Source:** Annual Reports of Thane Janata Sahakari Bank

Table No. 5.17 shows that the deposits ratios of Apna Sahakari Bank and Thane Janata Sahakari Banks. In Apna Sahakari Bank in the pre IT year, the ratio of Fixed deposits to total deposits was 53.96%, the ratio of savings deposits to total deposits was 37.85% and the ratio of current deposits to total deposits was 8.18%. Whereas in the Thane Janata Sahakari Bank the ratio of Fixed deposits to total deposits in the year 1999 was 64.57%, ratio of saving deposits was 28.50% and the ratio of current deposits was 6.93% respectively.

Over the introduction of information technology in both the banks the ratio has been changed. In the year 2007, in Apna Sahakari Banks the ratio of Fixed deposits to total deposits has been 61.64%, ratio of savings deposits 31.57% and the ratio of current deposits was 6.79%. Whereas the Thane Janata Sahakari Bank the ratio of Fixed deposits to total deposits has been 65.085, ratio of savings deposits 26.75% and the ratio of current deposits has been 8.17 % respectively.

## Deposit Mobilisation of Selected Urban Co-operative Banks

In the category of external sources of Finance, Deposits constitute the main component. Deposits are the mainstay of a bank and they constitute its life-blood. Generally the activities of a bank revolve around two things (1) Mobilization of Deposits and (2) Proper deployment / utilization of the same. Deposits and advances are, therefore, the main products of banking industry. The very definition of banking as accepting for the purpose of lending or investment, deposits of money from the public repayable on demand or otherwise, collaborates the fact. Both activities are independent in the sense that without deposits, advances are least possible, and if there is no advance, there is no question of mobilising the deposits, It is the size of the deposits that largely decides the lending activity of the bank and it is only when the lending increase's the other internal resources viz., share of capital and reserves are naturally augmented. Further deposits serve as cushion in absorbing the shocks of overdues enabling the bank to maintain an uninterrupted flow of credit which in of deposits promotes social well-being of the depositors as also the public at large by installing in them the habit of savings. Banks, therefore, can discharge their socio-economic responsibilities only if they accelerate the pace of deposit mobilization.

## Classification of Deposits

### Fixed Deposits (FD)

The term 'Fixed Deposits' means the deposit repayable only after the expiry of a specified period. Banks pay interest on the deposit according to maturity. These are further classified into short term and long term. The rate of interest on Fixed deposits depends upon the length of the time of the deposit. The longer the period, the higher is the rate of interest. They are also known as 'Time Deposits'. Fixed Deposits are the most suitable form of raising resources for co-operative banks.

### Saving Deposits (SD)

Saving deposit is means for small businessmen and individuals who wish to save a little out of their current incomes to safeguard their future and also to earn some interest on their savings.

## Current Deposits (CD)

Current Deposits also known as demand deposits. Current deposits are those which may be withdrawn by the depositor or transferred to someone else at any time without prior notice to bank. Therefore current deposits serve both as a means of payment and as a store of value. The rate of interest on current account deposits which form the bulk of demand deposits is nil. These are maintained by those who need liquid balance. Current deposits constitute the universal means of payment.

**Table No. 5.18: Share of Fixed Deposits to Total Deposits of Apna Sahakari Bank Ltd. and Thane Janata Sahakari Bank Ltd.**

**(Rs. in lakhs)**

| Year | Apna Sahakari Bank | | Thane Janata Sahakari Bank | |
|---|---|---|---|---|
| | Fixed Deposits | Total Deposits | Fixed Deposits | Total Deposits |
| 1 | 2 | 3 | 4 | 5 |
| Pre IT Year 1999 | 11087.80(53.95%) | 20548.16(100%) | 23784.62(64.57%) | 36833.95(100%) |
| Post IT Year | | | | |
| 2000 | 13721.10(55.52%) | 24710.23(100%) | 30952.21(66.23%) | 46730.61(100%) |
| 2001 | 16582.95(56.25%) | 29477.54(100%) | 40332.86(68.13%) | 59197.47(100%) |
| 2002 | 19439.16(59.24%) | 32809.66(100%) | 52229.94(71.16%) | 73388.76(100%) |
| 2003 | 22058.06(600.58%) | 36422.23(100%) | 53007.94(68.28%) | 77630.57(100%) |
| 2004 | 26199.76(61.16%) | 42836.44(100%) | 58567.70(67.15%) | 87213.21(100%) |
| 2005 | 29286.87(61.04%) | 47978.74(100%) | 61703.39(65.72%) | 93881.97(100%) |
| 2006 | 33662.35(61.12%) | 55069.70(100%) | 67080.98(62.51%) | 107305.91(100%) |
| 2007 | 40180.57(61.64%) | 65184.99(100%) | 86460.75(65.07%) | 132852.18(100%) |

**Source:** Annual Reports of Apna Sahakari Bank and Thane Janata Sahakari Bank

**Fig 5.10: Share of Fixed Deposits to Total Deposits in Apna Sahakari Bank Ltd. and Thane Janata Sahakari Bank Ltd.**

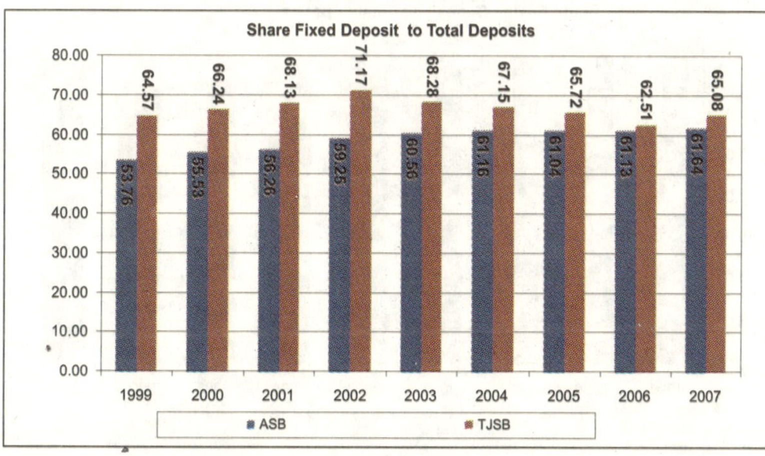

## Share of Fixed Deposits to Total Deposits

The ratio of Fixed deposits to Total deposits is higher in both Apna Sahakari Bank and Thane Janata Sahakari Bank (See Table 5.18). In Apna Sahakari Bank the ratio of Fixed deposits to Total deposits is ranging between 53.95% to 61.64% during the study. The proportion of Fixed deposits as a percentage of total deposits in 1999 was 53.95 % and it was 61.64% in 2007. The percentage of Fixed deposits to total deposits in Apna Bank is in increasing trend. In Thane Janata Sahakari Bank the ratio of Fixed deposits to total deposits is ranging between 62.51% to 71.16% during the study period. The proportion of Fixed deposits as a percentage of total deposits in 1999 was 64.57% and it was 65.07% in 2007. The percentage of Fixed deposits to total deposits in Thane Janata Sahakari Bank also is in increasing trend. It reveals that in both the banks percentage of Fixed deposits is major part of total deposits and it is continuously in increasing trend.

**Table No. 5.19: Share of Saving Deposits to Total Deposits**

**(Rs. in lakhs)**

| Year | Apna Sahakari Bank | | Thane Janata Sahakari Bank | |
|---|---|---|---|---|
| | Saving Deposits | Total Deposits | Saving Deposits | Total Deposits |
| 1 | 2 | 3 | 4 | 5 |
| Pre IT Year 1999 | 7778.97(37.85%) | 20548.16(100%) | 10497.65(28.49%) | 36833.95(100%) |
| Post IT Year | | | | |
| 2000 | 9357.16(37.86%) | 24710.23(100%) | 12476.21(26.69%) | 46730.61(100%) |
| 2001 | 10770.71(36.53%) | 29477.54(100%) | 15469.83(26.13%) | 59197.47(100%) |
| 2002 | 11525.57(35.12%) | 32809.66(100%) | 17126.76(23.33%) | 73388.76(100%) |
| 2003 | 12531.51(34.40%) | 36422.23(100%) | 19834.98(25.54%) | 77630.57(100%) |
| 2004 | 14343.25(33.48%) | 42836.44(100%) | 23175.68(26.57%) | 87213.21(100%) |
| 2005 | 16106.98(33.56%) | 47978.74(100%) | 25964.78(27.68%) | 93881.97(100%) |
| 2006 | 18033.62(32.74%) | 55069.70(100%) | 31410.83(29.27%) | 107305.91(100%) |
| 2007 | 20577.10(31.56%) | 65184.99(100%) | 35535.06(26.74%) | 132852.18(100%) |

**Source:** Annual Reports of Apna Sahakari Bank and Thane Janata Sahakari Bank

**Fig 5.11: Share of Saving Deposits to Total Deposits**

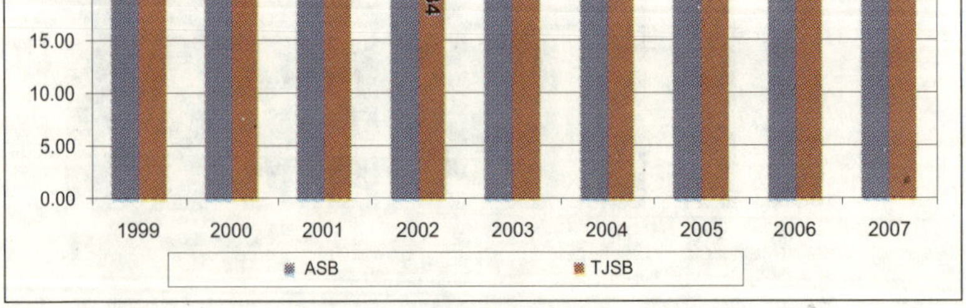

## Share of Saving Deposits to Total Deposits

The ratio of saving deposits to total deposits in Apna Sahakari Bank is ranging between 3.156% to 37.86% during the study period. The proportion of saving deposits as a percentage of total deposits in pre IT year 1999 was 37.86% and it was 31.56% in 2007. The percentage of saving deposits to total deposits in Apna Sahakari bank is in decreasing trend. In Thane Janata Sahakari bank the ratio of saving deposits to total deposits is ranging between 23.33% to 29.27% during the study period. The proportion of saving deposits as a percentage to total deposits in 1999 was 28.49% and it was 26.74% in 2007. The percentage of saving deposits to total deposits in Thane Janata Sahakari bank is in fluctuating trend.

**Table No. 5.20: Share of Current Deposits to Total Deposits**

**(Rs. in lakhs)**

| Year | Apna Sahakari Bank | | Thane Janata Sahakari Bank | |
|---|---|---|---|---|
| | Current Deposits | Total Deposits | Current Deposits | Total Deposits |
| 1 | 2 | 3 | 4 | 5 |
| Pre IT Year 1999 | 1681.39(8.18%) | 20548.16(100%) | 2551.68(6.92%) | 36833.95(100%) |
| Post IT Year | | | | |
| 2000 | 1631.97(6.60%) | 24710.23(100%) | 3302.19(7.06% | 46730.61(100%) |
| 2001 | 2123.88(7.20%) | 29477.54(100%) | 3394.78(5.73%) | 59197.47(100%) |
| 2002 | 1844.93(5.62%) | 32809.66(100%) | 4032.06(5.49%) | 73388.78(100%) |
| 2003 | 1832.66(5.02%) | 36422.23(100%) | 4787.65(6.16%) | 77630.57(100%) |
| 2004 | 2292.43(5.35%) | 42836.44(100%) | 5469.83(6.27%) | 87213.21(100%) |
| 2005 | 2584.89(5.38%) | 47978.74(100%) | 6212.80(6.61%) | 93881.97(100%) |
| 2006 | 3373.73(6.12%) | 55069.70(100%) | 8814.10(8.21%) | 107305.91(100%) |
| 2007 | 4426.32(6.79%) | 65184.99(100%) | 10856.37(8.17%) | 132852.18(100%) |

**Source:** Annual Reports of Apna Sahakari Bank Ltd. and Thane Janata Sahakari Bank Ltd.

**Fig 5.12: Share of Current Deposits to Total Deposits**

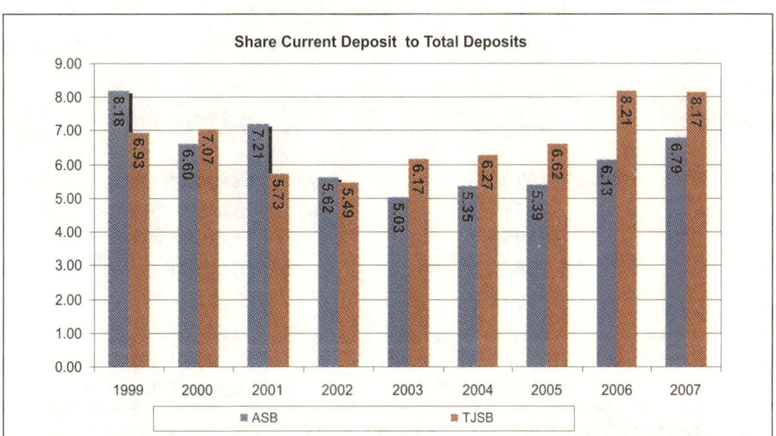

**Share of Current Deposits to Total Deposits**

The table No. 5.20 shows that the ratio of current deposits to total deposits in Apna Sahakari bank is ranging between 5.02% to 8.18% during the study period. The proportion of current deposits as a percentage of total deposits in pre IT year 1999 was 8.18% and it was 6.79% in 2007. In Thane Janata Sahakari Bank the ratio of current deposits to total deposits is ranging between 5.49% to 8.21% during the study period. The proportion of current deposits as a percentage to total deposits in 1999 was 6.92% and it was 8.17% in 2007. The percentage of current deposits to total deposits in Thane Janata Sahakari Bank is also in increasing trend. It reveals that in Apna Sahakari Bank and Thane Janata Sahakari Bank the percentage of current deposits to total deposits is in fluctuating trend.

**Table No. 5.21:Optimum Level of Loans and Advances of Apna Sahakari Bank Ltd. and Thane Janata Sahakari Bank Ltd.**

**(Rs. in lakhs)**

| Apna Sahakari Bank | | | |
|---|---|---|---|
| **Year** | **Deposits** | **Loans & Advances** | **Credit Deposit Ratio** |
| 1 | 2 | 3 | 4 |
| Pre IT Year 1999 | 20548.16 | 11999.70 | 54.50 |
| Post IT Year | | | |
| 2000 | 24710.23 | 13656.61 | 55.27 |
| 2001 | 29477.54 | 15718.13 | 53.32 |
| 2002 | 32809.67 | 18454.50 | 56.25 |
| 2003 | 36422.23 | 22433.15 | 61.59 |
| 2004 | 42836.44 | 22452.67 | 64.09 |
| 2005 | 47978.74 | 36268.30 | 75.59 |
| 2006 | 55069.71 | 41659.33 | 75.65 |
| 2007 | 65184.99 | 45849.61 | 70.34 |

**Source:** Annual Reports of Apna Sahakari Bank

| Thane Janata Sahakari Bank Ltd. | | | |
|---|---|---|---|
| **Year** | **Deposits** | **Loans & Advances** | **Credit Deposit Ratio** |
| 1 | 2 | 3 | 4 |
| Pre IT Year 1999 | 36833.95 | 22191.24 | 60.25 |
| Post IT Year | | | |
| 2000 | 46730.61 | 28040.93 | 60.01 |
| 2001 | 59197.47 | 37307.19 | 63.02 |
| 2002 | 73388.76 | 43368.26 | 59.09 |
| 2003 | 77630.57 | 51130.84 | 65.86 |
| 2004 | 87213.21 | 54219.77 | 62.17 |
| 2005 | 93881.97 | 58247.44 | 62.04 |
| 2006 | 107305.91 | 68042.85 | 63.41 |
| 2007 | 132852.18 | 90292.63 | 67.96 |

**Source:** Annual Reports of Thane Janata Sahakari Bank

**Fig 5.13: Credit Deposit Ratio of Apna Sahakari Bank Ltd. and Thane Janata Sahakari Bank Ltd.**

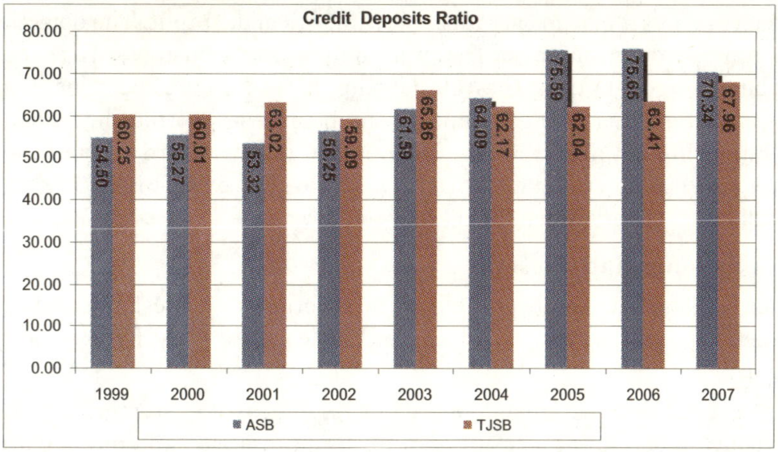


The Table No. 5.21 indicates that the deposits of Apna Sahakari Bank has increased by 317.23% from Rs. 20548.16 lakhs to 65184.99 lakhs, in the course of 8 years from 1999 to 2007, whereas such growth in respect of Thane Janata Sahakari Bank had increased by 360.67% from Rs. 36833.95 lakhs to Rs. 132752.18 lakhs during the aforesaid period.

Loans and Advances of Apna Sahakari bank registered an increase by 382.08% from Rs. 11999.70 lakhs to Rs. 45849.61 lakhs whereas such growth in respect of Thane Janata Sahakari bank was found fairly 406.88% in the course of 8 years from 1999 to 2007.

The credit deposit ratio of Apna Sahakari Bank is lowest i.e., 54.50% in the year 1999 and it was highest i.e., 75.65% in the year 2006. Whereas in respect of Thane Janata Sahakari Bank the credit deposit ratio is lowest i.c., 60.01% in the year 2000 and it was highest i.e., 67.96% in the year 2007.

## Customer Satisfaction Level in Selected Urban Co-operative Banks

In an era of mature and intense competitive pressures, many banks are focusing their efforts on maintaining a loyal customer base. This is particularly true in the financial services sector where deregulation has created an environment that allows consumers considerable choice in satisfying their financial needs. In response, many retail banks are directing their strategies towards increasing customer satisfaction and loyalty through improved service quality.

Satisfaction of customers is of paramount importance for any business organization inclusive of banking sector. It determines the future cash inflows to the business. The organization has to depend on its existing as well as new customers to keep itself growing. Attracting new customers involves considerable acquisition costs – such as advertising, promotion, follow-up and setup costs. The operating cost is also higher than for existing ones.

The longer any business keeps a customer the more profits are likely to flow in. In case the customer is not adequately satisfied and defects, the business. This not only incurs a loss due to unrecovered costs but it also misses an opportunity to make profit. The defection rate of the customers is a major determinant of the profitability of any business. Higher the defection rate, lower the average length of the relationship, with the customers leading to losses or reduced profits. Satisfied customers improve the businesses' bottom line not only through continued relationship but also through referrals and positive word of mouth feedback. It is said that to retain a customer is cheaper than that of to get new customer. For the attention of customer satisfaction is very much essential.

**Meaning of Customer Satisfaction**

Customer Satisfaction has been defined in several ways. Most important of them are 'Expectation performance interactions, Pleasure / Displeasure and the Evaluation of the benefits of consumption'.

It has also been defined as the 'degree of happiness a customer experiences with a company's product or service as a result of his or her interaction and inter-relationship of all the people within that company'. So many theories have been propounded. A brief discussion about some of these will be very much timely. Customer satisfaction is generally described as the full meeting of one's expectations.

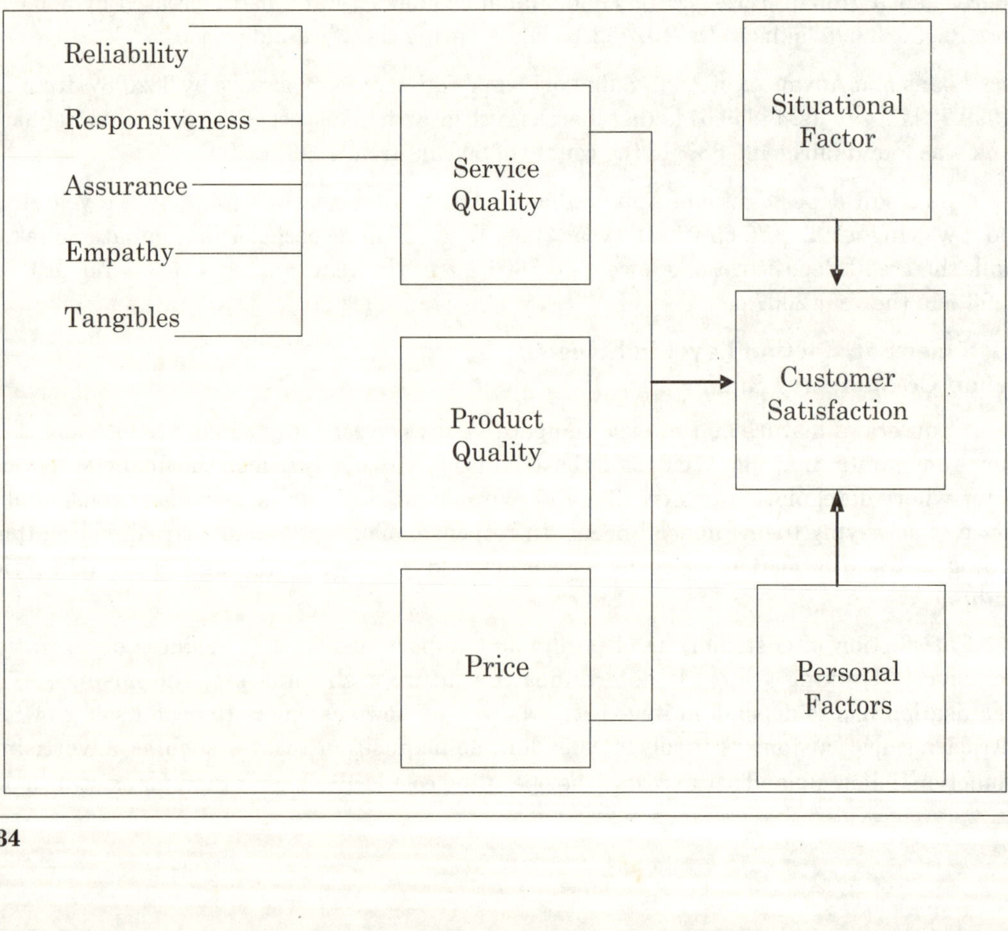

According to Richard L. Oliver, respected expert and long time writer and researcher on the topic of customer satisfaction, 'Satisfaction is the customer's fulfillment response. It is a judgment that a product or service features, or the product or service itself, provides a pleasurable level of consumption related fulfillment'. It means that satisfaction is customer's evaluation of a product or service in terms of whether that product or service has met the expectations. If it fails to meet the expectation the result ends in a dissatisfaction for the product or service'.

**Service Quality & Customer Satisfaction**

The delivery of expected service quality is prerequisite for the customer satisfaction. Customer satisfaction is also affected by situational as well as personal factors. And that is why it keeps on changing from time to time. It means that once the customer is satisfied, he can never be assumed satisfied always because of the situational and personal factors. Therefore in the present research care is taken to get representative samples along with different timings throughout the year.

In the modern, highly competitive business world, the key to sustainable competitive advantage lies in delivering high quality service that will, in turn, lead to satisfy customers. Customer satisfaction is considered a prerequisite of customer retention and loyalty, and can help to boost profitability, market share and return on investment. The research by Surechandar et.al., (J 38) also, shows, however, that service quality and customer satisfaction are closely related, and that an increase in one is likely to lead to a rise in the other.

Customer satisfaction is the feeling or attitude of a customer towards a product or service after it has been used. Customer satisfaction is a major outcome or marketing activity whereby it serves as a link between the various stages of consumer buying behavior. For instance, if customers are satisfied with a particular service offering after its use, then they are likely to engage in repeat purchase and try line extensions. Customer satisfaction is widely recognized as a key influence in the formation of customers' future purchase intentions. Satisfied customers are also likely to tell others about their favourable experience and thus engage in positive word of mouth advertising. It is seen that dissatisfied customer tell their bad experiences regarding services on their own to more people than the satisfied customer. But the satisfied customer speaks out only when asked about the services. Therefore it is better to keep customers satisfied that dissatisfied. This positive word of mouth advertising is particularly useful in collectivist Middle Eastern cultures like that of Abu Dhabi where social life is structured in a way to improve social relationship with others in the society (J 33). Dissatisfied customers, on the other hand, are likely to switch brands and engage in negative word of mouth advertising. Furthermore, behaviors such as repeat purchase and word-of-mouth directly affect the viability and profitability of a firm. A recent study conducted by Levesque and McDougall (J 24) confirmed and reinforced the idea that unsatisfactory customer service leads to a drop in customer satisfaction and willingness to recommend the service to a friend. This would in turn lead to an increase in the rate of switching by customers.

There can be potentially many antecedents of customer satisfaction as the dimensions underlying satisfaction judgments are global rather than specific. For instance, research on customer satisfaction has largely relied on the disconfirmation paradigm, which views satisfaction with products and brands as a result of two cognitive variables: pre-purchase expectation and disconfirmation. Pre-purchase expectations are beliefs about anticipated performance of the product, disconfirmation refers to the differences between pre-purchase expectations and post- purchase perceptions.

Improving customer satisfaction, and thereby retention rates, come from a variety of activities available to the firm. The existing evidence suggests that major gains in customer satisfaction are likely to come from improvements in:
Service quality;
Service features; and
Customer complaint handling.

**Levels of Satisfaction**

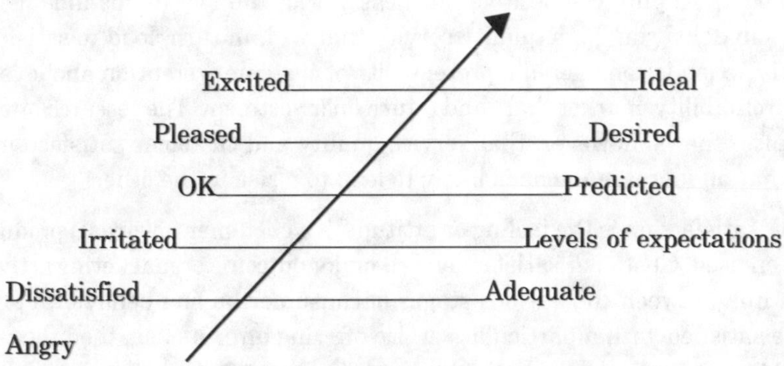


**Levels of Service Satisfaction**

**Satisfaction States and Levels of Consumer Expectation**

The retained customer is further committed to the product or the services and becomes brand loyal. The rewards to firms that establish a loyal customer base have been well documented. In general, increased loyalty leads to lower costs of servicing the firm's customers, reduced marketing expenditures, increased business from the existing customer base and greater profits. These rewards are particularly true in the retail banking sector. Customer satisfaction is considered as a necessary condition for customer retention and loyalty and therefore helps in realizing economic goals like turnover and revenue.

By increasing loyalty, a retail bank reduces its servicing costs (i.e., accounts do not have to be opened or closed, and credit ratings do not have to be established; gains knowledge of the financial affairs and needs of its customers (thereby allowing effective and efficient targeting); and has an opportunity to cross-sell existing and new products and services.

A review of the literature also suggests that expectations for service quality are likely to be based on perceptions of excellence, whereas satisfaction judgments are likely to be based on a broad range of non-quality issues. Research on customer satisfaction is often close associated with the measurement of service quality. While satisfaction is a feeling or an attitude of a customer towards a service after it has been used, service quality is simply essential too.

**Measurement of Customer Satisfaction**

From the literature it is found that there is direct relation between service quality and customer's satisfaction. If customer satisfaction is to be measured then perception of service quality is to be measured. There are various methods to measure the customer satisfaction i.e., service quality which are discussed earlier in the literature survey. In the present research the service parameters are divided into following four types and service quality is measured by point method.

**Personnel Factors**

Employees presence at counter

Employee's knowledge of job

Helpful and problem solving attitude

Promptness of employees'

Courteous treatment of employees of the bank

**Physical Factors**

Layout in Bank

Location of bank

Seating arrangement & facilities customers in bank

Lighting in bank

**Factors & Computer System**

ATM Services

E- Co-operative Systems

Smart Cards

E-Banking

ECS – Services

**Social Factors**

**Regular customer - bank meet**

Advertising of bank services

Innovativeness in bank services

Notice board for customer

The satisfaction level regarding above factors was measured on five points scale between totally satisfied to totally dissatisfied ones's.

The questionnaire was designed to measure the satisfaction level of the customers of selected urban co-operative banks. The importance of service parameters or indicators were also tested. About 20 questions were asked to test the parameter of importance and to find the level of satisfaction. The respondents were asked to tick mark (Ö) on the following scale.

| (1) | (2) | (3) | (4) | (5) |
|---|---|---|---|---|
| (not important) | (some what important) | (Neither imp or not imp) | (Somewhat important) | (highly important) |
| (1) | (2) | (3) | (4) | (5) |
| (always dissatisfied) | (some what dissatisfied) | (Neither sat nor dissat) | (Somewhat satisfied) | (always satisfied) |

For calculating the satisfaction level, respondents were segregated bank wise and data was tabulated in MS EXCEL. Satisfaction was measured on 5 point scale point 1 to 5 for always dissatisfied to always satisfied range. All points for 20 number, satisfying factors were added and % was found against 100% satisfaction.

**Data Collection and Interpretation**

Overall 330 samples were collected from Apna Sahakari Bank Ltd., Mumbai and Thane Janata Sahakari Bank Ltd., Thane. Out of them 150 sample from Apna Sahakari Bank Ltd and 180 from Thane Janata Sahakari Bank Ltd., Thane. The data has analysed with the following way.

**Demographic Analysis of Selected Urban Cooperative Banks**

Out of the total sample respondents, some of the samples had to be rejected due to insufficient data filled in questionnaire. Therefore at the end of 300 samples were analysed on the basis of demographic variables.

**Table No. 5.22: No. of Samples in Apna Sahakari Bank Ltd. and Thane Janata Sahakari Bank Ltd.**

| | **Apna Sahakari Bank** | **Thane Janata Sahakari Bank** | **Total** |
|---|---|---|---|
| **1** | **2** | **3** | **4** |
| No. of Samples | 140 | 160 | 300 |
| Percentages | 46.67 | 53.33 | 100 |

**Source :** Data compiled and computed by the Researcher

**Fig 5.14: No. of Samples in Apna Sahakari Bank and Thane Janata Sahakari Bank**

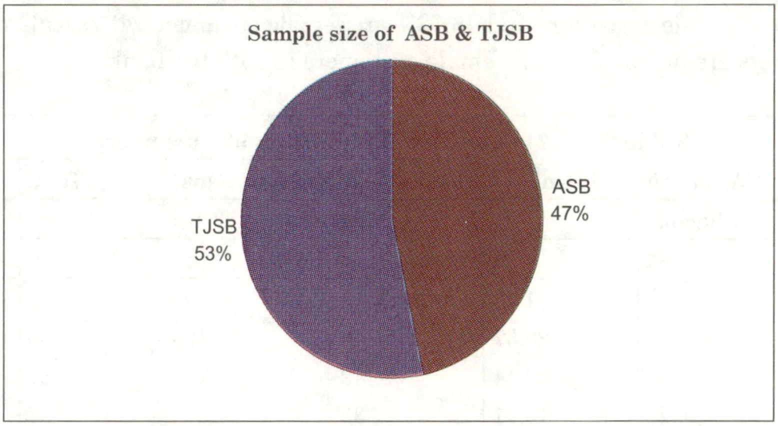


| Table No. 5.23: Gender-wise Distribution of Customers | | | | | | | | |
|---|---|---|---|---|---|---|---|---|
| | Apna Sahakari Bank Ltd | % | % | Thane Janata Sahakari Bank | % | % | Total | % |
| 1 | 2 | 3 | 4 | 5 | 6 | 7 | 8 | 9 |
| Males | 90 | 64.28 | [48.64] | 95 | 59.37 | [51.36] | 185 | 61.66 |
| Females | 50 | 35.72 | [43.47] | 65 | 40.63 | [56.53] | 115 | 38.34 |
| Total | 140 | 100 | | 160 | 100 | | 300 | 100 |
| **Source :** Data compiled and computed by the researcher | | | | | | | | |

**Fig 5.15: Genderwise Distriution of Customers Apna Sahakari Bank and Thane Janata Sahakari Bank**

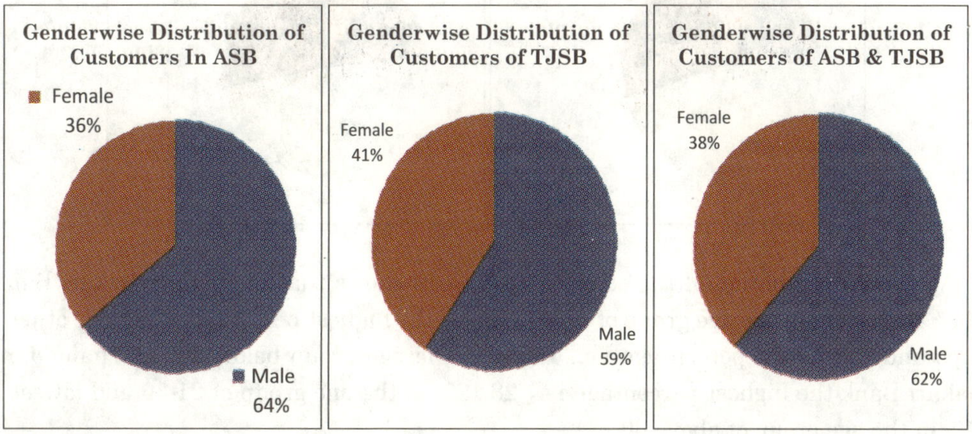

Table No. 5.23 shows that in Apna Sahakari Bank out of the total sample customers 64.28% are make customers and 35.72 are female customers. In Thane Janata Sahakari Bank bank 59.37% are male customers and 46.63% are female customers. It reveals that selected male customers are higher than the female customers in both the banks.

**Table No. 5.24: Age-wise Distribution of Customers**

| Age | Apna Sahakari Bank | | Thane Janata Sahakari Bank | | Total | % |
|---|---|---|---|---|---|---|
| | Sample | % | Sample | % | | |
| 1 | 2 | 3 | 4 | 5 | 6 | 7 |
| < 20 | 2 | 1.42 | 0 | 0 | 2 | 0.66 |
| 21 -30 | 40 | 28.57 | 45 | 28.12 | 85 | 28.33 |
| 31 - 40 | 45 | 32.14 | 42 | 26.25 | 87 | 29.00 |
| 41 - 50 | 22 | 15.71 | 35 | 21.87 | 57 | 19.00 |
| 51 - 60 | 20 | 14.28 | 25 | 15.62 | 45 | 15.00 |
| 60 > | 11 | 7.88 | 13 | 8.14 | 24 | 8.01 |
| Total | 140 | 100 | 160 | 4.31 | 300 | 100 |

**Source:** Data compiled and computed by the Researcher

**Fig 5.16: Customer wise Age Profile of Apna Sahakari Bank**

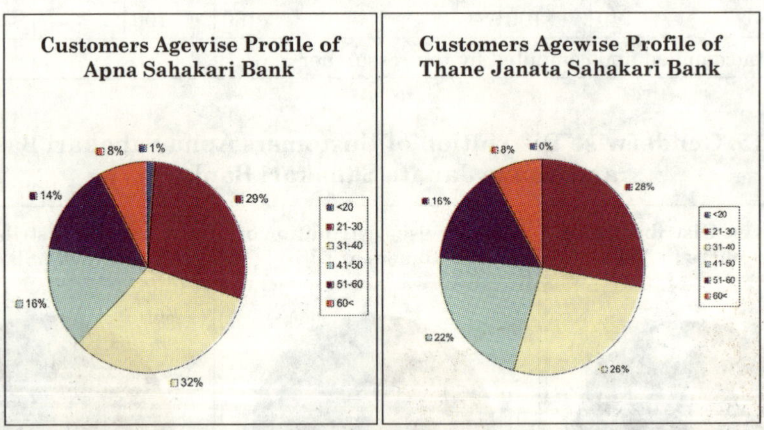


Age-wise distribution of the selected customers shows that in Apna Sahakari Bank is 32.14% customers in the age group of 31-40. This is the highest percentage than the other age groups and the lowest percentage i.e., 1.42% is the age group below 20. In Thane Janata Sahakari Bank the highest percentage i.e., 28.12% in the age group of 21-30 and lowest i.e., 4.31% in the age group of above 60.

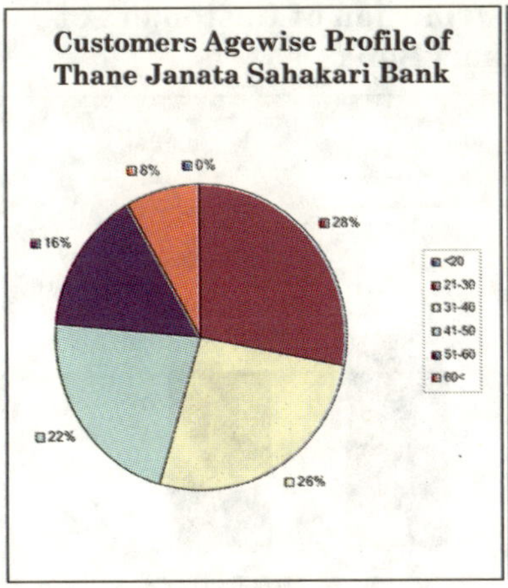


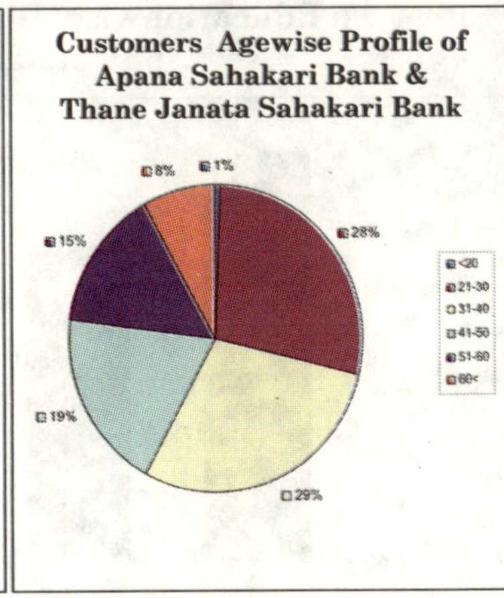


| Table No. 5.25: Education-wise Distribution of Customers | | | | | | |
|---|---|---|---|---|---|---|
| **Education** | **Apna Sahakari Bank Nos** | **%** | **Thane Janata Sahakari Bank Nos.** | **%** | **Total** | **%** |
| **1** | **2** | **3** | **4** | **5** | **6** | **7** |
| Upto SSC | 52 | 37.14 | 55 | 34.37 | 107 | 35.66 |
| SSC - UG | 40 | 28.57 | 45 | 28.12 | 85 | 28.33 |
| UG-PG | 25 | 17.85 | 32 | 20 | 57 | 19 |
| Other Technical & Professional | 23 | 16.42 | 28 | 17.5 | 51 | 17 |
| Total | 140 | 100 | 160 | 100 | 300 | 100 |

**Source:** Data compiled and computed by the Researcher

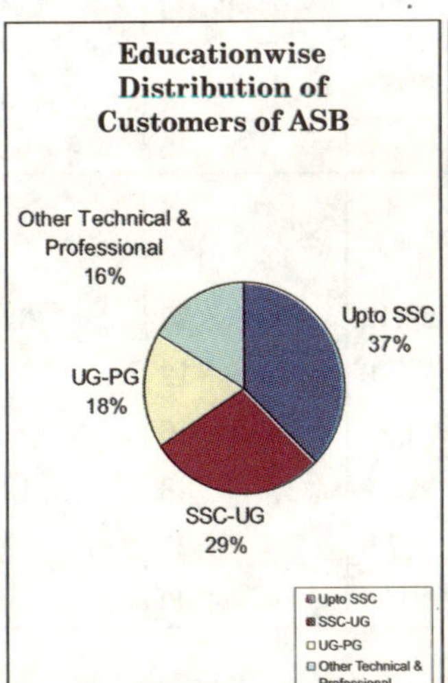


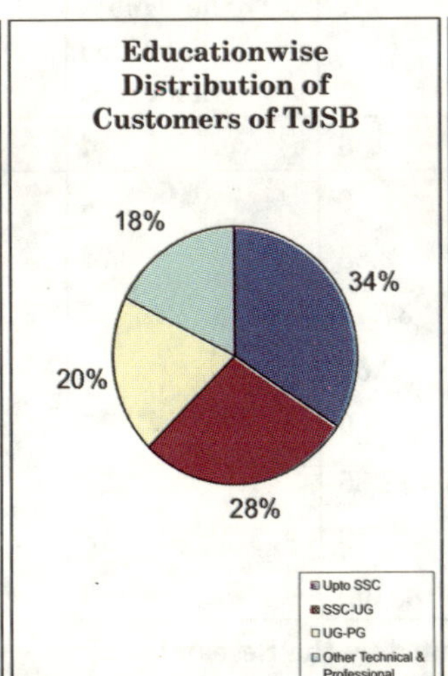


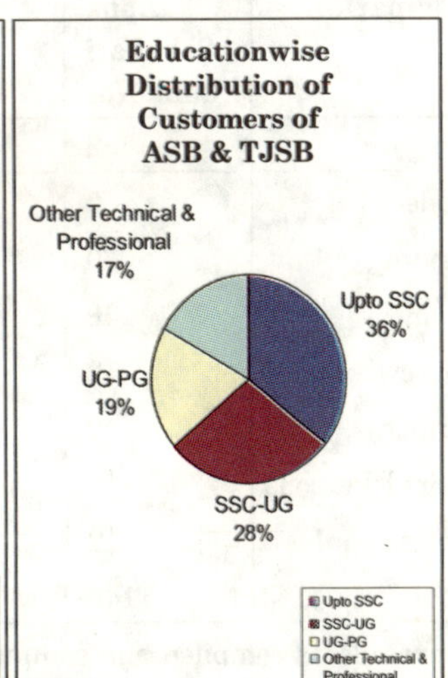

**Fig 5.17: Educationwise Distribution of Customers of Apna Sahakari Bank**

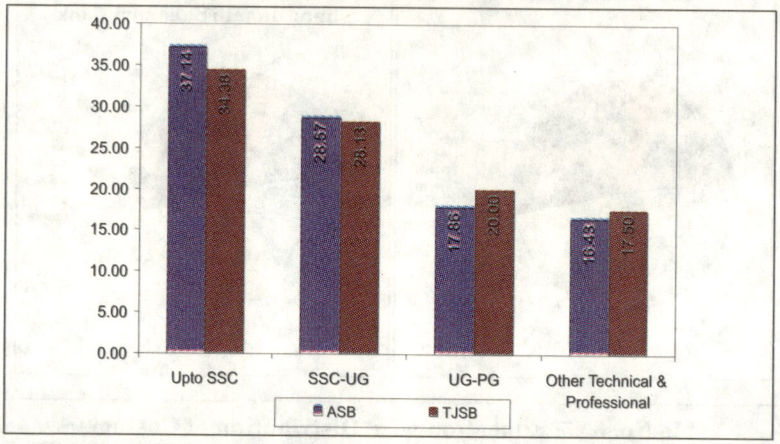


Education-wise distribution of the customers shows in Apna Sahakari Bank the highest percentage i.e., 37.14 are the customers educated upto SSC and lowest percentage i.e., 16.42 customer are completed other technical and professional courses. The customers from Thane Janata Sahakari Bank the highest percentage i.e., 34.37% are the custopmers educated upto SSC and lowest percentage i.e., 17.5% are completed other technical and profe4ssional courses.

**Table No. 5.26: Occupation-wise Distribution of Customers**

| Occupation | Apna Sahakari Bank Nos | % | Thane Janata Sahakari Bank Nos. | % | Total | % |
|---|---|---|---|---|---|---|
| 1 | 2 | 3 | 4 | 5 | 6 | 7 |
| Students | 0 | 0 | 4 | 2.5 | 4 | 1.33 |
| Service | 60 | 42.85 | 72 | 45 | 132 | 44 |
| Business | 38 | 37.14 | 45 | 28.12 | 83 | 32.68 |
| Housewives | 12 | 3.57 | 0 | 0 | 12 | 4 |
| Farmers | 0 | 0 | 6 | 4.28 | 6 | 2 |
| Retired Persons | 18 | 12:85 | 20 | 12.5 | 38 | 12.66 |
| Professionals | 12 | 3.59 | 13 | 7.6 | 25 | 3.33 |
| Total | 140 | 100 | 160 | 100 | 300 | 100 |

**Source:** Data compiled and computed by the Researcher

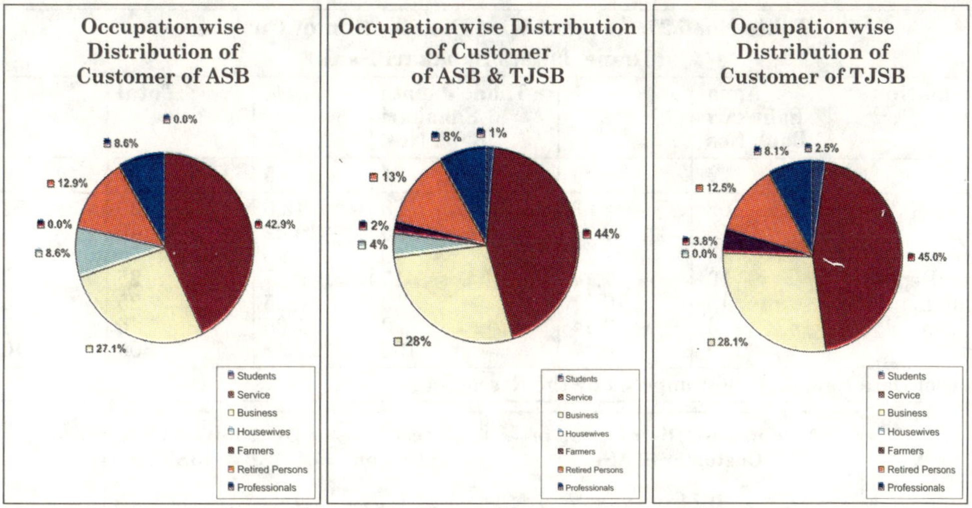


**Fig 5.18: Occupationwise Distribution of Customers of Apna Sahakari Bank and Thane Janata Sahakari Bank**

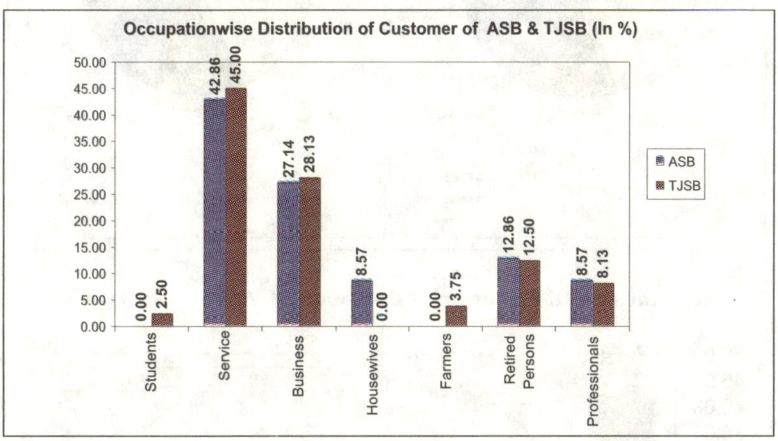


Occupation wise distribution of customers in the Apna Sahakari Bank shows that the customers from service occupation are highest i.e., 42.85% and lowest percentage from the other professional i.e., 3.59%. The Thane Janata Sahakari Bank shows that the customers from service occupation are higher i.e., 45.0% and lowest customer from student. It is found hat he customers from service occupation are highest in both the banks.

| Table No. 5.27: Account-wise Distribution of Customers (Thane Janata Sahakari Bank) | | | | | | |
|---|---|---|---|---|---|---|
| **Occupation** | **Apna Sahakari Bank Nos** | **%** | **Thane Janata Sahakari Bank Nos.** | **%** | **Total** | **%** |
| **1** | **2** | **3** | **4** | **5** | **6** | **7** |
| Saving | 62 | 43.3 | 68 | 42.6 | 130 | 53.35 |
| Loan | 15 | 10.71 | 25 | 15.62 | 40 | 13.33 |
| Current | 35 | 25 | 40 | 25 | 75 | 25 |
| Fixed Deposit | 10 | 7.14 | 15 | 9.37 | 25 | 3.33 |
| Recurring | 15 | 10.71 | 10 | 6.25 | 25 | 3.33 |
| Pension | 3 | 3.14 | 2 | 1.25 | 5 | 1.66 |
| Total | 140 | 100% | 160 | 100% | 300 | 100% |
| **Source:** Data compiled and computed by the Researcher | | | | | | |

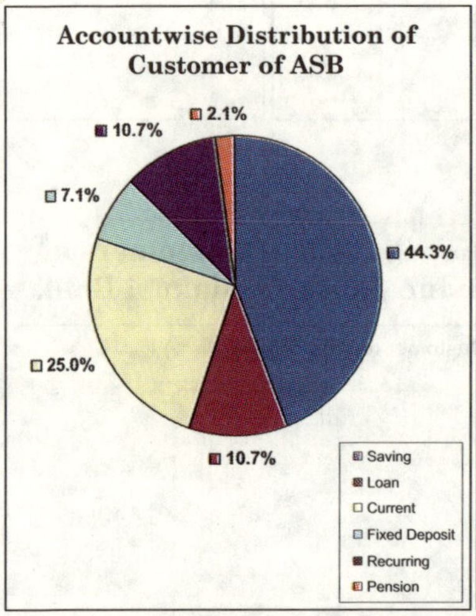


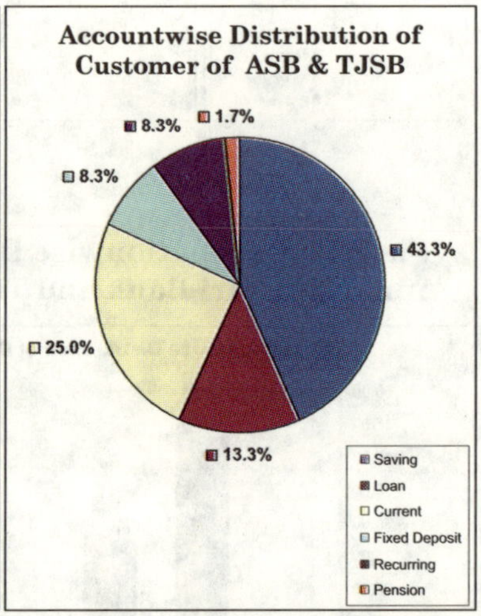


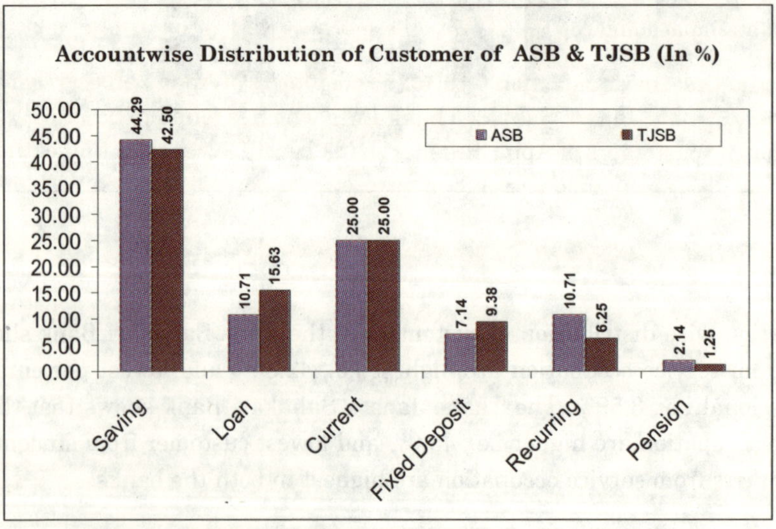

**Fig 5.19: Accountwise Distribution of Customers of Apna Sahakari Bank and Thane Janata Sahakari Bank**

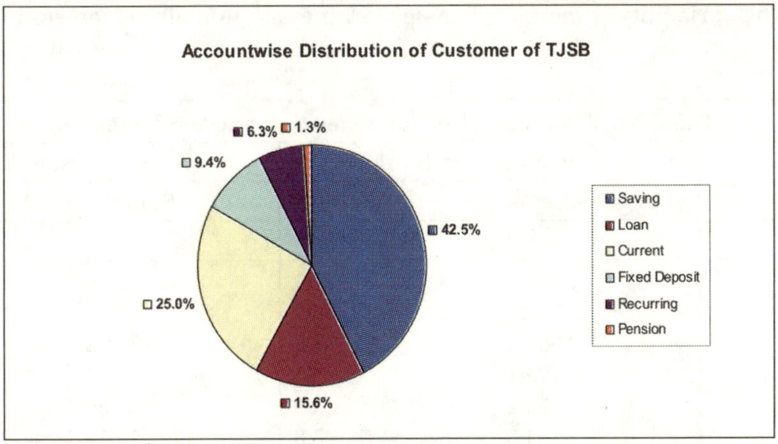


Account-wise distribution of customers shows that the customers from saving account ahs found highest i.e., 43.30% in Apna Sahakari Bank and 53.35% in Thane Janata Sahakari bank respectively. The customers from pension account are lowest i.e., 3.14% in Apna Sahakari Bank and only 1.66% in Thane Janata Sahakari Bank.

**Table No. 5.28: Satisfaction Level of Customers in Apna Sahakari Bank and Thane Janata Sahakari Bank**

| Particulars | Apna Sahakari Bank | Thane Janata Sahakari Bank |
|---|---|---|
| 1 | 2 | 3 |
| Satisfaction Level | 72.42 | 77.65 |
| Standard Deviation | 4.49 | 5.64 |

**Source:** Data compiled and computed by the Researcher

It is found that the satisfaction level of the customers of Apna Sahakari bank i.e., 72.42%, is less than the Thane Janata Sahakari bank Ltd., which is found to be 77.65% The Standard Deviation for the customers of Apna Sahakari bank is 4.49 lower than that of the customers of Thane Janata Sahakari bank which is 5.64. This shows the variability is more in case of customers of Thane Janata Sahakari bank than the customers of Apna Sahakari bank.

**Table No. 5.29: Gender-wise Customer Satisfaction Level**

| Gender | Apna Sahakari Bank | | Thane Janata Sahakari Bank | |
|---|---|---|---|---|
| | S.Level | S.D. | S. Level | S.D. |
| 1 | 2 | 3 | 4 | 5 |
| Males | 71.52 | 3.03 | 72.85 | 5.75 |
| Females | 74.95 | 4.12 | 85.31 | 5.85 |

**Source:** Data compiled and computed by the Researcher

Gender-wise analysis shows that the satisfaction level of female customers is more than the male customers. The trend is same in Apna Sahakari bank and Thane Janata Sahakari bank also. The variability is more for female customers than male customers in case of both the banks

**Table No. 5.30: Age-wise Customer Satisfaction Level (%)**

| Gender | Apna Sahakari Bank | | Thane Janata Sahakari Bank | |
|---|---|---|---|---|
| | S.Level | S.D. | S. Level | S.D. |
| 1 | 2 | 3 | 4 | 5 |
| < 20 | 70.1 | 3.81 | 0 | 0 |
| 21 - 30 | 71.32 | 3.52 | 74.7 | 5.51 |
| 31-40 | 65.24 | 3.6 | 71.42 | 5.84 |
| 41-50 | 72.41 | 3.51 | 73.4 | 5.9 |
| 51-60 | 65.52 | 2.91 | 68.59 | 6.01 |
| 6- > | 64.8 | 3.8 | 72.12 | 5.72 |

**Source:** Data compiled and computed by the Researcher

The Age-wise analysis reveals that the younger customers (21-30) age and middle aged customers (41-51 age) of the Apna Sahakari Bank and Thane Janata Sahakari Bank are more satisfied compare to the other age groups. Whereas the customers of age group of above 60 in Apna Sahakari bank is less satisfied compare to other age groups and in Thane Janata Sahakari bank the age group of 51-60 are less satisfied compare to the other age group.

**Table No. 5.31: Education-wise Satisfaction Level (%)**

| Gender | Apna Sahakari Bank | | Thane Janata Sahakari Bank | |
|---|---|---|---|---|
| | S.Level | S.D. | S. Level | S.D. |
| 1 | 2 | 3 | 4 | 5 |
| Upto SSC | 71.23 | 2.85 | 78.27 | 4.8 |
| SSC – UG | 69.72 | 4.2 | 74.26 | 5.43 |
| UG – PG | 65.52 | 2.43 | 70.42 | 5.79 |
| Other Technical | 68.71 | 3.22 | 69.3 | 6.23 |

**Source:** Data compiled and computed by the Researcher

The education-wise analysis reveals that the satisfaction level of educated class up to SSC is less compare to other educated class-in both the banks. In Apna Sahakari bank the satisfaction level is higher in educated group of SSC to UG and in Thane Janata Sahakari bank the satisfaction level is higher in the educated group of UG to PG. The variability of educated class of customer of Apna Sahakari bank is less than that of Thane Janata Sahakari bank.

| Table No. 5.32: Occupation-wise Satisfaction Level (%) | | | | |
|---|---|---|---|---|
| **Gender** | **Apna Sahakari Bank** | | **Thane Janata Sahakari Bank** | |
| | **S.Level** | **S.D.** | **S. Level** | **S.D.** |
| **1** | **2** | **3** | **4** | **5** |
| Students | 65.43 | 3.1 | 73.11 | 4.37 |
| Service | 68.72 | 3.8 | 79.42 | 5.75 |
| Business | 70.71 | 4.21 | 77.56 | 5.81 |
| Housewives | 69.42 | 4.31 | 75.42 | 6.74 |
| Farmers | 65.41 | 3.89 | 69.61 | 6.03 |
| Retired Persons | 64.4 | 3.21 | 71.74 | 6.41 |
| Professionals | 66.67 | 3.3 | 74.62 | 4.31 |
| **Source:** Data compiled and computed by the Researcher | | | | |

In case of Apna Sahakari Bank, the business, housewives, professionals category show higher satisfaction level than the customers like Farmers, Retired persons and student category. In case of Thane Janata Sahakari bank the service business, housewives, professionals, shows higher satisfaction level than the customers of student, retired persons and farmers. The variability is high in case of housewives customers of both banks.

| Table No. 5.33: Account-wise Satisfaction Level (%) | | | | |
|---|---|---|---|---|
| **Gender** | **Apna Sahakari Bank** | | **Thane Janata Sahakari Bank** | |
| | **S.Level** | **S.D.** | **S. Level** | **S.D.** |
| **1** | **2** | **3** | **4** | **5** |
| Saving | 65.41 | 4.41 | 69.42 | 6.1 |
| Loan | 61.39 | 5.3 | 71.42 | 6.12 |
| Current | 67.43 | 4.33 | 70.69 | 6.89 |
| Fixed Deposit | 61.21 | 5.43 | 70.41 | 5.47 |
| Recurring | 65.49 | 4.11 | 72.69 | 5.41 |
| Pension | 60.01 | 3.12 | 65.03 | 5.13 |
| **Source:** Data compiled and computed by the Researcher | | | | |

The table reveals that the satisfaction level in Apna Sahakari bank is higher in Current, Recurring, Saving and Loan account and in Thane Janata Sahakari bank it is in Loan, Recurring, Current and fixed account, while less satisfaction in Apna bank is in pension and fixed deposits while in Thane Janata Sahakari bank it is less in pension and saving account. The variability is higher in fixed account in Apna bank and in Thane Janata bank the variability is higher in current account.

## E-governance & Modernisation of Urban Co-operative Banks in the New Centenary

The advent and emergence of LPG's in almost all major economic and commercial undertakings/sections has greatly expanded and opened up Indian liberalization and globalization process which must continue, but utmost care must be taken up in modernization and up-gradation to save co-operative sector from being swallowed by the MNC's. The silent introduction to LPG's policies have agreeably impressed and affected the functions, objectives, and operations of many co-operative organizations including the co-operative banking sector (system) and therefore, the need and necessity to accept economic and environmental changes is highly indispensable in the open market economic system. Even, techno-economic changes have become very imperative and sin-quo-non for the growth and development of co-operative sector in this era.

## Role of E-governance in Urban Co-operative Banks

The current banking environment is fast moving, turbulent and unpredictable mainly because of the global competition and highly developed computerization/ mechanization systems. Every one is aiming at technology banking system (e-banking system). In fact, almost all organizations depend increasingly on Information Technology and management information system (MIS) which would enable the process of organizational adaptation to changing situation, resulting in to making organizations more efficient and effective in their working operations. The information systems and communication or Information Technology Enabled Services (ITES) play a crucial role of organizational adaptability, and enhance decision making process in many co-operative banking organizations. In this fast changing world, co-operative banking organizations must be geared to accept emerging changes and modify their strategies, inputs, communication, planning, organizing, control, coordination and technologies.

The implementation of computerization and moderniza-tion of co-operative banking systems can drastically and simultaneously increase the overall efficiency and decrease the cost of operations/transactions. This is a challenge for co-operative banking organizations in the new centenary. The technical innovations are constantly emerging out of the technical research activities and successfully implementing the innovative techno-banking system which actually will depend on the ability of the management and administration of the co-operative banks to accept to use it at any time. Government allows in a wide spectrum and scope for implementing electronic systems including electronic banking systems and also other automization processes like the automatic teller machines (ATM's) in many banking organizations to gain higher banking operational efficiency in the long run.

Moreover, co-operative banking organizations are facing difficulties in implementing the electronic systems in their operations and transactions. Though the government, through economic reforms packages, have obeyed and accepted for higher upgradation and modernization of banks, but still they face challenges in implementing computerization and mechanization process. The only viable option for them is to computerize and capture more benefits in the new centenary by offering high quality services and products. Yet, the co-operative banking industry faces tough challenges, and competitions through technological upgradation and they are expected to make frequent improvements in their productivity, profitability, viability and higher bank marketing efficiencies.

The LPG's policies are silently giving clear-cut options that those who do not want to change will be left on the wayside as competition would ensure the survival of the fittest. The liberalized system will pave the way for the importation of technology and also facilitates exportation of technology, to even to other developing countries. Therefore, modernization and upgradation of technology through domestic research and development for continuous improvement in the quality of products/services in co-operative banking organization becomes critical at this juncture. And hence, it is the duty and responsibility of co-operative banking organizations to reap the benefits emanating from electronic revolution.

Co-operative banking organization, to some extent, are characterized by corruption, rigidity, instability in business operations, constantly misuse of power, bureaucracy, redtapism, unnecessary procedures, delayed decision making process, inefficient budgeting, lack of accountability, lack of transparency, etc. The main aim of introducing e-governance and e-co-operative system is to improve the total working operations of the entire organization. It would lead to better service delivery to members and customers. By installing e-governance structures such as internet and information technology, the co-operative sector can effectively and efficiently handle the operations of functional areas of management, materials management, human resource management, personnel management, office management, MIS and IT. Similarly, they can improve their internal operational efficiency and even external operations. Moreover, functional areas such as planning, organizing, staffing, controlling, coordinating, communication, cooperation, reporting and budgeting can be handled in a better way if the e-governance is practiced and implemented. It would be easy for the sector to carry out viable and profitable investment opportunities, there would be an improvement in the administration and management. With the introduction of information and communication technology, provision of better services and information to members will be made possible in 24 hours a day, and seven days a week, making the members become e-members and encourage them to participate in all activities.

## Definition of E-governance

Governance is the application of information technology (IT) and communication process to transact all business processes effectively and efficiently functioning in order to achieve simple, speedy, moral, transparent, ethical, accountable, responsive, prompt dissemination of information, prompt delivery of quality services, improve productivity and profitability by using the latest skills and knowledge of information technology and electronic revolution.

E-governance of co-operative banking organization is simply the ability of co-operative banks to provide all access to services and products through electronic and mechanized system. The banks can provide on-line services because of dynamic revolution in information technology and communication system which have made everything possible in e-banking world. Even purchase (e-purchase) payment (e-payment), customers transactions, operations of all types, etc., are made electronically with complete use of latest methods of information and communication technology (ICT). Moreover, through e-governance, mechanization and computerization process, performance of co-operative banking organizations will be and effective and efficient in 21st century.

**Merits of Computerization**

An attempt is made to elicit the merits of computerization of co-operative banking sector. They are :

- By entering into computerization and mechanization systems co-operative banking sector can obtain higher efficiency of money exchange and overall transactional operations,
- co-operative banks can have economical bank charges and reduction in cost of transactions,
- there will exists a protection of privacy as it is not easy to access the customers particulars by outsiders and other agents,
- overall cost of reduction will be possible electronically,
- co-operative banking services will be standardized and customer focused approach will be put into operation. Moreover, all members and customers will be able to conduct the banking business electronically,
- very quick surfing of information/data will be made possible on account of complete computerization and mechanization,
- by installing e-banking system, it will pave way for time efficiency in the transactions/ operations,
- it will pave way for reduced number of bank branches, staff and overall general staff. A customer can be contacted anywhere in the world within seconds by a single bank which is electronically operated,
- it will provide increase in productivity, profitability, viability and less operating costs,
- it will provide less burden on employees as it will be quick to operate and easy to use, and
- it will provide less number of papers and paper work in the head quarters, network of branches, and other sections of the bank.

## Demerits of Computerization

⇨ There exists a limited scope for personal advice on banking services/transactions and products availability,

⇨ there are no direct relationships or direct customer contacts when the bank is fully computerized,

⇨ protection of secrecy and security issues may not also be possible where the bank's strengths or regulations had to be disclosed to the customers and clients for better usage of the system,

⇨ customers may have little or temporary loyalty to a bank, since they are easily accessible to other banking organizations which are providing more or less the same kind of services and banking products, and

⇨ competition from foreign banks which are using advanced electronic banking methods/ systems pose a direct threat to the co-operative banking organization and their branch networks.

Inspite of demerits, there are number of opportunities for growth as far as computerization and mechanization through electronic banking as a separate entity is concerned. Also, opportunities and benefits both for the banking organizations and providing efficient services to customers do not exist by way of adopting the electronic banking system.

## Opportunities of Computerization

Some of the major opportunities which include :

- The national and international potentiality and recognition of co-operative banks through computerization and mechanization. Moreover, an electronic banking system is abundant in the Indian economy.
- Transactions and communications might be increased between different banks and government agencies and also with customers around the globe, thus creating a global network for co-operative banking sector.
- The local or the regional market share of co-operative banking network may increase drastically through computerization.
- Access to global markets, national, regional, state and local markets are possible through information technology (IT) and communication by the use of electronic system of co-operative banks.
- They can easily effect technical innovative solutions for customer related problems are formed.

# Findings & Recommendations

Information Technology is entirely changing the way of banking business and considerably widened the range of products and increased the expectations and demands of the customer. Information technology has made the banking services faster, more efficient and more economical. In present research study the impact have been seen on the efficiency of Urban Co-operative banks, productivity, profitability and customer satisfaction level. Information technology have improved the Urban Co-operative banking operations.

In the earlier chapters, various issues connected with Urban Co-operative banking sector have been dealt with in broad details on the basis of data collected from both primary and secondary sources. In the first chapter the review have been taken of the Urban Co-operative banking movement concerned with three phases. Urban Co-operative banks have played an vital role in the development of the state of Maharashtra . This chapter also explains the conceptual framework of Urban Co-operative banking structure, emerging banking scenario, challenges and opportunities and the future of Urban Co-operative banking.

The second chapter deals with the growth and development of Urban Co-operative banks in three stages i.e., (1) Prior to March 1966 (2) After 1966 to 1996 and (3) After 1996. It also deals with the various committee reports on banking technology and emerging trends in banking technology in India and Maharashtra.

The third chapter is Review of Literature. This chapter comprises of available literature on Urban Co-operative banks and information technology, which is proved to be very useful in getting an insight into the main objective of the study and in finalizing the methodology. Near about 50 relevant reviews have been taken from the various journals, articles, books and other publications.

The fourth chapter is research methodology comprises of the important aspects like introduction, problem definition, objectives of the study, hypothesis, research design etc. The researcher has adapted the sampling procedure. Urban Co-operative banking sector is characterised by heterogeneity in terms of size, spread, profitability and professionalism. The researcher have selected case study approach to investigate and assessing the impact of information technology on business growth, profitability, productivity, deposit mobilization and customer satisfaction. In view of this the researcher have selected two UCBs from Maharashtra, one from Scheduled status and another one from Non-Scheduled status.

Following are the selected UCBs for present research study.

1. Thane Janata Sahakari Bank Ltd., Mumbai.

2. Apna Sahakari Bank Ltd., Mumbai.

Two assess the impact of information technology on customer satisfaction total 300 sample respondents have been selected. Out of these 160 (53.33%) samples from Thane Janata Sahakari

Bank and 140(46.67%) samples from Apna Sahakari Bank have been selected. The analysis and interpretations of the data have been made with reference to objective and hypothesis to be tested.

The Fifth Chapter is Data Analysis and Interpretations. This chapter comprises of two sections. Section-I deals with the profile of selected UCBs. The whole profile of The Janata Sahakari Bank and Apna Sahakari Bank represented with systematic manner. Section II deals with the data analysis and interpretation keeping in view the objective of the present study. On the basis of certain parameters interpretation have been made, such as profitability, trend analysis, ratio analysis, productivity, deposit mobilization and customer satisfaction etc.

The last chapter highlights the major findings and recommendations drawn on the basis of present research study. Following are the major findings and recommendations drawn on the basis of present study.

**Findings**

It is found that the major head of expenditure in both the selected banks is interest paid on deposits and borrowings. The expenses has increased by 65.62% to 67.66% during the period from 1999 to 2007 in Apna Sahakari Bank. While in Thane Janata Sahakari Bank the expenses of deposits and borrowings has reduced from 71.38% to 66.02% during the period from 1999 to 2007. The staff expenses of Apna Sahakari Bank has reduced from 22.99% to 20.92% during the study period, whereas in the Thane Janata Sahakari Bank the staff expenses has slightly increased from 15.63 % during the period from 1999 to 2007.

1. Profitability is the most important and reliable indicator of the performance so also it serves as an indicator of the capability of bank to increase its earnings over a period of time. After the introduction of Information Technology (post IT period) the growth rate of Apna Sahakari Bank has increased by 394.90 percent and the growth rate of Thane Janata Sahakari Bank has increased by 301.83. It is revealed that the growth rate of Net Profit has increased by more than 4 times and further more than 3 times in Apna Sahakari Bank and Thane Janata Sahakar Bank respectively, after the adoption of information technology during the study period from 2000 to 2007.

2. We have observed a strong relationship between introduction of technology and the profitability of sample banks while introduction of technology itself an off-shoot of competition on account of reforms, it has been noticed that the impact of technology is rather more broad based. It is observed that the sources of income of selected UCBs is Interest and discount, Commission, exchange and brokerage and other earnings. Interest and discount is the main source of income i.e., 95.48% share in Apna Sahakari Bank and 92.82% in Thane Janata Sahakari Bank Ltd. Hence it is found that the proportion of other earnings is very less compared to the interest and discount in both selected banks. It is also analysed that the total income of Apna Sahakari bank has been continuously increasing after the application of Information Technology (IT).

3. The broad classification of the earnings of UCB, are interest income and non-interest income. While the former accrues on account of lending operations, the latter depends on a banks ability to earn income from fee based activities. It is observed that the managements of the bank have attempted to reduce their expenditure by introducing Information Technology (IT) and suitable changes into the organizational structure. The expenses of the bank had been divided into four heads including (1) Interest paid on deposits and borrowings, (2) Staff expenses including salaries, allowances provident funds, bonus etc., (3) Other establishment expenses, (4) Other expenses.

4. The trends of the spread earned is an important criterion to judge the profitability of fund related business of banks spread is the difference between interest received and interest paid by the co-operative banks. It reveals that the spread ratio of Apna Sahakari Bank was 3.95 in the pre IT year 1999 and it has been reduced upto 3.66 in the year 2007. Whereas in Thane Janata Sahakari Bank the spread ratio has reduced from 5.30 to 4.61 during the IT introduction period i.e., from 1999 to 2007. In tunes with the market conditions, the spread of both banks is reduced and a falling spread has not impacted the profitability, as the latter has shown substantial growth in two banks.

5. The trends in burden means the difference between non-interest expenditure and non-interest income of the bank. It is observed that the burden ratio of Apna Sahakari Bank has been reduced from 2.94 to 1.60 during the period from 1999 to 2007 and the burden ratio of Thane Janata Sahakari Bank has been reduced from 2.67 to 1.61 during the same period respectively. It means the burden ratio of Apna Sahakari Bank and Thane Janata Sahakari Bank has been continuously declining after introducing the information technology

6. Trends in Net worth of Apna Sahakari Bank and Thane Janata Sahakari Bank includes the capital, reserves and surplus of the bank. The capital of Apna Sahakari Bank has increased from Rs. 285.66 lakhs to 1813 lakhs during the period of 1999 to 2007. It means the capital has increased by more than 6 times, the reserves has increased by 4 times and surplus has increased by 6 times. Whereas the capital of Thane Janata Sahakari Bank Ltd has increased by four-fold, Reserves increased by 36 times and reserves has increased by 4 times during the study period. It is also revealed that the percentage growth of capital, reserves and surplus of Apna Sahakari Bank and Thane Janata Sahakari Bank having continuously the increased trend. This is the significant positive impact of information technology.

7. Profitability of the selected UCBs is computed by calculating net profits as percentage of total income earned by UCBs. The ratio of net profit as percentage to total income reflects the income generating capacity of the banks. It is observed that the Net operating profit of Apna Sahakari Bank and Thane Janata Sahakari Bank shows significant effect. The percentage growth of net profit in Apna Sahakari Bank was 191.54 in 2000 and it has been increased to 657.16 in the year 2007. Whereas the percentage growth of net profit in Thane Janata Sahakari Bank was 113.08 in 2000 and it has been increased by 301.83 in

the year 2007. It means in both the banks the percentage growth of net profit is continuously increasing but the rate is higher in Apna Sahakari Bank as compared to Thane Janata Sahakari Bank.

8. An attempt has been made to analyse the productivity parameter. The purpose of the productivity analysis is to assess the impact of computerization on productivity of employees, by various indicators. It is observed that per employee deposits in Apna Sahakari Bank was Rs. 58.70 lakh in the year 1999 and it has increased to Rs. 201.18 lakhs during the study period from1999 to 2007. Whereas in Thane Janata Sahakari Bank, the per employee deposits in 1999 was Rs. 83.90 lakhs and it has increased by Rs. 312.59 lakhs during the period from 1999 to 2007.

9. Advances per employee which was Rs. 31.99 lakhs in 1999 has increased by Rs. 141.51 crore. However in Thane Janata Sahakari Bank per employee advances was Rs. 50.54 lakhs and it has increased by Rs. 212.45 lakhs in the year 2007. This clearly shows that the per employee advances has shown an increasing trend in both the banks but the growth rate was slightly higher in Apna Sahakari Bank compared to Thane Janata Sahakari Bank.

10. Per employee business (Deposits + Advances) of Apna Sahakari Bank was Rs. 90.70 lakhs and after application of information technology the per employee business has shown continuously an increasing trend and it has been Rs. 342.69 lakhs in the year 2007. The total growth per employee, business has been increased by 377.88 lakhs during the period from 1999 to 2007. However the same situation has been showing in Thane Janata Sahakari Bank was Rs. 134.45 lakhs in the year 1999 and it has increased by Rs. 525.04 lakhs during 1999-2007. It means the growth of per employee business has been increased by 390.50 percent during the study period. The per employee business growth rate is slightly higher in Thane Janata Sahakari Bank than that of Apna Sahaakri Bank.

11. It is observed that the per employee Net profit grew at the rate of 437.83 percent in Apna Sahakari Bank during the period from 1999 – 2007. Whereas in Thane Janata Sahakari Bank per employee net profit has grown at the rate of 311.57 percent. It is also found that the per employee net profit in Apna Sahakari Bank has increased from Rs. 0.37 lakhs to Rs. 1.62 lakhs during 1999 to 2007, while in Thane Janata Sahakari Bank it has increased from Rs. 1.90 lakh to rs. 5.92 lakhs during the said period. The growth rate of net profit in Apna Sahakari Bank is higher than the Thane Janata sahakari Bank after the application of information technology. It indicates that the impact of IT has positively been significant in both the banks, but it is higher in Apna Sahakari Bank as compared to Thane Janata Sahakari Bank.

12. The per employee earnings in Apna Sahakari Bank has increased from Rs. 7.59 lakhs to rs. 20.82 lakhs during 1999 to 2007, While in Thane Janata Sahakari Bank per employee earnings has increased from Rs. 12.06 lakhs to Rs. 32.93 lakhs during 199 – 2007. It is also found that the growth rate of both the selected banks has shown an increasing trend.

13. The ratio analysis is one of the important techniques, which provides great help to the management in planning and controlling of their activities. It is observed that in both the banks the ratio of interest and discount to total income is very high i.e., more than 92% during the study period. The ratio of commission exchange and brokerage to total income is very less i.e., in Apna bank this ratio has increased by 0.33 to 0.59 during 1999 to 2007 and in Thane Janata Sahakari bank it has increased by 2.02 to 2.65 during 1999 to 2007. Again the ratio of other earnings to total income is found less i.e., in Apna bank this ratio has increased by 2.7 to 3.93 during 1999 – 2007 and in Thane Janata Sahakari bank this ratio has increased by 2.99 to 4.52 during the said period. It reveals that in both the banks, after application of IT enabled service the ratio of interest and discount to total income have slightly reduced and other factors income has slightly increased.

14. The ratio of interest paid to total expenditure in Apna Sahakari bank was Rs. 62% in the year 1999 and it has increased upto 67.66 % in 2007, whereas in Thane Janata Sahakari Bank the ratio of interest paid to total expenditure was 71.38% in the year 1999, but it has slightly declined up to 66.02% in the year 2007. It shows there is a fluctuation over the period 1999 to 2007. The ratio of staff expenses to total expenditure in Apna Sahakari bank in the year 1999 was 22.19% and it has reduced upto 20.92% in the year 2007, whereas in Thane Janata Sahakari Bank it was 15.63% in 1999 and it has reduced upto 14.12% in the year 2007. It clearly indicates that, after the IT enabled services in both the banks the staff expenses is reducing not in significant proportion.

15. Deposit ratio analysis shows that in pre IT year 1999, in Apna Sahakari Bank the Fixed deposits to total deposits was 53.96%, the ratio of saving deposits to total deposits was 37.85% and the ratio of current deposits to total deposits was 8.18%. Whereas in the Thane Janata Sahakari bank the ratio of fixed deposits to total deposits in the year 1999 was 64.57%, ratio of saving deposits 28.50% and the current deposits was 6.93% respectively. The ratio has been changed after the application of Information Technology in both the banks. In the year 2007 in Apna bank the ratio of fixed deposits to total deposits has been 61,64% ratio of saving deposits 31.57% and the ratio of current deposits 6.79%, whereas in Thane Janata Sahakari Bank the ratio of fixed deposits to total deposits has been 65.08%, ratio of saving deposits 26.75% and the ratio of current deposits has been 8.17% respectively.

16. It is found that after application of Information Technology the total deposits of Apna Sahakari bank has increased by 317.23 percent during the study period 1999-2007. Whereas in Thane Janata Sahakari bank the total deposits has increased by 360.67 percent during the same period. It means the deposit mobilization is growing rapidly in both the banks, but the rate of growth of deposit mobilization is higher in Thane Janata Sahakari bank during the study period.

17. The Researcher has observed that the credit deposit ratio of Apna Sahakari bank was 54.50% in the pre IT year 1999, after it has been continuously increasing upto year 2006

(i.e., 75.65%). However in the year 2007 it has been declined upto 70.34%. Whereas in Thane Janata Sahakari bank the credit deposit was 60.25% in the year 1999, after that it shows continuously increasing trend upto 67.96% in the year 2007. It clearly indicates that due to adoption of Information Technology credit deposit ratio has been rapidly increasing and it affects positively in the operations of banking business.

18. Among the three ratios Fixed deposits as a percentage of total deposits, saving deposits as a percentage of total deposits and current deposits as a percentage of total deposits, the fixed deposits as percentage of total deposits was higher during the study period and the second major ratio was saving deposits as percentage of total deposits. The following results are obtained regarding credit deployment (1) In absolute terms total credit is in the increasing trend in both the banks, (2) Priority sector advances are also in the increasing trend, (3) Credit-Deposit ratio is in increasing trend.

19. It is found that there is direct relation between service quality and customers satisfaction. There are various methods to measure the customer satisfaction. In the present research the service parameters are divided into following four types, and service quality is measured by point method. (1) Personnel Factors, (2) Physical Factors, (3) Factors and Computer System, (4) Social Factors. The Satisfaction level regarding above factors has been measured on five points scale between totally satisfied to totally dissatisfied. The questionnaire was designed to measure the satisfaction level of the customers of selected UCBs. Overall 300 samples were collected from both the banks. Out of them 140 sample from Apna Sahakari Bank Ltd, Mumbai (Non-Scheduled bank) and 160 samples from Thane Janata Sahakari Bank Ltd., Thane (Scheduled Bank) of the Maharashtra State. The following findings were obtained regarding the parameter of customer satisfaction.

20. The age-wise analysis reveals that the younger customers (21 to 30) and middle aged customers (41-51 age) of Apna Sahakari Bank and Thane Janata Sahakari Bankare more satisfied compared to other age groups.

21. The education-wise analysis reveals that the satisfaction level of educated class upto SSC is less compared to other educated class in both the banks. In Apna Sahakari bank the satisfaction level is higher in the educated group of UG and PG. The variability of educated class of customer of Apna Sahakari bank is less compared to Thane Janata Sahakari bank.

22. It is found that the overall satisfaction level of Thane Janata Sahakari bank is higher (i.e. 77.65) compared to the Apna Sahakari bank (i.e. 72.42). This shows that the variability is more in case of customers of Thane Janata Sahakari bank compare to the customers of Apna Sahakari bank.

23. In today's financial systems, usage of IT is fundamental to the survival and growth of the institutions. IT usage not only helps banks hold and reduce their cost of operations, several developments in the Information and Communication Technology (ICT) enable the institutions to proffer higher profitable products and services to their constituents. IT

has become not just an enabler, but also the distinguishing and differentiator , it also provides competitive advantage and edge to its user. Further, current regulatory and supervisory compliance demands that the institutions have a very sound usage of IT systems for their operations.

Gender-wise distribution of sample customer shows that out of the total customers, male customers were 48.64% in Apna SahakariBank (ASB) and 51.36% in Thane Janata Sahakari Bank. Again comparatively the% of male customers is higher (61.66%) in both the banks than the female (38.34%) customers.

**Recommendations**

1. It is observed in sample banks that there is no adequate infrastructure to achieve proper automation and integration of various communication networks. It is recommended that they should have to create adequate infrastructure and introduce appropriate technologies suiting to their requirements. Simultaneously they also have to make arrangement of educating and training the bank staff and also the customers so as to enable them to adapt the changes on the technology front.

2. It is observed that the silent introduction of LPG policies have agreeably impressed and affected functions, objectives and operations of co-operative banking sector. Information systems and communication play a very crucial role for organizational adaptability to accept emerging changes and modify their strategies. The sample banks are computerized but there is a need of modernization and upgradation of technology through domestic research and development for continuous improvement in the quality of products and services. By installing e-governance structures in urban co-operative banks can effectively and efficiently handle operations of functional areas of management, MIS and IT. The Urban Co-operative Banks can provide on-line services because of dynamic revolution in IT and communication system which have been made everything possible in e-banking world. Moreover through e-governance, mechanization and computerization process, performance of co-operative banking organizations will be made effective and efficient in 21st century.

3. Effective management of Information Technology (IT) is foremost and critical for the success and survival of any organization. This critically arises from changing role of IT in conducting business operations, the increasing dependence on information systems etc. For a successful organization, to understand and manage the risks associated with implementing new technologies is essential. Thus management needs to have an appreciation for and a basic understanding of the risks and constraints of IT in order to provide effective direction and adequate controls.

4. If IT is used in a scientific manner, following benefits may be earned by Co-op Banks. (1) Offering new and innovative Financial products, (2) Get accurate information which will help in time and effectively, (3) Maintain good Management Information System (MIS) and (4) Improvement in head office and reconciliation to improve customer service.

5. To absorb the latest and advanced technology in banking sector there is a need of education and training of staff on IT. Adequate budgetary allocation for the purpose, needs to be given. The training establishments of the banks should be strengthened with adequate personnel and other infrastructure facilities, to impart necessary IT training to the staff-at all levels. The bank may if necessary have to tie-up arrangements with some specialized institutions imparting training in IT to conduct customized training programmes for the bank staff.

6. Providing incentives to employees for acquiring specialized knowledge and skill in IT related matters will act as boost to increase the quality of the IT based talent within a bank. It will also attract more people to be inducted into this area from within as well as from outside. The incentive may be in the form of financial benefits or better promotional opportunities.

7. Outsourcing Software Technology would be a better option for banks to resort to in the context of rapid changes taking place in the IT industry so that the fruits of latest developments are available to the banks.

8. In the UCBs to develop in house capability and to perform management audit of IT departments, it is necessary that each UCB needs to devise a computer audit manual and appropriate methodologies systems for conducting computer audit. All new applications should be subject to pre-installation audit in addition to periodical audit.

9. In order to survive national and international banking, there is a need to introduce latest trends in urban co-operative banking technology, such as e-mail, single window concept, Anytime banking, Tele-banking and Home-banking, Electronic Funds Transfers, Electronic Clearing/Settlement, Cash Management etc. This will lead to growth of urban co-operative banking, accelerate the control, improve customer service, facilitate managerial decisions making and ultimately the profitability and productivity of banks.

10. In Urban Co-operative banking there is a need of new focus on customer and his needs, new risk management practices, modern credit management skills, product development and marketing skills for operating in electronic environment will be helpful to increase their profitability and productivity.

11. The sensitive nature of the banking business and the rapid spread of Information Technology. In this industry make it incumbent for regulators, bank management and users to become more conscious about the security risks involved and the need for security and controls in information technology.

12. While computerization brings with it a whole host of benefits such as reduction in costs, increased efficiency and productivity, Faster time to market and vastly superior customer service, bank managements also need to be mindful that computerization carries. Its own set of security risks and the types of control needed to effectively manage these risks are different from those in a manual environment.

13. Minimum information technology infrastructure in UCB's considering the concentration of small UCB's, the lack of uniformity in the levels of computerization and inadequate awareness about the efficacy of computers in enhancing competitiveness. It is necessary to arriculate minimum IT infrastructure which should exist in each UCB regardless of its size, location or profitability.

14. There is a strong feeling and recommendation that every bank should prepare a vision document on Information Technology being adopted and to be adopted in future.

15. The essence of qualified and trained staff in of utmost importance therefore once in two year each officer/staff should be given training and sensitized in banking related IT activities.

16. To keep abreast with the technology and upgrade, every bank should posses dedicated IT professional and a separate IT wing to cater all the needs.

17. The Reserve Bank should not grant licences, henceforth, without bank adopting core banking solution.

18. It is necessary to articulate the minimum IT infrastructure which should exist in each urban Co-operative Bank regardless of its size, spread, location, or profitability and it should include computerized MIS reporting, automated backened accounting and computerized front end i.e., customer interface.

19. The State Government and Reserve Bank should combinedly set up a center to support state level IT infrastructure for the Urban Co-operative Banks; also the services rendered by center to be determined by cost for that Bank.

20. It is observed in the present study that the E-CRM has not been developed so fast inspite of IT applications in other areas. In the present competitive scenario there is a need to develop the E-CRM system. E-CRM related to using IT for Customer Relationship Management. A good E-CRM system will be helpful to UCBs for providing excellent customer service, to capture as much information as possible from customers and analyse it in real time, so as to promptly optimize product design, marketing strategy etc. Further that it will be possible to give quick answers of all customers queries, differentiated offerings and automated gathering and sharing of all information will be possible.

21. Reserve Bank of India (RBI) has taken various steps for corporate governance in the Indian banking system. However it is observed that the practices of good corporate governance and e-governance system is not effectively implemented in the UCBs under study.

Therefore it is recommended that the UCBs should strive to build up the practices of good co-operative governance and E-governance which will be more beneficial to make the sound investment policy, better credit risk management, appropriate internal control systems, adequate automation, better customer services, Human resource development etc. and they should explore emerging areas like micro finance, adequate mechanization and proactive policies towards customers and shareholders.

**References :**


[1] B. Janki, (2002) : 'Unleashing Employee Productivity : Need for a Paradigm Shift, Indian Banking Association Bulletin, Vol. XXIV, No.3, (March) pp. 7-9.

[2] Bajaj, K.K. (2000), 'E-Commerce Issues in the Emerging Hi-Tech. Banking Environment'. The Journal of The Indian Institution of Bankers, (Jan-March).

[3] Bajaj, K.K. (1999) : E-Commerce, The Cutting Edge of Business, (New Delhi : Tata McGraw Hill Publication Company Ltd.)

[4] Benton, E. (1990) : Bank Fraud : Exposing the Hidden Threat to Financial Institutions. (McGraw – Hill Companies)

[5] Bhasin, T.M. (2001) : E-Commerce in Indian Banking. Indian Banking Association Bulletin, Vol. XXII Nos. 4 &5 (April-May)

[6] Bhattacharya, A. (1999) : 'The Impact of Liberalization on the Productive Efficiency of Indian Commercial Banks', European Journal of Operational Research 98, pp. 332-45.

[7] Birla Institute of Scientific Research, (1981), Banks Since Nationalization. (New Delhi : Allied Publishers Pvt. Ltd.)

[8] Clifford E. Kirsch. (1996), The Financial Services Revolution : Understanding the changing Roles of Banks, Mutual Funds and Insurance Companies. (McGraw-Hill Companies).

[9] Federick F., Reichheld & Phil. S. (2000), E-Loyalty' Harvard Business Review, (July-Aug)

[10] Husain, F. (1988), Computerization and Mechanization in Indian Banks (New Delhi : Deep & Deep Publications).

[11] Johri and Jauhari, (1994), Role of Computers in Banking Operations Systems. (New Delhi : Himalaya Publication House).

[12] Kaveri, V.S. (2001), 'Loan Default and Profitability of Banks', IBA Bulletin, Vol. XXIII No. 1 (January).

[13] Nair, S.NB. (2000), 'E-Commerce and The Emergence of E-Banking', IBA Bulleting, Vol. XXII, No. 10 (October).

[14] Niranjan, (2000), 'Internet Banking is Here', Business World, (3rd April).

[15] Pathrose, P.P. (2001), Hi-Tech', Banking – Prospects and Problem' IBA Bulletin, Vol. XXIII, No. (July).

[16] Rangarajan, C. (2000), 'Banking in the Hi-Tech Environment', The Journal of the Indian Institute of Bankers, (January-March).

[17] Rao, N.V. (2000), 'Changing Indian Banking Scenario : A Paradigm Shift', IBA Bulletin, Vol. XXIV, No.1, pp. 12-20.

[18] Rao, P.K. (1999), "IT in Financial Services Industry : Innovations and Implications', Chartered Secretary, (September).

[19] Sabnani, P. (2000), 'University Banking', IPA Bulletin, Vol. XXII, No.7 (July).

[20] Sarker, P.C. and Das, A. (1997), 'Development of Composite Index of Banking Efficiency : The Indian Case', RBI Occasional Papers 18,1.

[21] Saxena, M. (2001), 'Bankers' Choice : Teach it or Leave it', Strategic Marketing, (February), pp. 42-50.

[22] Shah, S.G. (1977), 'Bank Personal : Manpower for Banking Productivity, a Commerçe (September 24).

[23] Shanti, S. (1984), Customer Services in Banks. (Bombay : Himalaya Publishing House).

[24] Shapiro, C. (2000), 'Will E-Commerce Erode Liberty', Harvard Business Review (May-June).

[25] Shasrti, R.V. (2001), 'Technology for Banks in India Challenges', IBA Bulletin, Vol. XXIII, No.3, (March).

[26] Singhal's, S. (1987), Banks and Customers : A Behavioral Analysis. (New Delhi : Shri Ram Centre for Industrial Relations and Human Resources).

[27] Swamy, B.N.A. (2001), 'New Competition, Deregulation and Emerging Changes in Indian Banking : An Analysis of Different Banks Groups', The Journal of The Indian Institute of Bankers, Vol. 72, No.3, (July-September), pp. 3-22.

[28] Vageesh, N.S. (2000), 'New Private Banks : New Kids on the Block', Business Line, (March).

[29] Vijay, K. and S. Annamalai, (2002), 'Job Satisfaction Among Bank Employees : Cadre-Wise – A Case Study, Pranjan, Vol. XI, No.1, (January-March).

[30] Verghese, S.K. (1983), 'Profits and Profitability of Indian Commercial Banks in the Seventies', NIBM.

[31] Verma, D. (2000), 'Banking On Change', ICFAI Reader, (May), pp. 69.

[32] Wadikar, S.A. (1980), Private Sector Banking in India since 1969 – A Study in its Operations, Ph.D. Thesis (Unpublished).

[33] Zahir, M.A. (1980), 'Transfer Price Mechanism for Performance Evaluation', Reading in Management, pp. 413-422.

[34] Dr. Patil, Y.S., Programme on Strategic Issues in Computerization of Co-operative Banks for Core Banking, Any Branch Banking, Tele Banking, 1-5 August 2006.

[35] Patil, (2000),

[36] Kulkarni, Suresh, (2006), 'Golden Rules for bank Computerization', Cooperative Perspective, Vol. 37, No.3, October-December 2002.

[37] Divekar, Devdutta A., 'Cooperative Banks and Information Technology', Cooperative Perspective, Vol. 37, No. 3, October-December, 2002.

[38] Bakshi, Sunil, (2006), 'Security Policy for Information and Related Technology', Cooperative Perspective, Vol. 37, No.3, October-December

[39] Velanganni, 'E-Governance and Modernization (Mechanization of Cooperative Banking Organizations in the New Centenary, Cooperative Perspectives, Vol. 40, No. 1, April-June-05

[40] Edwinraj, D. Joel, (2005), 'Information Technology : The Emerging Driving Force in Cooperative Banks', Cooperative Perspective, Vol. 40, No.1, April-June'06.

[41] Gulati, V.P. Web Based Information System for Indian Banking Industry, Programme on Economising Information Technology Implementation (10-14 December 2005), organized by....... Pune

[42] Das, Prasun Kumar, The Indian Banker, A Monthly Journal published by the Indian Bank's Association, May-2007, Vol. II, No.5.

[43] Kakkad, Ratish, Electronic Banking : Indians are Becoming High Tech, NICM, Bulletin, Vol. III, No.12, Dec.2006.

[44] Patil, Y.S., Priorities in bank Automation : Customer Viewpoint, Programme on Managing IT implementation in Co-op banks VMNI of Co-op Pune.

[45] Bakshi, P.M., 'Electronic Commerce and the Law of Contracts, The Journal of Business Perspective Jan-June, 1999, pp. 48-50.

[46] Naik, (2007), National Insurance Academy, Pune.

[47] Kakkad, Web Security and Commerce by Simson Grafinkel and Gene Spafford.

# *Epilogue*

Financial inclusion is being accorded the top most priority by the Government and the Reserve Bank of India (RBI). It is the central part of the policy agenda which needs to be carried forwarded through use of cost-effective technological solutions.

Financial inclusion is important for the poor as it provides them opportunities to build savings, avail credit, make investments. And it equips them to meet emergencies. A combination of regulatory mandates, cost effective technology solutions and implicit and explicit incentives has been used to increase financial penetration of affordable banking services particularly in the rural and unorganized sectors.

Sadly, India ranks low when compared with the OECD countries and select Asian peer group contries in respect of financial penetration. The untapped potential with regard to financial inclusion needs to be harnessed using cost effective technology solutions and appropriate business models that make small value transactions viable, argues the latest RBI Report (2010) on Trends and Progress of Banking Industry in India.

Out of the 600,000 habitations in the country, only about 5.0 percent have a commercial bank branch. Just about 40 percent of the population across the country has bank accounts, and this ratio is much lower in the north-east region of the country. People with debit cards comprise 13 percent and those with credit cards comprise only 2.0 percent.

**Role of UCBs & The RBI Vision Document**

In 2005, the Reserve Bank of India (RBI) prepared a Vision Document for Urban Co-operative Banks (UCBs) in order to improve their working. In the document, RBI acknowledged that UCBs are an important part of the financial system in India. "It is, therefore, necessary that the UCBs emerge as a sound and healthy network of jointly owned, democratically controlled, and ethically managed banking institutions providing need based quality banking services, essentially to the middle and lower middle classes and marginalized sections of the society," RBI said

The role of RBI could, thus, be to frame a regulatory and supervisory regime that is multi-layered to capture the heterogeneity of the UCB sector and implement policies that would provide adequate elbowroom for the sector to grow in a non-disruptive manner, the document stated.

The State and Central governments could recognize that the UCBs are not just co-operative societies but they are essentially banking entities whose management structure is that of a co-operative. They should recognize the systemic impact that inefficient functioning of these entities in the sector could have.

Consequently, it would be in the interest of the sector if they support, facilitate and empower the RBI to put in place mechanisms and systems that would enable these UCBs to perform their banking functions in a manner that is in the overall interest of the depositor and the public at large, the document stated.

The RBI displayed the Vision Document in the public domain on its website, seeking feedback on the issue, stating its objectives. These are:

- To rationalize the existing regulatory and supervisory approach keeping in view the heterogeneous character of entities in the sector
- To facilitate a focused and continuous system of supervision through enhanced use of technology.
- To enhance professionalism and improve the quality of governance in UCBs by providing training for skill up-gradation as also by including large depositors in the decision making process / management of banks.
- To put in place a mechanism that addresses the problems of dual control, given the present legal framework, and the time consuming process in bringing requisite legislative changes
- To put in place a consultative arrangement for identifying weak but potentially viable entities in the sector and provide a framework for their being nurtured back to health including, if necessary, through a process of consolidation
- To identify the unviable entities in the sector and provide an exit path for such entities.

It has been nearly six years since the RBI set about to streamline the working of UCBs and the results can be seen in their annual performance balance sheets.

Today, it is a fact that the performance of UCBs has vastly been improved in terms of their focus and customer-profile. In its latest report on the Trends and Progress of Banking (2009-10), the Reserve Bank of India (RBI) praised the performance of the co-operative banks and their role in promoting financial inclusion.

"Co-operative banks, though account for a small proportion of the total business undertaken by the banking system in India, have a prominent place in the Indian financial landscape owing to their potential role in furthering financial inclusion as also because of financial inter linkages that these institutions have with the rest of the financial system," the RBI report said.

As a result of the on-going consolidation initiatives in the UCB sector, the profile of UCBs witnessed a shift in favour of financially sound banks. The UCB sector reported overall net profits as at end-March 2010. However, the spillover effects of the global financial turmoil caused a decline in the profitability during the last two years.

There was an overall improvement in the financial performance of rural co-operatives at end-March 2009 over the previous year. However, the asset quality deteriorated during the same period. Improving the financial soundness of these institutions is extremely important as the existing infrastructure of these institutions especially that of primary agricultural co-operative societies (PACS), can be leveraged upon for furthering financial inclusion. Addressing the lopsided geographical spread and the lopsided distribution of banking business of PACS across regions is important in this context.

Further, there is also an urgent need to improve deposit mobilisation by the long-term co-operative credit institutions both from the point of view of diversification of resources and financial inclusion. The declining trend in the disbursal of loans from RIDF and the number of Kisan Credit Cards issued by co-operatives is a source of concern that requires urgent attention.

In 2009-2010, The Urban Co-operative Banking sector reported overall net profits as at end-March 2010 with improved asset quality. The overall financial performance of the rural co-operative sector witnessed some improvement at end-March 2009 over the previous year, though the asset quality deteriorated. However, the financial position of ground level institutions in the rural co-operative sector is a cause for concern as they reported losses alongside a high NPA ratio. Further, the role of the co-operative sector in the Kisan Credit Card Scheme, in terms of number of cards issued as well as amount of credit sanctioned, exhibited a declining trend during the recent years.

According to the RBI report, the wide network of co-operatives, both urban and rural, supplements the commercial bank network in its efforts to deepen financial intermediation by bringing large number of small depositors/borrowers under the formal financial network.

During 2009-10, the Platinum Jubilee year of the Reserve Bank, the flagship project was the outreach programme aimed at financial inclusion and financial literacy. The Reserve Bank chose 160 remote unbanked villages to convert them into villages having 100 per cent financial inclusion with each household having at least one credit facility along with effective grievance redressal mechanism and awareness.

Banking analysts are extremely optimistic that India's efforts at bringing about a revolution in financial inclusion will be successful, with banks, including the Urban Co-operative Banks playing a vital role.

## The India vs Bharat Debate

Finally, I would like to briefly look at the issue of India vs Bharat, which keeps cropping up time and again when the anomalies in economic development are discussed and debated.

It is not a tale of two nations at war as the title implies. In fact, it is the tale two notions complimenting each other. The two, India and Bharat, can survive and thrive only when they support each other.

The general perception is that India and Bharat are at conflict. But I see them more as complimentary. India collapses without Bharat's support. Bharat withers away without India's prop. In today's context, India is an urban entity, thronging with a 300-million strong middle-class with tremendous purchasing power, mostly living in cities and bigger towns. On the other hand, Bharat constitutes the rest of the population thronging in villages and the rural country, with agricultural as its backbone. Today, India's popular image is that of a country on the fast track of industrialization, driven by advanced technology. The fact is India's economy is agriculture-based. Nearly 70 percent of the country's billion plus population depends upon agriculture and allied activities for its livelihood. The impact of agriculture on the economy is clearly seen when the country is bestowed with a good monsoon. The demand for every consumer item shoots up, including bullion. But the failure of a single monsoon can trigger inflation and a sharp drop in the sale of all verieties of consumer goods

The general perception of the country that is projected both in the print and electronic media is that while the India of malls and markets is shining, the Bharat of villages is suffering. Occasional surveys and studies reveal that vast sections of Indian population survive on an income as low as Rs 20 per day. It sounds bizarre against the claims that India is marching ahead in the 21st century as an economic powerhouse.

There is a view that Bharat represents the cultural and spiritual heritage and traditions that are more than 2,000 years old. Its millions of people comprise simple living farmers, farm and manual labourers. In spite of their poverty, illiteracy, they are proud sons of this soil. In fact, most of the soldiers who fight for this country are the sons of farmers.

However, the debate of India versus Bharat still continues. As recently as on 21 November 2011, eminent personalities from across different walks of life participated in a panel discussion on the topic of *'India versus Bharat – Can they ever Meet?,'* organized by Presidency University, Kolkata, in association with the Times of India.

The outcome of the debate, *'whether India's progress is a holistic one or a part of the nation has never benefited from the development over the years,'* was interesting as much as it was thought-provoking because the panelists were divided on their opinions.

West Bengal State Municipal Affairs Department Secretary Alapan Bandopadhyay, IAS, had an interesting, real-life story to tell. He recalled how one of his IAS batch mates could not mention his address in their service directory as he lived on a footpath with his vegetable vendor mother. But he rose to become one of the main persons in charge of the municipal areas of the very city where once he had no address. Bandopadhyay showed the trajectory of the journey of the man coming from Bharat and becoming part of India.

Educationist Prasanta Roy argued that India and Bharat do engage daily and one needs the other. But journalist Suman Chattopadhyay felt India and Bharat are still different. "One India is moving very fast and the other is lagging behind. There is a dichotomy and the reality on the ground for a tribal from Madhya Pradesh, or a slum dweller from Mumbai or Kolkata is that it is moving very slowly," he said. This opinion was shared by another journalist, Utpal Chatterjee.

Educationist Rajat Kanta Roy said that India has not done "too badly in terms of civilized behaviour", and looked back at the Bharatvarsha where Emperor Ashoka said that people should not speak ill about other sects and instead learn from their tenets.

Very interestingly, journalist and author, Hiranmay Karlekar said that 'India and Bharat have been living together for some time but are yet to be married.' "I am not bothered as long as they are together, there will be hitches and glitches and that's how a relationship evolves," he quipped.

Writer, translator and teacher SV Raman pointed out that 'whether we call it Bharat or India, it was important that there is development, and upward mobility did not just mean possessing a mobile phone.'

Presenting an example that overwhelmingly unites India and Bharat, writer Boria Mazumdar asked, "When Sachin comes out to bat, does he represent Bharat or India?" "Sachin represents both," Mazumdar said, adding, "when India and Bharat both come together and there is the confluence of both, emotions flow and the country celebrates."

More the debate, the better for both India and Bharat!

At present, land acquisitions in rural areas and villages by various states have thrown up the question of development at what cost? It has also opened the issue of India vs Bharat yet again. Is India encroaching upon Bharat? Or is India sharing its wealth with Bharat? Only the future will tell !

# UCBs - Figures at a Glance

**Grade-wise Distribution of Deposits and Advances of Urban Cooperative Banks**
(As at end-March 2011)

| Grades | Number of UCBs | Percentage Share to Total | Amount of Deposits | Percentage Share to Total | Amount of Advances | Percentage Share to Total |
|---|---|---|---|---|---|---|
| 1 | 2 | 3 | 4 | 5 | 6 | 7 |
| I | 845 | 51.3 | 1,34,691 | 63.5 | 86,916 | 63.7 |
| II | 497 | 30.2 | 55,130 | 26.0 | 35,701 | 26.2 |
| III | 172 | 10.5 | 10,206 | 4.8 | 6,487 | 4.8 |
| IV | 131 | 8.0 | 12,004 | 5.7 | 7,237 | 5.3 |
| **Total** | **1,645** | **100.0** | **2,12,031** | **100.0** | **1,36,341** | **100.0** |

**Merger and Amalgamation of Urban Cooperative Banks**
**Year-wise Progress in Mergers/acquisitions**

| Financialyear | Proposals received in RBI | NOCs issued by RBI | Merger effected (Notified by RCS) |
|---|---|---|---|
| 1 | 2 | 3 | 4 |
| 2005-06 | 24 | 13 | 4 |
| 2006-07 | 32 | 17 | 15 |
| 2007-08 | 42 | 28 | 27 |
| 2008-09 | 16 | 26 | 22 |
| 2009-10 | 26 | 17 | 13 |
| 2010-11 | 17 | 13 | 11 |
| 2011-12* | 1 | 6 | 3 |
| **Total** | **158** | **120** | **95** |

*:Upto June 30,2011

**State-wise Progress in Mergers/acquisition**

| States | 2005-06 | 2006-07 | 2007-08 | 2008-09 | 2009-10 | 2010-11 | 2011-12 | Total |
|---|---|---|---|---|---|---|---|---|
| 1 | 2 | 3 | 4 | 5 | 6 | 7 | 8 | 9 |
| Maharashtra | 2 | 12 | 14 | 16 | 6 | 6 | 2 | 58 |
| Gujarat | 2 | 1 | 7 | 2 | 2 | 1 | 1 | 16 |
| Andhra Pradesh | – | 1 | 3 | 1 | 3 | 2 | – | 10 |
| Karnataka | – | – | 2 | 1 | – | – | – | 3 |
| Punjab | – | 1 | – | – | – | – | – | 1 |
| Madhya Pradesh | – | – | – | – | – | 1 | – | 1 |
| Uttarakhand | – | – | 1 | 1 | – | – | – | 2 |
| Chhattisgarh | – | – | – | 1 | – | 1 | – | 2 |
| Rajasthan | – | – | – | – | 2 | – | – | 2 |
| **Total** | **4** | **15** | **27** | **22** | **13** | **11** | **3** | **95** |

**Distribution of Urban Cooperative Banks by Size of Deposits and Advances**

(As at end-March 2011)

(Amount in ₹ crore)

| Deposit base | Distribution of UCBs by Size of Deposits | | | | Advances base | Distribution of UCBs by Size of Advances | | | |
|---|---|---|---|---|---|---|---|---|---|
| | Number of UCBs | | Deposits | | | Number of UCBs | | Advances | |
| | Number | Percentage share in total | Number | Percentage share in total | | Number | Percentage share in total | Number | Percentage share in total |
| 1 | 2 | 3 | 4 | 5 | 6 | 7 | 8 | 9 | 10 |
| D e" 1000 | 28 | 1.7 | 83,867 | 39.6 | Ad e" 1000 | 17 | 1.0 | 45,487 | 33.4 |
| 500 d" D < 1000 | 41 | 2.5 | 28,899 | 13.6 | 500 d" Ad < 1000 | 27 | 1.6 | 19,057 | 14.0 |
| 250 d" D < 500 | 91 | 5.5 | 30,212 | 14.2 | 250 d" Ad < 500 | 50 | 3.0 | 17,335 | 12.7 |
| 100 d" D < 250 | 206 | 12.5 | 31,631 | 14.9 | 100 d" Ad < 250 | 148 | 9.0 | 22,642 | 16.6 |
| 50 d" D < 100 | 245 | 14.9 | 17,219 | 8.1 | 50 d" Ad < 100 | 182 | 11.1 | 12,463 | 9.1 |
| 25 d" D < 50 | 318 | 19.3 | 11,442 | 5.4 | 25 d" Ad < 50 | 259 | 15.7 | 9,323 | 6.8 |
| 10 d" D < 25 | 418 | 25.4 | 7,115 | 3.4 | 10 d" Ad < 25 | 446 | 27.1 | 7,297 | 5.4 |
| D < 10 | 298 | 18.1 | 1,646 | 0.8 | Ad < 10 | 516 | 31.4 | 2,737 | 2.0 |
| **Total** | **1,645** | **100.0** | **2,12,031** | **100.0** | **Total** | **1,645** | **100.0** | **1,36,341** | **100.0** |

**Tier-wise Distribution of Urban Cooperative Banks**

(As at end-March 2011)

(Amount in ₹ crore)

| Bank Tier Type | No. of banks | | Deposits | | Advances | | Assets | |
|---|---|---|---|---|---|---|---|---|
| | Number | Percentage Share to Total | Amount | Percentage Share to Total | Amount | Percentage Share to Total | Amount | Percentage Share to Total |
| 1 | 2 | 3 | 4 | 5 | 6 | 7 | 8 | 9 |
| I | 1,279 | 77.8 | 40,779 | 19.2 | 24,918 | 18.3 | 52,377 | 19.2 |
| II | 366 | 22.2 | 1,71,252 | 80.8 | 1,11,423 | 81.7 | 2,20,924 | 80.8 |
| Total | 1,645 | 100.0 | 2,12,031 | 100.0 | 1,36,341 | 100.0 | 2,73,301 | 100.0 |

**Liabilities and Assets of Urban Cooperative Banks**

(As at end-March 2011)

(Amount in ₹ Crore)

| Item | Scheduled UCBs | | Non-Scheduled UCBs | | All UCBs | |
|---|---|---|---|---|---|---|
| | 2010 | 2011 | 2010 | 2011 | 2010 | 2011 |
| 1 | 2 | 3 | 4 | 5 | 6 | 7 |
| **Liabilities** | | | | | | |
| 1. Capital | 1,612 | 1,871 | 3,955 | 4,395 | 5,567 | 6,267 |
| | (1.6) | (1.6) | (3.0) | (2.9) | (2.3) | (2.3) |
| 2. Reserves | 10,377 | 11,066 | 14,153 | 15,195 | 24,531 | 26,260 |
| | (10.0) | (9.3) | (10.6) | (9.9) | (10.3) | (9.6) |
| 3. Deposits | 80,208 | 92,428 | 1,02,943 | 1,19,602 | 1,83,150 | 2,12,031 |
| | (77.2) | (77.3) | (77.2) | (77.8) | (77.2) | (77.6) |
| 4. Borrowings | 1,783 | 2,718 | 557 | 1,571 | 2,340 | 4,289 |
| | (1.7) | (2.3) | (0.4) | (1.0) | (1.0) | (1.6) |
| 5. Other Liabilities | 9,916 | 11,483 | 11,766 | 12,973 | 21,682 | 24,455 |
| | (9.5) | (9.6) | (8.8) | (8.4) | (9.1) | (8.9) |
| **Assets** | | | | | | |
| 1. Cash in Hand | 586 | 648 | 1,604 | 1,709 | 2,190 | 2,357 |
| | (0.6) | (0.5) | (1.2) | (1.1) | (0.9) | (0.9) |
| 2. Balances with Banks | 10,290 | 11,010 | 10,238 | 12,880 | 20,528 | 23,890 |
| | (9.9) | (9.2) | (7.7) | (8.4) | (8.7) | (8.7) |
| 3. Money at Call and Short Notice | 407 | 651 | 1,023 | 485 | 1,431 | 1,136 |
| | (0.4) | (0.5) | (0.8) | (0.3) | (0.6) | (0.4) |
| 4. Investments | 31,107 | 33,480 | 48,063 | 53,595 | 79,170 | 87,075 |
| | (29.9) | (28.0) | (36.0) | (34.9) | (33.4) | (31.9) |
| 5. Loans and Advances | 50,647 | 61,772 | 61,789 | 74,569 | 1,12,436 | 1,36,341 |
| | (48.7) | (51.7) | (46.3) | (48.5) | (47.4) | (49.9) |
| 6. Other Assets | 10,859 | 12,005 | 10,657 | 10,498 | 21,516 | 22,503 |
| | (10.5) | (10.0) | (8.0) | (6.8) | (9.1) | (8.2) |
| **Total Liabilities/ Assets** | **1,03,896** | **1,19,566** | **1,33,374** | **1,53,736** | **2,37,271** | **2,73,302** |
| | **(100.0)** | **(100.0)** | **(100.0)** | **(100.0)** | **(100.0)** | **(100.0)** |

**Note:** Figures in parentheses are percentages to total liabilities/assets.

**Investments by Urban Cooperative Banks**

(Amount in ₹ Crore)

| Item | As at end-March | | Percentage Variation | |
|---|---|---|---|---|
| | 2010 | 2011 | 2009-10 | 2010-11 |
| 1 | 2 | 3 | 4 | 5 |
| **Total Investments (A+B)** | **79,169 (100.0)** | **87,075 (100.0)** | 21.6 | 10.0 |
| **A. SLR Investments (I to vi)** | **70,925 (89.6)** | **80,756 (92.7)** | 29.3 | 13.9 |
| i) Central Government Securities | 40,818 (51.6) | 52,372 (60.1) | 19.4 | 28.3 |
| ii) State Government Securities | 7,791 (9.8) | 10,127 (11.6) | 79.4 | 30.0 |
| iii) Other Approved Securities | 415 (0.5) | 576 (0.7) | 1.2 | 38.8 |
| iv) Term Deposits with StCBs | 6,326 (8.0) | 5,496 (6.3) | 19.8 | -13.1 |
| v) Term Deposits with DCCBs | 13,839 (17.5) | 10,861 (12.5) | 51.8 | -21.5 |
| vi) Others, if any | 1,736 (2.2) | 1,324 (1.5) | 13.1 | -23.7 |
| **B. Non-SLR Investments** | **8,244 (10.4)** | **6,319 (7.3)** | -19.4 | -23.4 |

**Note:** Figures in parentheses are percentages to total investments.

**Financial Performance of Scheduled and Non-Scheduled Urban Cooperative Banks**
(As at end-March 2011)

(Amount in ₹ Crore)

| Item | Scheduled | | Non-Scheduled | | All UCBs | | Percentage variation (All UCBs) | |
|---|---|---|---|---|---|---|---|---|
| | 2009-10 | 2010-11 | 2009-10 | 2010-11 | 2009-10 | 2010-11 | 2009-10 | 2010-11 |
| 1 | 2 | 3 | 4 | 5 | 6 | 7 | 8 | 9 |
| **A. Total Income (i+ii)** | **8,561 (100.0)** | **9,842 (100.0)** | **11,157 (100.0)** | **12,601 (100.0)** | **19,718 (100.0)** | **22,443 (100.0)** | **7.1** | **13.8** |
| i. Interest Income | 7,751 (90.5) | 8,989 (91.3) | 10,528 (94.4) | 11,860 (94.1) | 18,279 (92.7) | 20,849 (92.9) | 9.9 | 14.1 |
| ii. Non-Interest Income | 810 (9.5) | 853 (8.7) | 629 (5.6) | 741 (5.9) | 1,439 (7.3) | 1594 (7.1) | -19.1 | 10.8 |
| **B. Total Expenditure (i+ii)** | **7,347 (100.0)** | **7,809 (100.0)** | **9,500 (100.0)** | **10,770 (100.0)** | **16,847 (100.0)** | **18,579 (100.0)** | **12.7** | **10.3** |
| i. Interest Expenditure | 5,334 (72.6) | 5,536 (70.9) | 6,670 (70.2) | 7,601 (70.6) | 12,004 (71.3) | 13,137 (70.7) | 12.3 | 9.4 |
| ii. Non-Interest Expenditure | 2,013 (27.4) | 2,273 (29.1) | 2,830 (29.8) | 3,169 (29.4) | 4,843 (28.7) | 5,442 (29.3) | 13.6 | 12.4 |
| *of which:* Staff Expenses | 1,010 | 1,154 | 1,776 | 1,667 | 2,786 | 2,821 | 17.9 | 1.3 |
| **C. Profits** | | | | | | | | |
| i. Amount of operating profits | 1,214 | 2,033 | 1,657 | 1,832 | 2,871 | 3,865 | -17.0 | 34.6 |
| ii. Provisions, contingencies, taxes | 666 | 800 | 948 | 862 | 1,614 | 1,662 | -18.5 | 12.7 |
| iii. Amount of net profits | 548 | 1,233 | 709 | 970 | 1,257 | 2,203 | -19.6 | 75.3 |

**Note**: Figures in parentheses are percentages to their respective totals.

| **Select Financial Indicators of UCBs** | | | | | | |
|---|---|---|---|---|---|---|
| **Financial indicators** | **Scheduled** | | **Non-Scheduled** | | **All UCBs** | |
| | **2009-10** | **2010-11** | **2009-10** | **2010-11** | **2009-10** | **2010-11** |
| **1** | **2** | **3** | **4** | **5** | **6** | **7** |
| Return on Assets | 0.57 | 1.10 | 0.57 | 0.68 | 0.57 | 0.86 |
| Net Interest Margin | 2.54 | 3.09 | 3.12 | 2.97 | 2.86 | 3.02 |

**Non-Performing Assets of UCBs**

(Amount in ₹ Crore)

| **Items** | **Mar' 2010** | **Mar' 2011** |
|---|---|---|
| **1** | **2** | **3** |
| 1. Gross NPAs | 11,399 | 11,529 |
| 2. Net NPAs | 3,821 | 3,130 |
| 3. Gross NPA Ratio | 10.1 | 8.5 |
| 4. Net NPA Ratio | 3.9 | 2.5 |
| 5. Provisioning | 7,578 | 8,399 |
| 6. Coverage Ratio | 66.5 | 72.9 |

**Note**: 1. Coverage ratio is calculated as provisioning as percentage of gross NPAs.
2. Items 3, 4, and 6 are in percentages.

**Advances to Weaker Sections by Urban Cooperative Banks**
(As at end-March 2011)

(Amount in ₹ Crore)

| **Sector** | **Amount** | **Percentage share in total advances** |
|---|---|---|
| **1** | **2** | **3** |
| Agriculture and Allied Activities | 1,507 | 1.1 |
| *of which* 1. Direct Finance | 555 | 0.4 |
| 2. Indirect Finance | 952 | 0.7 |
| Small Enterprises | 11,928 | 8.7 |
| *of which* 1. Direct Finance | 9,991 | 7.3 |
| 2. Indirect Finance | 1,937 | 1.4 |
| Micro Credit | 1,000 | 0.7 |
| State Sponsored Organisations for SC/ ST | 96 | 0.1 |
| Educational loans | 399 | 0.3 |
| Housing loans | 4,021 | 2.9 |
| **Total** | **18,951** | **13.9** |

**A Profile of Rural Cooperative Banks**
(As at 31st March, 2010)

(Amount in ₹ crore)

| Item | Short-Term | | | Long-Term | |
|---|---|---|---|---|---|
| | StCBs | DCCBs | PACS | SCARDBs | PCARDBs |
| 1 | 2 | 3 | 4 | 5 | 6 |
| **A. No. of Cooperative Banks** | 31 | 370 | 94,647 | 20 | 697 |
| **B. Balance Sheet Indicators** | | | | | |
| i. Owned Funds (Capital + Reserves) | 11,871 | 31,370 | 12,479 | 4,510 | 5,165 |
| ii. Deposits | 79,150 | 1,46,404 | 35,286 | 759 | 461 |
| iii. Borrowings | 23,559 | 28,735 | 51,764 | 15,581 | 12,832 |
| iv. Loans and Advances Issued | 53,588 | 1,18,393 | 74,938 | 3,205 | 2,465 |
| v. Loans and Advances Outstanding | 49,629 | 1,07,466 | 76,480 | 17,000 | 11,482 |
| vi. Total Liabilities/Assets | 1,20,662 | 2,18,676 | 1,35,192 + | 25,562 | 25,037 |
| **C. Financial Performance** | | | | | |
| i Institutions in Profit | | | | | |
| a. No. | 29 | 322 | 40,936 | 10 | 276 |
| b. Amount of Profits | 462 | 1,659 | 1,132 | 127 | 123 |
| ii. Institutions in Loss | | | | | |
| a. No. | 2 | 47* | 41,679 | 9 | 416 |
| b. Amount of Loss | 209 | 523 | 2,347 | 155 | 538 |
| iii. Overall Profit (+)/Loss (-) | 253 | 1,136 | -1,215 | -27 | -415 |
| iv. Accumulated Loss | 575 | 4757 | – | 1,190 | 4154 |
| **D. Non-performing Assets** | | | | | |
| i. Amount | 4353 | 16,234 | 39,524 ++ | 5,642 | 4,841 |
| ii. As Percentage of Loans Outstanding | 8.8 | 12.9 | 41.3 | 33.2 | 42.0 |
| iii. Recovery of Loans to Demand (Per cent) | 91.8 | 75.7 | – | 41.0 | 41.5 |

**Financial Performance of State Cooperative Banks**

(Amount in ₹ Crore)

| Item | As at end-March | | Percentage Variation | |
|---|---|---|---|---|
| | 2009 | 2010 | 2008-09 | 2009-10 |
| 1 | 2 | 3 | 4 | 5 |
| **A. Income (i+ii)** | **7,590** (100.0) | **8,239** (100.0) | **22.5** | **8.6** |
| i. Interest Income | 7,281 (95.9) | 7,822 (94.9) | 21.8 | 7.4 |
| ii. Other Income | 309 (4.1) | 417 (5.1) | 44.1 | 35.0 |
| **B. Expenditure (i+ii+iii)** | **7,272** (100.0) | **7,985** (100.0) | **21.8** | **9.8** |
| i. Interest Expended | 5,729 (78.8) | 6,595 (82.6) | 24.9 | 15.1 |
| ii. Provisions and Contingencies | 451 (6.2) | 393 (4.9) | -16.9 | -12.9 |
| iii. Operating expenses | 1,092 (15.0) | 997 (12.5) | 29.3 | -8.7 |
| *of which, Wage Bill* | 512 (7.0) | 581 (7.3) | 11.8 | 13.7 |
| **C. Profits** | | | | |
| i. Operating Profits | 768 | 647 | 0.6 | -15.8 |
| ii. Net Profits | 318 | 253 | 43.8 | -20.4 |

**Note:** 1. Figures in parentheses are percentages to the total income/ expenditure.
2. Data for StCBs in Bihar, West Bengal, Manipur and Kerala are repeated for the year 2009-10. Source: NABARD.

**Soundness Indicators of State Cooperative Banks**

(Amount in ₹ Crore)

| Item | As at end-March | | Percentage Variation | |
|---|---|---|---|---|
| | 2009 | 2010 | 2009 | 2010 |
| 1 | 2 | 3 | 4 | 5 |
| **A. Total NPAs (i+ii+iii)** | **5,725** | **4,353** | -7.5 | -24.0 |
| i. Sub-standard | 1,627 | 1,332 | -41.9 | -18.1 |
| ii. Doubtful | 3,822 | 2,219 | 44.1 | -41.9 |
| iii. Loss | 276 | 802 | -62.5 | 190.6 |
| **B. NPAs to Loans Ratio** | **11.8** | **8.8** | | |
| i. Recovery to Demand (%) | 91.8 | 91.8 | | |
| ii. Provisions Required | 2,883 | 2,861 | 8.5 | -0.7 |
| iii. Provision Made | 3,310 | 4,438 | 10.3 | 34.1 |
| **Source:** NABARD | | | | |

**Liabilities and Assets of District Central Cooperative Banks**

(Amount in ₹ Crore)

| Item | As at end-March | | Percentage Variation | |
|---|---|---|---|---|
| | 2009 | 2010 | 2008-09 | 2009-10 |
| 1 | 2 | 3 | 4 | 5 |
| **Liabilities** | | | | |
| 1. Capital | 6,578<br>(3.4) | 7,309<br>(3.3) | 10.8 | 11.1 |
| 2. Reserves | 23,227<br>(11.9) | 24,061<br>(11.0) | 3.4 | 3.6 |
| 3. Deposits | 1,27,623<br>(65.2) | 1,46,404<br>(67.0) | 16.4 | 14.7 |
| 4. Borrowings | 27,663<br>(14.1) | 28,735<br>(13.1) | -13.9 | 3.9 |
| 5. Other Liabilities | 10,593<br>(5.4) | 12,168<br>(5.6) | 21.1 | 14.9 |
| **Assets** | | | | |
| 1. Cash and Bank balance | 12,917<br>(6.6) | 14,797<br>(6.8) | 21.8 | 14.6 |
| 2. Investments | 64,709<br>(33.1) | 75,913<br>(34.7) | 34.2 | 17.3 |
| 3. Loans and Advances | 99,429<br>(50.8) | 1,07,466<br>(49.1) | -1.8 | 8.1 |
| 4. Other Assets | 18,629<br>(9.5) | 20,500<br>(9.4) | -1.0 | 10.0 |
| **Total Liabilities/Assets** | **1,95,684**<br>**100.0** | **2,18,676**<br>**100.0** | **9.4** | **11.7** |

**Note:** 1. Figures in parentheses are percentages to total.

2. 'Reserves' include credit balance in profits and loss account shown separately by some of the banks.

3. Data for DCCBs of Bihar, West Bengal and Kerala are repeated for the year 2009-10, as the latest data were not available.

**Source:** NABARD.

**Financial Performance of District Central Cooperative Banks**

(Amount in ₹ Crore)

| Item | As at end-March | | Percentage Variation | |
|---|---|---|---|---|
| | 2009 | 2010 | 2008-09 | 2009-10 |
| 1 | 2 | 3 | 4 | 5 |
| **A. Income (i+ii)** | **16,302** | **17,713** | **24.1** | **8.7** |
| | **(100.0)** | **(100.0)** | | |
| i. Interest Income | 14,817 | 15,936 | 23.7 | 7.6 |
| | (90.9) | (90.0) | | |
| ii. Other Income | 1,485 | 1,777 | 28.6 | 19.7 |
| | (9.1) | (10.0) | | |
| **B. Expenditure(i+ii+iii)** | **14,949** | **16,576** | **12.6** | **10.9** |
| | **(100.0)** | **(100.0)** | | |
| i. Interest Expended | 9,413 | 10,330 | 19.6 | 9.7 |
| | (63.0) | (62.3) | | |
| ii. Provisions and Contingencies | 2,119 | 2,228 | -12.5 | 5.1 |
| | (14.2) | (13.4) | | |
| iii. Operating expenses | 3,417 | 4,018 | 14.7 | 17.6 |
| | (22.9) | (24.2) | | |
| *of which, Wage Bill* | 2,255 | 2,618 | 13.9 | 16.1 |
| | (15.1) | (15.8) | | |
| **C. Profits** | | | | |
| i. Operating Profits | 3,473 | 3,363 | 52.1 | -3.2 |
| ii. Net Profits | 1,353 | 1,136 | – | -16.0 |

**Note:** 1. Figures in parentheses are percentages to total.

2. Data for DCCBs of Bihar, West Bengal and Kerala are repeated for the year 2007-08.

**Source:** NABARD.

**Liabilities and Assets of State Cooperative Agriculture and Rural Development Banks**

(Amount in ₹ Crore)

| Item | As at end-March | | Percentage Variation | |
|---|---|---|---|---|
| | 2009 | 2010 | 2008-09 | 2009-10 |
| 1 | 2 | 3 | 4 | 5 |
| **Liabilities** | | | | |
| 1. Capital | 812<br>(3.2) | 821<br>(3.2) | -33.5 | 1.0 |
| 2. Reserves | 3,191<br>(12.6) | 3,688<br>(14.4) | 15.4 | 15.6 |
| 3. Deposits | 711<br>(2.8) | 759<br>(3.0) | 8.6 | 6.7 |
| 4. Borrowings | 15,849<br>(62.4) | 15,581<br>(61.0) | -1.6 | -1.7 |
| 5. Other Liabilities | 4,823<br>(19.0) | 4,713<br>(18.4) | 20.2 | -2.3 |
| **Assets** | | | | |
| 1. Cash and Bank Balance | 189<br>(0.7) | 197<br>(0.8) | -22.5 | 4.3 |
| 2. Investments | 2,941<br>(11.6) | 3,141<br>(12.3) | 15.6 | 6.8 |
| 3. Loans and Advances | 16,420<br>(64.7) | 17,000<br>(66.5) | -11.2 | 3.5 |
| 4. Other Assets | 5,836<br>(23.0) | 5,224<br>(20.4) | 67.3 | -10.5 |
| **Total Liabilities/Assets** | **25,386<br>(100.0)** | **25,562<br>(100.0)** | **2.5** | **0.7** |

**Note**: 1. Figures in parentheses are percentages to their respective totals.
2. Data for SCARDBs in the States of Maharashtra repeated from the year 2007-08.
3. SCARDB in Manipur is defunct.

**Source**: NABARD.

**Financial Performance of State Cooperative Agriculture and Rural Development Banks**

(Amount in ₹ Crore)

| Item | As at end-March | | Percentage Variation | |
|---|---|---|---|---|
| | 2009 | 2010 | 2008-09 | 2009-10 |
| 1 | 2 | 3 | 4 | 5 |
| **A Income (i+ii)** | **3,009** (100.0) | **2,012** (100.0) | **65.0** | **-33.1** |
| i Interest Income | 2,774 (92.2) | 1,737 (86.3) | 64.6 | -37.4 |
| ii Other Income | 235 (7.8) | 275 (13.7) | 69.3 | 17.1 |
| **B Expenditure (i+ii+iii)** | **2,960** (100.0) | **2,040** (100.0) | **43.2** | **-31.1** |
| i Interest Expended | 1,330 (44.9) | 1,303 (63.9) | 3.7 | -2.0 |
| ii Provisions and Contingencies | 1,390 (47.0) | 450 (22.1) | 147.7 | -67.7 |
| iii Operating expenses | 240 (8.1) | 287 (14.1) | 7.7 | 19.6 |
| *Of which, Wage Bill* | 194 (6.5) | 233 (11.4) | 19.7 | 20.3 |
| **D Profits** | | | | |
| i Operating Profits | 1,439 | 422 | 352.2 | -70.6 |
| ii Net Profits (+)/ Loss (-) | 49 | -27 | – | – |

**Note:** 1. Figures in parentheses are percentages to their respective totals.
2. Data for SCARDBs in the States of Maharashtra repeated.
3. SCARDB in Manipur is defunct

**Source:** NABARD.

**Liabilities and Assets of Primary Cooperative Agriculture and Rural Development Banks**

(Amount in ₹ Crore)

| Item | As at end-March | | Percentage Variation | |
|---|---|---|---|---|
| | 2009 | 2010 | 2008-09 | 2009-10 |
| 1 | 2 | 3 | 4 | 5 |
| **Liabilities** | | | | |
| 1. Capital | 1,515<br>(6.1) | 1,527<br>(6.1) | 69.4 | 0.8 |
| 2. Reserves | 3,493<br>(14.1) | 3,638<br>(14.5) | 15.0 | 4.2 |
| 3. Deposits | 400<br>(1.6) | 461<br>(1.8) | 17.8 | 15.2 |
| 4. Borrowings | 12,365<br>(49.8) | 12,832<br>(51.3) | 16.4 | 3.8 |
| 5. Other Liabilities | 7,073<br>(28.5) | 6,579<br>(26.3) | 32.8 | -7.0 |
| **Assets** | | | | |
| 1. Cash and Bank Balance | 236<br>(0.9) | 268<br>(1.1) | 86.2 | 13.6 |
| 2. Investments | 1,122<br>(4.5) | 1,167<br>(4.7) | 27.6 | 4.0 |
| 3. Loans and Advances | 11,268<br>(45.4) | 11,482<br>(45.9) | 13.7 | 1.9 |
| 4. Other Assets | 12,219<br>(49.2) | 12,120<br>(48.4) | 31.3 | -0.8 |
| **Total Liabilities/Assets** | **24,846**<br>**100.0** | **25,037**<br>**100.0** | **22.9** | **0.8** |

**Note:** Figures in parentheses are percentages to totals.
**Source**: NABARD

**Financial Performance of Primary Cooperative Agriculture and Rural Development Banks**

(Amount in ₹ Crore)

| Item | As at end-March | | Percentage Variation | |
|---|---|---|---|---|
| | 2009 | 2010 | 2008-09 | 2009-10 |
| 1 | 2 | 3 | 4 | 5 |
| **A. Income (i+ii)** | **2,022** (100.0) | **1,831** (100.0) | **29.2** | **-9.4** |
| i. Interest Income | 1,431 (70.8) | 1,292 (70.5) | 4.8 | -9.8 |
| ii. Other Income | 591 (29.2) | 540 (29.5) | 195.8 | -8.7 |
| **B. Expenditure (i+ii+iii)** | **2,221** (100.0) | **2,248** (100.0) | **15.3** | **1.2** |
| i. Interest Expended | 1,217 (54.8) | 1,138 (50.6) | 22.9 | -6.5 |
| ii. Provisions and Contingencies | 545 (24.6) | 596 (26.5) | -12.3 | 9.3 |
| iii. Operating expenses | 458 (20.6) | 513 (22.8) | 46.0 | 12.0 |
| *of which, Wage Bill* | 191 (8.6) | 285 (12.7) | -9.4 | 49.2 |
| **C. Profits** | | | | |
| i. Operating Profits | 347 | 180 | 32.5 | -48.1 |
| ii. Net Profits | -199 | -417 | – | – |

**Note:** Figures in parentheses are percentages to their respective totals.
**Source**: NABARD

| | Maharashtra | India |
|---|---|---|
| **Urban Co-Operative Banks** | 539 | 1645 |
| **Scheduled Co – Op Banks** | 38 | 53 |
| **Non Scheduled Co – Op Banks** | 501 | 1592 |
| **Multi State** | 23 | 42 |
| **Share Capital** | 2700 Cr | 6267 Cr |
| **Owned Funds** | 12,200 Cr | 26,260 Cr |
| **Deposits** | 1,38,124 Cr | 2,12,031 Cr |
| **Advances** | 90,260 Cr | 1,36,341 Cr |